THE MEDICAL GOSPEL OF LUKE

AS TOLD TO HIM BY MARY - THE MOTHER OF JESUS

DR A. T. BRADFORD

Thanks are due, as always, to my wife Gloria.

Published by Templehouse Publishing, London, England.

www.templehouse-publishing.com

ISBN 9780956479877

The author may be contacted via: info@templehouse-publishing.com

The Medical Gospel Of Luke

Introduction

As a later arrival on the first-century Judean-Christian scene, Luke (a medical doctor) took great pains to ensure the accuracy of his Gospel by interviewing eyewitness sources. Who were they? It is generally agreed that Jesus' disciple Peter served as Mark's primary source of information, while Matthew and John were of course part of 'the twelve' - the apostolic team that accompanied Jesus in his ministry. But what of Luke? This book sets out to examine the Gospel of Luke from eight perspectives: (1) who Luke's main 'eye-witness' source was and their influence, (2) a central (legal) reason for Luke writing both his Gospel and the Book of Acts, (3) who Theophilus (their recipient) was, (4) the influence of recent Roman history on the text, (5) the impact of the Jewish law on the narrative, (6) Jesus' use of humour, (7) local Judean use of Greek, reflecting Jewish thinking and culture and (8) Luke's medical language and background.

Luke was a faithful member of the Apostle Paul's ministry team; as he notes, 'Only Luke is with me' (2 Timothy 4:11). As in Acts (the other side of the Lucan coin), Luke has a particular concern with accurately informing a certain Roman, Theophilus, about the new spiritual movement of 'The Way' (Acts 24:14), as based on the life, death and widely attested bodily resurrection of Jesus, 'called Christ' (Matthew 1:16). Luke's prologue is unusual in containing a high proportion of legal language. Why is this? The answer has to do with the person Luke was writing to, evidenced by the title Luke gives him - 'Most Excellent' - a title Luke uses three times in Acts for different legal figures in Paul's various trials and legal hearings before Roman authorities. It is therefore highly likely that Theophilus was a legal counselor appointed to Paul's defense at his trial for his life before Caesar's court in Rome. This would explain the particular emphasis Luke gives in Acts to Paul's activities at the expense of the equally important apostolic ministry of Peter, and why the account of the growth of the church in Acts ends in something of a cliff-hanger - Paul under house-arrest in Rome. Luke is bringing Theophilus completely up-to-date with Paul's legal history. The Jews who sought Paul's execution had gone to the trouble of bringing a Roman lawyer named Tertullus with them from Jerusalem to Paul's trial under Felix (Acts 24:1-2). The Roman authorities treated Paul very well upon his arrival in Rome ('When we entered Rome, Paul was allowed to stay by himself, with the soldier who was guarding him' - Acts 28:16) and he would certainly have had access to legal representation at his trial in Rome. But he needed someone to document his involvement in the new faith to show that it was part of existing Judaism and so 'religia licita' (officially permitted) under the Empire's religious laws, and that he had not been contravening Roman law. He turned to his friend Luke.

But Luke was at something of a disadvantage. He was a later convert to the new faith that was 'turning the world upside down' (Acts 17:6) (or indeed, the right way up!). As a Gentile (Paul list him with the other Gentiles in Colossians 3: 11 and 14) who was not from the immediate region in which the Gospels are set (Eusebius states that Luke was born in Antioch in Syria) [1] he was somewhat of an outsider to the predominantly Judean and Jewish messianic community that comprised the early first century spiritual and cultural information-pool so central to the faith in general and Paul's legal defense in particular. Luke needed local knowledge.

So to whom did Luke turn as a primary source? The information found in chapters 1 and 2 point to one person and one person only - Mary, the mother of Jesus. All of the other players in the grand scenario that ushered the arrival of the Messiah onto the world stage were by that time long since dead. Only Mary had the knowledge of those sacred events, and only Luke's Gospel provides them. The Roman physician must therefore have gone to the mother of Jesus.

4

But there is another hitherto largely unnoted reason for supposing that Mary was Luke's primary source. Luke's Gospel is a female Gospel. Of the four Gospel biographies of Jesus, Luke's stands head and shoulders above the others in terms of feminine references. While all of the Gospels are, for the time period concerned, culturally unusual in emphasizing the role of women in Jesus' ministry, Luke's account leaves the other three far behind in its prevalence of female content. Whereas the Gospel of Mark has a feminine word content totaling 116, Luke has more than double that at 247 (see appendix). Matthew and John fall between at 153 and 130 respectively; hence Luke has around two-thirds more than them.

What does that tell us? Simply that Luke was being informed by women; in all likelihood by one woman in particular, and, given the preponderance of 'widow' references (nine as compared to Mark's three, Matthew's one and John's none), most likely a woman who had been widowed. Luke's opening content points to one widow in particular - Mary, the wife of Joseph and mother of Jesus. Mary has perhaps been somewhat unfairly treated by the predominantly Gentile scholarship that has shaped Christian understanding. Highly venerated by large sections of the Church, in some cases almost to approaching Jesus' own status, she has also been widely painted with the brush of a 'simple uneducated peasant girl.' This book will provide biblical textual evidence to the contrary - that Mary was, unusually, a highly educated person in the study that her society held in the greatest regard, the study of Scripture (see chapter 1).

This book is also written from the well-recognised view that Luke was a ('beloved') physician (Colossians 4:14). As a man of medicine myself, I much appreciate Luke's perspectives and his use of Greek medical and surgical terminology to illustrate Jesus' biography. Luke must have found Jesus' healing ministry fascinating. Here was a Roman clinician confronted by accounts of a Jewish teacher who punctuated his instructions about living with miraculous gifts of health and wholeness, acts that Luke knew to be humanly impossible but which he had personally witnessed in the life of his friend Paul (Acts 28:8-9). Luke's use of medical Greek terms mirrors that of Hippocrates (460 - 370 BC) and also other ancient Greek speaking physicians, as shall be evidenced.

Finally, this commentary is informed by the understanding that our English Bibles are two languages removed from the words Jesus and his contemporaries spoke (Aramaic and Hebrew to Greek, then to English). To fully grasp the meaning it is necessary to go beyond the English translation and tackle the Greek as used by first century Jews in Judea, in addition to considering the historic socio-cultural context. Because the Gospels contain so many transcriptions of conversations and descriptions of human interaction, one may also deploy an understanding of behavioural psychology. In my own case as a (medically and psychologically trained) Jewish believer in Jesus, a human behavioural analysis that has a particularly Jewish perspective, as well as an understanding of Jesus' Jewish humour.

To date, translations and commentaries have based themselves on traditional views that are at odds with the Jewish environment in which Jesus ministered, e.g. that he was an uneducated and itinerant man. His enemies among the parties of the Pharisees and Sadducees despised such people (as John 7:49 shows), yet they never describe Jesus as either uneducated or as an itinerant person - something that they would have been quick to do had that been the case. This book will challenge some of these traditional views with alternatives based on contemporary Roman historical records in addition to the methods of analysis described above. The commentary that follows is a verse by verse attempt to get beneath the surface of the Gospel narrative from a variety of perspectives and particularly informed by an understanding that the Scripture is the living and active word of God (Hebrews 4:12). I hope that through reading it the Jesus of the first century will become clearer and closer to the reader.

Chapter 1

1:1 'Inasmuch as many have undertaken to compile an account of the things accomplished among us'

'Many have undertaken' but only four accounts have reliably withstood the test of time. The biographical data contained in Matthew, Mark, Luke and John's Gospels stands out from the crowd of later 'apocryphal' works that missed the keystone elements of incarnation, sacrificial death and life-changing resurrection power of the Saviour of the world in all of his 'flesh-veiled' glory. The 'account' (Greek: '*diêgêsis*') Luke speaks of means a 'chronological narrative'*[i] which remains today a central feature of legal testimony. A judge will carefully examine a 'chronology' of an event or claim looking for signs of inaccuracy or embellishment. A chronology that bears the ring of truth remains a central part of any legal argument. 'Accomplished' here is '*plêrophoreô*', a compound word meaning 'most surely believed'* and again carries a legal meaning in terms of sworn truth. Luke is writing to the 'most excellent' Theophilus (verse 4), the same title used to describe the Roman judges Felix (Acts 23:26 and 24:3) and Festus (Acts 26:25) who sat in Roman legal judgement over Paul. The title evidences the standing held by Theophilus within the Roman jurisprudence system (see verse 4), supporting the view that Luke's Gospel formed part of Paul's legal defence in his 'trial-for-life' before Caesar's court in Rome.

1:2 'Just as they were handed down to us by those who from the beginning were eyewitnesses and servants of the word'

The truths Luke sets out have been 'handed down' ('given over' or 'furnished' to him) by, critically importantly, 'eye-witnesses from

---

[i] * Strong's Greek and Hebrew Dictionary

the beginning'. This is the first of many medical terms Doctor Luke uses. 'Eye-witness' is '*autoptês*', from which we derive the term 'autopsy'. The post-mortem truth about the life of the dead (but now raised) Jesus is to be told to Luke by those who had seen it all for themselves. While the apostles witnessed the resurrection, other than John, none of Jesus' male disciples had had the courage to witness Jesus' death at that most unclean and accursed of places, the Roman site of public execution known as Calvary. Mary, however, had witnessed both. At Luke's time of writing (around AD 60, given the dating of Acts to Paul's imprisonment) which of Jesus' followers still alive had been present 'from the *[very]* beginning'? Only Mary.

Who too had been a 'servant of the word'? 'Servant' here is '*hupêretês*' (literally, 'under-rower'), and was the commonly used term for a medical assistant. [2] It is also used in the New Testament for an 'attendant assistant', as in the case of its synagogue use in Luke 4:20 - 'And he closed the book, gave it back to the attendant and sat down.' By Luke's time of writing, Mary would have fully understood her prophetic statement of being the Lord's 'hand-maiden', over and above her being the mother of his incarnate being. This use of the word 'servant' points to Mary's role - no one else could be said to have 'attended' and physically 'served' the incarnate word in the person of Jesus more than his mother Mary.

1:3-4 'It seemed fitting for me as well, having investigated everything carefully from the beginning, to write it out for you in consecutive order, most excellent Theophilus; so that you may know the exact truth about the things you have been taught.'

Luke presents himself as a reliable historian who has 'investigated' (literally 'followed alongside') his statement of facts 'from the first'. Once again, Luke states that his account is to be in '*kathexês*' ('consecutive order'), as in a legal chronology, from 'the beginning'

- '*archê*', also meaning 'from first principles',[3] as in an 'ordered legal argument.' This is indeed the 'exact truth' (the truth, the whole truth and nothing but the truth). The Greek for 'exact' is '*asphaleia*', meaning 'certain and safe', from which we derive the term 'asphalt', used to provide a reliable road-surface on which to drive. The same word appears in the Septuagint as the Greek equivalent of the Hebrew word used for the 'pitch' with which Noah coated the ark (Genesis 6:14).

'Taught' ('*katêcheô*'), means 'to orally instruct and inform'.[4] Whilst this has a later connotation of religious instruction, it also has an earlier general meaning in relation to an oral instruction and information (e.g. 'instructed out of the Law' - Romans 2:18). Theophilus has already received an 'instruction' from Luke; Luke is now writing to him with further information. It seems very likely, given Acts' closing context of Paul's imprisonment awaiting trial in Rome, that 'his Excellency' Theophilus was being 'instructed' with a view to assisting Paul's legal defence.

'Most Excellent' is '*kratistos*', a title Luke records three times and used by three different figures in the book of Acts, in respect of Roman judges in the context of Roman trials. These are Acts 23:26 (the Roman commander Claudius Lysias Felix), Acts 24:3 (the Roman lawyer Tertulius to Felix) and Acts 26:25 (Paul to the new Roman governor Festus). '*Kratistos*' is associated in Roman history with those who wore the '*latus clavus*', this being a broad purple stripe along the edge of their toga, and which signified the Roman rank of Senator. According to tradition it was introduced by Tullus Hostilius (who ruled from 673-642 BC) from the Etruscans. [5] It is well-recognised by Roman historical authors as the distinctive badge of the Senatorian order [6] and is widely used in Roman literature to signify the Senatorial rank. [7] While only the emperor was permitted wear a purple toga, Senators could wear a white toga bearing the *latus clavus*' broad purple stripe, with the lower ranking Equestrian togas having a narrow purple stripe (the '*clavus augustus*'). The title Luke uses therefore indicates that both Luke and Acts were originally written for the attention of a senior Roman legal figure.

That such a person as a Senator would be involved in Paul's trial goes a long way towards explaining the alacrity of his appeal to Caesar - he knew that he had access to powerful friends in Rome. The extraordinary response of Claudius Lysias, the commander of the Roman fortress Antonia in Jerusalem, to information brought by a mere child, whom Lysias greets with great respect and which results in his committing 470 of his troops to securing Paul's transfer to Caesarea, also points to significant connections in Rome. Lysias was surely responding to whom he knew the boy's father to be (Paul's brother-in-law), hence the respect that Lysias shows the boy.

Paul's sister was therefore married to an important Roman official whom Lysias wished to impress by taking very seriously the word of his son - 470 of his troops would have represented a significant proportion of his garrison. When a little while later Gessius Florus (the second Roman governor after Porcius Festus - Acts 24:27), who was notorious for his cruelty, wanted to enter Jerusalem against a huge crowd of Jews, he sent only one centurion with 50 soldiers. [8] When the governors of Tiberias sent two of their number in embassy to Jerusalem at a time of great military unrest their escort numbered 100 soldiers. [9] 470 soldiers to escort one prisoner against the threat of local Jewish assassins was therefore a significantly large number.

'The things' that Theophilus is being 'instructed' in is '*logos*' - the 'word', used here in the sense of the 'account' that Luke is providing him with. Luke has 'instructed' Theophilus in a similar sense to the modern use of 'instructing' a solicitor. He is now providing a written chronology, having first given him an oral 'instruction'. Paul uses this word '*katêcheô*' in Romans 2:18 (KJV: 'instructed out of the law' ('*katêchoumenos ek tou nomou*'), a verb meaning 'to instruct', which often occurs in Greek papyri concerning legal instructions. [10]

1:5 'In the days of Herod, king of Judea, there was a priest named Zechariah, of the division of Abijah; and he had a wife from the daughters of Aaron, and her name was Elizabeth.'

Herod, called 'the Great' on account of his massive building projects (driven by a combination of a robust ego inflamed by a likely diagnosis of cerebral syphilis),[11] was not of Jewish descent. His father Antipater was a descendant of Edom (a people Judas Maccabeus had forcibly converted to Judaism in 165 BC), and his mother was an Arab from Petra in Jordan. He was given the title 'King of the Jews' by the Roman Senate under Octavian and Marc Antony while seeking the military reinforcements needed to re-capture Jerusalem following the Parthian invasion in 40 BC. Judea and the surrounding region was important to Rome both as a buffer zone between them and the hostile Parthian empire in the east, and also as a means of controlling the Mediterranean ports necessary for European food imports.

Herod had re-built the Temple in Jerusalem in grand style, thereby benefiting the Jewish priestly families that ran the sacrificial system of atonement that under-pinned the Jewish faith and sold the animals marked suitable for offerings. While it was not compulsory for a priest to marry within their own tribe (the Law stipulated only that they marry a virgin of pure Israelite descent (Leviticus 21:13),[ii] it was customary to do so. Luke introduces us in this verse to John the Baptist's father and mother - educated people from the religiously privileged and culturally important background of the priesthood.

[ii] 'He is to marry a virgin of his own people' (Leviticus 21:14).

1:6 'They were both righteous in the sight of God, walking blamelessly in all the commandments and requirements of the Lord.'

This concept of being 'righteous' to Jews in first century BC was different to our modern 'post-Paul' understanding of righteousness by faith. To be 'right with God' at that time meant that you kept the Law. Being at that time largely oral in form (the Oral Torah was not written down until around 200 AD), that meant being taught first-hand by rabbinic scholars. Hence 'righteous' meant being formally educated in the Law. Consequently Luke attests to John's parents' strict adherence to the largely oral Law's various obligations for ordinary life. The fact that Elizabeth was also 'blameless' illustrates her parent's practice of teaching their daughters the things of God, and not simply the sons, especially in families without a son. The majority of the Jewish populace at the time were not so fortunate. Their ignorance of the legal requirements of the Torah led to their frequently unwittingly break it, earning them the derogatory title of 'sinners' (Greek: '*hamartôlos*' - a term for one who 'misses the mark' or 'strays off the path' in relation to God's requirements).

1:7 'But they had no child, because Elizabeth was barren, and they were both advanced in years.'

Like many of the patriarchs before them, they were barren. And so the scene is set for a further intervention of the God who gives babies to those who cannot naturally have them. Childlessness was a severe stigma in Israel, where the rabbis ('*Yebamoth*' 64a) held it to be a breach of Genesis 35:11 (where Jacob is commanded to 'Be fertile and increase'). We are not told at what age Zechariah and Elizabeth had married, only that Elizabeth was barren and that their age now made having children impossible, thereby placing it firmly into the hands of the One for whom 'all things are possible' (Luke 1:37). 'Barren' ('*steiros*') is the first of five different obstetric and gynaecological terms that Doctor Luke employs in his Gospel, showing a range of detailed content that reflects on a female primary source as well as his own medical knowledge.

1:8-9 'Now it happened that while he was performing his priestly service before God in the appointed order of his division, according to the custom of the priestly office, he was chosen by lot to enter the Temple of the Lord and burn incense.'

Every male descendant of Aaron was automatically born into the priesthood. The priests were divided into twenty-four sections, and only at the compulsory feasts (Passover, Pentecost and the Feast of Tabernacles / Booths) were they all on duty. For the rest of the year each division served two periods of one week. [12] In this instance to 'enter the Temple' means to enter the Holy Place, a great honour that many priests never undertook owing to the duty being apportioned by lot. To 'burn incense' is '*thumiaô*', which was also the common medical term for fumigating using herbs and spices. [13] There were many thousands of priests, about a thousand in each division, and their Temple duties were allocated in the following way.

'Every morning and evening a sacrifice was made for the nation, consisting of a burnt offering of a one year old male lamb without spot or blemish (Numbers 28:3). With this there was also an offering of flour and oil and a drink offering of wine. Before the morning sacrifice and after the evening sacrifice, incense was burned on the altar in the Holy Place, with the priest chosen by lot. The lot was cast four times, though at different periods of the service. It was done in this manner. The priests stood in a circle around the president, who for a moment removed the headgear of one of their number, to show that he would begin counting at him. Then all held up one, two, or more fingers - since it was not lawful in Israel to count persons - when the president named some number, say seventy, and began counting the *[total]* fingers till he reached the number named, which marked that the lot had fallen on that priest. The first lot was for cleansing the altar and preparing it; the second, for those who were to offer the sacrifice, and for those who were to cleanse the candlestick and the altar of incense in the Holy Place.'

'The third lot was the most important. It determined who was to offer the incense. The fourth lot, which followed close on the third, fixed those who were to burn the pieces of the sacrifice on the altar, and to perform the concluding portions of the service. The morning lot held good also for the same offices at the evening sacrifice, save that the lot was cast anew for the burning of the incense.' [14]

Priests worked in groups ('divisions'), performing the tasks necessary to the continual function of sacrifice and offering, living around the clock in the Temple until their shift was over, whereupon they returned to their own towns. Given the large numbers of priests in each division it was quite possible that many would never be selected for the privilege of burning incense in the Holy Place, and once having been awarded a priest would not be eligible again (Talmud, *'Tamid'* 32a). Zechariah was chosen for that task.

1:10 'And the whole multitude of the people were in prayer outside at the hour of the incense offering.'

Outside the Holy Place at the heart of the Temple lay the Court of the Priests and adjacent to that lay the Court of Israel (men) with the Court of the Women beyond. Incense was burned at the hour of prayer, and Zechariah's role carried great meaning and significance for a large number of priestly on-lookers and the ordinary Jewish worshippers further away. The duties relating to the burning of incense were comparatively simple. 'The priest reverently removed what had been left on the altar from the previous evening's service; then, worshipping, retired backwards. The second assistant now advanced, and, having spread to the utmost verge of the golden altar the live coals taken from that of burnt-offering, worshipped and retired. Meanwhile the sound of the 'organ' (the Magrephah), *[a musical instrument struck by the incense offerers as they moved from the Court of the Priests into the Holy Place]*, heard to the most distant parts of the Temple, and, according to tradition, far beyond its precincts, had summoned priests, Levites, and people to prepare for whatever service or duty was before them. For this was the innermost part of the worship of the day. The celebrant priest, bearing the golden censer, stood alone within the Holy Place, lit by the sheen of the seven-branched candlestick. Before him, somewhat further away, towards the heavy veil that hung before the Holy of Holies, was the golden altar of incense, on which the red coals glowed. To his right (the left of the altar, that is, on the north side) was the table of shewbread; to his left, on the right or south side of the altar, was the golden candlestick. And still he waited, as instructed to do, till a special signal indicated that the moment had come to spread the incense on the altar, as near as possible to the Holy of Holies.' [15]

1:11-12 'And an angel of the Lord appeared to him, standing to the right of the altar of incense. Zechariah was troubled when he saw the angel, and fear gripped him.'

The priests held that only the first five books of the Bible (the Pentateuch) were authoritative. One of the distinctions between them and the Pharisaic Torah scholars (who regarded the whole of the Old Testament as inspired) was the question of angels. Did they exist or not? The priestly Sadducees held that they did not ('The Sadducees say that there is no resurrection, nor an angel, nor a spirit' - Acts 23:8). Imagine Zechariah's surprise and consternation then when one appeared to him! Luke's choice of word for 'troubled' is '*tarasso*'. This means 'to agitate' (literally 'to move to and fro', as in 'troubling the water' at the pool of Bethesda - John 5:4) and to

15

'render distressed' and to 'perplex the mind of one by suggesting scruples or doubts'. [16] Zechariah, in his great fear and trembling, suddenly began to have doubts about his disbelief in angels. This is not a good basis for the faith needed to listen respectfully to an angelic messenger.

The Talmud also shows that there was good reason for priests to be concerned regarding supernatural consequences to their entry into the Holy Place, whether they believed in angels or not. Tractate '*Yoma*' 19b reads, 'There was a Sadducee who had arranged the incense without, and then brought it inside. As he left he was exceedingly glad. On his coming out his father met him and said to him: "My son, although we are Sadducees, we are afraid of the Pharisees." He replied, "All my life was I aggrieved because of this scriptural verse: 'For I appear in the cloud upon the ark-cover.' *[Leviticus 16:2]* I would say: "When shall the opportunity come to my hand so that I might fulfil it. Now that such opportunity has come to my hand, should I not have fulfilled it?" It is reported that it took only a few days until he died and was thrown on the dung heap and worms came forth from his nose. Some say: 'He was smitten as he came out of the Holy of Holies.' For Rabbi Hiyya taught: 'Some sort of a noise was heard in the Temple Court, for an angel had come and struck him down on his face to the ground and his brethren the priests came in and they found the trace as of a calf's foot on his shoulder, as it is written: 'And their feet were straight feet, and the sole of their feet was like the sole of a calf's foot'' (Ezekiel 1:7). The priest had entered with a view to proving or disproving the Scripture; like Zechariah after him he did not believe in such supernatural things as angels and was apparently punished for his presumption.

1:13-14 'But the angel said to him, 'Do not be afraid, Zechariah, for your petition has been heard, and your wife Elizabeth will bear you a son, and you will give him the

name John. You will have joy and gladness, and many will rejoice at his birth.'

The angel takes pity on Zechariah's state of fear and doubt and reassures him that yes, prayer works! His wife is to give birth to a son who is to have the (non-family) name of John, who will bring not only joy but 'extreme joy'; 'gladness' being *agalliasis*, also meaning 'exuberant joy and exultation'.* The 'many' who will rejoice at his birth points to the widely felt impact of his ministry.

1:15-16 'For he will be great in the sight of the Lord; and he will drink no wine or liquor, and he will be filled with the Holy Spirit while yet in his mother's womb. And he will turn many of the sons of Israel back to the Lord their God.'

John's Nazirite vow [17] is foretold, being vows described by Moses in Numbers 6:1-8. 'Again the Lord spoke to Moses, saying, "Speak to the sons of Israel and say to them, 'When a man or woman makes a special vow, the vow of a Nazirite, to dedicate himself to the Lord, he shall abstain from wine and strong drink; he shall drink no vinegar, whether made from wine or strong drink, nor shall he drink any grape juice nor eat fresh or dried grapes. All the days of his separation he shall not eat anything, that is produced by the grape vine, from the seeds even to the skin. All the days of his vow of separation no razor shall pass over his head. He shall be holy until the days are fulfilled for which he separated himself to the Lord; he shall let the locks of hair on his head grow long. All the days of his separation to the Lord he shall not go near to a dead person. He shall not make himself unclean for his father or for his mother, for his brother or for his sister, when they die, because his separation to God is on his head. All the days of his separation he is holy to the Lord.' A Nazirite vow could be for a specific period of time (commonly 30 days) or for life; John's is to be for life just as Samson's was in the

Old Testament (Judges 13:5, though Samson was not faithful to it). The Talmud laid down some dispensations for life-Nazirites. 'A life-Nazirite, whenever his hair becomes burdensome, may thin it with a razor and then offer three animal sacrifices; whilst should he be ritually defiled, he must offer the sacrifice prescribed for defilement' (Talmud, '*Nazir*' 4a). John the Baptist is to be filled with the Spirit, the first New Testament character to be so described. Unlike the Old Testament craftsman Bezalel [iii] who was filled with the Spirit for the time needed to build the Tabernacle under the oversight of Moses (who possessed the plans for its construction, given to him by the Lord on Mount Sinai), John will be filled with the Spirit as an embryo, capable of leaping for joy in his mother's womb at the coming of Mary, newly pregnant herself with the Lord Jesus. Again, his ministry will impact 'many' in Israel, causing them to 'turn back' (Greek: '*epistrephô*') - 'to be converted.'*

1:17 'It is he who will go as a forerunner before him in the spirit and power of Elijah, to turn the hearts of the fathers back to the children, and the disobedient to the attitude of the righteous, so as to make ready a people prepared for the Lord.'

The 'fathers' spoken of here are probably primarily not natural fathers (if anything Jesus promised schism), [iv] but rather as was commonly used for the spiritual fathers of the nation - the Teachers of the Law, of which Nicodemus (John 3:10) is the first recorded example. It echoes the prayer of Elijah in 1 Kings 18:37. 'Answer me, O Lord, answer me, that this people may know that you, O Lord, are God, and that you have turned their heart back again.' Jesus

---

[iii] 'I have filled him with the Spirit of God in wisdom, understanding and knowledge' (Exodus 31:3).
[iv] 'Five members in one household will be divided, three against two and two against three' (Luke 12:52).

himself records that John embodied the ministry of Elijah ('If you are willing to accept it, John himself is Elijah who was to come' - Matthew 11:14).

The 'children' whose hearts are turned to the fathers primarily represent the 'lost sheep' of the house of Israel (Ezekiel 34:11-16), about whom Jesus (and by extension John) were especially concerned (Matthew 10:6) prior to the out-pouring of the Holy Spirit sending the gospel to the surrounding nations of the world.

The converse of the heart-turning of the spiritual fathers is a change in the heart attitude of the children. They are currently 'disobedient' ('*apeithês*', literally meaning 'without trust')* and consequently are weak in faith and not properly ready to meet the coming Messiah. They also lack the necessary tools to be 'righteous' ('right with God'), partly through a lack of teaching and partly because their underlying disposition reflects an indifference to the things of God that the righteous pursue. Had they had better teachers and a better attitude they would have been more 'prepared' for Jesus' eventual arrival. To be 'prepared' for the Lord is '*kataskeuazô*' - a term which when negated was used for workmen who were not ready to begin building.* How ready are we for his return?

1:18 'Zechariah said to the angel, "How will I know this for certain? For I am an old man and my wife is advanced in years."'

While this may seem like a reasonable question, it was a step too far in terms of unbelief. Zechariah and Elizabeth had been petitioning God for many years for the birth of a child. Zechariah appears to have not been expecting his prayers to be answered! So he asks the angel for a sign. How was a sign from an angel supposed to work for someone who did not in the first place believe that angels were a sign in and of themselves? Evidently the angelic appearance itself

19

was not an adequate sign and so Zechariah asks for another. One problem with a sign is that if the recipient is entrenched in unbelief then it is unlikely to have the desired effect, as Jesus indicated in his parable of the rich man and Lazarus (Luke 16:34), and will actually make the recipients' spiritual position worse through their rejection of the grace that it offers.

1:19-20 'The angel answered and said to him, "I am Gabriel, who stands in the presence of God, and I have been sent to speak to you and to bring you this good news. And behold, you shall be silent and unable to speak until the day when these things take place, because you did not believe my words, which will be fulfilled in their proper time."'

The angel Gabriel had centuries earlier been God's messenger to the prophet Daniel. 'I heard the voice of a man between the banks of Ulai, and he called out and said, "Gabriel, give this man an understanding of the vision"' (Daniel 8:16). Hebrews 1:14 tells us that angels are 'sent out to render service for the sake of those who will inherit salvation.' God in his foreknowledge had already given Gabriel, who had the honour on waiting on God's presence, the authority to bring a judgement on the unbelieving priest. 'Dumb' here is '*siôpaô*', meaning 'to be silent'.* His relatives' later use of signs to communicate with him (verse 62) suggests that he also lost his hearing.

1:21-23 'The people were waiting for Zechariah, and were wondering at his delay in the Temple. But when he came out, he was unable to speak to them; and they realized that he had seen a vision in the Temple; and he kept making signs to them, and remained mute. When the days of his priestly service were ended, he went back home.'

After the offering of incense it was the custom for the priest to go to the barrier separating the Court of the Priests from the Court of Israel and bless the people waiting there. [18] Zechariah's delay was an ominous sign to his waiting priestly colleagues and the people beyond. Had he collapsed or been struck down by God? When he appeared he was able to make signs to them as to what had happened. What they made of the angelic appearance in relation to their particular doctrine on the subject is not recorded. Dumbness was not a barrier to Zechariah's duties, which he, to his credit, completed before taking the great news home to Elizabeth.

1:24-25 'After these days Elizabeth his wife became pregnant, and she kept herself in seclusion for five months, saying, "This is the way the Lord has dealt with me in the days when he looked with favour upon me, to take away my disgrace among men."'

The 'disgrace' was on both sides of the marriage. The Talmud ('*Sanhedrin*' 36b) ordained that the childless scholar might not sit on the Sanhedrin. '*Nedarim*' 64b, among other Talmudic texts, accounted the childless as already dead, together with the pauper, the leper, and the blind. Such were the sympathies of the rabbinic scholars for common human conditions!

1:26 'Now in the sixth month the angel Gabriel was sent from God to a city in Galilee called Nazareth, to a virgin engaged to a man whose name was Joseph, of the descendants of David; and the virgin's name was Mary.'

Enter Mary. Nazareth, in the north of Israel, was home to Mary but not to Joseph who was from Bethlehem in Judea, 4 miles south of Jerusalem. What was a devout Jewish '*tekton*' (Matthew 1:19 and 13:5) from the south doing in northern Nazareth? Nazareth was a Jewish town 5 miles south and east of Sepphoris, the Roman

21

administrative headquarters of Galilee. As a devout Jewish *'tekton'* Joseph would have been one of the very few non-Hellenized artisans capable of training the highly separatist Jewish priests, one thousand of which were recruited by King Herod the Great [19] to build the new and improved Holy Place in the existing Court of the Priests between 18 and 12 BC. [20] As such, he would have been an obvious candidate to assist in the construction work in Sepphoris, also sponsored by King Herod and fortifying what was already a very strong strategic location; so called 'because it was perched on the top of a mountain like a bird' ('Sepphor' - Hebrew: *'Zippor'*, Talmud *'Megilah'* 6a). And as a devout and well-known figure amongst the community of priests, there were no doubt some who had daughters or nieces for whom they thought Joseph would be a good matrimonial prospect. Perhaps one such was Mary. There must have been a good reason for a daughter of Aaron to marry outside her own tribe and being the architect of Herod's Temple (Greek: *'architekton'* - 'master tekton') was certainly a good reason. Mary was 'betrothed' to Joseph - a legally binding contract that required divorce proceedings to end it. And so part two of Gabriel's mission commences - he visits Mary.

1:28-29 'And coming in, he said to her, "Greetings, favoured one! The Lord is with you." But she was very perplexed at this statement, and kept pondering what kind of salutation this was.'

Favoured indeed! Chosen from before the foundation of the world to be the God-bearer, to carry the embryo that was fully God and fully human in her womb for nine months, to give birth to him and to breast-feed him. Favoured indeed. 'Perplexed' is from the same word that describes her uncle Zechariah's reaction to Gabriel's appearance, meaning to be 'troubled' to the point of agitation and trembling. Gabriel had that sort of effect on people! Her subsequent reaction however is the first evidence given that Mary was both an intelligent and at that time unusually for girls, an educated person.

22

She 'pondered' Gabriel's greeting. The Greek here is *'dialogizomai'*, meaning 'to reason logically' in her mind; [21] *'logizomai'* being the root of the English word 'logic'. Mary is sometimes presented as being a simple, uneducated peasant girl. This view is completely contradicted by the text, as evidenced by the enormous breadth of scriptural knowledge that her song the 'Magnificat' contains, to say nothing of the depth of theological understanding illustrated.

This was evidently not the first day that the Lord had been 'with' Mary. The level of faith and trust she exhibited was certainly the product of years of faithful discipleship, in prayer, Tanakh (Hebrew Scripture) and Torah (Law) reading. The fact that she was female did not necessarily exclude her from these, especially within a priestly family, and Scripture quotations flow out of her in the manner of a Charles Wesley hymn. Her response of faith had been years in the making, youth or not, and illustrates that her meeting with Gabriel, despite his unusual message, was not likely to have been her first spiritual encounter with the God of her ancestors. Mary was spiritually prepared in a way that her elderly relative Zechariah, for all his years of priestly ministry, was not.

1:30-31 'The angel said to her, "Do not be afraid, Mary; for you have found favour with God. And behold, you will conceive in your womb and bear a son, and you shall name him Jesus."'

If Mary was getting over her fear of the angel's arrival, she was then immediately given another good reason to fear. Becoming pregnant in the betrothal stage, if not by your husband-to-be, was regarded as worse than adultery within Jewish Law (Talmud, *'Sanhedrin'*, 89a). Mary was risking summary execution for sexual unfaithfulness. While Jesus' name was a common one - Joshua (*'Y'shua'*), meaning 'Jehovah is salvation' - the manner of his conception was surely almost unbelievable, even to a woman with the level of faith that

Mary had. Isaiah 7:14 had spoken of an '***almah***' giving birth to a son - Immanuel - (God with us), and while the Septuagint had translated this as '***parthenos***' ('virgin'), the more common usage had remained as 'maiden'. Literal virgin-birth was not yet on the theological radar.

1:32-33 'He will be great and will be called the Son of the Most High; and the Lord God will give him the throne of his father David; and he will reign over the house of Jacob forever, and his kingdom will have no end.'

More reasons for fear! There was already a king called 'Great' reigning in Jerusalem, one supported by the might of the Roman Empire. True, the Jews did not regard Herod's ancestry as giving him a legitimate right to rule, but he had proved resilient to the efforts of the Parthians to displace him and had also managed to stay in power despite the political changes in Rome. If Mary's son was to take over the throne of David in Jerusalem, there was likely to be considerable trouble along the way. Gabriel's reference to David's throne and rule without end would surely have brought to Mary's biblically informed mind the words of Isaiah the prophet. 'For a child will be born to us, a son will be given to us; and the government will rest on his shoulders; and his name will be called Wonderful Counsellor, Mighty God, Eternal Father, Prince of Peace. There will be no end to the increase of his government or of peace, on the throne of David and over his kingdom, to establish it and to uphold it with justice and righteousness, from then on and forevermore. The zeal of the Lord of hosts will accomplish this' (Isaiah 9:6-7). Standing confronted by one of the angelic leaders of the Lord's 'hosts' (armies), Mary would have realised that all of this was only going to be possible by God's direct intervention. She had a choice to make - to trust or not to trust. She chose to trust.

1:34 'Mary said to the angel, "How can this be, since I am a virgin?"'

On the face of it, Mary's question can appear similar to Zechariah's (who drew a swift rebuke from Gabriel), but it is not. There are some important differences. Firstly the Old Testament has many accounts of the barren and aged conceiving according to the plans and purposes of God. But there were no instances in Israel's history of virgins conceiving and the scripturally-literate Mary is clearly not understanding Isaiah 7:14 in this way. Secondly, Mary's pregnancy would put her on a collision course with a death sentence, in contrast to Elizabeth's, which was a case of answered prayer. Thirdly, Mary's pregnancy would inevitably call into question the 'righteous' reputation of Joseph, her betrothed, as well as bringing shame onto her priestly family. There is thus a world of difference between her question and Zechariah's.

1:35-37 'The angel answered and said to her, "The Holy Spirit will come upon you, and the power of the Most High will overshadow you; and for that reason the holy child shall be called the Son of God. And behold, even your relative Elizabeth has also conceived a son in her old age; and she who was called barren is now in her sixth month. For nothing will be impossible with God.'

A bright cloud of God's presence would later 'overshadow' Peter, James and John on the Mount of Transfiguration; one would in a similar way overshadow Mary and combine with one of her own ova, from one of her ovaries, and implant the resulting embryonic blastocyst in her womb. The miraculous result - physical life that was both fully God and fully human - would be truly the Son of God. Mary would have rejoiced in the news of Elizabeth's pregnancy; she too was a woman of faith and knew that what was impossible to humankind was all too possible to God. Greek physicians divided human life into three distinct periods; [22] 'old age' (*'gêras'*) was the final one wherein any natural possibility of reproduction had ceased.

25

1:38 'And Mary said, "Behold, the bondslave of the Lord; may it be done to me according to your word." And the angel departed from her.'

'Bondslave' or 'handmaid' is the feminine form of '*doulos*', a slave. Wholeheartedly, and with great faith and trust, Mary places herself under the will of God. And nothing has ever been the same since. Gabriel must have been deeply impressed by the contrast in attitudes between the older male religious priest in the Temple in Jerusalem and the young faith-filled girl from Nazareth.

1:39-40 'Now at this time Mary arose and went in a hurry to the hill country, to a city of Judah, and entered the house of Zechariah and greeted Elizabeth.'

Mary went to the one place she could be certain that her story would be believed - the house of Zechariah and Elizabeth. This was much safer too - there needed to be a time period for Joseph to react to the unexpected news. The journey was approximately 80-100 miles (depending on the exact location of their house) and would have taken around a week to complete. Mary, haste notwithstanding, would have travelled with others journeying in the same direction. Elizabeth, now in her sixth month, is no longer 'in seclusion' - resting to guard against any possible miscarriage - but is still, as women then usually were, 'in the house'.

1:41 'When Elizabeth heard Mary's greeting, the baby leaped in her womb; and Elizabeth was filled with the Holy Spirit.'

Babies develop their sense of hearing at about 19 weeks gestation. [23] The in-utero John, now at around 29 weeks gestation, responds to the sound of Mary's voice, accompanying the much earlier embryonic presence of the Saviour of the world - both humankind and God fully and perfectly fused - and rapidly growing in size. Presumably John was already 'filled with the Spirit' (Luke 1:15); Elizabeth therefore is the first adult to be so described in the New Testament - further testimony to Luke's female primary source of information.

1:42-45 'And she cried out with a loud voice and said, "Blessed are you among women, and blessed is the fruit of your womb! And how has it happened to me that the mother of my Lord would come to me? For behold, when the sound of your greeting reached my ears, the baby leaped in my womb for joy. And blessed is she who believed that there would be a fulfilment of what had been spoken to her by the Lord."'

The prophetically anointed Elizabeth affirms the work of God in Mary before Mary has had a chance to explain anything. Mary is blessed among (not above) women; the infant Jesus receives a blessing too - 'blessed' is *'eulogeo'*, literally meaning to 'speak something good'.* Elizabeth's exceptional insight is that the infant Jesus is 'her Lord' (Greek *'kurios'* - 'Lord' or 'master'), surely used in the messianic sense, a term repeated in verse 45 where she endorses Mary's great faith in 'believing' (Greek: *'pisteou'* from *'pistis'* - faith) the word that the Lord had been spoken to her through Gabriel. According to Romans 10:17, 'faith comes by hearing'. The Greek there is *'akoe'*, also meaning 'the thing heard'.* God's word, when heard by the believer, has the power to engender faith in and of itself. Such was Mary's experience, now being confirmed by Elizabeth. She had heard the word of God from Gabriel, believed and trusted in it, and so experienced the fruit of the Holy Spirit actioning it within her own body, such was her faith.

1:46-47 'And Mary said: "My soul exalts the Lord, and my spirit has rejoiced in God my Saviour."'

And now the 'Magnificat' begins, a prophetic God-inspired song, and one rooted and grounded in Old Testament Scripture. The analysis that follows provides clear evidence for Mary being a scripturally well-educated person, because the song is laden with biblical references, and from each section of the Jewish Bible. It was the custom at the time to refer to a section of Scripture simply by quoting a few words from it (rather than the whole passage), relying on the Jewish audience's memorised knowledge of the text to recognise the original passage being referenced. Mary does both - whole lines of Scripture are quoted as well as many smaller portions. This was unusual for a woman at that time but less so in the case of a woman from a priestly family, especially if she was an only child (Luke 1:36 mentions her 'kinswoman' but not brothers or sisters). She also knows the sections of the Bible that the priestly caste did not consider to be authoritative, indicating that her study was wider than that expected from someone of her background. Mary's education is evidenced not just in her knowledge of the verses but also of their underlying theological meaning - she knows, for example, the difference between soul and spirit.

The theological wordbook of the Old Testament gives the original meaning of the word 'soul; as 'to breathe' (Hebrew: '*nephesh*')', hence it was held to reside in the lungs. The first mention of this word in Scripture is in Exodus 23:12: 'Six days do your work, but on the seventh day do not work, so that your ox and your donkey may rest and the slave born in your household, and the alien as well, may be refreshed.' '*Nephesh*' is translated here as 'refreshed' - equivalent in modern vernacular to 'having a breather.' But there is also another Hebrew word for breath - '*ruach.*' This word has three hundred and seventy-eight uses in Old Testament. On twenty-seven occasions the meaning is: 'breath.' On two hundred and thirty two occasions it is 'spirit'. Simply put, the soul is our breath (our human life), and the Spirit is God's life (his breath) in us. To 'exalt' the Lord is '*megalunô*' often (and somewhat unhelpfully) translated as 'magnify', which has a modern sense of 'enlarging' quite foreign to the original meaning, which is to 'extol', 'to make conspicuous, to deem or declare great, to esteem highly, to laud (in praise)'.* The Latin form of 'magnify' gave rise to the song's traditional name, 'The Magnificat'.

1:48a 'For he has had regard for the humble state of his bondslave'

God pays a special attention to the humble and lowly. As Jesus said, 'Blessed are the poor in spirit, for theirs is the kingdom of heaven' (Matthew 5:3). Mary echoes Psalm 136:23, about her God, 'Who remembered us in our low estate, for his loving-kindness is everlasting', and Psalm 138:6a, 'For though the Lord is exalted, yet he regards the lowly'. In the Jewish Bible the Psalms were part of the *'Ketuvim'* ('The Writings'), together with Ruth, Chronicles, Ezra, Nehemiah, Esther, Job, Proverbs, Ecclesiastes, Song of Songs, Lamentations and Daniel. To Mary's priestly family these (together with the other book of 'The Prophets') were quite distinct from the Pentateuch, which was the sole section regarded as authoritative.

'Regards' is *'epiblepô*, meaning 'to gaze upon'.* The Lord loves to gaze upon his children, especially those who have the quality of humility. He loves to think about them - how to bless them and use them within his kingdom. Mary will come back to this verse later in the prayer.

1:48b 'For behold, from this time on all generations will count me blessed.'

The thought here is the same as in Psalm 136:23, 'His loving-kindness is everlasting.' Mary knows that God's favour has eternal consequences. She will, by all people, be considered *'makarizô'* - 'blessed' or 'happy',* owing to God's favour towards her.

29

1:49a 'For the Mighty One has done great things for me'

Mary echoes Moses' words in Deuteronomy 10:21 - 'He is your praise and he is your God, who has done these great and awesome things for you which your eyes have seen.'

1:49b 'And holy is his name.'

This common-sounding phrase only occurs as such in one other passage in the Bible - Psalm 111. 'He has sent redemption to his people; he has ordained his covenant forever; holy and awesome is his name' (Psalm 111:9). Mary is experiencing in her own body the redemption of God's people. Her mind was already recalling the everlasting covenant that God made with her forefather Abraham (Luke 1:55). She is personally experiencing God's 'great and awesome things' (Deuteronomy 10:21). This is a result of the incarnation and is not supposed to be limited to Mary - all Christians are in-dwelt by the Holy Spirit and so can 'flesh-out' or 'incarnate' Jesus in their lives. His presence is supposed to bring about similar great and awesome things into our lives on a day-to-day basis.

1:50. 'His mercy is upon generation after generation toward those who fear him.'

This is an obvious and complete quotation from Psalm 103 verse 17. Mary clearly has a good grasp of the trans-generational nature of covenant in the plan of God, and will return to that them at the end of her Spirit and Scripture-inspired song. Psalm 103:17: 'The loving-kindness of the Lord is from everlasting to everlasting on those who fear him, and his righteousness to children's children.' God's covenant-keeping love is designed to be inter-generational. This does also require some effort on our part. As verse 18 goes on to say: 'To those who keep his covenant, and remember his precepts to do them.' Keeping the covenant precepts is our side of the bargain.

1:51 'He has done mighty deeds with his arm. He has scattered those who were proud in the thoughts of their heart.'

The 'arm of the Lord' (the Greek here indicated specifically the upper arm with the powerful biceps muscle) is commonly used to express God's power to free his people. For example, in Exodus 6:6, 'Say, therefore, to the sons of Israel, 'I am the Lord, and I will bring you out from under the burdens of the Egyptians, and I will deliver you from their bondage. I will also redeem you with an outstretched arm and with great judgments.'' His arm works in two directions - to save and free his people, but also to judge his enemies, and especially those forces of darkness that oppose him. Mary is drawing upon both of those Scriptural ideas, as expressed in Psalm 89:10, 'You yourself crushed Rahab like one who is slain; you scattered your enemies with your mighty arm.'

God always opposes the proud (James 4:6 and 1 Peter 5:5). This is the thought behind Proverbs 3:34, 'He scoffs at the scoffers, yet he gives grace to the afflicted.' It is resonant with what befell King Nebuchadnezzar, the mighty king of Babylon, when 'his heart was lifted up, and his mind hardened in pride, he was deposed from his kingly throne' (Daniel 5:20 KJV). Mary understands that pride is primarily a matter of the heart, which while sometimes hidden from men and women is always clearly, and very offensively, visible to God. One of the enemy's effective strategies is to lead God's people into pride, in order to bring them, unawares, into opposition to God.

1:52 'He has brought down rulers from their thrones, and has exalted those who were humble.'

Mary now dips into 'The Prophets' section of her Bible, again resonant of Nebuchadnezzar, who had been brought low to learn that humility before God was more important than any earthly power that

31

a human king might have. When Daniel's prophetic warning to him went unheeded, 'A voice came from heaven, saying, 'King Nebuchadnezzar, to you it is declared: sovereignty has been removed from you, and you will be driven away from mankind, and your dwelling place will be with the beasts of the field. You will be given grass to eat like cattle, and seven periods of time will pass over you until you recognize that the Most High is ruler over the realm of mankind and bestows it on whomever he wishes'' (Daniel 4:31-32). The text goes on to describe the prophecy's literal fulfilment.

Rulers often have human pride that brings them into opposition to God. But while God is bringing them down, there are others who are coming up - the humble - those who recognize their own limitations and hence their need of God. As Eliphaz had said to Job, 'He sets on high those who are lowly' (Job 5:11). Of course, kings don't have to be proud - in fact a day is coming when 'All the kings of the earth will give thanks to you, O Lord, when they have heard the words of your mouth. And they will sing of the ways of the Lord, for great is the glory of the Lord. For though the Lord is exalted, yet he regards the lowly, but the haughty he knows from afar' (Psalm 138:4-6). This Psalm is a natural one to quote after Mary's comment that 'He scatters the proud' - God still knows the proud, but from a 'scattered' distance.

1:53 'He has filled the hungry with good things, but has sent away the rich empty handed.'

This next verse contains another very obvious quotation from the Psalms, 'The hungry soul he has filled with what is good' (Psalm 107:9). Mary is echoing the words of the song of an earlier woman of faith - Hannah. 'The Lord makes poor and rich; he brings low, he also exalts. He raises the poor from the dust; he lifts the needy from the ash heap, to make them sit with nobles, and inherit a seat of honour' (1 Samuel 2:7-8).

'And sent away the rich empty-handed.' The Law (Deuteronomy 15:13), stated that when the Sabbath (seventh) year arrived and Jewish slaves were set free, their masters should be generous to them and so help provide for them at that time of transition - 'When you set him free, you shall not send him away empty-handed.' God is a generous master, but his grace is restricted in the case of those who insist in relying on themselves and their own natural strength and resources rather than upon him. Rich people often habitually trust in their riches and so are restricted in their ability to receive from God, because their trust is in themselves and not in him. As Jesus said, 'How hard it is for a rich man to enter the Kingdom of Heaven' (Matthew 19:23).

Riches are given by God in order to bless those in need, not to be hoarded away or used in ways that are solely self-indulgent, something that Jesus' half-brother James warned of graphically. James 5:1-5: 'Come now, you rich, weep and howl for your miseries which are coming upon you. Your riches have rotted and your garments have become moth-eaten. Your gold and your silver have rusted; and their rust will be a witness against you and will consume your flesh like fire. It is in the last days that you have stored up your treasure! Behold, the pay of the labourers who mowed your fields, and which has been withheld by you, cries out against you; and the outcry of those who did the harvesting has reached the ears of the Lord of Sabaoth *[Hebrew for 'armies']*. You have lived luxuriously on the earth and led a life of wanton pleasure; you have fattened your hearts in a day of slaughter.' Possessions are to be stewarded on behalf of him who gave them - the God who gives us 'richly all things to enjoy' (1 Timothy 6:17). While being properly taken care of, they should be held on to lightly so that the One who gave them can re-distribute them if he chooses to.

1:54 'He has given help to Israel his servant, in remembrance of his mercy.'

If God does not rush to the aid of those rich people who trust in themselves, whom does he hasten to help? One such are those who set themselves to serve him. Jacob (whose name means 'cheat' and 'supplanter') was re-named Israel (meaning 'one who has prevailed with God'); the limp that he carried after his night of all-in wrestling with God was a constant reminder to him of his new mission and of the futility of reliance upon human strength in doing the will of a supernatural God. As Isaiah would later prophecy, 'Do not fear, you worm Jacob, you men of Israel; I will help you, declares the Lord, and your Redeemer is the Holy One of Israel' (Isaiah 41:14).

'Mercy' is '*eleos*', meaning 'pity' and 'compassion'. God knows all about our human weakness ('remembrance' means 'to be mindful of'), yet he still chooses to build his kingdom through us. This is rather like us choosing to build a kingdom using ants. We can only fulfil God's purposes when it is his power that flows through us and around us, and not our own strength disconnected from him and his strength.

'Help' here is '*antilambanô*' and means to 'take hold of something to give aid'.* God 'helps' us by taking hold of the thing he has given us to participate in, and moving it forward in a way that would otherwise not be possible for us to do by ourselves. As Psalm 127:1 puts it, 'Unless the Lord builds the house, they labour in vain who build it.' While God wants us to join in with what he is doing, he does not want us to do so in a way that acts as if it is down to our strength and abilities to make it succeed. Rather he wants us to be fully reliant on him, while at the same time fully participating in it, not least in prayer, knowing that if God does not make it happen, then it is not going to happen. In that way God gets all the glory, and we get the pleasure of joining in with him as he works through us.

1:55 'As he spoke to our fathers, to Abraham and his descendants forever.'

This 'help that takes hold' that Jacob experienced is tied up in the covenant promises that God had made earlier to his forefather Abraham. In Genesis 17:7, God says that he 'will establish my covenant between me and you and your descendants after you throughout their generations for an everlasting covenant, to be God to you and to your descendants after you.' In promising 'to be God to you', the reality is one of a God who is more than capable of getting what needs to be done, done. He can manage without help from anyone else, though he may graciously choose to involve others in accomplishing his will, he has no need of them. But God does graciously allow his people to get involved in his work for their own good, growth in faith and character, and future eternal reward. When the patriarchs tried to fulfil God's will in their own strength, they failed (for example, Abram and Hagar producing Ishmael). When they trusted in God to do it (i.e. in faith), they had success (for example Abraham and his barren wife Sarah producing Isaac). By faith in Messiah all are the 'descendants of Abraham' and the faith (which also means the faithfulness) of Abraham.

1:56 'And Mary stayed with her about three months, and then returned to her home.'

Mary would have stayed with Elizabeth until it was safe for her to return; presumably she heard about the census and returned to re-join Joseph for the journey to his native town of Bethlehem. 'Return' is '*hupostrephô*', a term used twenty-four times in the Gospels. The fact that twenty-three of these are by Luke may well be due to it having been the Greek physicians' common medical term for the return of the symptoms of a disease. [24]

1:57-58 'Now the time had come for Elizabeth to give birth, and she gave birth to a son. Her neighbours and her relatives heard that the Lord had displayed his great mercy toward her; and they were rejoicing with her.'

Elderly primigravida (first-time) mother's obstetric labours and deliveries are fraught with possible complications, some of them life-threatening. But God over-ruled obstetric norms. As was the custom, the whole neighbourhood joined in the rejoicing over the 'mercy' ('*eleos*', also meaning 'compassion') shown to her by God.

1:59-63 'And it happened that on the eighth day they came to circumcise the child, and they were going to call him Zechariah, after his father. But his mother answered and said, "No indeed; but he shall be called John." And they said to her, "There is no one among your relatives who is called by that name." And they made signs to his father, as to what he wanted him called. And he asked for a tablet and wrote as follows, "His name is John." And they were all astonished.'

God's covenant with Abraham required that all male Jewish babies be circumcised on the eighth day (Genesis 17:11), combined with naming in a rabbinic '*brit*' ceremony that has survived to this day. Zechariah is still undergoing his enforced silence, but has had about 42 weeks to ponder his faith (or lack of it) and in particular his understanding of the supernatural. So common was it to name a firstborn son after the father that the rabbi concerned did not even bother to enquire as to the choice of name. The use of sign language together with the production of a small writing board (Greek: '*pinakidion*' - a small writing tablet) allowed Zechariah to settle the matter, to the surprise of his relatives. The boy was to be named John, the shortened form of Jehohanan, which means 'Jehovah is gracious'.

1:64-66 'And at once his mouth was opened and his tongue loosed, and he began to speak in praise of God. Fear came on all those living around them; and all these matters were being talked about in all the hill country of

Judea. All who heard them kept them in mind, saying, "What then will this child turn out to be?" For the hand of the Lord was certainly with him.'

Their surprise did not end there. Zechariah's mouth was opened and so was his tongue ('loosed' is an addition, being not present in the original Greek text) - opened to the prophetic word of God (verses 68-79) concerning his son John and to God's praise in general. This miraculous event provoked *'phobos'* ('fear') in the surrounding region, almost certainly a fear of the Lord. John was marked out as a special child by his conception, by the Holy Spirit (who filled him in the womb) and by the miracle of his father's recovery of speech at his *'brit'* ceremony. God's 'hand' with him signifies a powerful anointing. John appears next not as a priest like his father but as a rabbi with his own disciples, some of whom change their allegiance to Jesus. His time 'in the desert' (Matthew 3, Mark 1) indicates his likely participation in the life of the separatist religious community of the Essenes. This was an ultra-orthodox Jewish community that practiced consecrated celibacy, and with which Jesus himself appears to have had contact. The man carrying water (Luke 22:10) indicates that the house that hosted the Last Supper had neither women nor children in it, hence was likely a celibate household.

1:67-68 'And his father Zechariah was filled with the Holy Spirit, and prophesied, saying: "Blessed be the Lord God of Israel, for he has visited us and accomplished redemption for his people."'

Now it is Zechariah's turn to be filled with the Holy Spirit. He begins with the common Hebrew blessing of God himself, and with especial regard for God's interventions in the life of his people Israel. The Greek for 'visited' is *'episkeptomai'*, which also means to 'look upon, inspect and examine with the eyes'.* The thought here is that of the prophet Hanani. 'For the eyes of the Lord move to and fro throughout the earth that he may strongly support those whose heart is completely his' (2 Chronicles 16:9). God is constantly on the look-out for those whose hearts are inclined towards him, and he visits them to bless them, that they may be resourced to be a blessing to others. 'Redeem' (Greek: *lutrôsis*'), means 'to release upon payment of a ransom'. [25] Early on is his prophesy, Zechariah is looking, perhaps unbeknown to him, beyond the ministry of his son John to the Messiah who would pay the price of sin's ransom.

1:69 'And has raised up a horn of salvation for us in the house of David his servant.'

Or, as Psalm 148:14 puts it, 'He has raised up for his people a horn, the praise of all his saints.' (NIV). A 'horn' was a metaphor for (usually kingly) strength. The strength of Messiah (a member by direct descent from the family and so 'house' of David) is spelled out in terms of salvation, meaning deliverance, preservation and safety. [26] The word for 'servant' that Zechariah uses here to describe David is *'pais'* (literally meaning 'child'), a term used for an attendant who was considered to be part of the family rather than simply a slave. David is reckoned as part of the covenanted family of Almighty God, and so are we.

1:70-71 'As he spoke by the mouth of his holy prophets from of old, "Salvation from our enemies and from the hand of all who hate us."'

The history of Israel is chequered with accounts of God saving his people from the hands of their enemies. The Levites had proclaimed, following the people's return from exile in Babylon, 'When they cried to you in the time of their distress, you heard from heaven, and according to your great compassion you gave them deliverers who delivered them from the hand of their oppressors' (Nehemiah 9:27).

Israel even today is hated by many who desire her destruction; it is God who ensures her safety and her part in his eternal plans.

1:72-73 'To show mercy toward our fathers, and to remember his holy covenant, the oath which he swore to Abraham our father.'

God's mercy (kindness and goodwill) is directed to all men, but especially those with whom he has made a covenant. The covenant with Abraham was put into place so that all the nations of the earth could benefit (Genesis 22:18 and 26:4), not just Israel as the natural descendants via Isaac, the child of promise. This 'oath' or 'pledge' to Abraham was about to come to fulfilment with the birth of the Messiah whose coming John would herald.

1:74-75 'To grant us that we, being rescued from the hand of our enemies, might serve him without fear, in holiness and righteousness before him all our days.'

Being 'rescued' is a concept linked to 'salvation' ('deliverance'), again, from enemies 'who hate us' (verse 71). The result is that the people are free to 'serve' God without fear to undermine their faith in him. 'Serve' is '*latreuo*', which means 'to minister' and especially 'to worship', and is used by Luke twice in that way in Acts (7:42 and 24:14). Such service and worship is performed in holiness - set apart to God, or as Paul would later put it, 'Created to be like God in true righteousness and holiness' (Ephesians 4:24, NIV). 'Righteousness' here again means right with God 'in accordance with God's standards', which were embodied in Torah. It meant to live in a way that was 'right' with God'.* This is the way in which Paul used the term to describe his life as a Pharisee prior to his coming to the righteousness that is by faith in Christ - 'As to the righteousness which is in the Law, found blameless' (Philippians 3:6) - a right standing that could not save, but was an outcome of legal obedience.

1:76 'And you, child, will be called the prophet of the Most High; for you will go on before the Lord to prepare his ways'

John is to receive the title of 'prophet of the Most High', in the same way that his father Zechariah is prophesying - under the inspiration of the Holy Spirit. Zechariah is prompted by the Spirit to quote the Old Testament prophet Malachi (3:1). '"See, I will send my messenger, who will prepare the way before me. Then suddenly the Lord you are seeking will come to his Temple; the messenger of the covenant, whom you desire, will come," says the Lord Almighty' (NIV). John is to be the voice that calls, 'Clear the way for the Lord in the wilderness; make smooth in the desert a highway for our God' (Isaiah 40:3). The Roman army would deploy divisions of wood-cutters and engineers to literally prepare 'a way' for the coming of their empire, and John's ministry is to be the spiritual equivalent. The Greek for 'go on before' is *proporeuomai*, a term used for a herald * that went ahead of a king announcing the fact of his impending arrival, so that the people might be ready to receive him.

1:77 'To give to his people the knowledge of salvation, by the forgiveness of their sins'

The salvation and deliverance that John would herald would be on the basis of sin being forgiven. 'Forgiveness' here is *aphesis*, which means 'pardoned' from the term to 'let go' and was used in the sense of being pardoned for wrongdoing by 'remitting' the offence. The penalty for sin is to be remitted and we are to be set free from the power of sin by Messiah's sacrificial death and subsequent resurrection.

1:78 'Because of the tender mercy of our God, with which the Sunrise from on high will visit us'

Zechariah is looking forward to the end of the dark night of the 400-year silence following the Book of Malachi, and the rising of the true spiritual sun. He is echoing Isaiah - 'The people who walk in darkness will see a great light; those who live in a dark land, the light will shine on them' (Isaiah 9:2). Already the early reflections of the sun's rays are appearing, before the sun itself has risen above the horizon. Once again, Zechariah uses the term 'visit' - God is coming to inspect the spiritual state of his people. John's task is to help them to be ready to pass the inspection.

1:79 'To shine on those living in darkness and the shadow of death, to guide our feet into the way of peace.'

Psalm 107:10-11 now is quoted. 'There were those who dwelt in darkness and in the shadow of death, prisoners in misery and chains, because they had rebelled against the words of God, and spurned the counsel of the Most High.' People need to be helped out of their spiritual darkness - God promises to 'break the bonds' (Psalm 107:14) of all those who respond to him, and to lead them into peace, with him and with themselves. To follow is our responsibility.

1:80 'And the child continued to grow and to become strong in spirit, and he lived in the desert until the day of his public appearance to Israel.'

According to the Talmud [27] the age for commencing public speaking 'with authority' as a teacher of the Law was 30. John underwent his spiritual preparation in the wilderness, not at all in the sense of being on his own - he could not have been regarded as a rabbi if he had - but perhaps within the community of the Essenes, evidence of whom has been found in the Qumran desert. [28] As an ultra-orthodox Jewish teacher, John would command great respect in Israel, but with a slightly different message to the normal - a message of repentance that announced Messiah's arrival.

Chapter 2

2:1-3 'Now in those days a decree went out from Caesar Augustus, that a census be taken of all the inhabited earth. This was the first census taken while Quirinius was governor of Syria. And everyone was on his way to register for the census, each to his own city.'

Luke uses Caesar's Latin title 'Augustus' instead of the Greek equivalent ('Sebastos'). Luke is very careful throughout the Gospel and Acts to be respectful to Romans. In seeking the legal aid of a senior Roman legal figure, Theophilus, on behalf of his friend and ministry colleague Paul, Luke was passing on material that was to be integral to a legal defence. Augustus had eventually succeeded to the throne of the Roman Empire after the assassination of Julius Caesar, and reigned from 27 BC to 14 AD. He regarded his censuses among his most important acts, [29] firstly because of their use in estimating taxation revenues but also because he was concerned that the population he ruled was declining in numbers, of especial concern for future military service. One such census is recorded as being decreed in 8 BC, and a 1-2 year time lapse would be quite usual for the border zones of the Empire such as Palestine. Jesus is believed to have been born between 7 and 6 BC, based upon Herod's death in 4 BC and Josephus' account of an accompanying lunar eclipse. [30]

Quirinius ruled as governor in Syria from 6-7 AD, [31] and undertook a census recorded by Luke in Acts 5:37. He took over from Herod the Great's older son Archelaus (Josephus, 'Antiquities' 18, 26), who had proved himself to be too much like his father for the local populace to tolerate. There has therefore been debate regarding how the census travel of Jesus' birth fits with Luke's information. The most probable answer (given Luke's phenomenal historical accuracy) lies with the common English translation of the passage - in the Greek text the word 'while' ('while Quirinius was governor') does not appear. Additionally, 'first' (*'prôtos'*), also means 'former' or 'before', [32] and 'governor' is not in the noun form but the verb form (*'hêgemoneuô'* - 'to govern'). The passage can therefore also be rendered, 'This was the census before Quirinius governed Syria.' Luke takes it for granted that his audience knows who Quirinius was (Publius Sulpicius Quirinus, 51 BC - 21 AD).

Josephus noted the effects on non-citizens of this decree in Judea in 6 AD: 'Now Cyrenius *[Quirinius]*, a Roman senator, and one who had gone through other magistracies, and had passed through them until he had been consul, and one who, on other accounts, was of great dignity, came at this time into Syria, with a few others, being sent by Caesar to be a judge of that nation, and to take an account of their substance. Coponius also, a man of the equestrian order, was sent together with him, to have the supreme power over the Jews. Moreover, Cyrenius came himself into Judea, which was now added to the province of Syria, to take an account of their substance, and to dispose of Archelaus' money; but the Jews, although at the beginning they took the report of a taxation heinously, yet did they leave off any further opposition to it' ('Antiquities' 18, 1). This makes the premise that there were two rulers with the same name unlikely. Syria was an important region in the Roman world as it served both as a buffer against their Parthian enemies further east and as a means of holding the Mediterranean ports important for importing food to Rome. It was to the Syrian legion that Herod the Great had turned for the military resources to overthrow the Parthian invasion of 40 BC and so re-take Jerusalem in 37 BC.

Most people did not travel far from their place of birth, and the Roman's required that people be numbered in their 'own *[native]* city'. A Roman census document from 104 AD discovered in Egypt records that citizens were specifically commanded to return to their original homes for the census. [33] This is because the family and tribal records were kept there.

2:4-6 'Joseph also went up from Galilee, from the city of Nazareth, to Judea, to the city of David which is called Bethlehem, because he was of the house and family of David, in order to register along with Mary, who was engaged to him, and was with child. While they were there, the days were completed for her to give birth.'

As has been said above, the likeliest reason for a Judean '*tekton*' to be in Nazareth was its proximity to the Roman construction going on in Sephorris. Joseph had to travel back to his family's home in Bethlehem, with his betrothed wife-to-be Mary, now in an advanced stage of pregnancy. Joseph would no doubt have been relieved to have a good reason to take Mary out of what would have been an awkward situation in Nazareth. The commonly portrayed children's nativity-play notion of Mary and Joseph having nowhere to stay in Bethlehem is an extraordinary one. Joseph would have gone to the house of his father Jacob, where his mother and other female relatives would have taken care of Mary and the imminently arriving baby. Mary was situated in the family home when her labour pains began - the idea of the couple going from place to place while she was in labour offends against the text ('native town'), and Luke's comment 'while they were there' (rather than labour starting while they were arriving). Even without Joseph's parents help, the near-Eastern culture of aiding travellers, especially a 'son of David', renders the idea of going from inn to inn (even if there had been more than one inn in a small village so close to Jerusalem) absurd.

2:7 'And she gave birth to her firstborn son; and she wrapped him in cloths, and laid him in a manger, because there was no room for them in the inn.'

Once again the translators veer away from Biblical Greek and also from common sense. Luke's New Testament word for 'inn' is not the word being used here. That word is '*pandocheion*', as featuring

44

in the parable of the Good Samaritan (Luke 10:34). The Greek here in verse 7 is '*kataluma*', which is only used in the New Testament to mean 'guest room' (Mark 14:14 and Luke 22:11). While it is true that people would lodge travellers in their guest-rooms, this is very different to an inn. Bethlehem, being walking distance of Jerusalem, had little need of an inn, and the idea of Joseph going to an inn in preference to his family home is ludicrous, particularly given his need of familial assistance with Mary's labour and delivery.

But the census meant that other far-flung members of Joseph's father Jacob's '*tekton*' offspring had also been required to make the journey home. Consequently the house guest-room was full, and certainly no place for the 12-hour labour of the primigravida Mary. But just as in our day and age space can be created by moving a car out of a garage and rendering it, at a pinch, warm and habitable, so there was an alternative place for Mary's labour - the family stable, kept clean to the hygiene standards of the religious Law the devout Jewish family adhered to. The animal's feeding trough provided a convenient and warm place to lay the newly wrapped infant Jesus. Doctor Luke's use of 'first-born' ('*prototokos*' - first birth/delivery/labour')* does not support the idea that Jesus was Mary's only child, especially given the fact that Luke was necessarily obtaining this information from Mary herself, and neither does Psalm 69 verse 8, where any notion of 'cousin' is ruled out. [v]

2:8 'In the same region there were some shepherds staying out in the fields and keeping watch over their flock by night.'

Shepherds were outcasts of religious Jewish society because their work necessarily made ritual cleansing impossible. However, it is

---

[v] 'I have become estranged from my brothers, and an alien to my mother's sons' (Psalm 69:8).

likely that these were not ordinary shepherds. According to the Jewish Talmud, Bethlehem was the place that the Temple flocks were grazed, providing the Temple with their own 'clean' supply of sacrificial lambs for sale in the Temple market. In the Talmud ('*Berakoth*', 2.3), Messiah is said to be born in 'the royal castle of Bethlehem', and Messiah was spoken of by the Jews of as 'the tower of the flock' (the '*Migdal Eder*'). [34]

Edersheim states: 'This '*Migdal Eder*' was not the watchtower for the ordinary flocks which were pastured on the barren sheep-ground beyond Bethlehem, but lay close to the town, on the road to Jerusalem. A passage in the Mishnah ('*Shekalim*' 7) leads to the conclusion that the flocks, which pastured there, were destined for Temple-sacrifices. In fact the Mishnah ('*Baba Kama*' 7) expressly forbids the keeping of flocks throughout the land of Israel, except in the wilderness, and the only flocks otherwise kept would be those for the Temple-services ('*Baba Kama*' 80a), and accordingly that the shepherds who watched over them were not ordinary shepherds.' The Law forbade contact with ordinary shepherds as being unclean because their isolation from religious observances and their manner of life, which rendered strict legal observance of hygiene laws impossible.

Temple flocks were out all year round - the Talmud refers to them as being in the fields thirty days before the Passover, that is, in the month of February, when rainfall is abundant. In the Talmud two opinions are expressed. According to one, the '*Midbariyoth*' or 'animals of the wilderness,' are those which go to the open at the Passover time, and return at the first rains (about November); while the wilderness-flocks remain in the open alike in the hottest days and in the rainy season, i.e. all the year round ('*Beitzah*' 40a). 'Thus Jewish tradition in some dim manner apprehended the first revelation of the Messiah from that '*Migdal Eder*' (the watch-tower of the flock), where shepherds watched the Temple-flocks all the year round.' [35]

These shepherds were being given the privilege of witnessing the arrival of the One whose own offering of himself on a cross would make their flock's contribution to Temple sacrifices no longer necessary. Those who cared for the Temple sacrificial lambs were the first outside Jesus' own family to see the Lamb of God who would take away the sins of the world (John 1:29). Jesus is believed to have been born at the time of, and in prophetic fulfilment of, the Feast of Tabernacles (September - October),[vi] and at that time of the year in Israel it is still warm enough for shepherds to sleep outside with their flocks.

2:9 'And an angel of the Lord suddenly stood before them, and the glory of the Lord shone around them; and they were terribly frightened.'

Jews believed that at the point of death an angelic spirit came to take them to Sheol, the place of the dead. This is why the disciples on stormy Lake Galilee, already in fear of drowning, are terrified by the sight that they believe to be a ghost (spirit) approaching them on the surface of the water (Matthew 14:26). Not knowing that it is actually Jesus, they believe that their fear of imminent death had been confirmed. Besides, angelic appearances normally do terrify people, especially when unexpected! Peter records that angels 'are greater in power and might' (2 Peter 2:11) - perhaps something of an under-statement when compared with ordinary men and women. The Old Testament prophet Daniel had a similar experience. 'I heard the voice of a man between the banks of Ulai, and he called out and said, "Gabriel, give this man an understanding of the vision." So he came near to where I was standing, and when he came I was frightened

---

[vi] 'The Word became flesh and tabernacled among us' (John 1:14).

and fell on my face' (Daniel 8:16-17). So did the Apostle John: 'I fell at his feet to worship him. But he said to me, "Do not do that; I am a fellow servant of yours and your brethren who hold the testimony of Jesus"' (Revelation 19:10). 'Glory' ('*doxa*') here is used in the sense of 'brightness'* - angels reflect the glory of God whose radiant face they behold (Matthew 18:10).

2:10-11 'But the angel said to them, "Do not be afraid; for behold, I bring you good news of great joy which will be for all the people; for today in the city of David there has been born for you a Saviour, who is Christ the Lord.'

'Good news' is '*euaggelizô*', a fitting choice of word in this instance, being derived from '*eu*' meaning 'good' or 'well' and '*aggelos*' meaning 'angel' (and occasionally 'messenger'). A good angel was bringing a 'good message'. David was from Bethlehem (1 Samuel 17:15 and 20:28), and it was that city that the prophet Micah had foretold would be Messiah's birthplace. 'As for you, Bethlehem Ephrathah, too little to be among the clans of Judah, from you one will go forth for me to be ruler in Israel. His goings forth are from long ago, from the days of eternity' (Micah 5:2). Jesus titles are '*sôtêr*' - 'Saviour' and '*Christos Kurios*' - 'Anointed Lord'; both are clearly messianic in nature.

2:12 'This will be a sign for you: you will find a baby wrapped in cloths and lying in a manger.'

Finding a baby wrapped in cloths (common enough) is the goal; the 'sign' is that the baby they would be looking for would be laying in a feeding trough - an uncommon enough scenario to be unmissable.

2:13-14 'And suddenly there appeared with the angel a multitude of the heavenly host praising God and saying,

"Glory to God in the highest, and on earth peace among men with whom he is pleased."'

The angelic army had no doubt been there all along, only now the shepherd's eyes were opened to see them. The glory referred to here is synonymous with praise [36] for the God who dwells in the highest place but who had now set up his tabernacle in human flesh. God's benevolent favour had overflowed from heaven and onto earth.

2:15-16 'When the angels had gone away from them into heaven, the shepherds began saying to one another, "Let us go straight to Bethlehem then, and see this thing that has happened which the Lord has made known to us." So they came in a hurry and found their way to Mary and Joseph, and the baby as he lay in the manger.'

The shepherds evidence their faith by the alacrity of their obedience to the angel's instructions. Joseph's father's stable would have had a direct opening to the outside thereby making the shepherds' search for the baby-occupied manger much easier.

2:17-18 'When they had seen this, they made known the statement which had been told them about this child. And all who heard it wondered at the things which were told them by the shepherds.'

The shepherds passed on the angel's message thereby explaining their sudden arrival; 'all who heard' implies a greater number than simply Joseph and Mary - Joseph's wider family in the house heard the news as well. Their reaction was 'to wonder' - '*thaumazô*' - 'to marvel'.*

2:19-20 'But Mary treasured all these things, pondering them in her heart. The shepherds went back, glorifying

49

and praising God for all that they had heard and seen, just as had been told them.'

'Treasured' here is '*suntêreô*', meaning 'to preserve carefully' * in her mind what the shepherds had related to them. Once again we see the intelligent, biblically informed Mary considering carefully in her mind what she has just heard, in a similar way to her reaction to the words heard from the angel Gabriel. Her 'remembering' was to be of the utmost help to Luke in compiling his Gospel and the many evidences of Jesus' messianic status that had led to the Apostle Paul putting his faith in him. 'To ponder' is '*sumballô*', from '*sum*', meaning 'together with', and '*ballô*', meaning 'to throw'.* Mary is 'throwing things that she has heard around in her mind', intelligently considering them as she seeks to make sense of them before God. For the shepherds, their response was to offer praise and thanks to God for Jesus' birth.

2:21 'And when eight days had passed, before his circumcision, his name was then called Jesus, the name given by the angel before he was conceived in the womb.'

Genesis (17:12) laid down the eighth day as the time for circumcision (even on the Sabbath day); it is also, with God's foreknowledge, the time when a baby's blood clotting factors have become sufficient for bleeding to stop quickly. It was also the ceremony ('*Brit*' - Hebrew for 'covenant') at which the baby would be named (as in Luke 1:39). Jesus' name in Hebrew is '*Y'shua*', which, transliterated, is 'Joshua'. We arrive at the English version of 'Jesus' by virtue of coming via Greek ('Iēsous') and then Latin ('IESUS') names, being transliterated into the available consonants of the language in question, while trying to keep to the existing recognised pronunciation as closely as possible.

2:22-24 'And when the days for their purification according to the law of Moses were completed, they brought him up to Jerusalem to present him to the Lord (as it is written in the Law of the Lord, 'Every firstborn male that opens the womb shall be called holy to the Lord'), and to offer a sacrifice according to what was said in the Law of the Lord, a pair of turtledoves or two young pigeons.'

Childbirth rendered a mother legally unclean for 40 days in the case of a boy, and 80 in the case of a girl (Leviticus 12:1-4). After that time had elapsed, the Law specified the sacrifices that must be brought. 'When the days of her purification are completed, for a son or for a daughter, she shall bring to the priest at the doorway of the tent of meeting a one year old lamb for a burnt offering and a young pigeon or a turtledove for a sin offering' (Leviticus 12:6).

In addition, the Law (Exodus 13:2) laid down that all firstborn males, be they human or animal, belonged to the Lord. While animals could be sacrificed, the baby boys had to be redeemed, as stated in Numbers 18:18. 'As to their redemption price, from a month old you shall redeem them, by your valuation, five shekels in silver, according to the shekel of the sanctuary, which is twenty gerahs.' Having a firstborn son was an expensive business.

Much has been made of the fact that Mary and Joseph offered the birds rather than a lamb. Scholars have consistently seen it as a sign of the family's poverty, as it was the Law's provision for the poor. But there was another very good reason for a Jew to make the cheaper of the two offerings (which were not means-tested), and so fulfil his legal obligations. All offerings, be they birds or animals, had to be purchased using 'the sanctuary shekel'. Ordinary money was not accepted; hence it had to be changed into the special Temple coins. And this was not a cheap process; the families of priests who

51

controlled the Temple market used an inflated exchange rate to gain enormous wealth for themselves.

Additionally, worshippers could not bring their own birds or animals as offerings - the priests would not accept them as being worthy of Temple sacrifice. The Temple market was the only place at which legally acceptable offerings could be obtained, and their prices were also grossly inflated, something that Jesus objected to on the occasions when he 'cleansed' the Temple markets (John 2:15, Matthew 21:12), as did other rabbinic figures. The Talmud records, 'It once happened in Jerusalem that the price of a pair of doves rose to a golden denar. Said Rabbi Simeon ben Gamaliel, "By this sanctuary, I shall not go to sleep tonight before they cost but a silver denar!" Then he entered the Beth Din and taught; 'If a woman had five certain births or five certain issues she need bring but one offering, and may then partake of sacrificial flesh, and she is not bound to bring the other offerings. Thereupon the price of a pair of birds stood at a quarter of a silver denar each.' [37]

The families of priests that ran the Temple market (becoming extremely rich in doing so) were at the opposite ideological end of the Jewish religious spectrum from the devout Jews that studied and taught Torah, and who were often, but not always, poor, because they spent so much of their time doing so. Accordingly there was a no love lost between these two sections of the Temple community. Joseph (Matthew 1:19) is described as being 'devout', i.e. 'righteous in relation to the Law' (c.f. the Apostle Paul's claim in Philippians 3:6, 'As to the righteousness which is in the Law, found blameless'). 'Law' necessarily included the Oral Law, indicating that Joseph was religiously well schooled. He would have been extremely reluctant to put any more money into the pockets of the already obscenely wealthy and ideologically opposed priests than the minimum sum necessary to meet his legal obligations. Hence he offered two birds rather than the much more expensive alternative of a lamb. This has no bearing on the family's later financial position - they had yet to receive the Magi's visit and the kingly gifts that they brought.

2:25-26 'And there was a man in Jerusalem whose name was Simeon; and this man was righteous and devout, looking for the consolation of Israel; and the Holy Spirit was upon him. And it had been revealed to him by the Holy Spirit that he would not see death before he had seen the Lord's Christ.'

Enter Simeon. Luke records that he was 'righteous' - again, meaning one who kept the Mosaic Law. The Greek here is, again, *'dikaios'*, from *'dikh'*, meaning 'justice'. Simeon was also 'devout'. The Greek here is *'eulabes'*, someone who has 'taken a good hold' (from *'eu'* - 'acted well' and *'lambano'* - 'taken or procured').* He had 'taken a good hold' on God's word and was living in the good of what he knew to be God's plan for the people of Israel concerning the coming Messiah, 'the consolation of Israel'. Three times Luke informs us that Simeon was touched by the Holy Spirit; he also had a 'prophetic' gifting. Many devout Jews were waiting expectantly for the coming of the Messiah, the anointed one from God (the Lord's Christ). The Messiah was seen as being a deliverer from oppression (such as the Romans imposed) and as a restorer of the spiritual life of the people of Israel, very much in the manner of their illustrious ancestor King David. Simeon would have been just such a devout Jew, in all probability dissatisfied with the political situation of an occupying foreign power and with the wealth-driven corruption of the ruling priestly families, and hoping to see the Messiah in his own lifetime.

2:27-32 'And he came in the Spirit into the Temple; and when the parents brought in the child Jesus, to carry out for him the custom of the law, then he took him into his arms, and blessed God, and said, "Now Lord, you are

releasing your bondservant to depart in peace, according to your word; for my eyes have seen your salvation which you have prepared in the presence of all peoples. A light of revelation to the Gentiles and the glory of your people Israel."'

Simeon may well have recognised Joseph as a Temple architect, with his young wife Mary (a fellow descendant of Aaron), and their new-born baby boy. There may already have been some unkind rumours about this child's conception; some certainly followed later, since John records (John 8:39-41), 'The Jews answered and said to him, "Abraham is our father." Jesus said to them, "If you are Abraham's children, do the deeds of Abraham. But as it is, you are seeking to kill me, a man who has told you the truth, which I heard from God; this Abraham did not do. You are doing the deeds of your father." They said to him, "We were not born of fornication; we have one Father: God."'

Simeon 'blessed' God - *'eulogeo'* meaning to 'praise', or to 'celebrate with praises' (from *'eu'* meaning 'well', and *'logos'* meaning 'a word') [38] in the traditional Levitical manner, the prophetic blessing that Christ would fulfil the word of the prophet Isaiah. 'I the Lord have called you in righteousness; I will take hold of your hand. I will keep you and will make you to be a covenant for the people and a light for the Gentiles' (Isaiah 42:6, ANIV). Did Simeon's taking of the baby in his arms give Mary a shock? Or would she remember what had already been said to her about Jesus?

2:33 'And his father and mother were amazed at the things which were being said about him.'

Despite Mary and Joseph having been visited by none other than the angel Gabriel and told of who Jesus was, she and Joseph still stood 'amazed' at Simeon's prophecy. Even though both had heard from

Gabriel, both parents 'marvelled' (KJV) in amazement. Mary had heard, 'He shall be great, and shall be called the Son of the Highest: and the Lord God shall give unto him the throne of his father David: and he shall reign over the house of Jacob for ever; and of his kingdom there shall be no end' (Luke 1:32-33, KJV). Joseph had heard, 'Thou shalt call his name Jesus: for he shall save his people from their sins' (Matthew 1:21, KJV). Those are much more awesome words than Simeon's. Yet Jesus' parents 'were amazed' at the words about him being a light to the Gentiles and the glory (praise) of Israel; qualifications that could be fulfilled by any prophet. They were therefore still coming to terms with understanding the words spoken of him.

2:34-35 'And Simeon blessed them and said to Mary his mother, "Behold, this child is appointed for the fall and rise of many in Israel, and for a sign to be opposed - and a sword will pierce even your own soul - to the end that thoughts from many hearts may be revealed."'

'Fall' here is '*ptosis*', the medical term given for a drooping eyelid; 'rise' is '*anastasis*' meaning 'resurrection'. For Mary, there was more - a 'long sword' would pierce her soul ('*psuche*') - 'that part where the breath of human life resides as the seat of all that perceives and feels humanly').* This is distinct from '*kardia*' - the heart - 'the place of thinking, reasoning and the will'. [39]

2:36-38. 'And there was a prophetess, Anna the daughter of Phanuel, of the tribe of Asher. She was advanced in years and had lived with her husband seven years after her marriage, and then as a widow to the age of eighty-four. She never left the Temple, serving night and day with fasting and prayers. At that very moment she came up and began giving thanks to God, and continued to

speak of him to all those who were looking for the redemption of Jerusalem.'

Enter Anna. Also prophetically gifted, she too spoke God's word to Mary and Joseph. Her name means 'grace' in Hebrew, and she is described as being the daughter of one whose name meant 'the face of God' (Phanuel). She was of the tribe of whom the Jewish patriarch Jacob had prophesied in Genesis 49:20, 'From Asher, his bread shall be rich, and he will yield royal delicacies.' At age eighty-four she was still going strong, doing the menial tasks (serving, '*latreou*', 'a hired menial'),* tasks that were possibly below the dignity of the priests to do, while praying and fasting. Timing again is perfect as she responds with 'a mutual agreement and acknowledgement in thankfulness to God' - '*anthomologeomai*'.* Anna comes and speaks of the Christ to all those whom God had likewise gathered to witness the coming of the one who would rescue the inhabitants of the twin hills of Jerusalem from the consequences of their sins.

2:39-40 'When they had performed everything according to the Law of the Lord, they returned to Galilee, to their own city of Nazareth. The child continued to grow and become strong, increasing in wisdom; and the grace of God was upon him.'

It is Matthew's account that describes the intervening journey to Egypt, after which the family return to Nazareth, a short distance from the town of Sepphoris (the Roman capital of Galilee) where the government buildings and fortifications would have created a demand for Joseph's skills as a '*tekton*' (who 'laid foundations'). [vii] Jesus, we are told, 'increased in wisdom', including the study of

---

[vii] 'Like a wise master builder [*'tekton'*] I laid a foundation' (1 Corinthians 3:10).

Torah and the Jewish oral rabbinic traditions - the teaching of centuries of accumulated rabbinic wisdom, with the status that this learning gave in his society. He was growing both naturally and in wisdom.

2:41-51 'Now his parents went to Jerusalem every year at the Feast of the Passover. And when he became twelve, they went up there according to the custom of the Feast; and as they were returning, after spending the full number of days, the boy Jesus stayed behind in Jerusalem. But his parents were unaware of it, but supposed him to be in the caravan, and went a day's journey; and they began looking for him among their relatives and acquaintances. When they did not find him, they returned to Jerusalem looking for him. Then, after three days they found him in the Temple, sitting in the midst of the teachers, both listening to them and asking them questions. And all who heard him were amazed at his understanding and his answers. When they saw him, they were astonished; and his mother said to him, "Son, why have you treated us this way? Behold, your father and I have been anxiously looking for you." And he said to them, "Why is it that you were looking for me? Did you not know that I had to be in my Father's house?" But they did not understand the statement which he had made to them. And he went down with them and came to Nazareth, and he continued in subjection to them; and his mother treasured all these things in her heart.'

All able-bodied Jews within the land of Israel were required to journey to Jerusalem for the three compulsory feasts: Passover, Pentecost and Tabernacles (Booths), as the Law required. 'Three times in a year all your males shall appear before the Lord your God in the place which he chooses, at the Feast of Unleavened Bread and at the Feast of Weeks and at the Feast of Booths' (Deuteronomy 16:16). All Jewish boys studied Scripture to age ten. At that point the less academically able moved into full-time training in their father's trade. The more able continued in schooling, learning the Mishnah (rabbinic law and traditions) until age 15. [40] Afterwards, only the very gifted boys would move on to the in-depth study of Scripture and Talmudic Law known as Midrash. This took place in the 'Hall of Study' (Bet Midrash), the most important of which was located in the Temple courts in Jerusalem, where the Doctors of Torah like Gamaliel taught their disciples.

The Bet Midrash is the hall that the Talmud records the great Jewish scholar Hillel (as a young man) almost freezing to death over the roof-window of in his desire to hear the Torah being expounded. 'It was reported about Hillel the Elder that every day he used to work and earn one *tropaik*, half of which he would give to the guard at the House of Learning, the other half being spent for his food and for that of his family. One day he found nothing to earn and the guard at the House of Learning would not permit him to enter. He climbed up and sat upon the window, to hear the words of the living God from the mouth of Shemayah and Abtalion... That day was the eve of Sabbath in the winter solstice and snow fell down upon him from heaven. When the dawn rose, Shemayah said to Abtalion, "Brother Abtalion, on every day this house is light and to-day it is dark, is it perhaps a cloudy day?" They looked up and saw the figure of a man in the window. They went up and found him covered by three cubits of snow. They removed him, bathed and anointed him and placed him opposite the fire' (Talmud, *'Yoma'* 35b).

The first recorded words of Jesus, aged twelve, come from such a teaching session in the Hall of Study in the Temple. His family's attendance at the feast is what was expected of a 'devout' family (Matthew 1:19). But, at age twelve, before his Bar-mitzvah and official entry into the world of adulthood in his society, something unusual happened. Jesus got separated from his parents in the crowd of pilgrims leaving the city after the festival and five days elapsed before he was reunited with them. He was found, as he put it, 'in his Father's house' (the Temple in Jerusalem). Passover, which commemorated the exodus of the Jews from Egypt under the leadership of Moses, and the establishment of the nation of Israel as a free entity in their own right, was the busiest, the holiest and most celebrated of all the Jewish feasts. Jerusalem was packed to overflowing with pilgrims - shortly after Christ's death, a count of the Passover lambs sacrificed put the number of worshippers at around 2.7 million. [41] So there was every possibility that a lively twelve-year-old boy might get separated from his mother and father. Eventually, Jesus was found by Mary and Joseph in the Temple courts - 'sitting among the Teachers (*'Didaskalos'* - 'Doctors' - of the Law) listening to them and asking them questions. Everyone who heard him was amazed at his understanding and his answers' (verse 47).

We may think that 'asking them questions' amounts to making enquiries to further his knowledge. Actually, it is also the Jewish rabbinic method of teaching, whereby the answer becomes obvious to the other person through the asking of questions. Rabbis taught through a process of asking questions that would provoke their hearers into elucidating truth for themselves. The venerable Doctors of the Law are amazed at Jesus' 'understanding' and 'answers'; hence, at the age of twelve, Jesus was teaching the teachers. From the Greek *'didasko'* ('to teach') is derived the title used by Luke - *'Didaskalos'* - the 'Doctors' (of the Law) - 'The Masters of Teaching'. These were the men who ran the rabbinic schools that taught the Torah and the oral traditions that became the Mishnah (the commentary that the rabbis had compiled on the Torah), men like Gamaliel, who were recognised and appointed by the Sanhedrin, the ruling Jewish council of elders. They debated the knottier aspects of Jewish law, and they were very good at it. Jesus had attached himself to the '***Didaskalos***' of his own free will at the age of twelve, and they had accepted him. That he was allowed to sit with them and listen was unusual in itself given that Jesus is not yet a legal adult. The Doctors of Torah were not child-minders, and Bet Midrash was certainly not a centre for lost and found children! Their extraordinary inclusion of Jesus at this young age indicates that they knew of his father Joseph (most likely as a Temple architect) and were caring for Jesus out of their honour of him until Joseph returned. What is extremely unusual is Luke's comment, 'Everyone who heard him was amazed at his understanding and his answers.' The One who had delivered the Torah to Moses on Sinai had arrived in their midst as a twelve year old boy, the son of Joseph, the Temple '***tekton***'.

What would their reaction have been to the arrival of such a brilliant youngster? They would certainly have made a response. The Law [42] laid down that boys must be trained to the level of their ability; Mishnah 8 therein speaks of the blessing upon the mother of Rabbi Joshua ben Hananaiah who carried him as a baby his cot to the Bet Midrash so that from his infancy his ears might become attuned to the sound of the study of the Torah. Jesus' mother and father would have been no less devout in their practice of Judaism. The Doctors of Torah are described by Luke as responding ecstatically to Jesus' grasp of Torah, and his talent was one they would not have allowed to slip through their fingers, for Jewish legal reasons as well as human academic appreciation. The Temple-based Doctors of the Law and senior rabbis saw, in the twelve-year-old Jesus, the most brilliant mind for their beloved Torah that they had ever come across. He could, with a few simple questions, clarify their most complicated arguments and legal issues and make beautiful sense out of them. When learned Law masters sat down with him, they were the ones who ended up being instructed in the Word of God. It seems, from this example, that no one could disciple Jesus because his understanding was so great that he excelled among the very greatest minds of the Temple courts.

'Amazed' here is '*existimi*', literally meaning 'to stand out', describing a state of sheer astonishment, meaning to 'throw into wonderment',* and these men, who lived for the Law of Moses, would certainly have acted to secure this young man for rabbinic training. No other reaction makes any sense from a human, and especially a Jewish psychological perspective, in men who would have been euphoric over such a star finding in a boy on the verge of legal manhood. The Doctors had a legal duty to train promising students for the benefit of the wider Jewish community as well as a natural personal interest. Josephus ('Antiquities' book 4, chapter 8, 12) records an injunction of Moses: 'Let the children also learn the laws, as the first thing they are taught, which will be the best thing they can be taught, and will be the cause of their future felicity.' Jesus would have been taught by Joseph and local rabbis at the Torah School attached to the synagogue in his native Nazareth, where the Law of Moses was learned by rote. He would then have been brought to Jerusalem for adult rabbinic training in the official theological schools that operated there from within the Temple courts, under the supervision of the Doctors of the Law. It was there that his future apostle, Saul of Tarsus, 'sat at the feet of Gamaliel' (Acts 22:3), a master of the Jewish Oral Law.

Jesus clearly had an amazing talent, one they would not have failed to secure for him rabbinic training, with the blessing of his father Joseph. The Doctors would have wanted him in their schools because in him they would have seen a new and golden age of Jewish wisdom and understanding unfolding. Here was a boy in the class of Moses and King David at a time when the pagan Romans had placed their image (a golden eagle) over the main Temple entrance. [43] They had also defiled the Temple precincts by building a garrison (named Antonia) there, even going so far as connecting it to the holy Temple courts themselves. National pride had taken a severe blow with the Roman occupation, and now Herod, an Idumean (the very people their illustrious ancestor Judas Maccabeus had conquered in the uprising against Hellenistic rule in 167 BC) was ruling over them. In Jesus, they would have seen a bright hope.

2:52 'And Jesus kept increasing in wisdom and stature, and in favour with God and men.'

Jesus returned to Nazareth and grew in wisdom (the Torah-based wisdom of his people) and stature (in relation to that wisdom), and favour with God and men - the men who taught the wisdom of his people Israel. Devout Jews with a son who was a widely recognised genius in Torah would seek for him further rabbinic scholarship, as that was what education stood for in their society and was what the Law required, as well as having great status. Having met him once, the Doctors of the Law in Jerusalem would also have ensured that his parents brought him for training. To have failed to do so would have meant breaking their own Law. Jesus was to be honed for greatness, with a view to producing the most brilliant theologian Israel had seen for centuries, like Gamaliel, who was one of the very few ever to be addressed as 'Rabboni' - Master Rabbi (as Jesus was - Mark 10:51 and John 20:16).

Luke's use of 'stature' here relates to Jesus' growth in wisdom, and is not a repeated reference to his growth in physical stature. The 'men' that he is growing in favour with are particularly the men who taught the wisdom of Torah - the rabbinic scholars. Jesus' clearly extraordinary talent assured him of a fast-track route in the Jewish educational process. The fact that Christ was later addressed by the same title (Doctor of the Law) as the men he met aged twelve explains what he was doing in the intervening eighteen years before re-emerging into public life aged thirty, the age the Mishnah accords to 'speaking with authority'. [44] He had, inevitably, gained academic parity with them in becoming a '*Didaskalos*' himself. There was no higher Jewish rabbinic office that a scholar could acquire, and there had never been a scholar with a greater ability than Jesus' ability.

Chapter 3

3:1 'Now in the fifteenth year of the reign of Tiberius Caesar, when Pontius Pilate was governor of Judea, and Herod was tetrarch of Galilee, and his brother Philip was tetrarch of the region of Ituraea and Trachonitis, and Lysanias was tetrarch of Abilene.'

Once again Luke's attention to detail comes through. He is careful, with his Roman audience in mind, to give pre-eminence to the Empire's historic perspective in preference to the Jewish priestly rule. Tiberius became sole Emperor in AD 14, however he ruled alongside Augustus from AD 11. After Herod the Great had died, his will was contested by his sons, necessitating the Emperor Augustus to decide the matter and ratify it. Augustus divided Herod's territory into four parts, with none having kingly authority. Instead, he appointed to each territory rulers directly subordinate to Rome. Archelaus, son of Herod's Samaritan wife Malthace and older brother of Antipas, was awarded the more prestigious region of Judea, and as an 'ethnarch' (superior to 'tetrarch'), perhaps out of respect for Herod's (disputed and unfulfilled) wish that Archelaus be king in his stead. However Archelaus was not a good ruler, and in 6 AD he was banished to Vienne in Gaul (near Lyons in France) after ruling for nine years. Rome appointed Pontius Pilate as procurator (and later as prefect) to govern in his place, making Judea a province under the Emperor's oversight and paying tax directly to Rome.

Malthace's younger son Antipas was appointed to rule over Galilee as a 'tetrarch' (ruler over one-quarter', although Herod's territory was being divided into three with the region of Abilene in Syria being added to the equation). It was Herod Antipas who would later execute John the Baptist and (unsuccessfully) attempt to interrogate Jesus at his trial at the request of Pilate. Philip was the son of Herod the Great by his fifth wife Cleopatra of Jerusalem. He was allocated

Ituraea and Trachonitis, the regions to the east of the River Jordan extending north towards Damascus, and reigned from 4 BC to 33 AD. It was this Philip who built Caesarea Philippi at the source of the River Jordan. [45]

Lysanias was not a descendant of Herod the Great. He was allocated the region adjacent to Galilee named Abilene, in Syria, northwest of Damascus and southeast of Mount Lebanon. This territory had not been under Herod the Great's rule; Augustus appears to have taken the opportunity to re-assign it at the same time as re-ordering Herod's territories.

3:2 'In the high priesthood of Annas and Caiaphas, the word of God came to John, the son of Zechariah, in the wilderness.'

Annas, son of Seth, was Jewish high priest. Josephus records 'Cyrenius had now disposed of Archelaus' money, and when the taxings were come to a conclusion, which were made in the thirty-seventh year of Caesar's victory over Antony at Actium, he deprived Joazar of the high priesthood, which dignity had been conferred on him by the multitude, and he appointed Ananus *[Annas]*, the son of Seth, to be high priest.' [46] Annas ruled from AD 7 until AD 14. Before the Parthian and Roman invasions, the office of high-priest had been hereditary and for life. Political intrigues changed all that; there are 38 high priests recorded as holding office between 37 BC and 26 AD. Annas was the head of the family which produced five high priests during the Herodian period (Josephus, 'Antiquities' 20, 9). These were Eleazar, Jonathan, Theophilus, Anan, and Matthias. His daughter was married to the high priest Joseph, who, under the surname of Caiaphas, held that office about ten years (27-37 AD).

It was into Annas' hands that Jesus was delivered for his first hearing, before being sent to Caiaphas (John 18:13). Caiaphas was the properly appointed high priest, and Annas, as his father-in-law and the former incumbent of the office, still exercised a great deal of the power attached to the position, from behind the throne.

Enter John the Baptist. The son of a priest (Zechariah), he was given the title of 'Rabbi' (John 3:26) and as such had disciples (Matthew 11:2 and Luke 5:33). Some scholars argue that the ordained office of rabbi was not in place at this time, and that the title was purely an honorary one. This is largely because Jerusalem's Talmudic records were completely destroyed during the Roman siege of Jerusalem in 70 AD. However the Babylonian Talmud refers to the Jerusalem-based scholar Gamaliel the Elder (mentioned in Acts 5) as *'rabban'*, and Jesus took pains to warn his disciples against the prevailing attitude of pride behind the contemporary use of the title 'Rabbi' - clear evidence of its use (and indeed misuse) in Israel at that time.

What was John doing in 'the wilderness'? It is known that the ultra-orthodox Jewish Essene's had partly withdrawn into the Judean desert region [47] to escape what they rightly saw as the corruption prevalent within the Temple priesthood and to preserve the Hebrew Scriptures (e.g. as the 'Dead Sea Scrolls'). Matthew 3:4 records that John's diet included 'locusts and wild honey'. 'Locusts' in general were a permitted food (Leviticus 11:22), however an alternative and more likely understanding is that *'akris'* ('locust') also refers to the bean of the same name from the indigenous tree *Ceratonia siliqua,* also called the 'Locust tree', which bears long leathery pods containing sweet edible pulp and resembling locusts. These trees are recorded in the Talmud ('*Ta'anit*' 23a) as growing locally. Because of the association with John the Baptist, the tree is also known as 'St John's bread'. Given the likely association of the house at which the Last Supper was eaten with the Essenes (who were noted for celibacy, there evidently being no women or children to carry water - Luke 22:10), it is probable that both John and Jesus had connections with this grouping of orthodox Jews. In any event, John is about to enter a prophetic ministry - the 'word of God came to him' there.

3:3 'And he came into all the district around the Jordan, preaching a baptism of repentance for the forgiveness of sins.'

'Baptism' (from '*bapto*' - 'to dip') was an accepted Jewish practice - a legal requirement to be cleansed from legal impurity. At the Temple steps there were pools in which worshippers dipped themselves in order to be clean according to the Law's requirements. John takes the practice and extends it to encompass an inner change, one based upon a change of heart and mind. 'Repentance' is '*metanoia*', from '*meta*' ('after') and '*noeô*' ('perception', 'understanding' and 'thinking').*

An internal change of perspective and way of thinking is required before a genuine change of behaviour (rather than simple externalism) can occur. Repentance was highly valued, the Talmud teaching that 'Great is repentance, because it brings about redemption, as it is said, 'And a redeemer will come to Zion, and unto them that turn from transgression in Jacob.' *[Isaiah 59:20]* Why will a redeemer come to Zion? Because of those that turn from transgression in Jacob.' [48] The descendents of Jacob were responding to John's renewed call to repent. 'Forgiveness' is '*aphesis*', meaning 'remission of a penalty' and 'release from bondage and imprisonment'.* 'Sins' is '*hamartia*', meaning to 'miss the target' (as in archery), rather than the other New Testament word for 'sin' ('*opheilêma*'), which means 'debt', as in a moral debt to God.

3:4 'As it is written in the book of the words of Isaiah the prophet, 'The voice of one crying in the wilderness, make ready the way of the Lord, make his paths straight. Every ravine will be filled, and every mountain and hill will be

brought low; the crooked will become straight and the rough roads smooth, and all flesh will see the salvation of God."

This Old Testament quotation that was seen as defining John's ministry is from Isaiah 40:3-5. 'A voice is calling, "Clear the way for the Lord in the wilderness; make smooth in the desert a highway for our God. Let every valley be lifted up, and every mountain and hill be made low; and let the rough ground become a plain, and the rugged terrain a broad valley. Then the glory of the Lord will be revealed, and all flesh will see it together; for the mouth of the Lord has spoken."' The context is that of the Israelites return from exile in Babylon. In those days the coming of kings and armies would be heralded by an advance party to proclaim their approach, obtain provisions for them and to make a smooth road for them by repairing holes and removing any obstacles, even to the point of earthworks and the felling of trees. Isaiah was prophetically commanding a new public road to be made for the return of the captive Jews from Babylon, who had the Lord himself as their deliverer.

'Crooked' is '*skolios*', 'scoliosis' being the medical term for a crooked spine. The flattening and in-filling of the surrounding terrain will help usher in and enable all of humanity to witness God's new initiative in Messiah.

3:7-9 'So he began saying to the crowds who were going out to be baptized by him, "You brood of vipers, who warned you to flee from the wrath to come? Therefore bear fruits in keeping with repentance, and do not begin to say to yourselves, 'We have Abraham for our father,' for I say to you that from these stones God is able to raise up children to Abraham. Indeed the axe is already laid at the root of the trees; so every tree that does not bear good fruit is cut down and thrown into the fire."'

John's ministry seems quite far removed from the concept of being 'seeker sensitive'. Matthew's account (3:7) indicates that it is the Sadducees and Pharisees in the crowd that John calls 'vipers', seeking a late repentance to escape God's impending judgement, just as a desert fire would drive out the local poisonous snakes. Better late than never, but there needs to be evidence of their 'change of thinking' (repentance) for it to be genuine. Reliance on their religion, if solely external, will not get them very far. God has no grand-children, only children with their own faith relationship with him. Reliance on the faith of a forefather is not going to work.

The image of the axe been laid to the root of the tree is reminiscent of God's judgement upon Nebuchadnezzar. 'An angelic watcher, a holy one, descended from heaven. He shouted out and spoke as follows: "Chop down the tree and cut off its branches"' (Daniel 4:13-14). Jesus taught that God would not spare Israel from this penalty if spiritual fruit was not forthcoming. 'A man had a fig tree which had been planted in his vineyard; and he came looking for fruit on it and did not find any. And he said to the vineyard-keeper, "Behold, for three years I have come looking for fruit on this fig tree without finding any. Cut it down! Why does it even use up the ground?" And he answered and said to him, "Let it alone, sir, for this year too, until I dig around it and put in fertilizer; and if it bears fruit next year, fine; but if not, cut it down"' (Luke 13:6-9). Since even branches that bear fruit are pruned, how much more will be cut off from those that do not? (John 15:2.)

'Fruit of repentance' was an important rabbinic concept. The Talmud taught: 'The goal of wisdom is repentance and good deeds, so that a man should not study Torah and Mishnah and then despise his father and mother and teacher and his superior in wisdom and rank, as it says, 'The fear of the Lord is the beginning of wisdom, a good understanding have all they that do thereafter'. It does not say, 'that do', but 'that do thereafter', which implies, that do them for their

68

own sake and not for other motives. If one does them for other motives, it were better that he had not been created.' [49] In rabbinic thought repentance was active ('He that has done repentance' - Talmud '*Kethuboth*' 22a), hence the crowd's response 'Then what shall we do?'

3:10-11 'And the crowds were questioning him, saying, "Then what shall we do?" And he would answer and say to them, "The man who has two tunics is to share with him who has none; and he who has food is to do likewise."'

John took a very practical approach to demonstrating a change to people's way of thinking. In the ancient world garments were commonly of two types. There was the under-garment (the '*chitôn*', often translated as 'tunic' and sometimes, confusingly, as 'coat'), which was worn next to the skin. Even poorer people would have a change of tunic, and one of them could be taken away lawfully in payment of a debt (Matthew 5:40). Jesus' '*chitôn*' was unusual and highly expensive in that it was seamless; consequently the soldiers who crucified him cast lots for it rather than tear it (John 19:23-24). Then there was the '*himation*', which was the outer garment, sometimes referred to as a 'mantle' or 'cloak'. This was what the High Priest tore on delivering his guilty verdict at Jesus' trial. The Law protected against having this outer garment taken in payment as it was also used as a blanket at night (Exodus 22:26-27).

If someone had no '*chitôn*' then they were very poor indeed, to the point of being destitute, a fact reinforced by the comparison with having no food. There is a Christian and also a simple human duty to help such people' however this does not mean that they no longer have any responsibility for themselves.

3:12-13 'And some tax collectors also came to be baptized, and they said to him, "Teacher, what shall we do?" And he said to them, "Collect no more than what you have been ordered to."'

Tax collectors (sometimes called 'publicans') were some of the most despised members of Judean society. They were educated Jews whose love of money had led them to work for the occupying Roman authorities and at the same time line their own pockets at the expense of their fellow countrymen. Interestingly, John does not tell them to stop representing the Romans, but rather to do their job honestly and not profit at others' expense. As the Apostle Paul would later write, taxes should be paid to those to whom they are due (Romans 13:6-7).

3:14 'Some soldiers were questioning him, saying, "And what about us, what shall we do?" And he said to them, "Do not take money from anyone by force, or accuse anyone falsely, and be content with your wages."'

Soldiers too were prone to abuse their power, by extortion and by false accusation, and thereby bolster their meagre and sometimes erratically paid wages. 'Use force' is *'diaseiô'*, a term unique to Doctor Luke in the New Testament, and was a medical term meaning to 'shake' [50] as with a fever. 'To accuse falsely' is *'sukophanteô'*, from which the word 'sycophant' is derived. This ancient word literally means 'to make figs appear'. In bygone Athens it was illegal to export figs and those who complained and informed on those who did often looked for their reward in a fawning type of way, hence the word came to mean a flatterer and one who uses words falsely. 'Content' with wages/rations is *'arkeô'*, which also means 'enough' or 'sufficient'.* John's admonition is again countering the love of money that so characterised the authority figures of the day.

3:15-16 'Now while the people were in a state of expectation and all were wondering in their hearts about John, as to whether he was the Christ, John answered and said to them all, "As for me, I baptize you with water; but one is coming who is mightier than I, and I am not fit to untie the thong of his sandals; he will baptize you with the Holy Spirit and fire."'

John's likeness in dress and ministry to the prophet Elijah would inevitably have raised messianic questions among the crowds. Was John the Messiah? John's response is to compare what he is doing with what the Messiah will do. John is immersing people in water. This was an outward sign of an inner repentance, a cleansing from the effects of the sins that the people were turning away from. But Messiah will be 'mightier' than that - the Greek here is '*ischuros*', meaning a 'powerful ability', and one not always predictable or under men's control, being used of extreme famine (Luke 15:4) and violent weather (Revelation 19:6). John, an ordinary man, is by comparison to Messiah, lesser in standing than a Gentile slave. The Law protected Jewish servants from the more unpleasant aspects of personal care of their masters such as foot washing; consequently wealthy Jewish households would employ a Gentile for such menial tasks. John describes himself as being unfit even for that in relation to the Messiah. Evidently God the Father was not quite of the same perspective given John's role in baptising Jesus, but the point is made that John's ministry and the Messiah's are not on level terms.

Messiah will immerse people in his own Holy Spirit and fire - a two-fold ministry, firstly empowering to serve (illustrated by the Spirit's baptism on the Day of Pentecost) and also the purification of believer's works, at any time but most notably described in 1 Corinthians 3:12-15. 'Now if any man builds on the foundation with gold, silver, precious stones, wood, hay, straw, each man's work will become evident; for the day will show it because it is to be revealed

71

with fire, and the fire itself will test the quality of each man's work. If any man's work which he has built on it remains, he will receive a reward. If any man's work is burned up, he will suffer loss; but he himself will be saved, yet so as through fire.'

3:17 'His winnowing fork is in his hand to thoroughly clear his threshing floor, and to gather the wheat into his barn; but he will burn up the chaff with unquenchable fire.'

Harvested grain would be beaten and then thrown into the air using a wide type of shovel known as a 'fan' or 'fork'. The lighter outer layer of chaff would be displaced by the wind allowing the kernels of grain to fall back to earth and be collected separately. The winnowing illustration is therefore one of separation for judgement; the wheat is saved and the chaff is burned. 'Unquenchable' is '*asbestos*', from which that fire-resistant material derives its name.

3:18-20 'So with many other exhortations he preached the gospel to the people. But when Herod the tetrarch was reprimanded by him because of Herodias, his brother's wife, and because of all the wicked things which Herod had done, Herod also added this to them all: he locked John up in prison.'

'Exhortation' is '*parakaleô*', meaning 'called on' in the sense of entreating someone to do something; 'proclaimed' is again, '*euaggelizô*' - literally, 'good messenger', as the angels were in chapter 2. John did not stop with those who came to him. The region's ruler, Herod Antipas, had acquired his half-brother Herod Philip I's wife Herodias while in Rome. The wife Antipas divorced in doing so was Phasaelis, daughter of King Aretas IV of Nabatea, the desert kingdom of modern-day Jordan, of which the red-rose city of Petra is the capital. Phasaelis returned to her father who in turn invaded Syria in revenge, taking Damascus from Rome, and thereby setting the scene for the later threat to the Apostle Paul's freedom (2 Corinthians 11:32). Antipas did not take kindly to John's criticism of the (illegal) marriage and had him imprisoned, whereby he suffered his death at the new wife Herodias' instigation (Matthew 14:6-12).

3:21-22 'Now when all the people were baptized, Jesus was also baptized, and while he was praying, heaven was opened, and the Holy Spirit descended upon him in bodily form like a dove, and a voice came out of heaven, "You are my beloved Son, in you I am well-pleased."'

Jesus was baptized 'to fulfil all righteousness' (Matthew 3:15) - 'the attribute of God pertaining to truthfulness and faithfulness'. [51] His baptism took place after all the other people had been baptised. This may have been because John and Jesus were related to each other through their mothers, who were kinswomen (Luke 1:36). Additionally the 'scouting' of Jesus into rabbinic scholarship following his meeting the Doctors of Torah in chapter 2 would mean that Jesus was a well-known figure by this point [52] and so John afforded him the dignity of being baptized last. Luke provides a further detail that the other Gospels omit, surely from Jesus' mother Mary. God spoke 'while he *[Jesus]* was praying'. And what did God say? That her son was also his Son. The words echo two Old Testament references; Psalm 2:7 and Isaiah 42:1. Psalm 2:7: 'I will surely tell of the decree of the Lord, he said to me, "You are my Son, today I have begotten you."' Isaiah 42:1: 'Behold, my Servant, whom I uphold; my chosen one in whom my soul delights *[Hebrew: 'ratsah' - 'pleased with']*, I have put my Spirit upon him.' And so Jesus, son of Mary, is announced from heaven as the Servant-Son of the Most High God.

3:23 'When he began his ministry, Jesus himself was about thirty years of age, being, as was supposed, the son of Joseph.'

Thirty is the age the Jewish law gives for commencing public teaching of Torah (with 'authority' - Tractate '*Avot*' 5). Prior to that, a person's rabbinic teaching ministry was confined to the hall of study (Bet Midrash), the place Luke describes Jesus as shining so brightly academically in chapter two. Jesus was 'about' thirty because the age of graduation was linked to the religious and academic calendar rather than an individual's actual birth date. Mary's influence again emerges with the word 'supposed' (to be the son of Joseph). Joseph was legally and societally Jesus' father, but Mary knew who his actual father was - God himself.

The genealogy that follows differs from the one in Matthew chapter one because it is Mary's own genealogy, details of which would have been supplied by Mary herself. Women's names almost never appear in Hebrew genealogies. If a family ended with the birth of a daughter as the only child, instead of listing her in the genealogy, the name of her husband was listed instead, as though he was the son of his father in law. The fact that the former Jewish scribe Matthew lists some women in his genealogy (of Joseph) is evidence of the changes that had occurred in Matthew's thinking as a result of Jesus' discipleship. 'Supposed' is '***nomizô***', also meaning 'thought to be'* from '***nomos***' - 'Law'. Joseph was recognised as Jesus' legal father. Who Jesus was culturally and societally, is whatever Joseph was. That is why it is so important to understand Joseph's humanity and standing in Jewish society - it is key to Jesus' humanity.

3:24-38 'The son of Heli, the son of Matthat, the son of Levi, the son of Melchi, the son of Jannai, the son of Joseph, the son of Mattathias, the son of Amos, the son of Nahum, the son of Hesli, the son of Naggai, the son of Maath, the son of Mattathias, the son of Semein, the son of Josech, the son of Joda, the son of Joanan, the son of Rhesa, the son of Zerubbabel, the son of Shealtiel, the son of Neri, the son of Melchi, the son of Addi, the son of

Cosam, the son of Elmadam, the son of Er, the son of Joshua, the son of Eliezer, the son of Jorim, the son of Matthat, the son of Levi, the son of Simeon, the son of Judah, the son of Joseph, the son of Jonam, the son of Eliakim, the son of Melea, the son of Menna, the son of Mattatha, the son of Nathan, the son of David, the son of Jesse, the son of Obed, the son of Boaz, the son of Salmon, the son of Nahshon, the son of Amminadab, the son of Admin, the son of Ram, the son of Hezron, the son of Perez, the son of Judah, the son of Jacob, the son of Isaac, the son of Abraham, the son of Terah, the son of Nahor, the son of Serug, the son of Reu, the son of Peleg, the son of Heber, the son of Shelah, the son of Cainan, the son of Arphaxad, the son of Shem, the son of Noah, the son of Lamech, the son of Methuselah, the son of Enoch, the son of Jared, the son of Mahalaleel, the son of Cainan, the son of Enosh, the son of Seth, the son of Adam, the son of God.'

Matthew's genealogy, from Abraham to Joseph, refers to 'sons' in the usual way - as natural generations. 'Abraham begat Isaac, and Isaac begat Jacob' and so on. Luke's use of 'son' varies, not only between referring to sons and sons-in-law, but also to natural sons and created sons such as Adam in his relationship to God. The other son-in-law listed is Salathiel, 'son' or son-in-law, of Neri, whose actual father was Jeconiah. In 1 Chronicles 3:17 we read: 'The sons of Jeconiah, the prisoner, were Shealtiel his son and Malchiram, Pedaiah, Shenazzar, Jekamiah, Hoshama and Nedabiah.'

Mary is therefore shown as the daughter of Heli, possibly an abbreviation of Heliachim (also meaning Joachim). Joseph, son of Jacob, and Mary; daughter of Heli, were of the same ancient family line: both came from Zerubbabel; Joseph from Abiud, his eldest son (Matthew 1:13), and Mary by Rhesa, the youngest (Luke 3:27).

Salathiel and Zorobabel were both directly descended from King Solomon.

Luke lists Salathiel as the son of Neri, who was descended from Nathan, Solomon's elder brother (1 Chronicles 3:5). If Neri had died without male children then Salathiel may have married the daughter of Neri and thereby reconnected the two branches of David's family (of Nathan and Solomon).

With Mary as his primary source, another reason for Luke's longer and more detailed genealogy emerges, other than the connection to Adam (Matthew's starts from Abraham). Mary, as a daughter of Aaron, came from a tribe whose lineage was especially vital in establishing the blood rights to their priestly ministry, and so she was well placed to share the details with Luke, telling her own story and that of her beloved Son to the Roman physician whose research was so vital to the legal defence of another Jewish scholar, the Apostle Paul.

Chapter 4

4:1-2 'Jesus, full of the Holy Spirit, returned from the Jordan and was led around by the Spirit in the wilderness for forty days, being tempted by the devil. And he ate nothing during those days, and when they had ended, he became hungry.'

Jesus, having been conceived by the Holy Spirit, and having received the fullness of the Spirit (landing on him in the form of a dove - Luke 3:32), is now 'led by the Spirit' (Matthew 4:1) into the Judean desert to be 'tested' ('tempted' is *'peirazô'* - 'to make trial of'* by the devil (Greek: *'diabolos'*, meaning 'slanderer' or 'accuser'). Being fully man, Jesus prepared for the test by fasting for forty days, as Moses had done when he was receiving the Law on Mount Sinai, thereby weakening him physically with hunger but strengthening him spiritually, by throwing his weight of reliance off his own abilities and more fully onto the strength that his Father would supply. The Gospel later gives the devil his name 'Satan' (Hebrew for 'adversary'), a term used by the Talmud in relation to Queen Vashti at the time of Esther. [53]

4:3-4 'And the devil said to him, "If you are the Son of God, tell this stone to become bread." And Jesus answered him, "It is written: 'Man shall not live on bread alone.'"

The three temptations the devil exposed Jesus to are rooted in his workings in what the Bible refers to as 'the world' - that part of God's creation that the devil, through man's sin, has gained an influence over. According to the Apostle John, the basis for the devil's work is threefold. 1 John 2:16: 'For all that is in the world, the lust of the flesh and the lust of the eyes and the boastful pride of life, is not from the Father, but is from the world.' The 'flesh' refers to the human body with its various passions and desires, of which extreme hunger would be an example. Jesus is tempted to use his miraculous powers to satisfy his hunger in a way contrary to God's creative order. The flat pieces of limestone in the Judean desert between the central plateau and the Dead Sea were similar to the locally produced loaves in size and shape. Bread however comes from grain and not from stone, and Jesus' miraculous powers were always subjected to his Father's ways. And so Jesus turns to the Scriptures for his answer - Deuteronomy 8:3, where Moses addresses the people of Israel. 'He humbled you and let you be hungry, and fed you with manna which you did not know, nor did your fathers know, that he might make you understand that man does not live by bread alone, but man lives by everything that proceeds out of the mouth of the Lord.' Jews in the time of Jesus referred to passages of Scripture by quoting a short section from it to denote the whole of the text. Deuteronomy chapter 8 is an exhortation to live in trusting dependency on the Lord, and in so doing to be led by him into the Promised Land - a land abundantly supplied with all the natural things needed to support life. The passage contains a reminder to the people of Israel that God supplied them with bread in the form of manna from heaven - no need then to transform rocks!

4:5-8 'And he led him up and showed him all the kingdoms of the world in a moment of time. And the devil said to him, "I will give you all this domain and its glory; for it has been handed over to me, and I give it to whomever I wish. Therefore if you worship before me, it shall all be yours." Jesus answered him, "It is written, 'You shall worship the Lord your God and serve him only.'"

Following the pattern of 1 John 2, the devil then tries to tempt Jesus through 'the lust of the eyes'. Matthew's Gospel (4:8) describes this temptation as taking place on a 'high mountain', from which the kingdoms of Judea could be seen. 'World' here can mean Judea, as used by the Pharisees in John 12:19 - 'The whole world has gone after him'. Having usurped authority over the earth to a limited degree through the fall, the devil then attempts to use what was not rightfully his to gain something else that was not rightfully his - Jesus' worship. The ludicrous idea of the co-creator Son of God (Proverbs 8:29-30) [viii] worshipping a created being (a fallen angel) must surely have brought a smile to Jesus' face.

Rather than argue with the devil over the technicalities regarding who owned the world's kingdoms, once again Jesus responds with Scripture. Deuteronomy 6:13: 'You shall fear only the Lord your God; and you shall worship him and swear by his name.' Worship is synonymous with spiritual service, and is to be given to God alone. The verse Jesus quotes is followed by: 'You shall not follow other gods, any of the gods of the peoples who surround you, for the Lord your God in the midst of you is a jealous God; otherwise the anger of the Lord your God will be kindled against you, and he will wipe you off the face of the earth' (Deuteronomy 6:14-15). The devil was seeking to bring about Jesus' self-destruction through idolatry.

4:9-12 'And he led him to Jerusalem and had him stand on the pinnacle of the Temple, and said to him, "If you are the Son of God, throw yourself down from here; for it is written, 'He will command his angels concerning you to guard you', and 'on their hands they will bear you up, so that you will not strike your foot against a stone.'" And Jesus answered and said to him, "It is said, 'You shall not put the Lord your God to the test.'"

The sanctuary (Holy Place) of Herod's temple had been built right up to and level with a large retaining wall that had been constructed

---

[viii] 'When he marked out the foundations of the earth; then I was beside him, as a master workman' (Proverbs 8:29-30).

on the eastern side of Mount Moriah. The combined height to the top of the royal portico totalled over 700 feet, and the Jewish Roman historian Josephus Flavius described the effect of looking down over the edge. 'This cloister deserves to be mentioned better than any other under the sun; for while the valley was very deep, and its bottom could not be seen, if you looked from above into the depth, this further vastly high elevation of the cloister stood upon that height, insomuch that if any one looked down from the top of the battlements, or down both those altitudes, he would be giddy, while his sight could not reach to such an immense depth' (Josephus, 'Antiquities', 15, 11).

The devil then appealed to the third category of temptation recorded in 1 John - the pride of life. This was both an appeal to Jesus' ability to do the miraculous, and also to demonstrate to all his identity as the long-awaited Messiah, who the prophet Malachi had said, 'Would suddenly come to his Temple' (Malachi 3:1). The devil backed up his suggestion by quoting Psalm 91:11-12. 'For he will give his angels charge concerning you, to guard you in all your ways. They will bear you up in their hands, that you do not strike your foot against a stone.' Unfortunately he omitted verse 13, which speaks of himself: 'You will tread upon the lion and cobra, the young lion and the *serpent* you will trample down.' The one who would 'bruise the serpent's head' (Genesis 3:15) knew the Scripture rather better, well enough to understand that the Psalm's reference to 'all your ways' precluded acts of deliberate recklessness such as jumping from Temple rooftops. 'All your ways' refers to the normal activities that God gives us to do, and not to stunt jumps.

Jesus responds by once again quoting from Deuteronomy chapter 6:16-19. 'You shall not put the Lord your God to the test, as you tested him at Massah. You should diligently keep the commandments of the Lord your God, and his testimonies and his statutes which he has commanded you. You shall do what is right and good in the sight of the Lord, that it may be well with you and that you may go in and possess the good land which the Lord swore to give your fathers, by driving out all your enemies from before you, as the Lord has spoken.' The passage refers to 'what is right and good in the sight of the Lord'; the sort of behaviour the devil was advocating did not fall into that category.

4:13 'When the devil had finished every temptation, he left him until an opportune time.'

Matthew's account (Matthew 4:11) describes angels attending to Jesus' needs after the testing was over. The devil left, but he would be back. The 'opportune time' would later come, in God's timing, through the love of money that dominated the life of Judas Iscariot.

4:14-15 'And Jesus returned to Galilee in the power of the Spirit, and news about him spread through all the surrounding district. And he began teaching in their synagogues and was praised by all.'

Having successfully completed his three rounds with the devil and thoroughly vanquished him, Jesus went back to the population centre that was the region of Galilee, empowered by the Holy Spirit - that member of the Godhead he had been in co-equal fellowship with for eternity past. It is sometimes thought that it was Jesus' miracles that won him the fame that Luke describes. It was in fact his teaching. John's Gospel (John 2:1-11) recounts the first of Jesus 'miraculous signs' at the wedding at Cana in Galilee, and the latter half of chapter 1 clearly describes Jesus functioning as a Rabbi, to such good effect that some of the disciple's of John the Baptist decide to switch their allegiance to him.

Jewish Temple scholar's entered public ministry in teaching Torah at age 30 ('*Avot*' 5). It was extremely unusual for the great minds among them to leave Jerusalem; rather they stayed in the Temple courts and taught their disciples there. Jesus differed in his ministry by taking his teaching and the good news of his Father's kingdom to the Jewish communities further afield, communities that would never otherwise have had the opportunity to be exposed to such a high level of rabbinic scholarship.

As an ordained graduate of the Temple's Bet Midrash Jesus had legal authority to teach both within the Temple courts and in the synagogues (not simply read from the scroll). When his disciples Peter and John later found themselves addressing a crowd in the Temple (Acts 3:11-4:3), they were promptly arrested and charged with the crime of 'teaching the people' (Acts 4:2), something that, as 'unschooled ordinary men' (Acts 4:13), they were not qualified or authorized to do. Jesus, on the other hand, taught completely unrestrained in the Temple courts, including debating Torah with different groups of the authorities who opposed him.

Jesus was able to teach 'with authority' (Mark 1:27) in their synagogues. While this is often thought of as meaning spiritual authority, the word '*exousia*' much more commonly means legal authority, which Jesus must have had to be teaching in the synagogues in the first place. Not only is he teaching, but his teaching is of such high quality as to be 'praised by all'. It continued in the same vein that so impressed and 'amazed' the Doctors of Torah in the Temple in Luke 2:41-52. And his mother Mary was no doubt present in those synagogues to hear her son, now the most celebrated Rabbi and Doctor of Torah that Israel had ever witnessed, and how justly pleased with and proud of him she must have been.

4:16 'And he came to Nazareth, where he had been brought up; and as was his custom, he entered the synagogue on the Sabbath, and stood up to read.'

Back in his hometown some 25 miles west and slightly south of Galilee, Jesus is afforded the same synagogue privileges by virtue of his rabbinic standing. Matthew and Mark's Gospels both recount the initial difficulty the townsfolk of Nazareth have in recognizing Jesus. 'Isn't this the **tekton's son** / **tekton**?', they ask (Matthew13:55 and Mark 6:3), and comment that Jesus' siblings are 'with them', implying that Jesus has not been with them. As a young rabbinic scholar Jesus would have left for further studies in Jerusalem aged 14-15, hence would have gone through much of puberty away from home. Returning as an adult with a company of disciples, he is therefore barely recognizable by those who had known him as a child. But they recognise his authority to teach by allowing him to do so in their synagogue. Until, that is, he offends them in what he says.

4:17-19 'And the book of the prophet Isaiah was handed to him. And he opened the book and found the place where it was written, 'The Spirit of the Lord is upon me, because he anointed me to preach the gospel to the poor. He has sent me to proclaim release to the captives, and recovery of sight to the blind, to set free those who are oppressed, to proclaim the favourable year of the Lord.''

Jewish synagogue services follow a yearly liturgical pattern; on the Saturday in question the readings included Isaiah 61:1-2. 'The Spirit of the Lord God is upon me, because the Lord has anointed me, to bring good news to the afflicted; he has sent me to bind up the broken-hearted, to proclaim liberty to captives and freedom to prisoners; to proclaim the favourable year of the Lord and the day of vengeance of our God; to comfort all who mourn.' This was particularly pertinent in the Father's timetable for Jesus' ministry, because it was a prophetic summary of the ministry of Messiah (Greek: '*Christos*'), meaning 'the anointed One'.

The 'gospel' is the '*euaggelizô*', literally, 'the good news' - news of a new kingdom, and especially good news for the poor, who were often denied justice and oppressed by the rich. Jesus is performing '*derash*', a rabbinic teaching method of connecting and comparing one passage of Scripture with another in order to amplify the meaning. He brings in Isaiah 42:7, where the Lord promises 'to open blind eyes, to bring out prisoners from the dungeon, and those who dwell in darkness from the prison.' 'Release to the captives' had a very particular meaning to the Israelite audience, harking back to the return of the exiles in captivity in Babylon. In 538 BC Cyrus the Great, the Persian conqueror of the Babylonian empire, had given the Jewish captives who had settled in Babylon (after the exile) permission to return. The Jewish scholars had shown Cyrus their scrolls of the prophet Isaiah, written 180 years earlier, in which the prophet had named a certain 'Cyrus' as being God's chosen servant to bring about the re-building of the Temple.

Josephus relates ('Antiquities' 11, 1), 'This was known to Cyrus by his reading the book which Isaiah left behind him of his prophecies; for this prophet said that God had spoken thus to him in a secret vision: "My will is, that Cyrus, whom I have appointed to be king over many and great nations, send back my people to their own land, and build my Temple." This was foretold by Isaiah one hundred and forty years before the Temple was demolished. Accordingly, when Cyrus read this, and admired the Divine power, an earnest desire and ambition seized upon him to fulfil what was so written; so he called for the most eminent Jews that were in Babylon, and said to them, that he gave them leave to go back to their own country, and to rebuild their city Jerusalem, and the Temple of God, for that he would be their assistant, and that he would write to the rulers and governors that were in the neighbourhood of their country of Judea, that they should contribute to them gold and silver for the building of the Temple, and besides that, beasts for their sacrifices.'

Despite Cyrus' royal patronage a large number of Jews decided to remain in Babylon where they had followed the prophet Jeremiah's words and settled there. 'Build houses and live in them; and plant gardens and eat their produce. Take wives and become the fathers of sons and daughters, and take wives for your sons and give your daughters to husbands, that they may bear sons and daughters; and multiply there and do not decrease' (Jeremiah 29:5-6). The Jews that returned had undergone the hard work of re-building the Temple and the city of Jerusalem, bringing back a spiritual light that the Jews who had not returned remained blind to. Messiah would open blind eyes (spiritual and natural) to what was important, and free the 'oppressed' (the Greek here is '*thraṓ*' meaning 'those broken into pieces'). Jesus' audience would certainly have had their Roman occupiers in mind at this mention of the oppressed!

'The favourable year of the Lord' or 'the year of the Lord's favour' would have put Jesus' audience in mind of the jubilee year, when debts were cancelled and land that had been used to secure a loan was returned to its original owner. Leviticus 25:10: 'You shall thus consecrate the fiftieth year and proclaim a release through the land to all its inhabitants. It shall be a jubilee for you, and each of you shall return to his own property, and each of you shall return to his family.' Messiah would cancel the debt of sin, once and for all.

4:20-22 'And he closed the book, gave it back to the attendant and sat down; and the eyes of all in the synagogue were fixed on him. And he began to say to them, "Today this Scripture has been fulfilled in your hearing." And all were speaking well of him, and wondering at the gracious words which were falling from his lips; and they were saying, "Is this not Joseph's son?"'

Rabbis taught from a seated position, as seen in John 8:2: 'Early in the morning he came again into the Temple, and all the people were coming to him; and he sat down and began to teach them.' Jesus announces to the assembled Nazarene townsfolk that he is the promised Messiah who has 'filled to the fullest' ('*plêroô*' - 'fulfilled') Isaiah's prophecies. Initially Jesus is well received, as any 'local boy made good' Temple scholar from his hometown might expect to be. Once again people are struggling to reconcile their memories of the pre-pubescent boy who had left town some 16 years earlier, with the returned bearded adult scholar and his company of disciples. But Jesus was not there to tickle their ears.

4:23-24 'And he said to them, "No doubt you will quote this proverb to me, 'Physician, heal yourself!' Whatever we heard was done at Capernaum, do here in your hometown as well." And he said, "Truly I say to you, no prophet is welcome in his hometown."'

Jesus seems to be responding to a perceived idea that his 'gracious words' were not sufficient, and that the Nazarenes wanted to see a demonstration of the miracles that they would have heard tell of from neighbouring Capernaum. Matthew's account (13:58) defines the root problem - their unbelief. Their familiarity with Jesus' immediate biological family (with Mary now at its centre following Joseph's apparent demise) [ix] seems to have been a stumbling block to accepting him as Messiah. Jesus counters the 'physician' proverb with another - prophets had always been looked down on in the places in which they had grown up. This 'physician' saying of Jesus' must have been of particular interest to Doctor Luke - it is not found in the other Gospels and is the sort of saying that a Jewish mother, justly proud of her son's ability to impart health and wholeness, would recall and so relate to a physician documenting her son's life.

[ix] 'Is not his mother called Mary, and his brothers, James and Joseph and Simon and Judas? And his sisters, are they not all with us?' (Matthew 13:55-56).

4:25-26 'But I say to you in truth, there were many widows in Israel in the days of Elijah, when the sky was shut up for three years and six months, when a great famine came over all the land; and yet Elijah was sent to none of them, but only to Zarephath, in the land of Sidon, to a woman who was a widow.'

Jesus is introducing the new covenant - a new dimension in God's spiritual economy. Israel, it seems, has been weighed in the balance and been found wanting. The fig tree is about to be dug around for the last time before it is judged for its lack of fruit. It is time in God's plan, as the prophets had foretold, for the Gentile nations of the world to be actively included in God's purposes. God was never exclusively concerned with Israel - he had always been concerned for all of his creation, not only for the covenanted sons of Abraham. Just as the first martyr Stephen would later do (Acts 7), Jesus emphasises occasions in Israel's history when God dealt, seemingly preferentially, with Gentiles.

In this, one of Jesus' earliest recorded discourses, we catch another glimpse of Luke's primary source. God's concern for widows was well known [x] and Mary, a widow herself, would have especially recalled her son's references to God's care for them. Sidon was a Phoenician region to the north of Tyre. (Zarephath, also known as Sarepta, is a coastal town in what is modern-day Lebanon and is now called Sarafand.) Elijah lived there during the severe drought and consequential famine recorded in 1 Kings 17. Elijah prayed for rain, which came at the end of the third year of drought (1 Kings 18:1). Rain usually fell heavily in Judea in October and in April, called the early and latter rains. In the preceding six months, there had been no

---

[x] 'He executes justice for the orphan and the widow, and shows his love for the alien by giving him food and clothing' (Deuteronomy 10:18).

rain as was normally the case between rainy seasons; consequently the nation went three years and six months without rain.

4:27 'And there were many lepers in Israel in the time of Elisha the prophet; and none of them was cleansed, but only Naaman the Syrian.'

Naaman's healing is recounted in 2 Kings chapter 5. The great Aramean military captain had humbled himself to Elisha's command and dipped himself seven times in what he regarded as the rather inferior local waters of the river Jordan; on the seventh his skin was made new like a babies' (2 Kings 5:14). Jesus' focus on Gentiles who received the grace of God while Jews did not is by now drawing forth the hidden animosity from his audience. He is provoking from them the reaction that will expose the true motives of their hearts.

4:28-30 'And all the people in the synagogue were filled with rage as they heard these things; and they got up and drove him out of the city, and led him to the brow of the hill on which their city had been built, in order to throw him down the cliff. But passing through their midst, he went his way.'

The peoples reaction is described as '*thumos*', form '*thuo*' ('to kill') - an eruption of anger that quickly boils over and then subsides. Just south of Nazareth is a rocky outcrop called 'The Mount of Precipitation', with a rock ledge overhanging a cliff edge. The people wish to perform a form of summary execution in the manner of the troops under the rule of Amaziah in 2 Chronicles 25:12. 'The sons of Judah also captured 10,000 *[sons of Seir]* alive and brought them to the top of the cliff and threw them down from the top of the cliff, so that they were all dashed to pieces.' Psychologically this is a very extreme response if religious prejudice were the sole motivator. It may well be that Jesus had also made a statement of divinity which would have appeared blasphemous and provoked a similar response (and evasion by Jesus) as that recorded in John 8:58-59 when Jesus appears to speak the unspoken name of God, 'I am'. 'Jesus said to them, "Truly, truly, I say to you, before Abraham was born, I am." Therefore they picked up stones to throw at him, but Jesus hid himself and went out of the Temple.' Jesus was miraculously preserved, maintaining an inner peace and serenity founded on his trust in his Father to keep him.

4:31-32 'And he came down to Capernaum, a city of Galilee, and he was teaching them on the Sabbath; and they were amazed at his teaching, for his message was with authority.'

Mark (2:1) records that Jesus had a 'home' base in Capernaum, on the north-west tip of Lake Galilee. Capernaum housed part of the local Roman garrison, commanded by a centurion. Matthew 8:5: 'When Jesus entered Capernaum, a centurion came to him, imploring him.' It lay on the border between Herod Antipas' kingdom and that of his brother Philip. Once again Jesus is amazing the Jews with his teaching, once again he is acting in an official capacity in their synagogues (verse 33) and once again he is recognised as having '*exousia*', denoting 'authority' (from the impersonal verb '*exesti*', 'it is lawful'. [54] Jesus is doing what all rabbis and Doctors of Torah did on the Sabbath - they discoursed on what was 'lawful' according to Torah, and they did so from a position of legal authority. What amazed the crowds is that unlike all the other authoritative legal and religious teaching which re-cycled older rabbinic knowledge, Jesus' teaching was 'new' (Mark 1:27). He also exercised a much higher degree of spiritual authority in miracles and deliverance; however, the authority that the crowds are recognising and acknowledging is the legal authority needed to teach in the synagogue and the Temple.

4:33-34 'In the synagogue there was a man possessed by the spirit of an unclean demon, and he cried out with a loud voice, "Let us alone! What business do we have with each other, Jesus of Nazareth? Have you come to destroy us? I know who you are - the Holy one of God!"'

Evil spirits were rather quicker on the uptake as to Jesus' true identity than most of the people he mixed with. The Greek used for 'cried out' is '*anakrazô*', from '*krazô*', meaning 'the croak of a raven'. The throaty croaking scream, demonically inspired, must have caused the hairs on the back of the congregation's necks to rise. The Talmud recognised the existence of demons, often attributing abortions to their work. [55] 'Go away' is the demon's message. 'Leave us alone - we prefer the comfortable religious status-quo.' The demon knew that he was marked out by God for judgement but was hoping for a stay of execution. The title it used to address Jesus is '*hagios theos*', meaning 'Holy God' - the Greek text has no 'one of' God. The demon knew Jesus to be God incarnate ('Holy God'), and was in fear for its future as a result.

4:35 'But Jesus rebuked him, saying, "Be quiet and come out of him!" And when the demon had thrown him down in the midst of the people, he came out of him without doing him any harm.'

Jesus did not need demons to the work of evangelism for him, any more than Paul and Silas needed the assistance of a demon-possessed slave girl in the book of Acts (Acts 16:16-18) in their work of preaching the Gospel in Roman Philippi in Asia Minor. He 'muzzled' the demon. 'Be quiet' is '*phimoô*', 'to muzzle' - rather stronger than the NASB (above) or the KJV's 'hold thy peace'. 'Come out' is '*exerchomai*' - 'to expel', and is in the imperative mood, meaning that it is a command. Commands are no use without the authority needed to back them up. Despite the demon throwing the man suddenly and violently to the ground, he rises unhurt and free of the demonic tormentor. Rabbis were known to exorcise demons; the Talmud records them using incense for this purpose. [56]

'Thrown' here is '*rhiptô*', a term used frequently by the Greek physician Hippocrates for fits, [57] as well as others, in relation to epileptic seizures. [58] Luke distinguishes this episode and its demonic origins from everyday epilepsy by noting that the man was unhurt - without '*blaptô*', a medical term for morbidity and the harmful consequences of an illness, [59] and also used in Mark 16:18 to denote freedom from any ill effects of poison.

4:36-37 'And amazement came upon them all, and they began talking with one another saying, "What is this message? For with authority and power he commands the unclean spirits and they come out." And the report about him was spreading into every locality in the surrounding district.'

'Amazement' typically accompanied Jesus' ministry, be it teaching or miracles. The 'message' is simply '*logos*' - 'the word' spoken. The one who was God's '*logos*' personified spoke the '*logos*', usually in short expressions of command, and the miraculous happened. These are no long, pleading intercessions. They are words spoken with all the Father's authority behind them and nothing and nobody can stand in their way. Authority ('*exousia*') in Jesus' life was both legal (in the context of the Jewish Torah that governed the society) and spiritual. The 'news' of the miraculous went ahead of Jesus into the surrounding region like the roaring of the sea ('news' is '*êchos*' - 'a sharp sound producing a reverberation/echo'), preparing people's hearts in faith to hear and respond to the gospel. As Mark (Mark 1:28) puts it, 'Immediately the news about him spread everywhere into all the surrounding district of Galilee.' Even demonic interventions were being turned to good effect.

4:38-39 'Then he got up and left the synagogue, and entered Simon's home. Now Simon's mother-in-law was suffering from a high fever, and they asked him to help her. And standing over her, he rebuked the fever, and it left her; and she immediately got up and waited on them.'

Here Dr Luke's medical knowledge comes to the fore. Simon's wife's mother was '*sunechô*' with a fever - 'seized by it' and 'in its grip', such that she was laid up in bed. 'Asked him to help' is '*erôtaô*' - to 'urge' or 'beseech', conveying an earnestedness lacking in the English rendering. Fever (literally here being 'mega-fiery heat') was a common cause of death in an antibiotic-less world, but fever, like demons, has to leave when Jesus tells it to. Peter's mother-in-law loses no time in expressing her gratitude with practical service in the traditional hospitality of the people of the time.

4:40-41 'While the sun was setting, all those who had any who were sick with various diseases brought them to him; and laying his hands on each one of them, he was healing them. Demons also were coming out of many, shouting, "You are the Son of God!" But rebuking them, he would not allow them to speak, because they knew him to be the Christ.'

As the Sabbath ends and it becomes lawful to carry a load, the townsfolk bring their sick to Jesus. They are '*astheneô*' - 'without strength', as in 'myasthenia' - muscle weakness. The diseases were of all shades, and amounted to the town's entire population of ill people ('all those who had any sick'). Jesus healed 'each one'. Once again, the demons are unable to keep quiet and once again Jesus gives them a stern telling-off. Jesus had no interest in receiving the testimony, accurate or not, of evil spirits. It would not be long before the Pharisees would accuse him of cooperating with them. 'The

Pharisees said, "This man casts out demons only by Beelzebul the ruler of the demons"' (Matthew 12:24). Jesus knew very well 'not to give the devil a foothold' (Ephesians 4:27, NIV).

Doctor Luke gives two details that the other Gospel writers omit in their account of this episode. The first is the mode of healing (laying on of hands) which represented simplicity completely at odds with the complex Greek cures. The second is the sheer diversity of the illnesses being cured and the fact that the same mode was used for healing all of them, despite their many differences of presenting symptoms.

4:42-44 'When day came, Jesus left and went to a secluded place; and the crowds were searching for him, and came to him and tried to keep him from going away from them. But he said to them, "I must preach the kingdom of God to the other cities also, for I was sent for this purpose." So he kept on preaching in the synagogues of Judea.'

Jesus, Mark tells us, was in the habit of rising early to pray (Mark 1:35). As the Son of God he was also, in his incarnation, fully man and so totally dependent on his Father to empower and direct him. His prayer life was both an expression of this and an example for us to follow. The crowds want to keep Jesus for themselves; however, if Jesus had stayed in Capernaum, it would have been overrun with others coming to him there. Jesus was on his Father's timetable in ministering the gospel's 'good news' to the region's other population centres. That was his Father's God-ordained mission, not simply his own. Once again, Jesus' ministry is functioning in the context of synagogue preaching, further evidencing his official standing within Judean theological and legal society.

Chapter 5

5:1-3 'Now it happened that while the crowd was pressing around him and listening to the word of God, he was standing by the lake of Gennesaret; and he saw two boats lying at the edge of the lake; but the fishermen had got out of them and were washing their nets. And he got into one of the boats, which was Simon's, and asked him to put out a little way from the land. And he sat down and began teaching the people from the boat.'

Galilee was famous not only for the lake (also called Lake Tiberias) and the associated fishing industry, but also for the large fertile plane to its north-western side that was called Gennesaret (from the Hebrew *'gan'*, meaning 'garden'). The region is mentioned in the Talmud on account of its fertility - 'Like earthy water, one brings fertile soil from the valley of Gennesaret.' [60] Its fruits were exported to Jerusalem, giving rise to a festival saying, 'Had we merely ascended in order to eat the fruits of Gennesaret in Jerusalem, it would have sufficed us.' [61] The large crowds that Jesus ministered to meant it was harder to get away afterwards and the imminent possibility of a crowd surge ('pressing' is *'epikeimai'* - 'to lie on') pushing the minister into the water. Jesus resorted to using a fishing boat as a floating pulpit. The lake contained many such craft; Josephus describes it as being 'full of ships', enough to evacuate the local inhabitants from the approaching Roman army (Josephus, 'Wars', 7, 11). The Talmud taught that fishing-nets were legally unclean through use, [62] which was an additional reason for their being diligently washed in a prescribed manner by the devout Jewish fishermen when finishing up the post-shift cleaning operations. Jesus was preaching in the early morning (after the fishermen had finished their night's work), and, as customary for rabbis, taught from a sitting position (e.g. Matthew 5:1 and the Sermon on the Mount).

5:4-5 'When he had finished speaking, he said to Simon, "Put out into the deep water and let down your nets for a catch." Simon answered and said, "Master, we worked hard all night and caught nothing, but I will do as you say and let down the nets."'

Simon Peter was in partnership with James and John (verse 10), whose mother Salome was sister to Mary the mother of Jesus (Mark 14:40 and Matthew 27:5). Consequently James and John were Jesus' cousins, something they would later try and use to their advantage in relation to positions of authority in what they then saw as the coming temporal kingdom in Israel (Matthew 20:21). That Simon Peter knew of Jesus and his legal standing in their society is evidenced in his choice of title - 'Master'. The Greek here is '*epistatês*', 'Chief' or 'Commander'. Peter is recognising that, in his teaching authority, Jesus is legally 'over' him. An earlier meeting between Simon Peter and Jesus is recorded in John 1:40-42. At that point Simon Peter's brother Andrew was already a rabbinic disciple of Jesus (John 1:40), having switched allegiance from Jesus' cousin John the Baptist. Mark's Gospel (believed to have been sourced from Peter himself) and Matthew's Gospel both formally record Peter becoming a disciple of Jesus, but in a much more sketch-like way (there is no mention of the boat-pulpit and the miraculous catch of fish). Luke's detail surely came from an 'eyewitness' of the Galilean seashore, quite possibly Mary herself.

Jesus is teaching Torah in the 'new' (Mark 1:27) manner of the gospel, in other words, the way that Torah had originally been intended by the One who first gave it, before successive generations of human rabbinic scholars distorted it. Jesus was widely recognised in Jewish society as a 'master' or 'doctor' (*'Didaskalos'*) of Torah, unsurprising given the effect that he had had on the doctors of Torah in the Temple at age 12. Simon's respect for Jesus is such that he puts aside his recent fishing knowledge of the local shoal movements and does as Jesus asks. In doing so he demonstrates the active element of faith, as one who has heard the word of Jesus, trusts it and obeys it. Jesus is about to cross effortlessly from teaching to performing the miraculous.

5:6-7 'When they had done this, they enclosed a great quantity of fish, and their nets began to break; so they signalled to their partners in the other boat for them to come and help them. And they came and filled both of the boats, so that they began to sink.'

The disciples-to-be throwing of the net was perfectly in time with God's provision; a provision that convinced them that it was not necessary to continue their human business pursuits. Instead they could avail themselves of Jesus' generous offer of being discipled by the greatest Torah scholar Israel had ever seen, a much sought after honour in a religious society that highly valued Torah but which only permitted a few to enter into the deepest study of it. Being a disciple of a teacher who also had miraculous powers as God's son meant that they never need worry about human provisions again. Jesus could even supply their Temple tax payments! ('"Go to the sea and throw in a hook, and take the first fish that comes up; and when you open its mouth, you will find a shekel. Take that and give it to them for you and me"' (Matthew 17:24-27).

5:9-11 'But when Simon Peter saw that, he fell down at Jesus' feet, saying, "Go away from me Lord, for I am a sinful man". For amazement had seized him and all his companions, because of the catch of fish which they had taken; and so also were James and John, sons of Zebedee, who were partners with Simon. And Jesus said to Simon, "Do not fear, from now on you will be catching men." When they had brought their boats to land, they left everything and followed him.'

Peter's initial reaction, remarkable for a religious Jew, is to switch title from 'Master' to 'Lord', in recognition of Jesus' divinity. He is immediately aware, through the sign that Jesus has performed, of his own sinfulness and of Jesus' holiness. This should be a normal consequence of the manifestation of the miraculous - not a 'media buzz', but a repenting of sin amidst a sense of the majesty and holiness of God. Having recognised Jesus' divinity through the miracle, Peter is naturally, as a Jew, concerned that he is about to die. The patriarch Jacob had expressed amazement that his 'life had been spared' (Genesis 32:30) despite his encounter with God. Similarly Manoah and his wife (Samson's parents) had expected to die having witnessed 'the angel of the Lord' perform a miracle (Judges 13:9-23). Jesus now speaks his first 'Do not fear', something he would do many times in relation to people's appropriately awe-filled responses to him. The disciples' roles are about to change from catching fish to catching men, a task that would need the same attitude of faith that Peter had shown in hearing, trusting and obeying the word that Jesus spoke in regard to the net. Zebedee's business would now be in the hands of his hired men. His sons had entered a life of discipleship to the greatest rabbi in Israel's history.

5:12-13 'While he was in one of the cities, behold, there was a man covered with leprosy; and when he saw Jesus, he fell on his face and implored him, saying, "Lord, if you are willing, you can make me clean." And he stretched out his hand and touched him, saying, "I am willing; be cleansed." And immediately the leprosy left him.'

Leprosy, a disease caused by Mycobacterium Leprae, damages the nerves necessary for the body's protective pain response and the early detection of tissue damage and infection. It particularly affects the skin and the respiratory mucosa, and to Doctor Luke it was understood to be incurable. Nowadays it is eminently treatable with anti-bacterials. It is transmitted by prolonged contact, and the Jewish hygiene laws insisted on separation. The Talmud devotes a whole tractate to the subject (*'Nega'im'*). In the synagogue there would need to be a separate partition made for the purpose if a leper was to be allowed to enter, and then he would have to be the first to enter and the last to leave. If persisting signs were found in their homes the entire house would be demolished and the rubble (legally unclean to the size of an olive) moved to an area designated as unclean, [63] thereby effectively making the leper homeless as well.

Doctor Luke would have seen many lepers and this one was a particularly severe case. Hippocrates divided lepers into three classes. [64] Luke himself describes two of these in his Gospel, here and in chapter 17 (the ten lepers). This chapter's example is the worse type. 'Covered' with leprosy is *'plêrês'* from *'plêthô'* - 'to be full',* as in 'smothered with it'; he had the tell-tale white marks all over him and no doubt also concomitant tissue injury and degeneration brought on by subsequent infection. This leper had no way of hiding his affliction and was taking an extreme risk of punishment for coming into the city instead of remaining in isolation outside, as the Law commanded - 'He shall live alone; his dwelling shall be outside the camp' (Leviticus 13:46).

He must have heard that there was a man there called Jesus who could miraculously heal, and so was prepared to take a risk as far as the Law was concerned. The leper is especially breaking the Law in coming up to Jesus' feet, something that must have rather alarmed Jesus' mother Mary. Having thus been made ceremonially unclean, Jesus is not therefore breaking the Law in touching the leper. In reality he was keeping a higher law - to love one's neighbour as oneself. The instant healing of the leper was further evidence of his divine status. As Job had said, 'Behold, how happy is the man whom God reproves. So do not despise the discipline of the Almighty. For he inflicts pain, and gives relief; he wounds, and his hands also heal' (Job 5:17-18). It was not technically necessary to touch the leper -

Jesus could and did heal equally effectively with a word of command. But it was a gracious expression of his compassion and fellow-humanity that he chose to do so. The One who had healed Miriam's leprosy (Numbers 12) was at work again.

5:14-16 'And he ordered him to tell no one, "But go and show yourself to the priest and make an offering for your cleansing, just as Moses commanded, as a testimony to them." But the news about him was spreading even farther, and large crowds were gathering to hear him and to be healed of their sicknesses. But Jesus himself would often slip away to the wilderness and pray.'

It took a priest to diagnose a person with leprosy (Leviticus 13:3) and it took a priest to pronounce them clean again. The fact that there was no cure for leprosy meant that in reality such pronouncements rarely (if ever) happened, spontaneous remission being very unlikely. In sending the newly healed leper, Jesus is sending a message to the priests in Jerusalem that God was doing something new.

Jesus was now becoming somewhat encumbered by the success of his own ministry, such that he was often surrounded by crowds who came both to hear his teaching as a new and popular 'Doctor of Torah' and to be healed by him. But Jesus was still dependent on his Father and prayer was vital to his functioning under his Father's direction. This meant early rising and going to uninhabited places for uninterrupted prayer.

5:17 'And it came to pass on a certain day, as he was teaching, that there were Pharisees and Doctors of the Law sitting by, which were come out of every town of Galilee, and Judaea and Jerusalem, and the power of the Lord was present to heal them.'

This is the first occasion in his Gospel that Luke introduces the Pharisees. The Jewish Roman historian Josephus Flavius provides a useful source of background information about this important group within Jewish religious life. 'The Pharisees are those who are esteemed most skilful in the exact explication of their laws... These ascribe all to providence and to God, and yet allow that to act what is right, or the contrary, is principally in the power of men, although fate does co-operate in every action. They say that all souls are incorruptible, but that the souls of good men only are removed into other bodies, but that the souls of bad men are subject to eternal punishment... Moreover, the Pharisees are friendly to one another, and are for the exercise of concord, and regard for the public' (Josephus, 'Wars', 2, 8).

Josephus' 'Antiquities' 13, 5: 'Now for the Pharisees, they say that some actions, but not all, are the work of fate, and some of them are in our own power, and that they are liable to fate, but are not caused by fate.' And 'Antiquities' 13, 10: 'The Pharisees have delivered to the people a great many observances by succession from their fathers, which are not written in the laws of Moses; and for that reason it is that the Sadducees reject them, and say that we are to esteem those observances to be obligatory which are in the written word, but are not to observe what are derived from the tradition of our forefathers. And concerning these things it is that great disputes and differences have arisen among them, while the Sadducees are able to persuade none but the rich, and have not the populace obsequious to them, but the Pharisees have the multitude on their side.'

The Pharisees were prominent for their piety and influential enough to have the support of the Jewish Queen Alexandra who reigned from 79-68 BC. She 'permitted the Pharisees to do everything; to whom also she ordered the multitude to be obedient. She also restored again those practices which the Pharisees had introduced, according to the traditions of their forefathers, and which her father-in-law, Hyrcanus, had abrogated. So she had indeed the name of the regent, but the Pharisees had the authority; for it was they who restored such as had been banished, and set such as were prisoners at liberty, and, to say all at once, they differed in nothing from lords' (Josephus' 'Antiquities', 11, 16).

Josephus goes on to say 'They follow the conduct of reason; and what that prescribes to them as good for them they do; and they think they ought earnestly to strive to observe reason's dictates for practice. They also pay a respect to such as are in years; nor are they so bold as to contradict them in anything which they have introduced; and when they determine that all things are done by fate, they do not take away the freedom from men of acting as they think fit; since their notion is, that it hath pleased God to make a temperament, whereby what he wills is done, but so that the will of man can act virtuously or viciously. They also believe that souls have an immortal rigor in them, and that under the earth there will be rewards or punishments, according as they have lived virtuously or viciously in this life; and the latter are to be detained in an everlasting prison, but that the former shall have power to revive and live again; on account of which doctrines they are able greatly to persuade the body of the people; and whatsoever they do about Divine worship, prayers, and sacrifices, they perform them according to their direction; insomuch that the cities give great attestations to them on account of their entire virtuous conduct, both in the actions of their lives and their discourses also' ('Antiquities', 18, 1).

The Pharisees were, therefore, the guardians of the Jewish religious Law and in particular the interpretation of the Scriptures. Nicodemus was speaking for (at least) the Pharisees on the Sanhedrin when he said to Jesus, 'Rabbi, we know that you have come from God as a teacher [*Didaskalos*' - *Doctor*']; for no one can do these signs that you do unless God is with him' (John 3:2). 'Doctors of the Law' is *nomodidaskalos*'. These were the men that ran the rabbinic schools in the Temple, hence Luke's statement that they 'had come out of Jerusalem', 120 miles away. They had come with more local Torah scholars to listen to Jesus' teaching in a formal capacity. These Doctors of the Torah-law, based in the Temple in Jerusalem, would probably have included some of the same men with whom Jesus had spent five days aged twelve (Luke 2), before returning there following completion of Mishnaic studies at age 14-15. These men would have been in large part older in years, and to make such a long journey to hear Jesus teach is a mark of the huge respect that Jesus was held in because of his amazing ability with Torah and Scripture in general. Such a meeting of the minds was not happening by chance. It would have had to be pre-arranged considerably earlier, and it is evident that Jesus is cooperating fully with it by continuing to teach in their presence. They were not the only ones who had come in a purposeful way; Luke tells us that the power of the Spirit was present too. Mary would have also been present at such a high-powered gathering in the presence of her learned son, and the Jewish populace in Capernaum must have been in anticipation of it as these senior scholars arrived over a period of days from their towns.

5:18-24 'And some men were carrying on a bed a man who was paralyzed; and they were trying to bring him in and to set him down in front of him. But not finding any way to bring him in because of the crowd, they went up on the roof and let him down through the tiles with his stretcher, into the middle of the crowd, in front of Jesus. Seeing their faith, he said, "Friend, your sins are forgiven you." The scribes and the Pharisees began to reason, saying, "Who is this man who speaks blasphemies? Who can forgive sins, but God alone?" But Jesus, aware of their reasonings, answered and said to them, "Why are you reasoning in your hearts? Which is easier to say, 'Your sins have been forgiven you,' or to say, 'Get up and walk'? "But so that you may know that the Son of Man has authority on earth to forgive sins," he said to the paralytic, "I say to you, get up, and pick up your stretcher and go home."'

The rabbinic scholars, arriving from their various towns over a period of days, had attracted a huge crowd at the door of Jesus' house in Capernaum. Anyone that was senior in terms of local scholarship in their society would have been present within to hear the youngest and most brilliant of Israel's Torah scholars expound God's word to them. Mark's account of this miracle underlines Jesus' popularity at this stage in his ministry - the house was full to bursting (Mark 2:4). At a certain point however, his teaching was interrupted by men on the roof excavating a hole some six feet by three feet in size and lowering a 'stretcher' through it. Whereas Matthew and Mark refer to it as a 'bed' and a 'pallet' respectively, Doctor Luke uses the medical term ('*klinidion*') employed by the Greek historian Dionysius of Halicarnassus (60 BC - 7 AD) [65] for the light couch on which the sick were carried.

Once again Doctor Luke stands out from the other Gospel writers in his choice of word for the disease the man had. His is '*paraluô*', meaning 'enfeebled by a paralytic stroke', [66] as opposed to the much more generic '*paralutikos*' ('paralytic') used in Matthew 9:2 and Mark 2:3.

Matthew's account has a special significance because in addressing the paralysed man Jesus uses the particular word 'son' in a familial sense. 'Son' occurs forty-one times in the four Gospels, but is only used by Jesus to an individual on this one particular occasion - the healing of the paralytic. This raises a question - where was this man's family? None of the Gospels' accounts of this miracle mentions them. In Israel then, as in much of the world today, the responsibility of care for an invalid fell to the family, yet there is nothing to indicate that they were present or had even been involved in sending him. Luke's account records Jesus as saying '***anthrôpos***' ('man'), however both Matthew's account (Matthew 9:2) and Mark's account (Mark 2:5, via Peter who like Matthew was undoubtedly present) have 'son' ('***teknon***'). This is often translated as 'child' but is the familiar word for the son of a father, as opposed to the more formal and more commonly used term for 'son', '***huios***'.

The most probable likelihood is that the man's own family had been unable or unwilling to care for his disability, possibly because of the legal and ritual uncleanness associated with bowel incontinence secondary to spinal cord injury, and so had passed his care over to others. In all probability this was the Jewish religious order the Essenes, who were noted for their care of the sick. Josephus ('Wars' 2, 8) records of the Essenes: 'They have no one certain city, but many of them dwell in every city... there is, in every city where they live, one appointed particularly to take care of strangers... These two things are done among them at everyone's own free-will, which are to *assist those that want it*, and to *show mercy*; for they are permitted of their own accord *to afford succour to such as deserve it, when they stand in need of it.*' This being the case, the man is likely to have faced a painful estrangement from his family and especially his parents. Jesus sees the faith of the friends who were evidently familiar with Jesus' ministry and highly respected it, and who had put their trust in him and his ability to heal. He rewards their trust, and makes no allusion to their having dug a hole in his roof. Jesus was, after all, as a '***tekton***' builder, as well as being a teacher, so to fix a roof was not a problem for him.

Jesus speaks to the man, and every word appears to have been chosen carefully. In Matthew's and Mark's accounts Jesus addresses the paralysed man as 'son' ('***teknon***'), meaning 'child of a family'. The man had no natural family around him, probably because of his disability, and so Jesus meets him at the point of his deepest need, deeper even than the need of forgiveness, his need for fatherhood and sonship. This was the one word that the man had stopped hearing and stopped being addressed by, because of the painful estrangement from his family that his disability and consequential uncleanness had occasioned. 'You are a son. You are a family member!' Jesus never said this in the Gospel records to any other living person - it is only used in parables. God the Father had reserved it for this moment, this lost one, this lost son. Jesus could have simply forgiven him and left him for the rest of his life in a state of familial rejection and loss of natural sonship, despite the hope of heaven. Instead, Jesus first restored him to sonship and then forgave his sins.

'Your sins are forgiven.' Many disabled people carry a burden of guilt for the difficulties they cause others in caring for them. In Israel at this time, there was also a commonly held notion that sickness and disability was linked to sin - a punishment for some wrongdoing, or for 'being bad'. Even in modern times many disabled people see themselves as being punished by God for something. All need forgiveness, but this man needed to be released from his particular burden of guilt, hence Jesus' 'Your sins are forgiven.' The second most pressing personal issue is dealt with. Jesus could have said straightaway, 'Be healed.' He didn't, because the man had two deeper needs - to know he was a son, and to know he was forgiven, and these had to be addressed first. In saying this Jesus is not only taking the place of God (a capital offence under the Jewish Law), but also pointing beyond the current Temple system to a day when its complex system of sacrifice and offering for sin would be replaced as a means of being forgiven by his own sacrifice of himself on a cross.

The experts in the Mosaic Law were not there all at the same time by accident; they would have been there by arrangement, something that Jesus must have been party to and was continuing to cooperate with by teaching in their presence. Jesus is quite comfortable with their presence in his home, despite any growing enmity towards him as one who did not uphold their own Mishnaic interpretations of the Law, which Jesus referred to as 'rules taught by men' (Mark 7:7). On no occasion do we find it recorded that Jesus' teaching is assailed, quite the reverse. His miraculous acts and deliverance ministry were held up for scrutiny - 'Some of them said, "He casts out demons by Beelzebul, the ruler of the demons"' (Luke 11:15) - but never his teaching, which was always held in high honour, even by his enemies. In saying 'Your sins are forgiven', Jesus appears to score a spectacular own goal, since the man himself had not sinned against Jesus, Jesus is therefore standing in the place of God, a blasphemous offence. He hands the scribes and Doctors of Torah, on a plate, a golden opportunity to disbar him from office, ruin his reputation as a teacher within the Jewish community, and even get him killed. In addition, the rabbinic law taught that sins were only forgiven if the sinner asked that they be forgiven (Talmud, 'Baba Kama' 92a: 'The offence would not be forgiven until he asks him for pardon'), and the paralysed man had not asked to be forgiven.

'Who is this man who speaks blasphemes?' If antagonistic to Jesus, as some may have been, their reaction would have been one of outrage - 'It's blasphemy! We can stone him! We've heard it - with witnesses!' This is their reasoning 'in their hearts.' Because only God can forgive sins, and this paralytic in the care of a religious order could not have sinned against Jesus personally - Jesus was standing in the place of God, which was illegal under the Law and meant the death penalty. Mark's account states: 'Immediately Jesus, aware in his spirit that they were reasoning that way within themselves, said to them, "Why are you reasoning about these things in your hearts?"' (Mark 2:8). 'Immediately' God the Father spoke to Jesus ('in his spirit') about their attitude, because it was crucial that the issue got addressed. Jesus asks: 'Why reason you those things in your heart?' 'Let me give you an illustration,' is the gist of Jesus' response. Matthew records: 'Which is easier to say - 'someone's sins are forgiven' *(you can't tell)* or, 'get up and walk?' *(Words in italics are mine)*. Obviously, it's the first. Only God can say and do the second, because miraculous power is needed. Anyone can 'say' the first. It might be blasphemy, or not, if the person who says it is actually God. But only God could 'say', and perform, such a miracle of healing as this.

'But so that you may know that the Son of Man has authority on earth to forgive sins', he said to the paralytic, 'I say to you, get up, pick up your stretcher and go home.' Jesus is saying to the other Torah teachers, 'That you may have an opportunity to receive what I have come to give - that you may be able to get beyond your own natural prejudices and into the eternal life of the kingdom of my Father', for this reason also I am performing this miracle.'

'Go home.' This would have been something equally amazing, for the man himself. Not, 'Go back to the house you have come from' or 'Return with your friends'. Rather, 'Go your way to your house / home' (Greek: '*oikos*', 'the place your family and father live').* He is told to go to where his own father lived, to the place that he had been separated from by his disability. Jesus restores the man, not only to full health and wholeness, but to his own natural family.

5:25-26 'Immediately he got up before them, and picked up what he had been lying on, and went home glorifying God. They were all struck with astonishment and began glorifying God; and they were filled with fear, saying, "We have seen remarkable things today."'

The man, being healed, immediately obeys Jesus. Luke, like Mark (2:12) tells us: 'And *immediately*, he rose and went forth.' No hesitation - he probably ran home to his father. The people watching 'were all amazed and glorified God' - even, and perhaps especially, any present who were opposed to Jesus. This miracle evidently changed their personal attitudes toward Christ completely. While others of the religious leaders would later object to Jesus and his ministry, Mark tells us that 'everyone' present (including the religious lawyers), praised God saying, 'We never saw anything like this!' (Mark 2:12). The Greek here is '*oida*', meaning 'to discover something' - 'to perceive something for the first time.'* They had discovered something about Jesus that changed their whole lives.

5:27-29 'After that he went out and noticed a tax collector named Levi sitting in the tax booth, and he said to him, "Follow me." And he left everything behind, and got up and began to follow him. And Levi gave a big reception for him in his house; and there was a great crowd of tax collectors and other people who were reclining at the table with them.'

Goods moving between the Roman rulers Antipas' and Philip's territories were subject to a variety of taxes. Levi, otherwise known as Matthew, is believed to have been a scribe in the Jewish rabbinic legal system prior to having betrayed his spiritual heritage in going to work for the despised occupying Roman army. Scribes qualified at age 30, [67] as highly educated people, and Levi would have been functioning as such for some years prior to being considered suitable educationally by the Romans for the responsible role of revenue collector, or indeed to have earned the considerable sum needed to purchase the right to operate the post. Given the number of tax collectors that attended his 'send-off' party he must have been functioning as a tax collector for many years to become so well known and popular with the 'great crowd' of his fellows, who came over what must have been a wide geographical area. Consequently he must have been around at least 50 years of age when he met Jesus. This is an important consideration in discounting the widely held idea that he wrote his Gospel after the fall of Jerusalem in AD 70. Given Jesus' year of birth (6-7 BC), Matthew would have had to be around 100 years old in order to write his Gospel after AD 70. In 'reclining at table' (in the prevailing Roman manner of eating and as at the final Passover meal) with 'sinners' (Matthew 9:11 and Mark 2:16) Jesus is flaunting the Oral Law's constraints in regard to food and legal cleanliness. The Oral Torah (eventually written down as the Mishnah we have today in around 200 AD) had deviated away from the written Torah (taught to Moses at Mount Sinai and the Tabernacle by the pre-incarnate Jesus himself - Exodus 33:11) [xi] in ways that Jesus set out to correct back to his original intention.

Scribes could become wealthy as a result of worming their way into widows' legal inheritance affairs (hence Jesus' denunciation about 'devouring widows' houses' in Matthew 23:14). They were therefore able to buy their way into the lucrative post of revenue collector, someone who had considerable latitude in their appraisal of the value of, and hence the duty charged, on the movement of goods. They could lend at high interest the money to pay the tax, or be bribed into acceptance of a lower tax charge, and so became even wealthier.

5:30-32 'The Pharisees and their scribes began grumbling at his disciples, saying, "Why do you eat and drink with the tax collectors and sinners?" And Jesus answered and said to them, "It is not those who are well who need a physician, but those who are sick. I have not come to call the righteous but sinners to repentance."'

Ever wary of taking on such a brilliant Doctor of Torah (as Jesus was known to be) the critical but cowardly resident legal experts

---

[xi] 'The Lord used to speak to Moses face to face, just as a man speaks to his friend' (Exodus 33:11).

pick on his disciples instead. Ever equally quick to defend them, Jesus answers with a proverb. The rabbis ranked the Roman revenue collectors in the same class as murderers, [68] but to Jesus Matthew was a fellow Jew who needed saving. Mary would have surely enjoyed relating this saying of her son's to her new friend, Luke the Roman '*iatros*' (physician). '*Iatros*' is used in the English word 'iatrogenic', meaning 'caused by a doctor' (usually in relation to harm inadvertently done). Those like the Pharisees who saw themselves as 'righteous' ('right with God') were satisfied with their self-won legal and religious standing in their society. The 'sinners' of which Jesus spoke did not primarily mean notorious criminals or the grossly immoral but were rather those ordinary Jews who did not know the Oral Torah well enough to keep it and so were continually 'missing the mark' ('*hamartôlos*' - 'sinners' by virtue of missing the mark that God's Law set). To 'repent' ('*metanoia*' - 'to change one's mind and way of thinking') requires recognising the need to change - a need that the Pharisees were blind to.

5:33 'And they said to him, "The disciples of John often fast and offer prayers, the disciples of the Pharisees also do the same, but yours eat and drink."'

Failing to win the 'kosher food' argument, the Pharisees and religious-legal experts try another line of questioning. How come Jesus' disciples like a party? After all Jesus' cousin, John the Baptist, offered a much stricter approach to food. Surely that was where true piety lay? Again, out of respect for Jesus' standing as a senior Torah scholar, they pick on the disciples rather than on Jesus himself.

5:34 'And Jesus said to them, "You cannot make the attendants of the bridegroom fast while the bridegroom is with them, can you?"'

Jesus' answer is to point them to the local Jewish pattern of wedding behaviour. Weddings were (and are) an extremely important part of Jewish life, such that for them even the obligations of the Feast of Tabernacles in relation to living in booths were suspended. [69] Fasting at a wedding would have been deeply insulting to the families of the married couple (especially the groom's, who prepared the wedding feast) and to the couple themselves. No religious Jew would dream of fasting at a wedding, the house of which was termed 'the house of feasting'. [70] The notion of 'making' wedding guests fast takes the insulting behaviour to an even worse level of offence. The 'sons of the bride-chamber' made the preparations on behalf of the bridegroom for three days prior to the ceremony [71] and then entered into the celebration with the newly married couple.

5:35 'But the days will come; and when the bridegroom is taken away from them, then they will fast in those days.'

Fasting was associated with mourning (Esther 4:3), as well as a spiritual preparation for worship and prayer (Daniel 9:3). 'Taken away' is '*apairô*', literally meaning to 'lift and carry away',* surely a prophetic nod towards the crucifixion, an appropriate time for mourning if ever there was one.

5:36-39 'And he was also telling them a parable: "No one tears a piece of cloth from a new garment and puts it on an old garment; otherwise he will both tear the new, and the piece from the new will not match the old. And no one puts new wine into old wineskins; otherwise the new wine will burst the skins and it will be spilled out, and the skins will be ruined. But new wine must be put into fresh wineskins. And no one, after drinking old wine wishes for new; for he says, 'The old is good.'"'

God has always been a God of the new as well as the old. 'Behold, I will do something new, now it will spring forth; will you not be aware of it?' (Isaiah 43:19). The human mind however often develops rigidity in its thinking that holds on to the last new thing (now become old), and so is often unable to receive the next new thing that God is doing or saying. The next new thing is therefore rejected. There is always a need to weigh and test each new thing against basic wisdom and Scripture (as Luke commends the Bereans for doing in Acts 17:11). However as recipients of the new wine of the new covenant, Christians need to be careful to avoid being so inflexible that they are unable to receive what God is now giving in a new way. Wine skins were made from goat's hide; once they had set to a specific initial tension they lost elasticity and would split if new wine fermented inside it, producing gas that raised the pressure within. The 'new' wine was often much sharper in taste, but new wine eventually becomes old wine, more mature and further developed in flavour. It is 'good' in the sense of being more pleasant ('*chrestos*'); the same word that Jesus uses for the 'easy' yoke that he invites those he calls to be joined to him in.

Chapter 6

6:1-2 'Now it happened that he was passing through some grain-fields on a Sabbath; and his disciples were picking the heads of grain, rubbing them in their hands, and eating the grain. But some of the Pharisees said, "Why do you do what is not lawful on the Sabbath?"'

Observant Jews would prepare their Sabbath food the day before, because making meals on the Sabbath itself legally constituted 'work' and so was forbidden. Jesus and his disciples were probably too busy to have prepared food, and so were hungry on their way to the local synagogue for the Sabbath service. His disciples therefore are picking ears of corn from the fields they have to pass by, rubbing the husk off in their hands and eating the grain. Gleaning by hand in this way was not theft, but was quite legal under Jewish Law (Deuteronomy 23:25) in respect of both grain and grapes.

It was the 'work' of picking and de-husking that the pharisaic religious lawyers were objecting to, on the grounds that any sort of threshing, even on this small scale, was prohibited on the Sabbath. This was a minor incident perhaps, but an offence nonetheless. The Pharisees, whose role it was to uphold the Oral Law, point this out to their rabbi-master, the respected Doctor of the Law who had such unconventional views in his regard to Mishnaic interpretation. The fact that they do not criticize Jesus personally evidences that Jesus was not himself picking and threshing; if he had been, they would have criticized him directly. Jesus always kept the Oral Law in so far as it did not contradict God's word; he had been trained in it and upheld it, as Matthew 23:2-3 shows. 'Jesus spoke to the crowds and to his disciples, saying: "The scribes and the Pharisees have seated themselves in the chair of Moses; therefore all that they tell you, do and observe, but do not do according to their deeds; for they say things and do not do them."'

Jesus was to clash with the Pharisees again over other issues of legal interpretation like 'Corban', which was the legal withholding of money, such as alms otherwise to be given to parents, if put for a 'higher' purpose such as the support of Temple offering and sacrifice (Talmud '*Nedarim*' 10a - '*korban la-adonai*' - 'a sacrifice to the Lord'). But it was the issue of what constituted the breaking of the Sabbath that caught the Pharisees' attention as a point about which they felt, in all good conscience, they really must oppose the master Rabbi from Nazareth and this apparent disregard for the Oral Torah in the attitude of these disciples for whom he was responsible.

6:3-5: 'And Jesus answering them said, "Have you not even read what David did when he was hungry, he and those who were with him, how he entered the house of God, and took and ate the consecrated bread which is not lawful for any to eat except the priests alone, and gave it to his companions?" And he was saying to them, "The Son of Man is Lord of the Sabbath."'

Jesus meets their objections head-on. 'Haven't you read?' constitutes a rabbinic challenge. He is saying, 'You have read this but you haven't understood it. So now I am going to explain it to you.' David, who was not a priest, placed himself and his companions in the position of priests and ate that which it was lawful only for the priests to eat. Indeed, they were aided and abetted in this technically illegal act by none other than the official priest, Ahimelech, himself (1 Samuel 21:1-4). Ahimelech had discerned that David's need of food was a more suitable use in God's agenda for the bread than its role in sitting before the altar going gradually drier and mouldier by the day, as time passed until the next Sabbath, when it was finally eaten by the priests themselves as the next batch was put out.

This 'bread of the presence' ('Shewbread' - Exodus 25:30) constituted 12 loaves, more than enough for a brief snack for David and the companions whom he was to meet - David only asked for five of them. This generous and faith-filled attitude of Ahimelech was to bring about his and his family's death at the hands of King Saul, David's enemy, through their betrayal by Doeg, the servant of Saul, who was also present (1 Samuel 22:18). Ahimelech had simply acted in charity towards those he genuinely thought to be in need (David and his companions), and was completely removed from any political implication (1 Samuel 22:14-15). The act of slaughter of the priests by Saul can be seen as a type of prophetic foreshadowing of the death Jesus who, along with many of his companions, was to die at the hands of the Jewish authorities of his day.

In the same way David's men were treated like priests, so Jesus is saying that his followers too stand in the place of priests. To pretend to be a priest was an extremely serious offence in Jewish eyes and must have infuriated the Pharisees, given the serious way in which they approached family lineage with regard to qualification for the role of priest. They must have considered that Jesus was placing himself and his followers above the dictates of the Oral Torah. They were not able to see that he was indeed the promised Messiah.

In Matthew's account of this incident (chapter 12), Jesus ratchets up the case he is making by comparing himself and his disciples to the Temple priests who necessarily worked on the Sabbath, and then still further by stating that he was greater than the Temple itself. This did not draw an accusation of blasphemy because of Jesus' *'tekton'* connection (via Joseph) to the building of the Temple [72] and the Jewish proverb quoted in Hebrews 3:3, 'The builder of the house is greater than the house.' Joseph, the Temple *'architekton'*, and his first-born son Jesus, could therefore legitimately be said to be 'Greater than the Temple', without breaking the blasphemy laws.

This precedes Jesus' saying 'The Son of Man is Lord of the Sabbath.' There has been much debate about what Jesus meant by the term 'Son of Man'. In a few simple words recorded in Matthew's Gospel, we find the definition and explanation. 'Lord of the Sabbath' was a Hebrew term for God. 'One greater than the Temple' was idiomatic language for God. The 'Son of Man' being 'Lord of the Sabbath' makes it, as used by Jesus, a clear title of divinity. Luke does not record the Pharisees' response at this point, and technically, Jesus could not be legally charged with blasphemy here because he had not defined who the 'Son of Man' was. But the Pharisees were soon to have a more solid opportunity to accuse this Rabbi who broke so blatantly with their oral traditions.

6:6-11 'On another Sabbath he entered the synagogue and was teaching; and there was a man there whose right hand was withered. The scribes and the Pharisees were watching him closely to see if he healed on the Sabbath, so that they might find reason to accuse him. But he knew what they were thinking, and he said to the man with the withered hand, "Get up and come forward!" And he got up and came forward. And Jesus said to them, "I ask you, is it lawful to do good or to do harm on the Sabbath, to save a life or to destroy it?" After looking around at them all, he said to him, "Stretch out your hand!" And he did so; and his hand was restored. But they themselves were filled with rage, and discussed together what they might do to Jesus.'

The man had a palsied hand, and Doctor Luke records that it was his right hand (the other Gospels omit this pertinent medical detail), hence likely to be the dominant hand. Stone masons worked with very large blocks of stone (the foundation stones in the Temple weighed in excess of 500 tons). [73] Working with large stone blocks carries risks of fractures; an upper arm fracture is often associated with traumatic nerve injury and consequential muscle wasting. The Church Father Jerome wrote in 398 AD concerning Matthew's account (chapter 12). "In the Gospel which the Nazarenes and Ebionites use (which I have lately translated into Greek from the Hebrew, and which is called by many or most people the original of Matthew), this man who had the withered hand is described as a mason, who prays for help in such words as this: 'I was a mason seeking a livelihood with my hands. I pray thee, Jesus, to restore me mine health, that I may not beg meanly for my food.'" Since masons fashioned the stones used by *'tektons'* in foundations and construction it is quite possible that the man was known to Jesus' own family of *'tektons'*.

But for whatever reason, this man's hand was withered. Could the Pharisees tempt Jesus into breaking the Law? The Law said medical healing on the Sabbath was illegal except in the case of an emergency where death might occur as a result of any delay. [74] This man did not meet the emergency criteria so there was no rush to perform any healing.

So they ask Jesus if is it lawful (according to their Law) to heal on the Sabbath. In Matthew's account (Matthew 12:11), Jesus replies in a way that they could understand, using the Law. God had made provisions for sheep. A sheep left in a pit would not die if left till evening, when the setting sun signified the end of the Sabbath day. A few extra hours would not hurt it. But the Law [75] allowed for carrying food to it and the work to assist in extraditing it, because of the principle in Jewish Law of relative loss. A sheep was considered a great loss - one worthy of work during the Sabbath day. So, if God was concerned about meeting the needs of natural sheep, how much more was he concerned to meet the needs of his spiritual sheep?

Jesus takes their legal principle and turns it on its head. He was saying that if it is right to do good of a certain value on the Sabbath, then it is evil to refuse to do good of a certain relative value. The man has the higher value. Therefore it is lawful (according to the principles of the Law) to do good on the Sabbath. And so Jesus speaks to the man, 'Stretch out your hand.' He is intentionally very careful not to do anything that could be interpreted as being healing or work. Asking someone to stretch out their hand was not work. Stretching out your hand was not work. Jesus is being very careful not to give unnecessary grounds for offence or accusation. He is also demonstrating his divine power in an even more convincing way; in this instance by healing from a distance and re-creating human tissue by his spoken word, in a way reminiscent of the creation account of Genesis chapter 1.

He is also asking the man to participate in his own healing, in calling on him to do the impossible. God may ask us to do, with him, the impossible; because anyone can do the possible but only God can do the impossible. As Luke 1:37 says, 'For with God nothing shall be impossible.' As we respond to his word, in simple trust and obedience, so the miraculous happens. The withered hand is made like the other hand, which would itself have been slightly overdeveloped due to the extra use required of it, there being no other hand to call upon. His good hand would have therefore had an excessive development of musculature. Jesus restored his withered hand to be 'just as sound as the other' (Matthew 12:13), in other words, perfect symmetry. Many people in that synagogue (including the man's possibly impoverished family) must have praised God for this extraordinary miracle of re-creation of damaged and dead tissue.

But the Pharisees, filled with 'rage' (the Greek here is '*anoia*' - also meaning 'folly' and, literally, 'without understanding') went and plotted how they might kill Jesus. His words regarding 'saving life or destroying it' had been addressed to them and they demonstrated the truth of them in plotting to harm him. A miracle that God has sent to them to confirm the truth about Jesus' remarks concerning his divinity had the opposite effect on them. Their hearts were so hardened that they now hated Jesus even more - this Rabbi, turned

Messiah-figure, who dared to undermine their religious system by pointing to the God who had designed it in the first place. Jesus was showing that the Law was not mainly a means of approaching God, (which was ultimately through trust and faith), but as a means of revealing to us our own inability to keep it. Sadly, the Law had become to them a means of pride in their own attainments, thus estranging them still further to the God who 'opposes the proud but gives grace to the humble' (James 4:6).

6:12 'It was at this time that he went off to the mountain to pray, and he spent the whole night in prayer to God.'

There was no other human being who could make a case for being less needful of prayer and expressing total dependency on the Father than Jesus, because Jesus was also himself fully God. But there was also no other human being who better understood the need for total dependency on the Father as the means of living in faith and trust. Jesus' prayer illustrates the same concept as his 40 days of fasting had done - a reliance on what the Father was doing and saying rather than simply his own wishes. For him there was naturally much less variance, but in our case our natures create a much greater difference. Jesus was modelling for us how to get rid of our own ideas and instead take on God's and his preferences - by praying in an attitude of faith, enabling working in an attitude of faith, knowing that 'unless the Lord build the house, the workers labour in vain' (Psalm 127:1).

6:13-16 'And when day came, he called his disciples to him and chose twelve of them, whom he also named as apostles: Simon, whom he also named Peter, and Andrew his brother; and James and John; and Philip and Bartholomew; and Matthew and Thomas; James the son of Alphaeus, and Simon who was called the Zealot; Judas

the son of James, and Judas Iscariot, who became a traitor.'

Jesus' night in prayer was particularly important because the spiritual succession of his three and a half year ministry was at stake. The 'apostles' were those 'sent off under orders' (*'apostellô'*),* and as such were a type of mission-team leader in the work of preparing places for Jesus' ministry to come to. Jesus had a large though variable number of other disciples, including, unusually for a rabbinic scholar, a number of women. Luke's Gospel informs us (Luke 8:3 - surely another of Mary's contributions) that these women, as well as having the role of 'disciples' (*'mathêtês'* - 'a learner')*, would also re-produce Jesus' amazing teaching after his death.

Their role of leading in being 'sent out on mission' necessitated that the twelve apostles be men. God went to a great deal of trouble in the creation of mankind to make men and women to be different. He did this in order that they might have particular and distinct complimentary roles in the running and overseeing of his kingdom. He also recognised man's intrinsic irresponsibility, illustrated by the Fall, remedying it by calling the man into a particular place of responsibility - governmental oversight. [76]

Jesus' core group of three men were Peter, James and John. These were the men who accompanied him up the Mount of Transfiguration (Mark 9:2) and went further with him in the garden of Gethsemane (Matthew 26:37). James and John were the 'sons of Zebedee'; their mother was Salome, also described as Jesus' mother's sister. 'Standing by the cross of Jesus were his mother, and his mother's sister, Mary the wife of Clopas, and Mary Magdalene' (John 19:25), c.f. 'There were also some women looking on from a distance, among whom were Mary Magdalene, and Mary the mother of James the Less and Joses, and Salome' (Mark 15:40). James' name in Hebrew is '*Ya-cob*' ('Jacob'), the change occurring by the need to fit the sound into successive generations of languages. Being Jesus' cousins they would have known him growing up and their fellow professional fishermen Simon and his brother Andrew had a natural set of existing relationships that would have surely reached into the circle of Jesus' own childhood acquaintances prior to his departure for Bet Midrash in Jerusalem at age 14. When these men were called, they were therefore not encountering Jesus for the first time and they were not abandoning their livelihoods on the basis of a split-second decision to follow Jesus. They were attaching themselves as rabbinic apprentices to the best known Rabbi in Israel, at a time when to be afforded such a position meant having an already high level of academic ability. These men had not progressed beyond the first stage of Talmudic and religious legal schooling which was completed by age 14; if indeed they had got as far as that stage of formal religious instruction. Many Jewish boys switched to their father's trade and out of education aged 8, when Tanakh (Scripture and basic Law) studies were completed. With God there is no problem in being a late developer! Philip too was an old friend of Peter and Andrew from Bethsaida (literally 'house of fishing'), a village on the northeast shore of Lake Galilee.

The amazing power that Jesus had to change people's lives is evidenced by the co-existing of Matthew, the quisling ex-tax collector and Roman appointee who is now rubbing shoulders with a revolutionary Zealot activist named Simon, who, just a matter of months earlier, might happily have killed a tax collector. Bartholomew is listed as Nathaniel by John (John 21:1). Bartholomew means 'son of Talmai' (Aramaic for 'farmer'), his family name, with Nathaniel, from the Hebrew '*natan*' ('given') and '*El*' ('God'), meaning 'gift from God', this being his given or familiar name. Thomas, also known as 'Didymus' ('the twin'), was a man who seems to have worn his heart on his sleeve and was so deeply affected by Jesus' betrayal and death that he could not risk being let down a second time by the other disciples' story of resurrection, which he did not at first believe. Like the others, with the exception of John, he was eventually to be martyred for his faith. If history had been kinder, he might have entered posterity as 'Thomas the Evangelist to India', or, 'Thomas the man who laid down his life for his faith'. Alas, it was not to be, and (on earth at least), he was stuck with the tag of 'Doubting Thomas'. Then there was James (son of Alphaeus) an honest man; one ready to ask for clarification (John 14:22).

There were two men named Judas. Judas the son of James, was also known as Labbaeus, and is thought to have been the author of the book of Jude. The other Judas (of Kerioth in Southern Judea, hence 'Iscariot'), was a man motivated by love of his country's freedom but also, sadly, by money. He seems to have wanted Jesus to take direct political action against the Romans; for him a dead Messiah was of no use - Jesus' speaking clearly of his death helped prompt Judas' act of betrayal (Mark 14:6-10). That Jesus made him treasurer of the group contains an insight into dealing with temptation - the tree of the knowledge of good and evil was always before Adam and Eve, in the 'middle of the garden' (Genesis 2:9). The fact that it was not out of reach meant that they had a daily choice to make in terms of not eating of its fruit, in obedience to God's command. Like Adam and Eve, Judas helped himself - to the communal funds (John 12:6). That this could go largely unnoticed demonstrates that the company of disciples was not so badly off as to be living hand to mouth. While Thomas is perhaps unfairly remembered for doubting, the name Judas is still firmly synonymous with treachery.

6:17-19 'Jesus came down with them and stood on a level place; and there was a large crowd of his disciples, and a great throng of people from all Judea and Jerusalem and the coastal region of Tyre and Sidon, who had come to hear him and to be healed of their diseases; and those

who were troubled with unclean spirits were being cured. And all the people were trying to touch him, for power was coming from him and healing them all.'

Whereas Matthew records 'the Sermon on the Mount', Luke records 'the Sermon on the Plain'. Given the Jewish humour in it, one might venture the conjecture that it is like the Sermon on the Mount but for those who didn't like heights! Jesus was immensely popular with the crowds for two main reasons. The first was his miraculous healings and the second was the quality of his Scripture and Torah exposition and wisdom, wisdom the people would normally have to travel to the Temple in Jerusalem to hear. Scripture and Torah were the two most highly prized elements of Jewish society, on a level comparative to that of modern popular sports in the West. Senior rabbinic academics did not usually travel. They stayed in the rarefied atmosphere of the Temple schools and largely taught their own disciples, who in turn relayed their teaching to others. To hear someone of Jesus' standing was considered a rare treat for the majority who were unfortunately cut off from this highest level of teaching. And of course there was the added attraction of his healing and deliverance ministry. Just as with the woman with the 'issue of blood' (Luke 8), power to be healed was available simply by touching him, without Jesus needing to say a word. 'Troubled' by evil spirits ('*ochleô*') is a medical term unique to Luke in the New Testament but used by Hippocrates [77] for a chronically continuing and vexatious condition.

Tyre and Sidon are the coastal regions of modern-day Lebanon (south of Beirut), over 100 miles north and west of Galilee. Jerusalem is 120 miles south of Galilee. Jesus is drawing enormous crowds who would have had to travel many days to hear him. With the efforts being made to touch him some form of crowd control must have been needed, but Scripture is silent on this subject; presumably 'Health and Safety' issues did not have the same profile in first century Judea as in the modern day western world!

6:20 'And turning his gaze toward his disciples, he began to say, "Blessed are you who are poor, for yours is the kingdom of God."'

Just as the Sermon on the Mount was addressed to his disciples that 'came to him' there (Matthew 5:1), so is the Sermon on the Plain. 'Poor' here (Matthew has 'poor in Spirit') is *'ptochos'*, meaning beggarly or destitute,* derived from *'ptosso'*, which means 'to crouch',* (as a roadside beggar would - a common first century sight). Jesus' disciples were not all poor (Matthew as a former tax collector was certainly not, given the size of the retirement feast that he put on; neither were the women who were supporting Jesus), but they had emptied themselves of their own ambitions and had chosen to be Jesus' disciples.

Those who are poor in spirit recognise their own human condition of spiritual impoverishment, of one who is in great need and who, unless his need is met, will die. Jesus was saying that the 'happy' ones ('blessed' is *'makarios'*, from *'makar'*, meaning 'happy'), who inherit the life of his kingdom (now, on this earth, to a significant degree, as well as in heaven) are those who can recognise their own spiritual beggarliness from a human perspective and so do not have any pretensions about their own status or knowledge, and are consequently not filled with pride.

The 'kingdom' of God (or of 'heaven' in Matthew's more Jewish-oriented version) is the area over which the King exercises his authority to rule with the acceptance of his subjects, as opposed to those who reject his rule and live their lives, knowingly or unknowingly, under the rule of the devil. Until Jesus returns there exists a state of conflict between these two kingdoms, however the day is coming when 'The kingdom of the world has become the kingdom of our Lord and of his Christ, and he will reign forever and ever' (Revelation 11:15).

6:21 'Blessed are you who hunger now, for you shall be satisfied. Blessed are you who weep now, for you shall laugh.'

'Hunger' here is '*peinao*' - 'to suffer want' - 'to be in need of food and basic provisions'* ('hunger after righteousness' - Matthew 5:6). Jesus, as in verse 3, is speaking of those who not only hunger physically, but are also acutely aware of their desperate need spiritually. They have come to the often painful realization that to rely on themselves and their own abilities, good and God given though they may be, is futile. When dependence is shifted off God and onto self, reliance is no longer fully on God; faith diminishes and 'without faith it is impossible to please him.' 'Weep' is '*klaiô*', which is considerably stronger than the English implies. It means to 'bewail', just as the semi-professional mourners at Jairus' house were wailing for his dead daughter (Luke 8:52). The sense is one of mourning for sin and the resultant poor and weakened spiritual position that its power inflicts on those ravaged by its influence. But wait, there's more! The good news is that a change is imminent. 'Laughter' is coming - that phenomenon the Scripture associates with deliverance from the sort of oppression that brings wailing. This was what the Jewish captives experienced when King Cyrus announced their release from Babylon - 'Our mouths were filled with laughter' (Psalm 126:2).

6:22-23 'Blessed are you when men hate you, and ostracize you, and insult you, and scorn your name as evil, for the sake of the Son of Man. Be glad in that day and leap for joy, for behold, your reward is great in heaven. For in the same way their fathers used to treat the prophets.'

There have been a number of instances where this situation has occurred since Jesus spoke these words, most recently in militantly atheist communist states on the one hand, and in militantly religious Islamic states on the other. There, Christians have been and still are reviled and suffer for their faith. Charities such as the Barnabas Fund are to be commended for the work they do in providing support. 'Hate' here speaks for itself. 'Ostracize' goes further, meaning to 'separate by boundaries as disreputable',* much as the Nazis placed European city Jews into ghettos prior to seeking to exterminate them. 'Scorn' is the rather stronger '*ekballô*' - 'to drive out violently',* in the way that Christians in northern Nigeria have been recently driven out by violent radical Islamists. For Jesus' audience of disciples, this phenomenon would occur in their lifetimes. But the 'scattering' that the persecution under the oversight of Saul of Tarsus (Acts 8:1) would be used for good - the propagation of the gospel. Jesus' denunciation of the scribes and Pharisees and their fathers in Matthew 23:29-36 details some examples of how the prophets had been persecuted in delivering the message that God had entrusted them with. They had both addressed the sin that was around them and looked ahead to Messiah's coming.

6:24-25 'But woe to you who are rich, for you are receiving your comfort in full. Woe to you who are well-fed now, for you shall be hungry. Woe to you who laugh now, for you shall mourn and weep.'

While there were some wealthy followers of Christ who supported him with their resources, they were few in comparison to the large number of ordinary and relatively poorer people in Judea and in Jesus' audience of disciples. The wealthy in Judean society definitely included those religious folk who had become rich through exploiting their positions, be it as priests who charged exorbitantly for sacrificial offerings, or the religious lawyers and scribes who worked the Law to their own gain (e.g. the scribes in relation to widows' houses - Matthew 23:14). Given the connection with the 'well-fed' (verse 25), it is likely that Jesus' gaze has now moved away from his disciples and to those religious authorities that his ministry went on to further denounce. These men were the spiritually obese of Matthew 13:15, overly fattened consequential to their doing so little of any value with the words that they had received from God. They were 'satisfied' - so self-satisfied that they saw no need for the type of messiahhood Jesus brought. They thought that they needed nothing, but their end, in refusing the grace of God, would be the 'mourning and weeping' of those excluded from the wedding feast of the Kingdom of Heaven. As Jesus would later say, 'Throw out the worthless slave into the outer darkness; in that place there will be weeping and gnashing of teeth' (Matthew 25:29).

The change of audience is further evidenced by Jesus' saying, 'Woe to you who laugh now.' Jesus has just promised his disciples laughter, and given the typically rabbinic approach to humour that his teaching illustrates, with its widespread use of puns and plays-on-words, Jesus' company of disciples must have been a joyful place where laughter abounded. Children will not voluntarily go to sour-faced people, but they had no hesitation in going to Jesus for a blessing (Matthew 19:13).

6:26 'Woe to you when all men speak well of you, for their fathers used to treat the false prophets in the same way.'

This verse brings the focus of Jesus' words back to his disciples, and Jesus' phrase 'their fathers' points back to the religious leaders whose wealthy self-satisfied lifestyles he had just denounced. 'Being spoken well of' is not a sin. The point Jesus is making is that if we set out our speaking or behaviour in order to be well spoken of, then our speaking or behaviour is with a false and unworthy motive. It is that of the false prophets who spoke flattering words that they might by them gain men's approval, such as those who surrounded the King of Israel in 1 Kings 22 before the genuine prophet Micaiah brought a true word from God. This clear saying of Jesus' should not be taken as a license to speak in a deliberately offensive way, in order to be ill-spoken of by those who oppose the gospel. As one of Jesus' audience that day later wrote, 'Always be prepared to give an answer to everyone who asks you to give the reason for the hope that you have. But do this with gentleness and respect' (1 Peter 3:15).

6:27-28 'But I say to you who hear, love your enemies, do good to those who hate you, bless those who curse you, pray for those who mistreat you.'

Jesus sets the bar at a level that only someone whose life had been transformed by the power of God in new birth could attain. What Jesus is commanding is humanly impossible to do, because fallen human nature is incapable of any more than a mere pretence at keeping this saying. Only when 'God's love has been poured into our hearts by the Holy Spirit whom he has given to us' (Romans 5:5) can Jesus' instructions be carried out, and even then it is by no means easy! The response required towards those whose hatred had driven them into ghetto-slums and then murdered some of them was to 'do good', and only an inner transformation could make that possible. 'To curse' someone in first-century Judea was much more than to simply swear at them. '*Kataraomai*' means to stand and 'call down execrations of evil' upon someone (from '*kata*' - 'down' and '*ara*' - 'a curse'). Jesus calls his followers to bless, and not to curse (Romans 12:14). 'Mistreat' is, again, a very weak translation of '*epêreazô*', which means 'to insult and treat abusively'.[78] The Christian response is to 'offer prayers' for those doing the persecuting.

6:29 'Whoever hits you on the cheek, offer him the other also; and whoever takes away your coat, do not withhold your shirt from him either.'

The abuses behind 'to mistreat' now become clearer. The fallen human nature, when struck will, as the fictional lawyer Jaggers remarks in the Dickens' novel 'Great Expectations', either 'beat (hit back) or cringe'. The human nature renewed in the image of Christ by the Spirit of God does neither - it turns the other cheek offering that for striking also. Once again the humanly-speaking impossibility of keeping Jesus' teaching is revealed. It is not supposed to be humanly possible, rather, it is supposed to need a Spirit-led inner change. Likewise the forcible removal of the outer garment which doubled as a blanket at night (the '*himation*') is, in a believer, supposed to be followed by the offer of the '*chitôn*' too. The Jewish Law (Exodus 22:26-27) prohibited the retention of the outer garment for debt payment. The 'shirt' ('tunic') by contrast was the main item of clothing worn next to the skin. Losing that would leave a man naked other than for the loincloth, which once again underlines the natural or human impossibility of what is being asked. The circumstances Jesus is describing here are those of a violent assault. It is possible that such extraordinary responses as those being depicted would communicate to the assailant the extraordinary nature of the Christian person being assaulted in a spiritually effective manner; they certainly demonstrate a trust in the God who gave the command in the first place.

Matthew's Gospel contains a passage of similar teaching, but with a subtle difference. Matthew 5:40: 'If anyone wants to sue you and take your shirt, let him have your coat also.' Here the scenario is Jewish legal process, not violent assault. As mentioned above, Jewish Law protected a debtor from losing his cloak. In this situation Jesus is saying that the believer should be so confident of his honesty in the matter under legal question that he is prepared to offer the protected garment as well.

6:30 'Give to everyone who asks of you, and whoever takes away what is yours, do not demand it back.'

Here the situation of abuse is continuing to be portrayed - the forcible 'taking away of what is yours'. The context is that of an oppressive regime behaving in an unjust way towards believers. Roman law provided a measure of protection for their occupied territories, though abuses of authority were regular and well-recognised. Jesus' teaching here would equally aptly fit the situation in which Christians find themselves in modern-day militantly atheistic states. The 'everyone who asks' is in the same group as those who can 'take away by force'.

The passage is not advocating mindless giving to anyone, whoever they may be, who wants to sponge off Christians as a means of effortless income. It is commanding a willingness to obey an abusive authority in the same way as giving both sets of clothing - the outer and the inner. This is similar to the Apostle Paul's teaching in Romans 13:1-2. 'Every person is to be in subjection to the governing authorities. For there is no authority except from God, and those which exist are established by God. Therefore whoever resists authority has opposed the ordinance of God; and they who have opposed will receive condemnation upon themselves.' The obedience being called out in such hostile situations is one based on trust in Father God's overall supervision and control over all the circumstances of our lives. The God who can provide bread from heaven does not need his children to 'demand back' what is his to give; they can re-give and keep on re-giving.

6:31-34 'Treat others the same way you want them to treat you. If you love those who love you, what credit is that to you? For even sinners love those who love them. If you do good to those who do good to you, what credit is that to you? For even sinners do the same. If you lend to those from whom you expect to receive, what credit is that to you? Even sinners lend to sinners in order to receive back the same amount.'

It is actually quite difficult to second-guess how someone might want to be treated. A much more simple and reliable rule-of-thumb is to consider what we know all too well - how we want to be treated - and then treat others the same way. We should not consider, however, that the Christian life is to be lived in a way consistent with others who also treat people with basic human kindness, care and concern. That would just make the Christian life look similar to, and perhaps a bit better, than the best-lived pagan lives. And that is not what Jesus is looking for. The 'sinners' referred to here are the *'hamartia'* - the everyday ordinary Jew unschooled in Oral Torah and the minutiae of the Law. They would however have been aware that the Law prohibited charging interest on a loan (Deuteronomy 23:19). 'Expect to receive' does not therefore mean 'with interest', rather it means to get your money or item loaned returned to you. Within a close-knit local community, this is not a huge risk to take. It is not a 'big deal', and here Jesus is expecting a whole lot more than that from his disciples who are to go beyond the bounds of what the culture around them does.

6:35-36 'But love your enemies, and do good and lend, expecting nothing in return; and your reward will be great, and you will be sons of the Most High; for he himself is kind to ungrateful and evil men. Be merciful, just as your Father is merciful.'

Jews would very rarely, like the rest of humanity, lend to their enemies, and certainly not without expecting to be re-paid. In fact a Jew lending to a Gentile was quite legally entitled to charge interest on the loan. Jesus' Jewish disciples are being told to not even expect to get the loan back. Once again, a huge reliance on the Father's overall control is being called out of them. They would need to grow into a place of faith that would enable them to do this. The underlying necessary new-birth to achieve this is illustrated by Jesus' use of 'sons' - *'huios'* - 'children' of a Father who has more

131

than enough resources to supply his children's needs without needing to be begged to do so. This Father is also big enough to be kind to those who ignore and reject him. His very nature forbids that he withhold his inherent kindness from the 'wicked' - *'ponêros'* (from *'poneô'* - 'to toil') - hence expressing 'especially the active form of evil.' [79] As the account of the similar episode of teaching in Matthew's Gospel puts it, 'He causes his sun to rise on the evil and the good, and sends rain on the righteous and the unrighteous' (Matthew 5:45). 'Merciful' here is *'oiktirmôn'*, from *'oiktirô'*, meaning 'to have pity or compassion'. [80] This is God's 'compassion for the ills of others', as Vine's New Testament Dictionary's definition of 'merciful' puts it. One day, however, the time for his compassionate patience will be over and he will come and judge what we have done towards others.

6:37 'Do not judge, and you will not be judged; and do not condemn, and you will not be condemned; pardon, and you will be pardoned.'

That coming judgement is, however, God's own prerogative. His disciples and children are supposed to leave any judging in the negative sense of condemnation up to him. *'Krino'* does, however, also mean 'to decide' in the objective sense, and there are a lot of things in society that Christians need to make a decision about. So Jesus is not excluding the place of wisdom in making a decision about something on an objective and scriptural basis. As he would later upbraid the crowd, 'And why do you not even on your own initiative judge what is right?' (Luke 12:57). It is certainly though not our place 'to condemn' -*'katadikazô'* - 'to pass sentence upon'. We do not have all the facts that are at God's disposal, hence we are in no place to 'judge' in that sense. As Jesus' followers, we all need to be forgiven. And to be forgiven, it is necessary to first forgive others. 'Whenever you stand praying, forgive, if you have anything against anyone, so that your Father who is in heaven will also forgive you your transgressions. But if you do not forgive, neither will your Father who is in heaven forgive your transgressions' (Mark 11:25-26).

6:38 'Give, and it will be given to you. They will pour into your lap a good measure, pressed down, shaken together, and running over. For by your standard of measure it will be measured to you in return.'

The best way to 'get' from God is to give to God, because it is impossible to out-give God. What is received may not be exactly of the same type as that which was given, but it will be superior in quality (being from God) and, as this verse says, drastically greater in quantity. 'Lap' is '*kolpos*', the upper body between the arms, and hence better translated 'bosom' or 'chest'. The Apostle John lay back against Jesus' '*kolpos*' at the Last Supper when they 'reclined at table' (John 13:23). The '*kolpos*' was the folded area at the front of the tunic that was gathered up by a belt and so provided a type of convenient pocket for carrying things in. 'Pressed' down is '*piezô*', a medical term unique to Doctor Luke in the New Testament but commonly used by physicians for the force needing to be applied to staunch wounds. [81] There is thus a rather energetic image of the giver being laid hands upon such that, for example, grain, is shoved into his garment which is then vigorously shaken to make room for more before pouring in such an excess quantity that some falls to the ground at his feet. Such is Jesus' graphic depiction of his Father's generosity.

'Your standard of measure' is a known example of a Jewish '*targum*' (an explanatory note found in rabbinic discourse attached to a particular portion of Scripture). The term arose from the need to translate from the Hebrew scrolls into the common language of Aramaic, and features in Ezra 4:17-18, 'And now the document which you sent to us has been *translated* and read before me.' The term then came to mean an explanation or 'unpacking' of the text in a synagogue teaching. 'Your standard of measure' is attached to Genesis 38:26, where Judah speaks of his daughter-in-law Tamar's righteousness as being greater than his (standard of measure of righteousness). 'Measured to you in return' is literally to 'measure again' ('*antimetreô*') - '*metreô*' being 'to measure', hence modern 'metric' measurements. The meaning here is that we will receive something back that is about double what we had given. The alternative - we will receive what we have given - makes no sense of the preceding sentence about abundance. God always gives back more than we give to him.

6:39 'And he also spoke a parable to them: "A blind man cannot guide a blind man, can he? Will they not both fall into a pit?'

Rabbis taught using humour extensively. We may not recognise it, or even find it funny if we do, but Jesus' audience would have been laughing at the mental image invoked by his use of this existing proverb, partly because they knew whom it was Jesus was really talking about. It is true that there are degrees of blindness and that a blind man with a walking aid may help lead another blind man, but that is to ignore the central point that Jesus is making. A blind person is best helped by someone who can see. The image of one blind person leading another to fall to the bottom of an excavation is not supposed to be politically correct. It is supposed to be funny in the comic sense. Jewish teaching tradition is the longest recorded collection of humour known to man. Whether an individual finds it funny or not is not the issue, because humour varies with personality, culture and the historic period under analysis. A sense of humour is still very much at work.

Matthew's Gospel (15:14) provides the whole context for this saying of Jesus. First century Judean society was led by men who prided themselves on their spiritual sight. They had entrenched themselves in religious scholarship to the extent of ignoring the consequences of their religious teaching. This was well illustrated by their invention of the 'Corban' law. The Rabbis and Pharisees recognised that this could lead to parental hardship but to them the upkeep of the Temple was much more important than providing for any needs of elderly parents. Jesus would later denounce such Pharisees as 'blind guides' (Matthew 23:16). Hence Jesus was not making fun of blind people. His audience knew exactly which 'blind men' he was referring to.

6:40 'A pupil is not above his teacher; but everyone after he has been fully trained will be like his teacher.'

It was not God's intention that these 'blind' teachers should be blind. The Pharisees had a responsibility to pass on Torah in a spiritually helpful way. That depended on the quality of the teaching and also on the ability of the disciple ('*mathêtês*' - 'a learner' of an older teacher). 'Teacher' here is '*Didaskalos*', translated as 'Doctor' in Luke 2. It is the term for the most senior of Torah scholars, as used of Gamaliel in Acts 5:34. In the context of Jewish teaching (rather than say, medicine), the term '*Didaskalos*' always means 'Doctor of the Law'. There are many Talmudic passages bemoaning the different approaches disciples took to imbibing spiritually based knowledge. But even the best disciple did not go beyond correctly representing his master's body of teaching. Jesus' society valued what they saw as the correct rendering of ancient teaching and traditions, and was consequently very careful to preserve them. So when Jesus took passages of Scripture and interpreted them in ways that his audience had not heard from other rabbis, he was seen as giving 'new' teaching.

An example of this can be seen at the beginning of Jesus' public ministry in Capernaum. Mark 1:21-27: 'On the Sabbath he entered the synagogue and began to teach. They were amazed at his teaching; for he was teaching them as one having authority, and not as the scribes. Just then there was a man in their synagogue with an unclean spirit; and he cried out, saying, "What business do we have with each other, Jesus of Nazareth? Have you come to destroy us? I know who you are - the Holy One of God!" And Jesus rebuked him, saying, "Be quiet, and come out of him!" Throwing him into convulsions, the unclean spirit cried out with a loud voice and came out of him. They were all amazed, so that they debated among themselves, saying, "What is this? A new teaching with authority!"'

Jesus' (correct) re-stating of Old Testament teaching was 'with authority' (Mark 1:22), but quite different to the scribes whose job it was to repeat the 'old' teaching. The difference between Jesus and the scribes was not one of legal authority to teach (Jesus could not have formally taught in the synagogue without legal authority, which the scribes shared). The difference was twofold - what Jesus was teaching ('new teaching' - Mark 1:27), in addition to a spiritual ministry and a place of authority that the public associated with an expectation of 'old' teaching. Without proper legal authority the societal norm would been to reject 'new' teaching, not receive it in a favourable way. What they were used to, and valued, was the old.

There were three reasons why Jesus' new teaching was well received. The first is that Jesus' scholarly standing was evident to all his contemporaries, who called him 'Doctor' (of Torah) and Rabbi. They knew who his father Joseph was and they knew of Jesus' background in Temple studies and were not labouring under the misapprehension that he was an itinerant, uneducated peasant. Secondly, they recognised his teaching to be contextually suited to their religious history, but just up on another, much higher, level. Jesus was pulling things out of Scripture and Torah that had never been seen before but which were, on close inspection, actually there in the texts. They had just been 'hidden'. Thirdly, his extraordinary genius was being further testified to by the miracles he performed.

The mark of a 'fully trained' Christian is to be 'like' their master. This is not supposed to be seen as some theoretical ideal, but as a practical outworking of the Holy Spirit in our minds (correct God-centric thinking), our lives (out-working the mercy and compassion of God) and our spirits (the miraculous interventions of God in our lives). When that is all happening, we will be 'like our Master'. To be 'perfect' here is *'katartizô'*, from *'artos'*, 'a joint'. It is the medical term for re-locating a dislocated joint. This re-fitting together of what is out of joint is not the same sense of complete moral perfection found in the other New Testament word for 'perfect' which is *'teleiôs'* ('moral perfection'). In the context of putting a dislocated joint back in place, becoming 'like Jesus' seems more do-able. As a doctor who has re-located a few dislocated joints, I know that joints in their sockets are definitely preferable for the patient than joints that are not. Life just works better that way!

6:41-42 'Why do you look at the speck that is in your brother's eye, but do not notice the log that is in your own eye? Or how can you say to your brother, "Brother, let me take out the speck that is in your eye", when you yourself do not see the log that is in your own eye? You hypocrite, first take the log out of your own eye, and then you will see clearly to take out the speck that is in your brother's eye."'

More rabbinic humour. Only this time, rabbinic *'tekton'* humour. All rabbis started out with secular professions, because the Law prohibited charging for teaching and legal interpretation (to minimise material influence). But the Law did not prohibit receiving gifts, so very senior rabbis were highly thought of enough to be able to give up their work and concentrate solely on teaching, being supported by gifts from wealthy followers. Jesus was one such rabbi - 'Many women were there, watching from a distance. They had followed Jesus from Galilee to care for his needs' (Matthew 27:55,

NIV). '*Tektons*' worked with big buildings - bigger than the typical one storey houses and therefore requiring a properly dug foundation ('Like a wise master *tekton* I laid a foundation' - 1 Corinthians 3:10). Big buildings required big roof-beams, and it is these of which Jesus is speaking. A 'log' here is a '*dokos*' - normally translated as a 'beam'. [82] The '*dokos*' in the roof of Herod's Temple were 100 feet in length, [83] and installing them 165 feet above the ground [84] was a job for an '*architekton*' - a 'master *tekton*' - an architect / structural engineer, not a carpenter. Joseph and Jesus were master '*tektons*'.

Rabbis loved to use hyperbole - the (often humourous) contrast between two grossly dissimilarly sized objects. In this case the roof-beam is contrasted with a 'speck' (of sawdust). The Greek here is '*karphos*', meaning a very small dry piece of wood or stalk, [85] as might very conceivably fly off into someone's eye while using a wood plane on long Lebanese cedars to rid the trunks of their outer bark prior to installing them in a roof. The image of someone with a 100 foot tree-trunk in their eye 'helping' someone with a speck of sawdust in their eye is intentionally hyperbolic and would have been hilariously funny to Jesus' Jewish audience, who, knowing Jesus' and Joseph's profession, would have much appreciated the '*tekton*' imagery. Only a '*hupokritês*' - 'an actor' (in this case a comic actor) would try and 'help' like that! Stop play-acting, Jesus is saying, get real and sort yourselves out before attempting the admirable task of helping others with slightly more minor issues.

6:43-44 'For there is no good tree which produces bad fruit, nor on the other hand, a bad tree which produces good fruit. For each tree is known by its own fruit. For men do not gather figs from thorns, nor do they pick grapes from a briar bush.'

The humour continues with a graphic image of a tree that bears only fruit that is already rotten! A tree that changes instantly from having developing buds to having decaying maggot-infested fruit is not the sort of tree anybody would want to keep. 'Good' is *'kalos'*, meaning 'beautiful' and 'fitting the circumstances very well';* also meaning the exact opposite of *'sapros'* - 'rotten'. Looking in a thorn bush for figs or in a briar (bramble) bush for grapes is another image that Jesus' audience would have found delightfully amusing. The parallel passage in Matthew 7:16 has the fruit being looked for amongst thorns and thistles. Doubtless Jesus gave this teaching in different ways and on more than one occasion; the version Luke records has *'batos'* - 'a bramble bush'.* This is significant because the fruit, leaves and new shoots of these bushes (especially blackberry bushes) were used extensively for medical purposes. The Greek physician Claudius Galen (c. 130 - c. 210 AD) devoted a whole chapter of one of his books to its uses. [86]

6:45 'The good man out of the good treasure of his heart brings forth what is good; and the evil man out of the evil treasure brings forth what is evil; for his mouth speaks from that which fills his heart.'

'Treasure' is an important word that is often misunderstood by those not familiar with Jewish ideas. Far from containing gold and jewels, marked with a cross on a pirate's map, this is instead a *'thêsauros'*. We use the word 'thesaurus' to mean a collection of definitions and alternative word uses. For the Jews, burying your most precious possessions for the sake of safety meant burying your leather or goat-skin Torah scrolls, wrapped in linen (as in the case of the Dead Sea Scrolls found in clay pots in 1947). The scrolls contained the 'words' of the thesaurus; only these are words from God that set their people apart from the rest of mankind. Luke uses a different word for 'good' than for the tree - *'agathos'*, meaning 'kind' and 'benevolent'. This man wants to give away what God has given him, out of the thesaurus within him of words from God - a treasury that, like the man, is also *'agathos'*, because both have been shaped by

God. The rabbinic polar opposite in this hyperbole is the 'evil' man with his 'evil' treasure. Both are '***ponêros***' - the stronger of the New Testament words for evil and a fitting contrast to '***agathos***'.

The 'heart' is '***kardia***', which, in the modern-day west, stands for the seat of the emotions. But in the first-century near-east it stood for the seat of thought, understanding, will and intentions, [87] - what we call 'the mind'. As we train our minds with God's word and all that is good, so the contents can overflow out of our mouths. 'Speaks' is actually '***prophero***' - 'To bring forth', from '***phero***' meaning 'To bear', used in 'bearing fruit' (John 15:2), thus linking this saying to the fruit tree saying of verse 43. The image of the 'rotten fruit tree' has been switched to the 'rotten fruit man', one with evil fruit proceeding from his mouth as the (bad) fruit does from the corresponding tree. A mouth filled with evil-tasting maggot-infested fruit is a powerful mental image, one that would have kept Jesus' audience riveted on the discourse.

6:46-49 'Why do you call me, 'Lord, Lord', and do not do what I say? Everyone who comes to me and hears my words and acts on them, I will show you whom he is like. He is like a man building a house, who dug deep and laid a foundation on the rock; and when a flood occurred, the torrent burst against that house and could not shake it, because it had been well built. But the one who has heard and has not acted accordingly, is like a man who built a house on the ground without any foundation; and the torrent burst against it and immediately it collapsed, and the ruin of that house was great.'

Another '***tekton***' builder image and yet more humour - a great way to end this collection of Jesus' humorous teachings. As in 1 Corinthians 3:10, the work of the '***tekton***' is contextualised by building with foundations. Most houses were built on firm (rocky) ground upon which a single storey structure could be built directly onto without a need for under-pinning. In Matthew's account, the word 'sand' is used and the amusing story has since become immortalised as 'The foolish man who built on sand'. Actually even Matthew's choice of word ('*ammos*') means 'sandy ground' * from '*psammos*' - 'sand'. Not even rabbinic humour would stretch to the absurdity of a man building on pure sand. Luke's account has '*gê*', meaning simply 'ground'. This is where the '*tekton*' came in handy. What sand content in soil was so great as to warrant needing a foundation? Very sandy soil can be built on but requires a deep foundation - deep enough to hit the rock beneath. The expense involved meant that this was not likely to happen, but the opinion of a '*tekton*' would be needed. Any house that was built without a foundation on sandy soil was likely to be washed away in the sudden and torrential biannual rains. It would not need to be in a river bed, simply an area prone to flooding, where one might be conceivably foolish enough to build. Making a mistake over soil types and their required foundation depths was a common problem, and one that Jesus is likely to be alluding to in Luke 13:4, in the context of a tower that had recently collapsed in Siloam killing 18 people. This would have been of particular interest to a '*tekton*' like Jesus, for whom foundations were a speciality.

Jesus is keen to use the story about these two easily-recognisable situations to reinforce the point that the '*tekton*' needs to be obeyed in regard to building and that this particular '*tekton*' likewise needs to have his life-teaching acted upon. Faith may be described as putting into action the word that is heard from God (Romans 10:17). Jesus would later set out the standard by which he knew whether or not people truly loved him. It would be by their obedience to his word. As Jesus would later say, 'If you love me, you will keep my commandments' (John 14:15).

7:1 'When he had completed all his discourse in the hearing of the people, he went to Capernaum.'

The fact that Jesus kept a 'home' (Mark 2:1 and 2) in Capernaum (not Nazareth) which is described as being on the larger size ('many were gathered together') is evidence that he did not come from a poverty-stricken background. '*Tektons*' were specialist builders and would have been well remunerated, even without the expensive gifts the Magi had brought to the family. That Jesus gave that up to follow his Father's mission renders this all the more significant. There is nothing especially noble about having no choice with regard to living a simple, 'poorer' lifestyle, if that is what you are born into. If however you voluntarily give up wealth (as, for example, Francis of Assisi would later do) you are better able, by means of personal example, to encourage a 'rich young ruler' to do likewise (Mark 10:17-22). As previously mentioned, Mary and Joseph's 'offering of the poor' is equally likely to have been due to the conflict between the wealthy priests who ran the Temple market and the scholars who opposed them. Joseph gave the minimum needed to fulfil the Law, because the offering was not means-tested and the priests were at the opposite end of the religious spectrum to the scholars.

7:2-5 'And a centurion's slave, who was highly regarded by him, was sick and about to die. When he heard about Jesus, he sent some Jewish elders asking him to come and save the life of his slave. When they came to Jesus, they earnestly implored him, saying, "He is worthy for you to grant this to him; for he loves our nation and it was he who built us our synagogue."'

All the Gospels portray centurions (here and at the Cross) in a very positive light, and Luke is writing to Theophilus, who was likely to have been a Roman senator and lawyer. Such care for a servant was rare amongst Romans who saw their slaves as 'living tools', [88] to be discarded when broken. This Roman is a 'God-fearer', a proselyte to Judaism but one who had decided to do without the covenant sign of circumcision, although still committed enough to build a synagogue for his Capernaum subjects. As a *'tekton'* it is quite possible that Jesus knew about the synagogue's construction; if so he now also knew who had funded it. The Jewish elders have no doubts about Jesus' ability to heal. They seem to doubt Jesus' willingness to extend his ministry to a Gentile, in that they *'parakaleô'* Jesus - 'call him alongside' (to help) [89] 'earnestly', which is *'spoudaiôs'* - 'with haste'.* In the Greek text 'save' the life of the slave is not the usual *'sôzô'* in the sense of healing but rather the more unusual *'diasôzô'*, a term Doctor Luke employs frequently in Acts. It was the common medical term for bringing a patient through a particularly dangerous episode of illness [90] and was also used in surviving a shipwreck (e.g. Acts 27:44). The case is clearly an urgent one and the elders are looking to re-pay a debt of gratitude to the centurion. In Jesus, they had just the man for the job. Despite the Oral Law's prohibitions regarding Gentile contact, Jesus responds, gets up and goes.

7:6-7 'Now Jesus started on his way with them; and when he was not far from the house, the centurion sent friends, saying to him, "Lord, do not trouble yourself further, for I am not worthy for you to come under my roof; for this reason I did not even consider myself worthy to come to you, but just say the word, and my servant will be healed."'

The centurion not only demonstrates great faith, he is also aware and considerate of the stipulations around Jewish legal cleanliness. As soon as he gets word of Jesus' approach, he sends 'friends', probably Jewish, to explain the underlying humility behind his reason for not having come personally himself. His choice of title with which to address Jesus is '*kurios*', 'Lord', derived from '*kuros*' meaning authority. For a loyal Roman citizen, there was only one '*Kurios*', and that was Caesar. So for the centurion to address Jesus with that title was to put his loyalty to Caesar into question, a very dangerous thing to do in the Roman army. As well as humility and spiritual recognition of Jesus' status, the centurion has an equally impressive understanding of faith.

He understands that faith is a response to a spoken word of authority from God. Romans 10:17 states that 'faith comes by hearing ('*akoe*' - 'the thing heard'),* and what is heard from the word of God.' There was no debating an order in the Roman army. A thing was said from a position of authority, was heard and obeyed. God's word has the added advantage of creating within the person who hears it the power to be changed, overcome obstacles and to obey, even if it means getting out of a boat onto a stormy lake (Matthew 14:29).

7:8-10 '"For I also am a man placed under authority, with soldiers under me; and I say to this one, "Go!" and he goes, and to another, "Come!" and he comes, and to my slave, "Do this!" and he does it." Now when Jesus heard this, he marvelled at him, and turned and said to the crowd that was following him, "I say to you, not even in Israel have I found such great faith." When those who had been sent returned to the house, they found the slave in good health.'

'Go' and 'Do this' are all expressed in the imperative Greek mood, indicating commands to be obeyed, and 'Come' is in the indicative mood, indicating a fact that has occurred - the servant had already started to come. In all of them the response is obedience to what is recognised as a chain of command, an authority that goes beyond, to Caesar in the Roman case and to God in the centurion's understanding of Jesus' authority. This grasp of how faith works amazed Jesus, whose comment about relative levels of faith included the faith of his own disciples. That a Gentile could arrive at such a place without the immediate benefit of Jesus' discipleship was a testimony to God's over-riding grace and the ability of the Holy Spirit to work in unexpected places. 'Good health' is '*hugiainô*', a word that in all the Gospels is only used by Doctor Luke, and means 'sound' and 'whole' in all respects. [91] Jesus' authority works over a distance and in every way.

7:11-12 'Soon afterwards, he went to a city called Nain; and his disciples were going along with him, accompanied by a large crowd. Now as he approached the gate of the city, a dead man was being carried out, the only son of his mother, and she was a widow; and a sizeable crowd from the city was with her.'

Twenty miles from Capernaum, at Nain, two crowds meet - or as the KJV reads, 'many' meet 'much' people. Once again, Luke's widow-source Mary, the mother of Jesus, surfaces with a widow's story to tell. For a widow to lose her only son was a financial disaster, as well as a loss of standing in a religious society where rabbis taught that sons were more blessed than daughters. (Talmud '*Baba Bathra*' 16b: 'Happy is he whose children are males'.) Processing the deceased was a major part of mourning. The Talmud states that in Galilee the crowd would walk in front of the body; whereas in Judea they would follow it. [92] There are rock tombs some ten minutes walk outside the town and it is likely to have been there that the noisily wailing funeral procession was heading as they left Nain. As the two crowds met, there would have necessarily been some delay on both sides to navigate the roadway. In such delays God is apt to work. The climate and Jewish tradition necessitated burial as soon as was reasonably possible. Mary and Martha did not wait for Jesus to arrive before burying Lazarus. The body was enshrouded in cloth strips and carried on a type of stretcher to the tombs outside the city.

145

7:13-15 'When the Lord saw her, he felt compassion for her, and said to her, "Do not weep." And he came up and touched the coffin; and the bearers came to a halt. And he said, "Young man, I say to you, arise!" The dead man sat up and began to speak. And Jesus gave him back to his mother.'

This is Luke's first use of '*splagchnizomai*', meaning 'to feel compassion' - literally 'to be moved in one's bowels'.* After the nervous system itself, the bowel is the most densely innervated organ in the human body. Its neuro-vascular supply is known as the 'splanchnic plexus'. For the ancient world it therefore represented the seat of the emotions. When confronted with a very disturbing sight it is physiologically normal to feel 'sick to the stomach' - a kind of hollow feeling in the solar plexus accompanied by a sensation of nausea. Jesus is strongly moved and actually commands the widow to 'Stop weeping!' - in the imperative Greek mood, being a command. Jesus is the perfect example of someone who channelled his normal human emotions into supporting and driving forward spiritual action. This is evidenced by his 'going up a gear' in terms of the miraculous (feeding the five thousand and walking on water) after learning of the murder of his cousin John the Baptist at the hands of Herod Antipas (Matthew 14).

Jesus does not pray to his Father to raise the man to life. Jesus did nothing other than what he 'saw' the Father do (John 5:19), so, acting on what he had heard and seen from his Father he commands (also in the imperative mood) the man to '*egeirô*', meaning 'wake up' or 'sit up!' (from a lying-down position). [93] Jesus did not launch into a long prayer but simply spoke a brief word of command to the dead man who 'sat up' ('*anakathizô*', this being a medical term [94] used for someone well enough to be 'sitting up in their bed') and began to '*laleo*' ('to tell out') to the crowd his version of events.

What he said, presumably about having been dead, is not recorded, but Jesus 'gave' him back to his mother. What a gift!

7:16-17 'Fear gripped them all, and they began glorifying God, saying, "A great prophet has arisen among us!" and "God has visited his people!" This report concerning him went out all over Judea and in all the surrounding district.'

The inhabitants of Nain 'glorify' God in the sense of praising him; they do not worship Jesus because they have not yet understood him to be the Messiah in the sense of God incarnate. They are in all likelihood recalling the time when one of their great prophets Elijah raised back to life the son of the widow of Zarephath (1 Kings 17:17-24). 'God has visited' is '*episkeptomai*', a medical term for a doctor visiting an ill patient. It was used of 'visiting the sick' in Matthew 25:36 ('I was sick and you visited me'). The news ('*logos*' - 'a spoken word') of such an extraordinary publically attested miracle would have, and did, spread like wildfire.

7:18-19 'The disciples of John reported to him about all these things. Summoning two of his disciples, John sent them to the Lord, saying, "Are you the Expected One, or do we look for someone else?"'

John the Baptist is by this time in Herod Antipas' dungeon (Matthew 11:2). Unlike the populace of Nain, John is thinking about Jesus in terms of Messiah status. 'Expected One' is '*Erchomai*', meaning 'the person coming',* and 'look for' is '*prosdokaô*' - 'to watch for expectantly'.* John, in prison and awaiting death, is seeking confirmation that his ministry of 'preparing the way' for his more illustrious cousin has not been in vain.

7:21-23 'At that very time he cured many people of diseases and afflictions and evil spirits; and he gave sight

to many who were blind. And he answered and said to them, "Go and report to John what you have seen and heard: the blind receive sight, the lame walk, the lepers are cleansed, and the deaf hear, the dead are raised up, the poor have the gospel preached to them. Blessed is he who does not take offence at me."'

Jesus reply starts with a comprehensive messianic demonstration of healing, miracles and deliverance. The Messiah was expected to perform miracles. Isaiah 35:4-6: 'The recompense of God will come, but he will save you. Then the eyes of the blind will be opened and the ears of the deaf will be unstopped. Then the lame will leap like a deer and the tongue of the mute will shout for joy.' Jesus is going even beyond that expectation by raising the dead. Luke divides Jesus' healings in the Greek manner of both chronic and acute disease. 'Diseases' is '*nosos*' (a long, on-going illness or infirmity), whereas the work of 'evil' spirits is '*ponêros*'. This term was used by the second century physician Galen of Pergamon to describe the quick onset of poison and the need for an equally rapid remedy. [95]

The poor were not able to easily avail themselves of rabbinic scholarship; for them simply staying alive was hard enough without the eight hours of daily study that the rabbis required. Jesus, as a renowned Torah scholar, is bringing 'good news' to them - they don't need that now! They can be made right with God by putting their trust in him. The main takers of offence at Jesus' ministry were the scribes and Pharisees. They saw him as a Torah teacher who was apparently betraying the faith he stood for by claiming to be God - a capital offence rendered much worse by his senior teaching position in their society. 'Offence' is '*skandalizô*' - 'to scandalise', meaning 'to cause someone to stumble'.* Jesus is saying that we will be blessed ('*makarios*' - 'happy') if we do not 'stumble' over his teaching and his claim to divinity, as the Pharisees did. It is possible John also may have been struggling with this apparent and serious breach of Jewish Law. Antipas' prison was not likely to have been conducive to maintaining his faith in understanding Jesus' mission.

7:24 'When the messengers of John had left, he began to speak to the crowds about John. "What did you go out into the wilderness to see? A reed shaken by the wind?"'

John had ministered out of the Judean desert, most likely not as a hermit but as a part of the ultra-orthodox Jewish Essene community that had withdrawn there away from the materially corrupted and Roman polluted Temple worship in Jerusalem. Herod the Great had fixed the imperial golden eagle over the main gate [96] and attached the Temple Courts to the unclean Roman fort Antonia. Jesus, aware of the crowd's devotion in making the uncomfortable pilgrimage to hear John's teaching, seeks to bring the crowd to a correct understanding of who John really was in God's kingdom. Lest some of them had interpreted his remark about 'offence' as a backhanded rebuke of his cousin, Jesus reassures them that was not his intention. 'Reeds' were common locally and their waving in the breeze had made them a proverb for those who were easily swayed in their opinions, or as Paul would later put it, 'Tossed to and fro and carried about by every wind of doctrine' (Ephesians 4:14).

7:25 'But what did you go out to see? A man dressed in soft clothing? Those who are splendidly clothed and live in luxury are found in royal palaces!'

If not a reed then what? 'Soft' clothing is '*malakos*', meaning 'effeminate', and was also used to describe men who had homosexual intercourse with boys.* They are 'gorgeously dressed' and in '*truphê*' - 'luxury'. The word comes from '*thruptô*', meaning 'effeminate and delicate living'. Who could Jesus possible have had in mind? Josephus records that John was imprisoned by Herod Antipas in his palace at Machaerus: 'Now some of the Jews thought that the destruction of Herod's army *[by King Aretas of Nabatea following Antipas divorcing his daughter]* came from God, and that very justly, as a punishment of what he did against John, that was called the Baptist: for Herod slew him, who was a good man, and commanded the Jews to exercise virtue, both as to righteousness towards one another, and piety towards God, and so to come to baptism; for that the washing would be acceptable to him, if they made use of it, not in order to the putting away of some sins, but for the purification of the body; supposing still that the soul was thoroughly purified beforehand by righteousness. Now when others came in crowds about him, for they were very greatly moved by hearing his words, Herod, who feared lest the great influence John had over the people might put it into his power and inclination to raise a rebellion, (for they seemed ready to do any thing he should advise) thought it best, by putting him to death, to prevent any mischief he might cause, and not bring himself into difficulties, by sparing a man who might make him repent of it when it would be too late. Accordingly he was sent a prisoner, out of Herod's suspicious temper, to Machaerus, the castle I before mentioned, and was there put to death' (Josephus, 'Antiquities' 18, 5, *words in italics are mine*).

Herod Antipas had been heavily influenced by Greek lifestyle choices, including homosexuality and bisexuality. Was John like that? Once again Jesus employs hyperbole to make his point. A more exact opposite to the straight-talking, camel-skin wearing John would be hard to imagine, and at the time of Luke's writing Antipas was very much out of favour with Rome having been exiled to Gaul under suspicion of sedition.

7:26-27 'But what did you go out to see? A prophet? Yes, I say to you, and one who is more than a prophet. This is the one about whom it is written, 'Behold, I send my

messenger ahead of you, who will prepare your way before you.'

Third try. The people were familiar with their illustrious history of men and women who had been inspired by God to deliver his message to his often recalcitrant people. But wait! John was more. Jesus quotes to them the well-known verse from Isaiah 40:3, 'A voice is calling, "Clear the way for the Lord in the wilderness; make smooth in the desert a highway for our God."' There is also a nod to Malachi 3:1, '"Behold, I am going to send my messenger, and he will clear the way before me. And the Lord, whom you seek, will suddenly come to his Temple; and the messenger of the covenant, in whom you delight, behold, he is coming," says the Lord of hosts.' John is fulfilling the one who would prepare Messiah's way with his prophetic message of repentance.

7:28 'I say to you, among those born of women there is no one greater than John; yet he who is least in the kingdom of God is greater than he.'

A new kingdom is coming, one that John is hearing about the first signs of. A new covenant is about to be established between God and mankind, sealed in Messiah's blood, which will admit believers into the family of God by the indwelling of the Holy Spirit. John will sadly be martyred before this comes about, but up until then, with the exception of Jesus himself, John is indeed the greatest, in the plan of God, of those born of women.

7:29-30 'When all the people and the tax collectors heard this, they acknowledged God's justice, having been baptized with the baptism of John. But the Pharisees and the lawyers rejected God's purpose for themselves, not having been baptized by John.'

The crowd contained a contingent of tax collectors, perhaps drawn all the more to Jesus by the presence of a former tax collector, Matthew, among his company of disciples. 'Acknowledged God's justice' is '*dikaioô*', meaning 'to show to be righteous',* from '*dikaios*', meaning 'correct, right, or righteous'.* By entering into John's baptismal ministry, they had agreed with God and God's messenger that his way was right, whereas the better informed (in theory) Jewish legal experts who had come from Jerusalem to check the orthodoxy of John's teaching had rejected it.

7:31-35 '"To what then shall I compare the men of this generation, and what are they like? They are like children who sit in the market place and call to one another, and they say, 'We played the flute for you, and you did not dance; we sang a dirge, and you did not weep.' For John the Baptist has come eating no bread and drinking no wine, and you say, 'He has a demon!' The Son of Man has come eating and drinking, and you say, 'Behold, a gluttonous man and a drunkard, a friend of tax collectors and sinners!' Yet wisdom is vindicated by all her children."'

Jesus likens those who had rejected John's baptism to fickle children who were difficult to please. If the teaching had not come from them they would not receive it. John? Too austere! Jesus? Not austere enough! Shockingly, they had attributed John's fasting to demonic possession. Jesus' willingness to shun their Oral Law's food practices and eat with the ritually unclean earned him the slanderous label of gluttony and alcohol excesses, for which there is not the slightest evidence. Certainly none of his accusers, who kept well away from 'sinners' who did not know or keep the Oral Law, would have been present to act as eye-witnesses. Their title 'friend of sinners', though used in a derogatory way, was however true and has lasted across the centuries as testimony to Jesus' mission to redeem the lost. 'Wisdom vindicated by her children' appears as a Jewish proverbial saying, meaning that people can always justify their own stance, be they correct or not.

7:36 'Now one of the Pharisees was requesting him to dine with him, and he entered the Pharisee's house and reclined at the table.'

Jesus' high legal standing in Jewish academic society is the reason why one of his enemies would be willing to invite him to dinner but not, owing to his underlying animosity, offer the usual social courtesies. Jesus is quite comfortable to eat with his enemies - they too needed a physician, despite their ignorance of the fact.

7:37-38 'And there was a woman in the city who was a sinner; and when she learned that he was reclining at the table in the Pharisee's house, she brought an alabaster vial of perfume, and standing behind him at his feet, weeping, she began to wet his feet with her tears, and kept wiping them with the hair of her head, and kissing his feet and anointing them with the perfume.'

The woman is expressing great gratitude to Jesus for forgiveness, healing, deliverance or possibly all three. She is doing so in an extremely extravagant way, both materially and emotionally. The letting down of her hair evidences that she was not a respectable woman. Adult women in that day kept their hair covered by reason of modesty; as Paul later said, to 'uncover her head was to dishonour her head' (1 Corinthians 11:5). [97] Large houses in Jesus' day had courtyards in which meals were taken, being cooler there than indoors. 'In the house' included the courtyard of the house, a semi-public area into which an outsider might easily gain access, for example, to receive alms or to hear teaching given there. Simon has seen the woman but has not, for reasons of common cultural

153

practice, ordered that she be removed. He has permitted her to remain. But what he then sees disgusts him, both as a display of indecent behaviour on the part of the woman and Jesus' apparent lack of care of what people thought about his receiving it. Why would a senior and legally 'clean' rabbinic scholar permit such intimate contact with such an obvious sinner? What is going on here?

7:39-40 'Now when the Pharisee who had invited him saw this, he said to himself, "If this man were a prophet he would know who and what sort of person this woman is who is touching him, that she is a sinner." And Jesus answered him, "Simon, I have something to say to you." And he replied, "Say it, Teacher."'

What people say to themselves is always heard by God the Father and what God hears God can communicate to others who are listening to him. Jesus was always listening to his Father and therefore was informed of what Simon is thinking, thereby re-affirming his credentials as a genuine prophet (though much more than a prophet). In 'answering' Simon's thoughts, he speaks to Simon as a rabbinic scholar, a position that Simon has huge respect for, despite his uneasiness with Jesus' disregard for certain points of Oral Torah. 'I have something to say to you' means, 'I have something to teach you' (formally, as a Jewish legal scholar). 'Say' is '*epo*', also meaning 'to command'. * Simon acknowledges this in the choice of title in his reply to Jesus. 'Teacher' here is '*Didaskalos*', also meaning 'Master' (of Jewish Law) and 'Doctor' as used to the legal experts Jesus met in the Temple aged 12 (Luke 2:46). Jesus is about to make a point central to Jewish legal thought and practice, namely that of proportionality.

In Jewish Law, the punishment was proportional to the offence and conversely the reward was proportional to the measure of loyalty and

154

devotion that had been expressed. Simon is about to receive a legal lesson from the greatest religious and legal teacher Israel had seen, and at least at first he is keen to hear it.

It was normal courtesy (Genesis 18:4, 19:2, 24:32) to offer a guest water to wash their feet with on entering a home, for reasons of comfort but also for hygiene preservation within the home in an era marked by very dirty streets. It was normal courtesy to greet a guest with a kiss. Even Judas carried out this common courtesy (Matthew 26:49), although in his case as a treacherous mark of identification for the following soldiers sent to arrest Jesus. It was normal courtesy to anoint a guest with a few drops of perfumed oil, in part to counter any other less pleasant odours that the heat of the day might have produced. None of these acts represented unusual devotional courtesy. The fact that Simon had denied Jesus all three was, in contrast, expressive of disproportionate discourtesy, discourtesies that Jesus had hitherto been too polite as a guest to remark upon. But Simon's discourteous thinking about the woman and by extension Jesus had been a step too far for Jesus to remain silent about.

7:41-43 '"A moneylender had two debtors: one owed five hundred denarii, and the other fifty. When they were unable to repay, he graciously forgave them both. So which of them will love him more?" Simon answered and said, "I suppose the one whom he forgave more." And he said to him, "You have judged correctly."'

Simon, as a Jewish legal teacher himself, one representing the strict party of the Pharisees, (men who saw themselves as being the guardians of the Law and its correct interpretations), has no problem with the concept. The proportionality rule says the more you have been let off a debt, the more grateful you would (or at least should!) be. Such an unusual occurrence as being 'let off by a moneylender' would be remarkable in itself, but to be let off a debt equal to one and a quarter years' wages (based on a 6 day working week) would be an act of quite extraordinary disproportionate generosity. A disproportionate response was appropriate. Well judged, Simon!

7:44-46 'Turning toward the woman, he said to Simon, "Do you see this woman? I entered your house; you gave me no water for my feet, but she has wet my feet with her tears and wiped them with her hair. You gave me no kiss; but she, since the time I came in, has not ceased to kiss my feet. You did not anoint my head with oil, but she anointed my feet with perfume."'

Rabbis loved to use humour. Since the woman had entered and begun her socially disgraceful, over-the-top exhibition of love and devotion, Simon had 'seen' very little else! Simon's 'no water for you, Jesus', had been replaced by the woman's purer saline tear solution of repentance, love and gratitude for sins forgiven and a life re-born anew with God. Simon's 'no kiss on the cheek for you, Jesus', had been replaced by the repeated kissing of Jesus' (hitherto unwashed and so still probably rather dirty) feet. Simon's 'no oil for your head, Jesus', had been replaced by a disproportionally massive quantity of disproportionately expensive perfume (not just perfumed oil) poured out in abundance over Jesus' feet. Jesus does not even mention the sacrifice the woman made in drying his feet with her hair). And the woman did not yet know about the Cross - that was to come! What disproportionate love and devotion. What was the reason for it? She knew forgiveness and new spiritual life.

7:47 '"For this reason I say to you, her sins, which are many, have been forgiven, for she loved much; but he who is forgiven little, loves little."'

Jesus, the more senior Jewish legal scholar, draws the inevitable legal conclusion based on proportionality. Little forgiveness received leads to little love being expressed. Massive forgiveness received leads (or should lead) to massive love being expressed. Simple as that, Simon!

7:48-50 'Then he said to her, "Your sins have been forgiven." Those who were reclining at the table with him began to say to themselves, "Who is this man who even forgives sins?" And he said to the woman, "Your faith has saved you; go in peace."'

The woman had not sinned against Jesus. Therefore Jesus is taking the place of God in remitting, as a Jewish legal scholar, her sins (against God and other people), something that only God could do. That would have been bad enough if it had come from an itinerant Jewish peasant, but it had not. To come out of the mouth of a senior *'Didaskalos'* of Torah was another thing altogether. For the majority, who at this point did not believe Jesus to be God, it meant one thing only. Blasphemy. And blasphemy from a 'Doctor of Torah' was disproportionately much, much worse than from a peasant 'nobody'. And so their question - 'Who is this man?' And the unspoken question rang louder still in Simon's courtyard - 'What should be done about it?', because the Law required Jesus' execution.

But none of these legal questions bothered the woman. Her trust in words previously spoken by Jesus had saved her. Her extravagant love came from her grasp of that fact. She went away 'in peace' (*'eirênê'* - 'a state of tranquility and exemption from rage'),* rage Jesus' enemies felt when they heard his apparent 'blasphemies' in forgiving sin and taking God's role upon himself. Jesus, speaking in Hebrew, would no doubt have said *'Shalom'* - the 'total wholeness and well-being' that Jesus' new spiritual birth gives.

Chapter 8

8:1-3 'Soon afterwards, he began going around from one city and village to another, proclaiming and preaching the kingdom of God. The twelve were with him, and also some women who had been healed of evil spirits and sicknesses: Mary who was called Magdalene, from whom seven demons had gone out, and Joanna the wife of Chuza, Herod's steward, and Susanna, and many others who were contributing to their support out of their private means.'

Mary, Jesus' mother, who in all likelihood accompanied Jesus to the house of Simon the Pharisee, would been equally disgusted by Simon's disproportionate lack of common courtesy and would have been similarly delighted by his treatment of the woman, and especially the clever way Jesus drew Simon into the obvious implications. Luke further benefits from female influence in providing the 'real story' of where Jesus' team's necessary financial support came from. Far-seeing religious men with the money to put to the cause? No. From women! 'Contributing to their support' is actually a single word in the Greek text '*diakoneô*', meaning 'to minister'* in the sense of serving (and hence the English word 'deacon'). It is the same word that Matthew uses to describe the angels' attending to Jesus in his weakened state after his 40 day fast and the three 'rounds' (as in a boxing-ring) with the devil. Jesus' day-to-day life thereafter is not noted as punctuated by regular angelic apparitions, but is marked by regular help from women of the same sort of usefulness to him as the angels had earlier been.

Jesus was breaking new ground as a rabbi in teaching women both in private and in public, to the point of including them among his disciples. Luke (or Mary) makes special mention of the three more notable of these women among the 'many others'. Mary Magdalene is the first to be mentioned. 'Magdalene' means 'from Magdala', a town to the south of Capernaum and a Sabbath-day's journey from Tiberias. It was known for its dye-works, [98] and the manufacture of fine wool. [99] 'Of whom much has been forgiven' of the previous chapter equally well applies to those 'from whom many demons have been expelled.' Hence Mary Magdalene is synonymous with those who loved Jesus 'much', enough to linger at his grave and become the first eye-witness of his resurrection, and so the very first messenger of it, to a group of dispirited and unbelieving men.

Joanna, like Mary Magdalene, was another woman whose great love for Jesus drew her to want to be near even to his corpse (Luke 24:10). Perhaps these women had actually dared to believe Jesus' saying that he would rise on the third day (Mark 9:31). Luke tells us that Joanna was married to the Roman-appointed Herod Antipas' steward. She may have resided at Machaerus, that 'black fortress' (for so the name means) built originally by Herod the Great and where John the Baptist had been unjustly imprisoned and murdered by Antipas. It may well be that her support of Jesus came indirectly, and rather ironically, from the Roman tyrant that had killed Jesus' cousin John, after John had spoken out against Antipas' marriage to his half-brother Philip I's wife Herodias.

In any event, Joanna would surely have been aware of the miraculous healing of the 'royal official whose son was sick at Capernaum' (John 4:46). For all we know, the 'royal official' may have been Chuza himself and the boy Joanna's own son. Speculation? Definitely. But it is one plausible explanation for how Chuza's wife happened to be travelling with this Jewish scholar and spend her husband's money so freely on Jesus' upkeep and that of his apostolic team. Of Susanna, nothing is known or even surmised, other than her name (Hebrew for 'graceful lily'), and that she is likely to have been another grateful beneficiary of Jesus' power to heal all who came to him.

8:4 'When a large crowd was coming together, and those from the various cities were journeying to him, he spoke by way of a parable.'

Why parables? The Greek is '*parabole*', meaning to 'place two things (earthly and spiritual) side by side for comparison'.* Jesus frequently employed parables as stories to illustrate his points, thereby getting around people's conscious mental barriers to spiritual truth. The crowds would not have the advantage of the first-hand explanation that Jesus' disciples received; instead, their response to the spiritual content of the parable would be reflective of their own heart's receptivity or lack thereof. Jesus describes the spiritual condition of the religious folk of his day as having been prophesied about in Isaiah 6: 9-10 and quoted below in verses 9 and 10.

8:5-8 'The sower went out to sow his seed; and as he sowed, some fell beside the road, and it was trampled underfoot and the birds of the air ate it up. Other seed fell on rocky soil, and as soon as it grew up, it withered away, because it had no moisture. Other seed fell among the thorns; and the thorns grew up with it and choked it out. Other seed fell into the good soil, and grew up, and produced a crop a hundred times as great.'

A sower was a common sight. Jesus' audience would have been aware that much of the widely scattered seed would be wasted, either because it missed the target, got eaten by birds, got scorched or got squeezed out by the local weed (thorny bramble) population. Some, however, would find its way to good soil and produce a return. Jesus tells the crowd: 'Pay attention!' ('He who has ears to hear, let him hear'), because to hear the word of God with a disposition of trust in it is how faith ignites in your innermost being. As Paul told the Roman church, 'Faith comes by hearing and hearing by the word of Christ' (Romans 10:17). As previously mentioned, 'hearing' is *'akoe'*, which equally means 'the thing heard'.* Jesus (verse 11), told his disciples that the 'seed' stood for the word of God. Will the 'word heard' generate faith in the hearts of those who have heard it? It depends on the state of their heart. The word is sown having 'gone out'. If the word is kept within the four walls of the church, it is unlikely to bear the fruit it is intended to by the One who supplies the seed to be sown into the lives of those who have yet to hear it. As 2 Corinthians 9:10 states, 'Now he who supplies seed to the sower and bread for food will supply and multiply your seed for sowing and increase the harvest of your righteousness.'

8:9-10 'His disciples began questioning him as to what this parable meant. And he said, "To you it has been granted to know the mysteries of the kingdom of God, but to the rest it is in parables, so that seeing they may not see, and hearing they may not understand."'

By the first century AD, mysticism had become recognized as a part of Jewish life (e.g. the writings of Philo Judaeus of Alexandria, 20 BC - 50 AD, a Hellenized Jewish philosopher writing in Egypt). The concept of mysteries (*'musterion'*: 'hidden spiritual truth' - revealed only to a chosen few)* was well understood. Parables would be understood by those whose hearts were pure enough to receive the message, and like non-germinated seeds they would remain sitting in the subconscious minds of the rest. For some, eventually the penny would drop and the lights of comprehension would come on. Jesus said that if you have this quality of right standing with God ('given' means it is 'gifted' to you, unearned and undeserved), then you are in line for a whole lot more because, like the sower, God the Father is lavish in what he gives. 'Seeing they may not see, and hearing they may not understand' is a quotation from Isaiah 6:9-10. 'Go, and tell this people, "Keep on listening, but do not perceive; keep on looking, but do not understand." Render the hearts of this people insensitive, their ears dull, and their eyes dim, otherwise they might see with their eyes, hear with their ears, understand with their hearts, and return and be healed.' The Hebrew language used there is very clear. It describes someone who has become morbidly obese. The Hebrew '*shaman*' of Isaiah 6:9 means to 'grow fat', and Matthew's account describes some of Jesus' audience as '*pachuno*' (Matthew 13:15) meaning to 'thicken with fatness',* such that their ears and eyes have closed over with fat to the point of causing deafness and blindness. This can in fact happen in the really grossly obese. Matthew implies that the closing of eyes and ears has a voluntary element to it in addition to being a consequence of spiritual obesity.

Some of Jesus' Jewish audience had become so well fed on God's word but with so little correct practical application, that they had become spiritually obese and so incapable of seeing and hearing spiritually, let alone of moving much. Sadly, this is pertinent to the spiritual condition of many Christians today, who are often overfed and under-worked. The devil is quite happy to see people fed to the point of obesity if it will prevent them from gaining the genuine understanding of the heart that leads to a true conversion ('*epistrepho*' - 'to turn / return', as per the Hebrew '*shuwb*' of Isaiah 6:10) * under God's healing power of restoration. God's purpose in feeding and giving is that what is given be freely passed on to others.

8:11-14 '"Now the parable is this: the seed is the word of God. Those beside the road are those who have heard; then the devil comes and takes away the word from their heart, so that they will not believe and be saved. Those on the rocky soil are those who, when they hear, receive the word with joy; and these have no firm root; they believe for a while, and in time of temptation fall away. The seed which fell among the thorns, these are the ones who have heard, and as they go on their way they are choked with worries and riches and pleasures of this life, and bring no fruit to maturity.'"

While the 'good soil' of verse 15 is speaking of believers (who have received the word), the first three types of soil can be applied to non-believers and believers alike. 'Beside the road' is soil but it has been trodden hard by many travellers and was rather like the road itself - impervious to seed. The seed might just as well have fallen on the road - it is food for birds and little else. Indifference to God's word mainly affects unbelievers but can affect spiritually hardened Christians as well. Since the devil does not want God's word hanging around, he is quite happy to see it disposed of. The shallow soil does not allow the germinating seed to gain any root depth; consequently the scorching heat withers it. The depth we get to with God is largely a direct consequence of choices we make. Likewise 'weeds' generally only grow because the gardener tolerates them and does not deal with them in time to prevent them producing seeds of their own. If enough rubbish is allowed into a Christian's life then it will choke the activity of God, and so render the person unfruitful.

'Worries' here is '*merimna*', also meaning 'cares and anxieties' of the type that Paul warned of - 'Be anxious for nothing, but in everything by prayer and supplication with thanksgiving let your requests be made known to God' (Philippians 4:6). 'Riches' is '*ploutos*', meaning an 'abundance of external possessions'* that tempt the owner to self-reliance rather than reliance on God. God is not somehow against 'pleasures'. Psalm 16:11: 'You will make known to me the path of life; in your presence is fullness of joy; in your right hand there are pleasures forever.' But this life's pleasures can easily crowd God out of the picture.

8:15 'But the seed in the good soil, these are the ones who have heard the word in an honest and good heart, and hold it fast, and bear fruit with perseverance.'

The heart condition of the hearer is vitally important to determining whether a 'co-mingling' with faith will occur, or, as Paul later put it, 'hearing with faith' (Galatians 3:2) - whether faith will be ignited in the heart thereby empowering a godly obedience to the word heard. 'Honest' and 'good' are both words that could be translated as 'good'. 'Honest' is '*kalos*', the same word used for the 'good fruit' of the tree in chapter 6. It denotes moral beauty. Strong's Dictionary defines it as meaning 'beautiful, handsome, excellent, eminent, choice, surpassing, precious, useful, suitable, commendable, and admirable'. The second description of the fruitful heart is 'good' - '*agathos*', which Vine's Dictionary defines as good 'in its character or constitution, and is beneficial in its effect'. What's the difference?

The beauty intrinsic to '*kalos*' had been touched by God - tinged with his own nature. It looks very much like God, who is intrinsically good. The nature of '*agathos*' is the human out-working towards others of that touch from God. Because God is involved in both, they are very closely appositioned (rather like soul and spirit, or joint and marrow). The word not only is to be heard, but also 'held fast' to ('take possession of' lest the birds of distraction carry it away), and 'persevered' with ('steadfast patience'). It is important to recognise that growth has a seasonal and timing element and is influenced by the environment that the imperishable seed of God's word is in. 1 Peter 1:23: 'You have been born again not of seed which is perishable but imperishable, that is, through the living and enduring word of God.' Breaking up fallow ground [xii] and clearing it of weeds is necessary in order to have good soil.

8:16-17 'Now no one after lighting a lamp covers it over with a container, or puts it under a bed; but he puts it on a lampstand, so that those who come in may see the light. For nothing is hidden that will not become evident, nor anything secret that will not be known and come to light.'

[xii] Jeremiah 4:3: 'Break up your fallow ground, and do not sow among thorns.'

Like much of Jesus' teaching, there is more than one level of meaning at work. The first is the well-known application, reinforced by children's songs ('This little light of mine...'), exhorting the believer to live in such a way that God's handiwork is visible to all. This is the context of a similar saying of Jesus in Matthew 5:15. But the teaching in Mark 4:21-23 is different and it is this other version that appears here in Luke. This gives a second and quite different application which, to Jesus' Jewish audience, was likely to have been their first understanding - that Jesus is speaking of the light of Torah - God's word. The 'lamp' and 'light', to the Jews, was what proceeded forth from Torah and Scripture in general - spiritual light to live by, as the Talmud also states: 'Rabbi Judah said: 'Light' means the Torah' (Tractate 'Megilah' 16b).

The Scripture declares, 'Your word is a lamp to my feet and a light to my path' (Psalm 119:105), and, 'For the commandment is a lamp and the teaching is light; and reproofs for discipline are the way of life' (Proverbs 6:23). In his word, the Torah and the prophets, God had lit a lamp to guide the steps for all humanity. Jesus' ministry was fulfilling Psalm 119:130 - 'The unfolding of your words gives light; it gives understanding to the simple.' God's word often comes to us in a 'folded' form. We can understand some of it immediately - a lot of it even - but there is much that remains below the surface and can only be seen by digging deeper and with the guidance of the Holy Spirit, who breathed the word into being in the first place. God had intended his word be held aloft by the Jews ('Put on a lampstand') for all the nations to see; instead they had buried it under layer upon layer of legal minutiae.

Jesus was bringing forth 'hidden' truth from God's word and making it 'evident'. Isaiah had prophesied of Jesus: 'I am he, I am the first, I am also the last. Surely my hand founded the earth, and my right hand spread out the heavens; when I call to them, they stand together' (Isaiah 48:12-13). He had also said, 'Come near to me,

165

listen to this: From the first I have not spoken in secret, from the time it took place, I was there. And now the Lord God has sent me, and his Spirit' (Isaiah 48:16). In around 6 BC, the triune God had arrived by the Spirit in the womb of Mary, and now, as an adult senior Torah-teacher, he was proclaiming that which he had never intended to be kept 'secret'. It was to 'be known' and 'come to light' from within the gloom of traditional rabbinic Judaism. 'Come to light' is *phaneros*, meaning to be 'made plainly known and recognised openly'.*

There is more humour here too. The oil lamp (*'luchnos'*) provided a small flame, enough to illuminate a small room. Jesus was well aware that depriving the flame of air under a cover would prevent combustion causing the flame to expire. Putting it under bedclothes would set fire to the bed - plenty of light then! These are deliberate examples of extreme and intentionally ludicrously funny behaviour. Lamps were designed to fit into an elevated stand to provide the maximum benefit. The version in the Sermon on the Mount has: 'Let your light shine before men in such a way that they may see your good works, and glorify your Father who is in heaven' (Matthew 5:16). Our lives are supposed to be showrooms of the character and work of God, for the benefit of those who do not yet know him.

This is a process, but still a very visible one. Some of those works will be hidden, visible only to the Father who ordained them before the foundation of the world (Hebrews 4:3). As Paul (beneficiary of so much of Jesus' Temple teaching) would later say, 'The sins of some men are quite evident, going before them to judgment; for others their sins follow after. Likewise also deeds that are good are quite evident, and those which are otherwise cannot be concealed' (1 Timothy 5:24-25). Not only will the nature of our works be exposed (1 Corinthians 3:12-15), but also, 'Every careless word that people speak they shall give an accounting for it in the day of judgment' (Matthew 12:36).

8:18 'So take care how you listen; for whoever has, to him more shall be given; and whoever does not have, even what he thinks he has shall be taken away from him.'

The Torah-word nature of this teaching now becomes more apparent. Torah was largely received by listening. The oral form would not be written down until around 200 AD. To understand God's perspective, rather than man's, you had to listen with 'care'. This is '*blepô*', meaning 'to see and discern mentally with understanding'.* This calls for God's illumination over his word. With the 'listening' part we are back to how faith is received, via 'the thing heard', '*akoê*', of Romans 10:17. 'How we listen' to the word that we hear determines the amount and quality of the fruit it will bear in our lives. If the word meets with trust and an obedient response, it has the power in and of itself to produce spiritual change that transforms the hearer into the likeness of Christ. If it meets with unbelief or disinterest, it becomes simply birdseed. A response of faith generates good soil and the better the soil, the more fruit bearing word-seeds it in turn will produce. A 'blessed cycle' is generated that has far-reaching consequences of effectiveness in God's service and so more fruit that will remain' (John 15:16) to an eternal reward. The opposite 'vicious cycle' of ignoring and disobeying God's word causes a spiritual weakness that makes us vulnerable to an opposing ministry - one that comes only to steal and destroy (John 10:10).

Hearing and listening, in an active disposition of the dependent trust that is faith, will always lead to 'more' being given, because it supplys the foundations on which true growth can occur. 'All other ground is sinking sand' - what you thought was true ('what he thinks he has') turns out to have been not quite correct after all. It was a misunderstanding, a false reality that is no basis for a growing experiential faith relationship, and will not stand the light of heaven's searching gaze. It will be 'taken away' and replaced by the real thing - what the author of all truth wants all his children to hear.

8:19-21 'And his mother and brothers came to him, and they were unable to get to him because of the crowd. And it was reported to him, "Your mother and your brothers are standing outside, wishing to see you." But he answered and said to them, "My mother and my brothers are these who hear the word of God and do it."'

'Hearing and doing' is the essence of faith. The word, when heard (or read), has the ability to create faith in the heart of the hearer (Romans 10:17), assuming the hearer is open to receiving the word in a disposition of trust. This faith becomes complete through an active obedience to the word that has been heard. As James (Jesus' half-brother, who had presumably heard this teaching often enough to know it by heart) would later write, 'Prove yourselves *doers* of the word, and not merely hearers who delude themselves.' And, 'One who looks intently at the perfect law, the law of liberty, and abides by it, not having become a forgetful hearer but an effectual *doer*, this man will be blessed in what he does' (James 1:22 and 25, *italics are mine*). Faith is by nature active, enabling us to walk into the works that God has already prepared ahead of time for the faith-inspired believer to do - 'We are his workmanship, created in Christ Jesus for good works, which God prepared beforehand so that we would walk in them' (Ephesians 2:10).

Jesus had 'brothers' that accompanied Mary on her concerned journey to check up on her celebrity son. '*Adelphos*' (from '*delphus*' - 'womb') means natural bothers and half-brothers; it also denotes 'spiritual brothers'. In the New Testament however it is not used to mean 'kinsmen' (which is '*suggenês*' - 'male relative'). Psalm 69:8 makes it clear that Mary had other sons: 'I have become estranged from my brothers, and an alien to my mother's sons.' While Joseph may have been married prior to marrying Mary, and, if so, had children by that marriage, Mary was a virgin when Jesus was conceived. Jesus' brothers are recorded as being named 'James,

Joseph, Simon and Judas' (Matthew 13:55). The Church father Eusebius' writings note that James, known as 'The Just' (*'dikaios'*, here used as a title that James shared with his father Joseph - Matthew 1:19), had Temple privileges of the type that the Gospels' record Jesus as having. This is the James that went on to lead the embryonic church in Jerusalem and whom the second-century chronicler Hegesippus records was martyred for refusing to denounce the messianic status of his older half-brother Jesus.

The passage does not imply that Jesus was so disrespectful of his mother that he refused to go out to her. It simply records that he took the opportunity to affirm the second use of *'adelphos'*, namely the spiritual one. It was, and would continue to be, more important to be in a faith-based spiritual relationship with him than in a natural one. The members of his natural family each had their own journey of faith to make in coming to a realisation of who this son of Mary's womb really was. For Mary herself, relating this perhaps painful saying to Luke, that journey would be the hard road to the Roman site of execution at Jerusalem named Calvary.

8:22-23 'Now on one of those days Jesus and his disciples got into a boat, and he said to them, "Let us go over to the other side of the lake." So they launched out. But as they were sailing along he fell asleep; and a fierce gale of wind descended on the lake, and they began to be swamped and to be in danger.'

The theme of hearing the word spoken and obeying in trust continues into this episode. Jesus had not said, "Let us go and endanger our lives in a storm." Rather, he had said "Let us go over to the other side." No mention there of drowning! Lake Galilee, being on the receiving end of an east-west wind-funnel formed by the surrounding hills, was notorious for sudden and violent storms, which the Gospel writers describe as *'seismos'* - 'shaking', as in an earthquake. The storm being described here is even more violent. It is a '*leilaps*' - 'whirlwind, a tempestuous wind, a squall - never a single gust nor a steady blowing wind, however violent, but a storm breaking forth from black thunder clouds in furious gusts, with floods of rain'.* The many fishermen among Jesus' disciples were under no illusions of the danger they were in. Many of their colleagues would have drowned under similar weather conditions. They were in '*kinduneuô*' - literally 'in peril' of their lives.

8:24-25a 'They came to Jesus and woke him up, saying, "Master, Master, we are perishing!" And he got up and rebuked the wind and the surging waves, and they stopped, and it became calm. And he said to them, "Where is your faith?"'

Meanwhile, Jesus is peacefully sleeping. No one likes being woken prematurely out of a much-needed nap! Instead of immediately rebuking the disciples for their lack of trust ('*pistis*' - 'faith') in the word that he had spoken about 'crossing over to the other side', Jesus rebukes the wind and the waves and they stop. What other choice did they have?

8:25b 'They were fearful and amazed, saying to one another, "Who then is this, that he commands even the winds and the water, and they obey him?"'

The disciples have yet to learn that faith does not prosper in an environment of fear, but rather in a relaxed disposition of trust. They stay in 'fear mode' only now it is a fearful realisation of who this senior Jewish legal scholar, that some of them had known from their youth, might actually be. The maker of wind and waves has authority over them as men too. The disciples were coming into the shocking realisation of the incarnation - Creator God had come among them in the form of a Jewish '*tekton*' from nearby Nazareth.

8:26 'Then they sailed to the country of the Gerasenes, which is opposite Galilee.'

Happily now out of peril, the journey continued the six miles across the lake to the Gerasenes. The 'Gerasenes' (also known as the 'Gergasenes' and the 'Gadarenes') was part of the Roman overseen, but largely autonomous, region of the Decapolis (ten cities) on the eastern shore of Lake Galilee. The 'ten cities' of the Decapolis are mentioned by the Roman historian Plint the Elder. [100] They are Gerasa (Jerash) in Jordan, Scythopolis (Beth-Shean) in Israel (a city west of the Jordan River), Hippos (Hippus or Sussita) in Israel, Gadara (Umm Qais) in Jordan, Pella (west of Irbid) in Jordan, Philadelphia (modern day Amman, the capital of Jordan), Capitolias (Beit Ras) in Jordan (now Dion, Jordan), Canatha (Qanawat) in Syria, Raphana in Jordan and Damascus to the north.

8:27-29 'And when he came out onto the land, he was met by a man from the city who was possessed with demons; and who had not put on any clothing for a long time and was not living in a house, but in the tombs. Seeing Jesus, he cried out and fell before him, and said in a loud voice, "What business do we have with each other, Jesus, Son of the Most High God? I beg you, do not torment me." For he had commanded the unclean spirit to come out of the man. For it had seized him many times; and he was bound with chains and shackles and kept under guard, and yet he would break his bonds and be driven by the demon into the desert.'

Matthew's account (8:28-34) mentions that there were two demon-possessed men that met Jesus here. Luke's account focuses on one of them; perhaps because he was the most disturbed and violent of the two. Doctor Luke would have had experience of both the mentally ill and the demonised, and he is the only Gospel writer to point out the length of their (demonically derived) affliction. The rabbis also recognised the reality of demonic empowerment - the Talmud refers to a demon called 'Destruction' in this regard. 'The gate is smitten with destruction. Mar, son of Rabbi Ashi said: I have personally seen him, and he gores like an ox' (Talmud, '*Sotah*' 48a).

This man clearly had supernatural strength, enabling him to break metal chains. Naked (the mentally disturbed were noted to tear their existing clothing to shreds) [101] and living in the limestone caverns outside Gerasa where the cities dead were buried, he terrorized the neighbouring population who were all too familiar with the work of evil spirits when they 'laid hold by force' ('seized') men such as this. Jesus himself had already recognized and begun to exercise his far greater authority over the evil spirits. They have no difficulty recognizing in Jesus the person whom the disciples had just so recently begun to understand him to be. 'Son of the Most High God' is the same title announced to Mary by the angel Gabriel (Luke 1:32). The man's form of address would therefore have especially registered in the mind of Mary, when the disciples later related the episode to her. Its significance to her would cause it to remain in her memory before being passed on to Luke.

8:30-31 'And Jesus asked him, "What is your name?" And he said, "Legion"; for many demons had entered him. They were imploring him not to command them to go away into the abyss.'

'Legion', the Roman term for between three and six thousand troops, was indeed 'many' evil spirits, all competing among themselves to bring about ruin and destruction. The Talmud taught that demons could speak, [102] and these demons begin to speak to Jesus concerning their eventual fate. The spirits are expecting 'torment' (verse 28). The Greek here is '*basanizô*', also meaning 'to examine using torture', [103] and related to '*basanismos*', used in the book of

172

Revelation to describe the fate of those who worship 'the beast' who opposes Jesus' return. 'The smoke of their *torment* goes up forever and ever; they have no rest day and night, those who worship the beast and his image, and whoever receives the mark of his name' (Revelation 14:11). The 'abyss' (**'abussos'** - 'the bottomless pit') that the spirits are seeking to temporarily avoid is not the place where this eventual 'torment' occurs, but rather the place where demons dwell and in which they are kept imprisoned by 'an angel *[but clearly somewhat greater than the demons in authority]* coming down from heaven, holding the key of the abyss and a great chain in his hand' (Revelation 20:1, *words in italics are mine*).

8:32-34 'Now there was a herd of many swine feeding there on the mountain; and the demons implored him to permit them to enter the swine. And he gave them permission. And the demons came out of the man and entered the swine; and the herd rushed down the steep bank into the lake and was drowned. When the herdsmen saw what had happened, they ran away and reported it in the city and out in the country.'

The local Gentiles had communal herds of pigs that the demons suggest as a suitably 'unclean' place to go to in the meantime. In Matthew's account, Jesus confines himself to one word - there is no dialoguing - simply 'Go!' (Matthew 8:32). Archaelogists have found ruins of an ancient city 'right over against the plain of Gennesaret, which still bear the name of Kersa or Gersa.' [104] Just to the south of Gersa there is a steep bluff which descends abruptly on a narrow ledge of shore, [105] a cliff described as steep 'as nowhere else by the lake'. [106] The panicking swine, unlike migrating lemming rodents (which can swim) charge down the steep slope and drown in the lake. Now it is the herdsmen's turn to panic. Their sudden loss of livelihood causes them to rush away with the news of this extraordinary Jewish teacher's visit.

173

8:35-37 'The people went out to see what had happened; and they came to Jesus, and found the man from whom the demons had gone out, sitting down at the feet of Jesus, clothed and in his right mind; and they became frightened. Those who had seen it reported to them how the man who was demon-possessed had been made well. And all the people of the country of the Gerasenes and the surrounding district asked him to leave them, for they were gripped with great fear; and he got into a boat and returned.'

More fear of Jesus. Just as the disciples had been in fear (*'phobeo'*) of the man whose word commanded the wind and waves to be calm, now the local townsfolk are in fear (*'phobeo'*) of the man who could command demons to leave. In giving the demons permission to enter the swine, Jesus dealt a blow to the material prosperity of the region, and the local Gentile townsfolk arrive to see for themselves what had happened. Before they had been frightened of the demon-possessed man. Now that he is made well they are still frightened, only this time of Jesus' power. They might have been grateful that the region was now safe from demonically inspired attack or indeed happy that the man was restored to his right mind, but in fact they were 'overcome with fear' and begged Jesus to leave the region. They now have *'megas phobos'* ('great fear'); they are unable to cope with Jesus and so implore him to leave. But Jesus did not leave them without a witness to his care for them, as well as for demoniacs.

8:38-39 'But the man from whom the demons had gone out was begging him that he might accompany him; but he sent him away, saying, "Return to your house and describe what great things God has done for you." So he went away, proclaiming throughout the whole city what great things Jesus had done for him.'

While the townsfolk are begging Jesus to go, the newly freed man was begging Jesus to take him with him. But Jesus had another role in mind. 'Return home and tell how much God has done for you' is Jesus' commission of the first Gentile evangelist to the Gentiles.

8:40-42 'And as Jesus returned, the people welcomed him, for they had all been waiting for him. And there came a man named Jairus, and he was an official of the synagogue; and he fell at Jesus' feet, and began to implore him to come to his house; for he had an only daughter, about twelve years old, and she was dying. But as he went, the crowds were pressing against him.'

Returning west across the lake, Jesus is greeted by a different audience - a Jewish one who welcome him and which had been eagerly looking for his return. This appears to have been on behalf of one of their local dignitaries, a 'synagogue ruler' named Jairus. It is likely that the illness of his only daughter (*'thugatêr'* - 'a female *[prepubescent]* child')* had prompted the local people to search for the one they knew from many experiences had the power to heal her. But Jesus had last been seen heading for Gentile territory and it was not likely that the more legally encumbered religious Jews would have been willing to follow him there. On sighting his return the people tell Jairus, who leaves his daughter's sick-bed to throw himself at Jesus' feet. Jesus was in huge demand and a great crowd gathers, through which Jesus and his disciples have to push their way to make progress toward Jairus' home.

8:43-48 'And a woman who had a haemorrhage for twelve years, and could not be healed by anyone, came up behind him and touched the fringe of his cloak, and immediately her haemorrhage stopped. And Jesus said, "Who is the one who touched me?" And while they were all denying it, Peter said, "Master, the people are

175

crowding and pressing in on you." But Jesus said, "Someone did touch me, for I was aware that power had gone out of me." When the woman saw that she had not escaped notice, she came trembling and fell down before him, and declared in the presence of all the people the reason why she had touched him, and how she had been immediately healed. And he said to her, "Daughter, your faith has made you well; go in peace."'

Jesus never rushed - he always moved in peaceful accordance to his Father's schedule. When answering this emergency call to the sickbed (and ultimately deathbed) of a '*thugatêr*' - 'daughter' - and being interrupted by an elderly lady with a long-term problem of the same duration as the life of the girl, he is not at all put out, despite the woman being legally unclean. Leviticus 15:19 commanded that 'When a woman has a discharge, if her discharge in her body is blood, she shall continue in her menstrual impurity for seven days and whoever touches her shall be unclean until evening.' Rabbinic law devoted a whole tractate to menstrual uncleanness and the law was strict - even the hands of those who carried a defiled bed were unclean. [107] Undeterred, she touches Jesus' '*kraspedon*' - the 'hem' of his cloak, from which small tassels hung, in accordance with the Law's command. Numbers 15:37-39 reads, 'The Lord also spoke to Moses, saying, "Speak to the sons of Israel, and tell them that they shall make for themselves tassels on the corners of their garments throughout their generations, and that they shall put on the tassel of each corner a cord of blue. It shall be a tassel for you to look at and remember all the commandments of the Lord."'

Jesus is aware that a spiritual contact has been made. Power has left him - power that the Father has released in response to the faith of the older woman. What is Jairus feeling at this point? His daughter is dying. Couldn't this woman have waited a few minutes more? This delay, in Jairus' mind, may cost is daughter her life, indeed, the following verse (verse 49) brings the news of her death. There is no hiding for the older lady. While bleeding she had been legally unclean and should not have been a part of the crowd that pressed so hard around Jesus that Peter felt the need to remind him of it. But rather than her touch of Jesus' rabbinic tassels rendering him unclean, her faith has caused his 'cleanness' to heal her and make her whole and clean for the first time in twelve years - her bleeding 'stopped.' Luke is the only New Testament writer to use this otherwise common word ('*histêmi*' - 'to stop' or 'to stand') in a medical way (Matthew's account has 'made well' and Mark's has 'dried up'). It was widely used by physicians to describe cessation of gynaecological discharge and bleeding. [108] Doctor Luke is also quite clear that her healing was beyond the reach of physicians ('Could not be healed'), unlike the less well medically informed Mark (presumably via Peter) who says, 'She had endured much at the hands of many physicians, and had spent all that she had and was not helped at all, but rather had grown worse' (Mark 5:26). Mark may not have had good experiences of physicians; if so Luke is setting the record straight - the woman was incurable.

Jesus would have been acutely aware of Jairus' distress at this unlooked for delay. Recognising that Jairus is not at this stage thinking clearly, in the panic he is experiencing, Jesus takes the opportunity to pass an underlying and almost subliminal message of faith, encouragement, trust and hope to the increasingly anxious father. Jesus does so by addressing the woman. But he is actually communicating with Jairus. What does Jesus say? 'Daughter ('*thugatêr*'), take courage, your faith ('*pistis*') has healed you ('*sozo*')'. With those words (Luke 8:48) echoing in Jairus' mind, he is confronted with the fact of the death of his '*thugatêr*' and hears Jesus repeat, almost verbatim, these words again to him.

8:49-50 'While he was still speaking, someone came from the house of the synagogue official, saying, "Your

177

daughter has died; do not trouble the Teacher anymore." But when Jesus heard this, he answered him, "Do not be afraid any longer; only believe, and she will be made well."

Jesus had spoken to the older lady, curiously addressing her as 'Daughter' (*'thugatêr'*), the only occasion on which Jesus ever addressed an individual, rather than a group of women in this way. He said, "Daughter, your faith has made you well; go in peace." Jairus is now addressed directly with the same words. 'Do not be afraid (*take courage*), only believe (*have faith* - *'pistis'*),* and she (your *'thugatêr'*) will be made well (*'sozo'*).'* The title the messenger refers to Jesus with is, once again, *'Didaskalos'* - 'Doctor' (of Torah), referencing his legal standing in Israel. The synagogue ruler had sought the help of someone considerably senior to him in terms of Jewish legal stature, but he would certainly have needed this double encouragement, first (indirectly) to the older lady and then reinforced to Jairus directly when the dreaded news arrived.

8:51-53 'When he came to the house, he did not allow anyone to enter with him, except Peter and John and James, and the girl's father and mother. Now they were all weeping and lamenting for her; but he said, "Stop weeping, for she has not died, but is asleep." And they began laughing at him, knowing that she had died.'

Mourning for the dead played a major part in Jewish religious society. Semi-professional mourners were hired for the occasion, and doubtless there would have been many unpaid joining them out of a very real and genuine sense of grief at the girl's untimely demise. The mourning flutes ('The pipers for the dead') [109] could be heard from afar, greeting Jesus' and Jairus' arrival at the family home. Rabbis frequently used the expression 'to sleep' to mean 'to die.' Jesus would do so again in reference to Lazarus (John 11:11). The crowd of mourners evidently have rather less respect for Jesus than Jairus had. Their reaction to the '***Didaskalos***' is '***katagelaô***' - 'derisive laughter'.* They knew a dead body when they saw one and they knew that the girl was dead. Such scorn is not a good basis for faith and does not deserve to be rewarded with the direct sight of a miracle. Jesus (Mark 5:40) 'put them outside', remaining alone with his three closest disciples, Jairus, his wife and their lifeless daughter.

8:54-56 'He however took her by the hand and called, saying, "Child, arise!" And her spirit returned, and she got up immediately; and he gave orders for something to be given her to eat. Her parents were amazed; but he instructed them to tell no one what had happened.'

The Lord and Giver of life recalls the girl's spirit, and recreates any brain and other damage caused by the temporary absence of breathing. Mark's account (Mark 5:41) gives Jesus' exact words. "*Talitha kum*" is Aramaic, the very words the daughter would have heard every morning from her mother or father. "Little girl, it's time to get up." Or in modern parlance, "Wakey wakey, little girl." With these tender words the '***thugatêr***' was restored to her awestruck parents. The ever-practical Jesus arranges for a meal to be brought - being dead must have left her in need of the energy the food would provide. The reaction of Jairus and his wife is '***existêmi***' - 'amazement' - exactly what the Doctors of Torah had experienced on hearing the twelve year old Jesus (Luke 2:47).

Twelve-year-old Jesus. Twelve-year-old daughter. And twelve years of physical and legal misery ended for an older woman. Some nineteen years later, Jesus was still amazing people. Jairus and his wife are now faced with the challenge of keeping what had happened to themselves. Perhaps the disappointment of not witnessing the miracle would teach the mourners to think twice before giving way to derisive laughter in the face of one so senior in their society.

Chapter 9

9:1 'And he called the twelve together, and gave them power and authority over all the demons and to heal diseases.'

Jesus' instructions to the girl's parents did not extend to Peter, James and John, who would have lost no time in telling the remaining nine disciples what had gone on inside Jairus' house. No better encouragement then for a missionary journey and the opportunity to, for themselves, repeat the recent events of deliverance for the demoniac and healing for the sick.

9:2 'And he sent them out to proclaim the kingdom of God and to perform healing.'

'Proclaim' is '*kêrusso*', meaning 'to preach' and 'proclaim openly after the manner of a herald'.* In the New Testament, 'preaching' always occurs outside the church, to those that need to hear about salvation. What happens within the church is always referred to as 'teaching', something that much of the modern church would do well to remind itself of. It is rarely that non-Christians enter the church. 'Preaching' therefore needs to happen where they are - outside the walls of the church. Those in the Church are often treated as though they still need to be saved, rather than fed though the teaching of the word, so that their faith can grow and develop. The signs of miraculous healings were expected to accompany the proclamation of the 'good news' of the gospel, both to confirm the message of salvation and to draw attention to it. This was the continued pattern in the early church, as seen in Acts 8:5-6. 'Philip went down to the city of Samaria and began proclaiming ('*kêrusso*') Christ to them. The crowds with one accord were giving attention to what was said by Philip, as they heard and saw the signs which he was performing.' The frequent absence of the miraculous in the context of evangelism in today's western world is a sad reflection on prevalent low level of faith; something that God does not intend.

9:3-6 'And he said to them, "Take nothing for your journey, neither a staff, nor a bag, nor bread, nor money; and do not even have two tunics apiece. Whatever house you enter, stay there until you leave that city. And as for those who do not receive you, as you go out from that city, shake the dust off your feet as a testimony against them." Departing, they began going throughout the villages, preaching the gospel and healing everywhere.'

As official representatives of the greatest Torah-teacher Israel had ever seen or heard (and one that performed astounding miracles as well), it would be an unbelieving and hard-hearted town indeed that would not welcome Jesus' disciples. The emphasis on faith and trust continues with the instruction to travel light and rely on God to provide whatever was needful. Similarly the house they were led to enter was to be trusted to be the right place to stay. If subsequently rejected, don't waste time in disputing - there were a lot of other towns and villages that had yet to have the benefit of Jesus' extended ministry. So get moving! 'Shaking off the dust' is a Talmudic reference to legally unclean territory. 'Foreign' cities might have to be traversed in the course of a legitimate journey but their very dust was considered to legally defile and on leaving, the Law required that it be shaken clean. [110] This was not the case with Samaritan roads and houses. [111] Jesus is saying that villages and towns in Israel that ejected his disciples were behaving in a manner worse than Samaritans. Matthew's parallel account clarifies the fact that Jesus was at that time ministering to Israel. 'Do not go in the way of the Gentiles, and do not enter any city of the Samaritans; but rather go to the lost sheep of the house of Israel' (Matthew 10:5-6). 'Shaking off the dust' of a town was a sign to the inhabitants that, despite their Jewish heritage, they were actually behaving worse than their

181

despised Samaritan neighbours. Jesus' warning was: 'Truly I say to you, it will be more tolerable for the land of Sodom and Gomorrah in the day of judgment than for that city' (Matthew 10:15).

9:7-9 'Now Herod the tetrarch heard of all that was happening; and he was greatly perplexed, because it was said by some that John had risen from the dead, and by some that Elijah had appeared, and by others that one of the prophets of old had risen again. Herod said, "I myself had John beheaded; but who is this man about whom I hear such things?" And he kept trying to see him.'

Jesus' ministry brought him great fame, both as a '***Didaskalos***' now operating provincially (not simply in the Temple Courts) and as a worker of miracles. When Herod Antipas heard of it, he was 'perplexed' because of the different popular views regarding the source of the power that Jesus was operating in. 'Perplexed' is '***diaporeô***', a particularly strong term unique to Luke's writings, also used by him of the priests' reaction to finding the apostles having escaped from prison leaving the doors locked behind them (Acts 5:23-24). It was a medical term used by the Greek physicians for marked impairment of the mental faculties. [112] Antipas would eventually get his wish, but when he finally did, Jesus had nothing to say or do for him. Luke 23:8-9: 'Herod was very glad when he saw Jesus; for he had wanted to see him for a long time, because he had been hearing about him and was hoping to see some sign performed by him. And he questioned him at some length, but he answered him nothing.' As the murderer of John the Baptist (Jesus' cousin) at the behest of his new wife (illicitly acquired from his half-brother Philip in Rome), Herod would get nothing but silence from Jesus. These words from Herod, surely spoken in his own palace, are further evidence of the presence there of a resident who was a supporter of Jesus' apostolic team (possibly Chuza, Herod Antipas' steward - Luke 8:3).

9:10-11 'When the apostles returned, they gave an account to him of all that they had done. Taking them with him, he withdrew by himself to a city called Bethsaida. But the crowds were aware of this and followed him; and welcoming them, he began speaking to them about the kingdom of God and curing those who had need of healing.'

Jesus makes time and space for a proper debrief of his team. Andrew, Peter and Philip were from Bethsaida (John 1:44), on the northeast edge of Lake Galilee. Jesus went there for private team-building time with the men he was training to represent him. But good news travels quickly and Jesus is still very much in demand. Rather than stick to the schedule, Jesus discerns his Father's hand at work and instead of being annoyed at the 'interruption', welcomes them with true grace. 'Welcoming' is '*dechomai*', also meaning 'to receive someone by taking them by the hand.'* Many came seeking healing, but Jesus' 'first things first' approach meant teaching them - proclaiming Kingdom values so that their greater spiritual needs would be dealt with - and then setting about healing all those who had need of it. Doctor Luke's medical background comes through again with his use of need of 'healing', this being '*therapeia*', the established term for 'medical treatment', [113] from which we derive the term 'therapeutic.'

9:12-14 'Now the day was ending, and the twelve came and said to him, "Send the crowd away, that they may go into the surrounding villages and countryside and find lodging and get something to eat; for here we are in a desolate place." But he said to them, "You give them something to eat!" And they said, "We have no more than five loaves and two fish, unless perhaps we go and buy food for all these people." (For there were about five thousand men.)'

Bethsaida was not large enough to have accommodated the huge crowd (probably ten or fifteen thousand at a minimum given the number of adult males). Even five thousand could not have been accommodated. Jesus is ministering in the large open spaces outside of town - *'erêmos'* means the 'large uninhabited wilderness'* that surrounded Bethsaida. Given the sheer numbers needing prayer for healing and the time that this needed, evening had already come. The Jews spoke of two evenings, the first when the sun was setting, and the second when it had actually gone below the horizon but still reflected its rays off the sky (twilight) before the pitch black of (a moonless) night fell. The disciples are naturally concerned that such a large crowd be given time to disperse and sufficiently spread out such that that the surrounding area can accommodate their need to be fed and find lodging. This is a genuinely practical observation, but Jesus had other less conventional ideas. 'You give them something to eat' is not what the disciples would have been expecting to hear!

There is a widespread belief that the 'lad' (John 6:9: *'paidarion'* - 'boy')* who provided the five loaves and two fish was sharing his own lunch with Jesus and his disciples. While this paints a rather sweet picture, it is erroneous, unless he was a fore-runner of the obese fictional English schoolboy (with a voracious appetite) Billy Bunter! The 'loaves' in question are *'artos'*, about an inch thick and about ten inches across. They were intended to provide bread for two adults, although one might be eaten by someone particularly hungry. The popular notion of enough bread for ten men being the meal provisions for one pre-pubertal boy warrants a more detailed inspection. Wherever large crowds gathered, as in most parts of the world today, sellers of food would also come. These family-run operations would send their children out with the food to sell to those who had not brought their own or who had run out and wanted more. John's account of this incident plays out Jesus' agenda in more detail. Jesus is 'testing' Philip (one of the three disciples who had grown-up in Bethsaida) about what it is they should do.

John 6:5-9 - 'Jesus said to Philip, "Where are we to buy bread, so that these may eat?" This he was saying to test him, for he himself knew what he was intending to do. Philip answered him, "Two hundred denarii worth of bread is not sufficient for them, for everyone to receive a little." One of his disciples, Andrew, Simon Peter's brother, said to him, "There is a lad here who has five barley loaves and two fish, but what are these for so many people?"' Mark's version contains Philip's answer as a question - 'Shall we go and spend two hundred denarii on bread and give them something to eat?' (Mark 6:37). This contradicts the view that the disciples were somehow living hand-to-mouth in a state of near poverty. They clearly had the resources needed to buy the bread, should it have been available to purchase. The problem was, Jesus' 'local knowledge' disciples knew that it was not available, at least not at that hour of the day. One of the other three locals, Andrew, picks up on Jesus question about 'buying bread' (and not apprehending a little boy's lunch) by helpfully drawing Jesus' attention to the nearby 'lad' selling food. But even the ever-helpful Andrew hadn't the faith to put five and two together and make five (or thirty) thousand.

9:14-17 'And he said to his disciples, "Have them sit down to eat in groups of about fifty each." They did so, and had them all sit down. Then he took the five loaves and the two fish, and looking up to heaven, he blessed them, and broke them, and kept giving them to the disciples to set before the people. And they all ate and were satisfied; and the broken pieces which they had left over were picked up, twelve baskets full.'

Possibly somewhat disappointed that his disciples had not quite passed the test (John 6:5), Jesus begins his practical demonstration of trusting God with what you have got in doing God's will. Most English translations of this passage (such as the NASB above) accord with the other three Gospels: 'Have them sit down.' The

185

Greek of Luke's account, however, has 'have them lie down', being '*kataklinô*', 'to recline',* which was the manner of eating associated in Israel with freemen rather than of slaves, who normally ate standing up. Talmud '*Pesahim*' 10.1; 37b relates, 'Rabbi Levi said: "Since it is the way of slaves to eat standing, here we eat reclining to show that we were released from bondage and are free."' The accounts in Matthew 14:19 and Mark 6:39 have 'Ordering the people to sit down' ('*anaklinô*') and John 6:10 has 'Have the people sit down' ('*anapiptô*'). Luke is the only New Testament writer to use '*kataklinô*', and here it is in the active voice ('to make'), in accord with the medical usage that Greek physicians employed for placing patients in the correct position for operations or baths. [114]

In the description of Jesus' blessing and breaking the bread, English translations again veer away from the Greek 'original'. The words 'them' above (in connection to the bread) are not present in the Greek text. The passage illustrates the normal Jewish practice of 'saying grace', which is to pray a prayer of thanks before eating. Before involving his disciples in breaking and distributing the food, Jesus first prayed the customary blessing over the food, whereby God is blessed for the food and not simply God's blessing asked upon the food. The same incorrect translation is found in Mark 6:41: 'He blessed *the food* and broke the loaves' - '*the food*' is not present in the Greek text. Jesus simply 'blessed and broke the loaves'. He would have prayed the normal Jewish prayer of thanks for a meal - 'Blessed are you, Lord our God, King of the Universe, who brings forth bread form the earth.' God is blessed for the thing that God has given. Where the twelve disciples got the twelve baskets from into which to collect the leftovers is not stated. Possibly they were their own (previously consumed) lunch baskets!

9:18-20 'And it happened that while he was praying alone, the disciples were with him, and he questioned them, saying, "Who do the people say that I am?" They

answered and said, "John the Baptist, and others say Elijah; but others, that one of the prophets of old has risen again." And he said to them, "But who do you say that I am?" And Peter answered and said, "The Christ of God."'

More tests. How would the disciples' feedback on Jesus' ministry differ from the crowd's opinions? This time the disciples (with Peter as spokesman) passed the test. What a shame Peter couldn't keep it up! While Luke discretely omits Peter's subsequently over-reaching himself in upbraiding Jesus on announcing his impending death (such negativity!), Matthew and Mark do not. Mark 8:31-33: 'And he began to teach them that the Son of Man must suffer many things and be rejected by the elders and the chief priests and the scribes, and be killed, and after three days rise again. And he was stating the matter plainly. And Peter took him aside and began to rebuke him. But turning around and seeing his disciples, he rebuked Peter and said, "Get behind me, Satan; for you are not setting your mind on God's interests, but man's."' But the answer Peter had given was still correct, as Jesus affirms in Matthew 16:17. 'Jesus said to him, "Blessed are you, Simon Barjona, because flesh and blood did not reveal this to you, but my Father who is in heaven."' Jesus was indeed the promised Messiah, of God. Jesus gave the credit where the credit was due - to his Father. Peter (and the others) had received revelation from the Father and they had accepted it. And being generally speaking, good soil, and working under Jesus' direction of clearing the ground of their own lives to make it even better, they would be soon bearing even more good fruit.

9:21-22 'But he warned them and instructed them not to tell this to anyone, saying, "The Son of Man must suffer many things and be rejected by the elders and chief priests and scribes, and be killed and be raised up on the third day."'

Jesus had not come as the type of Messiah that most religious Jews expected. Not even John the Baptist, who was 'more than a prophet' (Luke 7:26) and 'the greatest born of women' (Luke 7:28) had discerned the distinction in the Old Testament scriptures that pointed to Messiah as being both the 'suffering Servant' of Isaiah 53 and also the 'righteous Judge' of Psalm 98:8-9 and Joel 3:12. Jesus was going to fulfil the first category at his first coming (to die a sacrificial death for the sins of the world), and the second category at his second coming, when 'We shall all stand before the judgement-seat of Christ' (Romans 14:10).

The Jews were expecting the second type of Messiah - one who, like their illustrious ancestor Judas Maccabees under the Greeks' rule, would throw off the Roman yoke and lead Israel to being, once again, top of God's class among the nations. Jesus would be rejected by the authorities not only because many of them preferred the comfortable Roman status quo that the Empire's *religio licita* ('legally valid religion') status gave the Jewish faith (along with the peace to practice it to their material advantage), but also because of Jesus' claims to be God. At some point this would inevitably cause him to fall foul of the Jewish blasphemy laws and the legal requirement to execute such a person, be they a legal scholar or not. The part about 'being raised on the third day' appears to have fallen upon deaf ears, if the emotional and psychological responses to Jesus' manner of death are anything to go by. The unbelief with which the male apostles greeted the good news brought to them by the women indicates that the apostles did not quite take this in - 'But these words appeared to them as nonsense, and they would not believe them' (Luke 24:11). Mark's account of their reaction to the resurrection statement that followed the Mount of Transfiguration reads: 'They seized upon that statement, discussing with one another what rising from the dead meant' (Mark 9:10). Their minds had yet to be opened to its meaning.

9:23 'And he was saying to them all, "If anyone wishes to come after me, he must deny himself, and take up his cross daily, and follow me."'

Some of Jesus' followers (e.g. Simon the Zealot) would have been initially very much in the second category of direct political and military Messiah-action, and the rest may have shared a similar view. James and John later went so far as to recruit their mother to assist them in their claim for a large slice of the temporal political cake. 'The mother of the sons of Zebedee came to Jesus with her sons, bowing down and making a request of him. And he said to her, "What do you wish?" She said to him, "Command that in your kingdom these two sons of mine may sit one on your right and one on your left" (Matthew 20:20-21). Jesus disabuses them of any such triumphalistic thinking by referencing his own death and hence the similar fate that his disciples should expect to be rewarded with in their imitation of their master. They had already 'come after him' in discipleship and they could expect the same treatment that he was going to get - a violent demise. And in fact all except John met with such a death, and even the 'beloved' John suffered a fair amount of abuse prior to his eventual exile to the island of Patmos. Disciples literally 'followed' behind their rabbinic masters, 'in the dust of their feet' as the Talmud said, 'Dust thyself with the feet of the wise.' [115]

9:24 'For whoever wishes to save his life will lose it, but whoever loses his life for my sake, he is the one who will save it.'

'To save' is '*sozo*', meaning 'safety', 'rescue' and a type of re-cycling re-creation.* It is used in the aorist tense, meaning that 'the concept of the verb is considered without regard for past, present, or future time'.* It is therefore used in the on-going sense that 'salvation' has a beginning (new birth 'from above' - John 3:7), a continuing middle part involving sanctification (being changed into

189

Jesus' likeness) and an ultimate end - receiving a new and immortal body rather like Jesus' post-resurrection body, as described in 1 Corinthians 15:53. [xiii] This on-going '*sozo*' process involves a series of small and large choices - whether to go our own way or to go Jesus' way. By such choices is a disciple made known to the watching world. These daily choices mean 'losing' independence and self-rule in an equally on-going way. 'Will lose it' and 'Will save it' are both in the rather more final future tense - an event that has not already occurred but which will.

9:25 'For what is a man profited if he gains the whole world, and loses or forfeits himself?'

Here is another example of extreme rabbinic comparison using hyperbole. 'Losing yourself' is the greatest loss of all; the diametric opposite of gaining everything. 'Loses' is '*apollumi*', also meaning 'to destroy' oneself and 'to put out of the way entirely'.* History is littered with examples of men and women who acquired huge wealth only for it to destroy them, leaving them emotionally and spiritually empty to the point of taking their own lives. To 'forfeit' is '*zêmioô*', meaning to 'do damage to'.* Paul used it to describe the loss incurred under the fire of testing of believer's works of wood, hay and straw (1 Corinthians 3:12-13).

9:26 'For whoever is ashamed of me and my words, the Son of Man will be ashamed of him when he comes in his glory, and the glory of the Father and of the holy angels.'

'Ashamed' is '*epaischunomai*' - a strong form of '*aischunô*' meaning 'to shame and dishonour' * and 'a feeling of fear or shame

---

[xiii] 'For this perishable *[body]* must put on the imperishable, and this mortal must put on immortality' (1 Corinthians 15:53).

that prevents a person from doing the right thing'. [116] If the believer is ashamed of Christ in an on-going way (aorist tense again), then Jesus will be ashamed of them at a future time. This is a pity, because Jesus in his glory, the Father's glory and the angels' glory too will be a sight well worth being associated with.

9:27 'But I say to you truthfully, there are some of those standing here who will not taste death until they see the kingdom of God.'

The disciples are about to get a preview of the 'glory' ('***doxa***' - 'brightness')* of the kingdom that will accompany its returning King. The king is the one with the right to rule. Jesus' right to rule is not currently universally acknowledged, but the day is coming when 'at the name of Jesus every knee will bow, of those who are in heaven and on earth and under the earth' (Philippians 2:10). On that day, 'Every eye shall see him' in that glory (Revelation 1:7). Certain ones of the disciples would soon know what it would be like.

9:28-29 'Some eight days after these sayings, he took along Peter and John and James, and went up on the mountain to pray. And while he was praying, the appearance of his face became different, and his clothing became white and gleaming.'

Jesus three 'core-group disciples' often experienced moments that the rest missed out on, such as the raising of Jairus' daughter (Luke 8:54). There wasn't always room for all twelve, and besides, Jesus would have known that there was a limit to what Judas could be trusted with. The Mountain of Transfiguration is traditionally thought to be Mount Tabor (1880 feet high) in Galilee, or possibly more likely, Mount Hermon in the Golan Heights (over 9000 feet high). While praying, Jesus begins to radiate pure light. The glory of the Creator was unveiled in his servant-Son, so powerfully as to end

191

all theological argument and in a way that left the three permanently changed. For John, Jesus' cousin through his mother, there was a finality that left no grounds for dispute. 'The Word became flesh' - with DNA similar to his! - 'and lived for a while among us. We saw his glory, the glory of the only begotten from the Father, full of grace and truth' (John 1:14). 'Seeing his glory' left no room for any doubts. John, most beloved of disciples, would later 'see Jesus in his glory' again, while in exile on the island of Patmos. Revelation 1:14-15: 'His head and his hair were white like white wool, like snow; and his eyes were like a flame of fire. His feet were like burnished bronze, when it has been made to glow in a furnace.' Mark's account (Mark 9:3) of the transfiguration (via Peter) states that Jesus' clothes were whiter 'than any fuller *[launderer]* could whiten them.' 'Gleaming' in Luke's account is a rather weak (NASB) translation of '*exastraptô*', which means 'to flash like lightning'. [117] Glow-worms 'gleam'; lightening is an altogether different proposition.

Jesus' face too 'became different' (changed in appearance) in his natural state of glory. That is one reason why the disciples on the Emmaus road were unable to recognise him and so related to him as a visitor to Jerusalem rather than as someone they knew. Their eyes were only supernaturally opened when Jesus had blessed and broken the bread at their table. Man's facial features are a poor substitute for the divine, and the Nazarene that they had known had by then been raised from death and the poor shell of humanity transformed to a glory that spoke of an eternity at his Father's side.

9:30-31 'And behold, two men were talking with him; and they were Moses and Elijah, who, appearing in glory, were speaking of his departure which he was about to accomplish at Jerusalem.'

Moses and Elijah are already enjoying the bright, new and immortal bodies that come with the third and final stage of the salvation process. Jesus' regular prayer kept him in step with his Father, and the upcoming stage of his mission evidently warranted a conference with the man to whom Jesus had entrusted the Law many years earlier on Mount Sinai, as well as the prophet whose ministry Jesus' cousin John had fulfilled. His 'departure' (meaning his death) is his '*exodus*', one thing that Moses had had plenty of experience of. Jesus' death would open a way through the 'Red Sea' of sin and death, that all mankind might have the chance of crossing over to the new life on Canaan's heavenly shore. Jesus is starting to fix his gaze on the Cross.

9:32-33 'Now Peter and his companions had been overcome with sleep; but when they were fully awake, they saw his glory and the two men standing with him. And as these were leaving him, Peter said to Jesus, "Master, it is good for us to be here; let us make three tabernacles: one for you, and one for Moses, and one for Elijah", not realizing what he was saying.'

Just as they later would in Gethsemane, Jesus 'core-team' succumbs to sleep. Perhaps the radiant light of Jesus' glory, augmented on a much lesser extent by the further brightness of Moses and Elijah's arrival, penetrated their eyelids into wakefulness. Ever ready to engage his mouth before his brain, Peter slips into religious mode with the generous offer of booth construction that marked, and still marks today in orthodox Jewish circles, the Feast of Tabernacles. Elijah and Moses are ready to return to heaven, but Peter wants them to stay, perhaps to team-up with Jesus. If so, God had other ideas.

9:34-36 'While he was saying this, a cloud formed and began to overshadow them; and they were afraid as they entered the cloud. Then a voice came out of the cloud, saying, "This is my Son, my Chosen One; listen to him!" And when the voice had spoken, Jesus was found

alone. And they kept silent, and reported to no one in those days any of the things which they had seen.'

Mountaintops attract clouds, but this was no meteorological phenomenon. Rather, it was another visual manifestation of the glory of God. The very presence of God naturally and quite appropriately inspires fear and awe, as the many episodes of prostration in the Scripture evidences, and so the disciples are struck with '*phobeô*' ('fear') as they are overshadowed. If the cloud hadn't done this, the voice would certainly have done so. Manuscripts vary at this point. The NASB renders the Father calling Jesus '*eklegô*' - 'chosen', whereas the KJV render is as '*agapêtos*' - 'beloved', as at Jesus' baptism. No doubt the Father spoke both. The 'lovely dwelling place' of Psalm 84 verse 1 is, in Hebrew, 'The tabernacle of the beloved one', meaning that a beloved person is God's tabernacle. Jesus was both chosen for the mission of salvation and is indeed beloved. All should 'listen to him.' When the disciples regain their senses they find that Moses and Elijah have left. They keep their own counsel, no doubt on strict instructions from Jesus.

9:37-40 'On the next day, when they came down from the mountain, a large crowd met him. And a man from the crowd shouted, saying, "Teacher, I beg you to look at my son, for he is my only boy, and a spirit seizes him, and he suddenly screams, and it throws him into a convulsion with foaming at the mouth; and only with difficulty does it leave him, mauling him as it leaves. I begged your disciples to cast it out, and they could not."'

Down to earth with a bump! From the quiet of the mountain top to the noise of the crowd. From the manifestation of the glory of God to a manifestation of the demonic. From the faithfulness of Moses and Elijah to the lack of faith of the disciples, who were unable to cast out the unclean spirit. From the Father calling the disciples to listen to the Son, to a human father calling Jesus' attention to his own demonised son.

The father knows very well who Jesus is humanly-speaking. He addresses Jesus as '***Didaskalos***' - 'Doctor' (of Torah). Jesus is being appealed to as someone who had senior legal teaching authority in Israel, and, as Nicodemus had observed (John 3:2), was also further authorised by the God of Israel to perform miraculous signs.

These signs were important in affirming the 'new' message of the Kingdom that Jesus' ministry inaugurated. They continued to be important to the early Church for the same reason (Acts 8:6), and are supposed to feature in the announcing of the 'good news' today, because the ministry of Jesus in this regard is unchanged.

From a medical perspective the boy is manifesting some of the symptoms of grand mal epilepsy. There is however a subtle but demonic twist to them. Epileptics collapse in a manner similar to a simple faint. They are not 'violently thrown to the ground' (verse 2); it is only subsequent to abnormal brain electrical impulses and oxygen deprivation that convulsions occur. Mark's account (Mark 9:22) adds the father's observation, 'It has often thrown him both into the fire and into the water to destroy him.' This clearly indicates the work of a demonic agency. Epileptics do not manifest any compulsion to throw themselves into fire or water; they are not able to move in any particular direction at all. The Greeks classified epilepsy as a 'sacred disease' [118] and the Talmud records it to be 'a concealed bodily defect' which could originate from being 'overtaken by a demon.' [119] Epilepsy was not the only illness with possible spiritual links; the Talmud records asthma as being so [120] as well as blindness. [121] The father's request that Jesus 'look at' his son is '***epiblepô***', a particular medical term for examining a patient'. [122] Luke's word for foaming ('***aphros***') is also a particularly medical one used to describe epileptic fits. [123]

Mark's Gospel contains the desperate appeal the man makes to Jesus to rectify the disciple's inability to help. "'If you can do anything, take pity on us and help us!' And Jesus said to him, "'If you can?' All things are possible to him who believes." Immediately the boy's father cried out and said, "I do believe; help my unbelief!"'" (Mark 9:22-24). The father's faith is surely not likely to be greater than that of the disciples, who had personally witnessed many great signs and wonders. The father had 'begged the disciples' to no avail. Now he was begging their Master.

9:41-43 'And Jesus answered and said, "You unbelieving and perverted generation, how long shall I be with you and put up with you? Bring your son here." While he was still approaching, the demon slammed him to the ground and threw him into a convulsion. But Jesus rebuked the unclean spirit, and healed the boy and gave him back to his father. And they were all amazed at the greatness of God.'

Jesus' rebuke shows that he is upset, not just with the demon and its abuse of the child but also with the lack of faith of his disciples and indeed all those who represented an inability to put their trust in him because of 'unbelief' ('*apisito*' - 'absence of faith'). But the demon would have to respond to a word of command from Jesus, whereas the disciples' shortage of trust would take a little longer to remedy, indeed it persisted beyond Jesus' resurrection appearances. ('When they saw him, they worshiped him; but some were doubtful' - Matthew 28:17.) Matthew's account (Matthew 17:21) records Jesus' comment that 'prayer and fasting' were needed for this type of demon; perhaps the disciples were not as prepared in this regard as Jesus undoubtedly was. The generation that earned Jesus' particular reprobation was also 'perverted'. This is '*diastrephô*', literally meaning 'to turn away from',* and so become 'distorted' and 'twisted' out of shape. [124] The remedy for this distortion is repentance - to 'change the mind's way of thinking' such that it reflects God's.

Demonic violence is further expressed in the word 'slammed' - '*rhêgnumi*' - a Greek wrestling term used by Hesychius of Jerusalem (a fifth century Christian scholar) meaning to 'break asunder'.* Mark provides us with the words of Jesus' rebuke: 'You deaf and mute spirit, I command you, come out of him and do not enter him again' (Mark 9:25). Jesus identifies the spirit when he might just have easily have said 'Go!', as he did to Legion (Matthew 8:32). There is no formula for demon removal, it relies totally on the authority (or delegated authority) of the one making the command. Authority cannot be 'claimed', it is given by God and received by those to whom God has given responsibility. Mark's account describes the demon's last act of defiance, a vigorous convulsion that left the boy 'like a corpse' (Mark 9:26), but not so dead as to be unresponsive to the touch of Jesus, the Lord and Giver of life (Isaiah 42:5). The boy had been struck to the ground, and now it is the turn of the crowd to be struck - with amazement at God's greatness. 'Amazed' is '*ekplêssô*', meaning to 'be struck out of self-possession and astonished.' *

9:43-45 'But while everyone was marvelling at all that he was doing, he said to his disciples, "Let these words sink into your ears; for the Son of Man is going to be delivered into the hands of men." But they did not understand this statement, and it was concealed from them so that they would not perceive it; and they were afraid to ask him about this statement.'

Perhaps the crowd's amazement sent the disciples' minds into rhapsodies of anticipated fame, popularity and rulership that would surely come with the kingdom of such a Messiah as this, one who could out-wrestle the strongest demon. If so, Jesus was quick to disabuse them of any such grand illusions. His road led to the Cross, not to the ruling seat in the Sanhedrin, currently occupied by the High Priest, and he would be 'delivered' (*'paradidômi'* - 'betrayed') [125] into that man's hands and to death. 'Sink in to your ears' is *'tithêmi'*, meaning 'to establish or set in place there.' * This involves reflecting and meditating on the word God has spoken. Psalm 119:99 says, 'I have more insight than all my teachers, for your testimonies are my meditation'. This was certainly true of the twelve year old Jesus in the five days he spent in the company of the Doctors of Torah (Luke 2:41-50). The disciples' inability to understand is also partly because God chose to conceal it from them. Proverbs 25:2 states, 'It is the glory of God to conceal a matter, but the glory of kings is to search out a matter.' God often conceals things, in order that we might have the pleasure of searching them out. This involves prayer, study and meditation, in an attitude of trusting that God rewards those who seek with a 'find' ('Seek and you will find' - Luke 11:9). People who very much want one particular thing to happen (e.g. Messianic kingship) are often sub-consciously reluctant to entertain an alternative less attractive possibility (e.g. death by crucifixion). This all too human psychological tendency may have contributed to the disciples' reluctance to seek Jesus' further clarification as to their future.

9:46-48 'An argument started among them as to which of them might be the greatest. But Jesus, knowing what they were thinking in their heart, took a child and stood him by his side, and said to them, "Whoever receives this child in my name receives me, and whoever receives me receives him who sent me; for the one who is least among all of you, this is the one who is great.'

The disciples were plagued by a human desire to 'be great', and this issue of disputing their relative standings would raise its ugly head on other occasions, none more shocking than at Jesus' 'Last Supper' following the occasion of Jesus' act of holy servanthood expressed by his washing his disciple's feet. Luke 22:24: 'There arose also a dispute among them as to which one of them was regarded to be greatest.' The Father would frequently reveal the thoughts of people's hearts to Jesus, such as Simon the Pharisee (Luke 7:39-40) and the Scribes (Matthew 9:4) when it was necessary to do. Evidently this was one such necessary occasion.

Children figured often in Jesus' illustrations of the values of his 'upside-down' kingdom. [xiv] In Hebrew society at the time they had no legal standing, and so could be likened to one who was 'the least'. This legal position is stated by Paul in Galatians (4:1), 'I say as long as the heir is a child, he does not differ at all from a slave although he is owner of everything.' Jesus, though legally entitled to total rulership, came as a humble servant, one who would subjugate his 'rights' to the will of his Heavenly Father, and 'empty himself, taking the form of a bond-servant' (Philippians 2:7).

In God's economy, the 'little' people in his service are in fact the 'great', because they embody the essence of what is needed to be spiritually great - the recognition that they can achieve nothing of themselves but only in total reliance on their Father in heaven. This is the basis of working faith - active trust in God and his ability rather than one's own abilities, good and God-given though they may be. Children are generally aware of their own inability to get things done; they are under few illusions of their own power and authority and cannot therefore substitute their own for things that only God can achieve. 'Greatness' in the kingdom is based on realisations such as these because they support and engender the faith without which it is 'impossible to please God' (Hebrews 11:6).

[xiv] Acts 17:6 'They drew Jason and certain brethren unto the rulers of the city, crying, "These that have turned the world upside down are come hither also"' (KJV).

Little ones' (including children) in Jesus' service should be received as one would receive Jesus himself.

9:49-50 'John answered and said, "Master, we saw someone casting out demons in your name; and we tried to prevent him because he does not follow along with us." But Jesus said to him, "Do not hinder him; for he who is not against you is for you."'

Jesus' act of 'receiving' the child for purpose of illustration may have prompted the all too recent incident of their inability to deliver the demon-possessed boy. Apparently others were starting to act in Jesus' authority against the demonic, and had been rebuked by the disciples for being 'unofficial'. Jesus' statement 'who is not against you is for you' is addressed to those on the 'inside', seeking to represent him in a positive way and based on the way Jesus modelled for all his disciples to follow, even the 'unofficial' ones. This perspective is quite different from those who sought to oppose Jesus from the 'outside', as represented by the unbelieving Pharisees. To them Jesus said, 'He who is not with me is against me; and he who does not gather with me scatters' (Matthews 12:30).

9:51-53 'When the days were approaching for his ascension, he was determined to go to Jerusalem; and he sent messengers on ahead of him, and they went and entered a village of the Samaritans to make arrangements for him. But they did not receive him, because he was travelling toward Jerusalem.'

Jesus is now beginning the physical ascent southwards to Mount Zion and Mount Moriah, the place of the Temple of Herod and the city of Jerusalem outside of which his sacrifice would be made. 'Messengers' is *aggelos*, as in 'angelic messenger';* an advance party of disciples sent ahead of Jesus to make preparations (such as accommodation and purchase of food provisions) for the large company of men and women that followed Jesus. From Galilee to Jerusalem entails passing through Samaria, the area inhabited by the half-Jews descended from the northern tribes of Israel that split away from Judea after Solomon's death and who had inter-married with the surrounding non-Jewish people groups.

In 740 BC Israel had been exiled by the Assyrian king Sargon II and his son Sennacherib. 'Then the king of Assyria carried Israel away into exile to Assyria, and put them in Halah and on the Habor, the river of Gozan, and in the cities of the Medes' (2 Kings 18:11). In consequence, 'Every nation still made gods of its own and put them in the houses of the high places which the people of Samaria had made, every nation in their cities in which they lived... They also feared the Lord and appointed from among themselves priests of the high places, who acted for them in the houses of the high places. They feared the Lord and served their own gods according to the custom of the nations from among whom they had been carried away into exile. To this day they do according to the earlier customs; they do not fear the Lord, nor do they follow their statutes or their ordinances or the law, or the commandments which the Lord commanded the sons of Jacob, whom he named Israel' (2 Kings 17:29-34).

The Samaritans had built their own temple on Mount Gerizim (about halfway between Nazareth in the north and Jerusalem in the south). Their allegiance to their own version of their faith was subject to considerable political expediency. When the Greek king Antiochus III ('the Great' - c. 241 - 187 BC) made war on the Jews, seeking to hellenise them, the watching Samaritans were quick to 'declare themselves free from such accusations, and agreeable to their petition, that their temple be (re)named the Temple of Jupiter Hellenius. [126] The Samaritans' objection to Jesus' coming may have been because they sought recognition of their own temple. The religious tensions meant that they also frequently opposed pilgrimages of religious Jews from the northern region of Galilee to the Temple in Jerusalem.

9:54-56 'When his disciples James and John saw this, they said, "Lord, do you want us to command fire to come down from heaven and consume them, even as Elijah did?" But he turned and rebuked them, and said, "You do not know what kind of spirit you are of; for the Son of Man did not come to destroy men's lives, but to save them." And they went on to another village.'

James and John (who were cousins to Jesus) were not called 'the Sons of Thunder' (Mark 3:17) for nothing! Aggrieved by the aggressive attitude of the Samaritans' rejection, they respond with some aggression of their own, albeit religious aggression! In 2 Kings 1:10, Elijah had called down fire on the men who had come to arrest him. James and John had not yet fully grasped the distinction between the old covenant and the new one of 'grace and truth' (John 1:14) that Jesus' ministry inaugurated. 'Rebuke' ('*epitimaô*') means 'to censure severely';* they are embodying the exact opposite of the attitude that Jesus wanted to see in his disciples. Given the area concerned, 'another village' means another of the Samaritan's villages. Jesus had already been a huge hit in one (John 4:39-42), where he had stayed following his ministry to the Samaritan woman at the well, and there were doubtless others also where he was known and welcome.

9:57-58 'As they were going along the road, someone said to him, "I will follow you wherever you go." And Jesus said to him, "The foxes have holes and the birds of the air have nests, but the Son of Man has nowhere to lay his head."'

Matthew (8:19) identifies this 'someone' as a scribe, a senior member of Jewish legal and religious society, a highly educated person and usually wealthy. Jesus was always clear that those who followed him understood that, despite his popular adulation, fame and glory would not be the lot of his disciples. The time was coming when those closest to him would deny they even knew him, out of fear for their lives (John 18:25-27). In the meantime the disciples' lot would be that of a traveller, with no permanent place of abode.

9:59-60 'And he said to another, "Follow me." But he said, "Lord, permit me first to go and bury my father." But he said to him, "Allow the dead to bury their own dead; but as for you, go and proclaim everywhere the kingdom of God."'

'Follow me' was the rabbinic invitation to enter into a discipleship relationship with a master of Torah. To be invited to join the school and company of a '*Didaskalos*' ('Doctor' of Torah) of Jesus' standing was an honour indeed. But this person, as opposed to the scribe, offers an excuse that suggests he may have had 'cold feet'. Perhaps he had over-heard Jesus' comment about being put to death (verse 44). His excuse is to be allowed to wait until his duty to care for his father had run its course by his father's eventual death. 'Bury my father' did not mean that his father was already dead - burials occurred very soon after death - but that he would have that obligation in the future. Jesus, knowing that there are others who could and would perform the office of burial, encourages the man to think again and instead 'announce' the new kingdom that was arriving.

9:61-62 'Another also said, "I will follow you Lord; but first permit me to say good-bye to those at home." But Jesus said to him, "No one, after putting his hand to the plough and looking back, is fit for the kingdom of God."'

Elisha (1 Kings 19:19:21) had been given permission to say good-bye to his parents, but he had then returned and burned his plough in order to sacrifice his ox! A man cannot plough a straight line looking anywhere other than straight ahead. Jesus is looking for disciples who will follow him on the straight road to Calvary. That meant choosing for him and therefore often against close family members. ('If anyone comes to me, and does not hate his own father and mother and wife and children and brothers and sisters, yes, and even his own life, he cannot, be my disciple' - Luke 14:26.) 'Fit' here is *euthetos*, a term not employed by the other Gospel writers but used solely by Luke. *'Euthetos'* was the common medical term for a properly placed bone [127] and was widely employed [128] by the physician pharmacologist and botanist Pedanius Dioscorides (c. 40-90 AD) a Roman army surgeon who (like the Apostle Paul) was born in Cilicia, now part of modern day Turkey. Jesus the physician is committed to making those he calls 'fit for purpose'.

Chapter 10

10:1 'Now after this the Lord appointed seventy others, and sent them in pairs ahead of him to every city and place where he himself was going to come.'

Jesus ministered in all the towns and cities in Israel (Matthew 9:35) and some in Samaria as well. He facilitated this by preparing the people for his coming to them by sending pairs of disciples ahead (no 'lone-rangers' here!). They would alert the local populace so that they were ready to assemble and receive his ministry, as one who was a senior legal scholar of Torah, when he arrived. The twelve apostles have done this already (Matthew 10:1), now another tier of ministers get their chance to go out and put into practice what Jesus had taught them.

10:2 'And he was saying to them, "The harvest is plentiful, but the labourers are few; therefore beseech the Lord of the harvest to send out labourers into his harvest."'

There were very many towns and villages between Jesus and Jerusalem, each one containing many people who would respond to Jesus' phenomenal combination of miraculous healing and inspired original Torah-teaching. Jesus was preparing his followers to multiply his ministry; to replicate it and then train others to replicate it further. But as we saw a few verses earlier, not all that followed him were ready or willing to pay the price of discipleship. Prayer was necessary because only through a faith-oriented dependence on God to supply the need could the harvest be met.

10:3-4 '"Go; behold, I send you out as lambs in the midst of wolves. Carry no money belt, no bag, no shoes; and greet no one on the way."'

There was to be no illusions as to the nature of the opposition that they would face, in the form of both natural and spiritual 'wolves'. But these are no ordinary 'lambs', these are lambs watched over by the Father, protected and provided for as children of the Lord of the universe. As such they have no need of self-reliance and need not be troubled regarding daily provisions, which Jesus had taught that any competent father would provide, never mind someone as wonderful as his Heavenly Father. Matthew 6:30: 'If God so clothes the grass of the field, which is alive today and tomorrow is thrown into the furnace, will he not much more clothe you?' The injunction to abstain from greeting those on the way is likely to be because such a greeting, made in the elaborate eastern style of stopping for repeated social enquiries and blessings, would inevitably result not only in delay but also in offers of hospitality and hence a diversion from the urgent tasks at hand. Jesus did not forbid receiving greetings made towards his disciples, only their own stopping to make such greetings themselves.

10:5-7 '"Whatever house you enter, first say, 'Peace be to this house.' If a man of peace is there, your peace will rest on him; but if not, it will return to you. Stay in that house, eating and drinking what they give you; for the labourer is worthy of his wages. Do not keep moving from house to house."'

The disciples' greeting of 'Peace' would certainly have been the Hebrew '*shalom*', meaning a holistic sense of well-being, soundness and welfare in general.* This blessing would be brought about by God if the house's inhabitants were receptive of it. If not, it would still establish its purpose, only towards those who gave the blessing. Hospitality was, and still is, central to middle-eastern culture, and was to be received with thanks, without 'shopping around' for a better deal. To do so would have been to create enmity between neighbours, such slights being equivalent to an insult. The Apostle

206

Paul would later (1 Timothy 5:18) make the same point by putting the proverb, 'The labourer is worthy of his wages', alongside the Law's command of Deuteronomy 25:4 - 'You shall not muzzle the ox while he is threshing'.

10:8-9 '"Whatever city you enter and they receive you, eat what is set before you; and heal those in it who are sick, and say to them, 'The kingdom of God has come near to you.'"

The households of Samaritan cities would not be serving kosher food. Just as the Samaritan woman's bucket had not been legally clean for Jesus to obtain a drink from (John 4:9), so their food would not be legally clean for religious Jews to eat. The disciples were to eat what was provided without questioning, just as Paul would later instruct the church at Corinth to do in relation to food previously offered in an idol's temple and later sold on the open market (1 Corinthians 8:7-8). Miraculous healing accompanying the preaching of the gospel was an integral expectation of Jesus and he has not changed over the intervening period. [xv] While our level of faith may not match that of the seventy Jesus commissioned, there is no reason to suppose that the gospel message of grace would not similarly benefit from signs and wonders accompanying it. They provide an important piece of evidence that the rule of God has in fact arrived.

10:10-12 '"But whatever city you enter and they do not receive you, go out into its streets and say, 'Even the dust of your city which clings to our feet we wipe off in protest against you; yet be sure of this, that the kingdom of God has come near.' I say to you, it will be more tolerable in that day for Sodom than for that city.'"

[xv] 'Jesus Christ is the same yesterday and today and forever' (Hebrews 13:8).

Samaritan cities, as seen above, were likely to refuse a Jewish teacher bound for Jerusalem. Jews regarded foreign cities' dust as legally unclean, hence this command would be not have been new to Jesus' disciples. Jesus, however, is applying the command to all cities that rejected him, not just the foreign ones. For a Jew to see another Jew wiping off the soles of his feet in judgement against him would have been something truly extraordinary. Jesus' command is made even more explicit by the reference to that most impure of towns, Sodom, home to Abraham's nephew, Lot (Genesis 19:1). Genesis 13:13 records, 'The men of Sodom were wicked exceedingly and sinners against the Lord.' Sodom was destroyed from heaven by fire and brimstone (Genesis 19:24-15); others who rejected Jesus' much greater ministry than that of Lot could expect a greater judgement.

10:13-15 '"Woe to you, Chorazin! Woe to you, Bethsaida! For if the miracles had been performed in Tyre and Sidon which occurred in you, they would have repented long ago, sitting in sackcloth and ashes. But it will be more tolerable for Tyre and Sidon in the judgment than for you. And you Capernaum, will not be exalted to heaven, will you? You will be brought down to Hades!"'

Though Jesus visited all the Jewish towns and villages (Matthew 9:35), the Gospels only contain a record of a relative few. Chorazin (on the northern edge of Lake Galilee) is an example of a town that the Gospels do not mention elsewhere, but which apparently saw the same miracle-based evidence of Jesus' claims as all the rest. Bethsaida (home of Peter, Andrew and Philip) certainly had its fair share, but with apparently little lasting effect on the spiritual state of the other residents. Again, its judgement would be proportional to its knowledge. Tyre and Sidon (port cities on the Mediterranean) had benefited from the prophetic ministry of Ezekiel (Ezekiel chapters 26-28), but had not been persuaded to turn to the God of Israel. Jesus says had he been there in place of Ezekiel, then they would have done and that will be taken into account in the final judgement of all things depicted in the Book of Revelation. 'I saw the dead, the great and the small, standing before the throne, and books were opened; and another book was opened, which is the book of life; and the dead were judged from the things which were written in the books, according to their deeds' (Revelation 20:12). Capernaum was a prosperous trading centre under Roman protection, for which the Jewish merchants there would have given thanks to God ('exalting their town to heaven'); Jesus on the other hand sees its spiritual poverty and warns of the consequences if left unchanged. The scholarly section of Jesus' Jewish society believed in an after-life that was divided into two sections prior to the final judgement: paradise and Hades. This is clearly depicted in Jesus' teaching on the rich man and Lazarus (Luke 16:19-31), where Hades is shown as a place of flame and torment (Luke 16:24), as opposed to the place of comfort enjoyed by the righteous poor man Lazarus alongside the patriarch Abraham.

10:16 '"The one who listens to you listens to me, and the one who rejects you rejects me; and he who rejects me rejects the One who sent me."'

The seventy disciples that Jesus is sending out on the mission to prepare the way for him understand that their role of representation is bound to that of their Master. Christians represent Christ, and should therefore live in such a way that fosters the acceptance of him rather than provoking an unnecessary rejection of themselves by a poor witness that will aggravate others into rejecting the One they represent.

10:17-19 'The seventy returned with joy, saying, "Lord, even the demons are subject to us in your name." And he said to them, "I was watching Satan fall from heaven like

lightning. Behold, I have given you authority to tread on serpents and scorpions, and over all the power of the enemy, and nothing will injure you."'

The seventy had been given responsibility for a mission. With that came the authority to act on behalf of their commissioner - they could do the same things that he did. The great commission of Matthew 28:18-20 certainly encompasses the same type of spiritual authority, as Mark's version (Mark 16:15-18) shows. Mark's account similarly mentions the divine authority over serpents, and protection from them, be they figurative of spiritual opposition ('the power of the enemy') or actual snakes, and the protection enjoyed by the Apostle Paul on Malta when he was bitten by one (Acts 28:3-5). Jesus' comment about Satan falling may have more than one sense of interpretation. The man spiritual victories that the seventy accomplished may have forced Satan out of heaven (in which Job 1:6 [xvi] shows that he retains a measure of access) and onto the earth to attend to his affairs there. Jesus would also have witnessed first-hand the devil's original ejection from the ranks of the senior angelic beings on the occasion of his initial rebellion, prior to mankind being created. There may also be a warning here to the seventy not to let their recent success go to their heads in the way that pride did to the devil, occasioning his spiritual demise.

10:20 '"Nevertheless do not rejoice in this, that the spirits are subject to you, but rejoice that your names are recorded in heaven."'

The last inference of spiritual warning against pride plays out into this warning. What is important is that the spiritual success or failure rests in the hands of the One whose hands their names are engraved

---

[xvi] 'Job 1:6: 'There was a day when the sons of God came to present themselves before the Lord, and Satan also came among them.'

upon. 'Can a woman forget her nursing child and have no compassion on the son of her womb? Even these may forget, but I will not forget you. Behold, I have inscribed you on the palms of my hands; your walls are continually before me' (Isaiah 49:15-16).

10:21 'At that very time he rejoiced greatly in the Holy Spirit, and said, "I praise you, O Father, Lord of heaven and earth, that you have hidden these things from the wise and intelligent and have revealed them to infants. Yes Father, for this way was well-pleasing in your sight."'

Jesus' relationship with his heavenly Father was one of joy. 'Rejoice' is *'agalliaô'*, also meaning 'exceeding gladness', from *'hallomai'* - 'to spring up'. [129] Jesus literally 'jumped for joy' by the influence and out-working of the Holy Spirit. His 'praise' of his Father is *'exomologeô'*, also meaning 'to acknowledge openly and joyfully.'* Prior to the out-pouring of the Holy Spirit on the day of Pentecost (Acts 2), the workings of the Spirit had been confined to the prophets and those appointed to specific tasks in God's service. In Jesus' day, access to God was confined to the elite priestly families and those Jews with the time and opportunity to study Torah to a high level. These are the 'wise and intelligent' that Jesus refers to here - those that had benefitted from senior religious education. But it had not led the majority of them to a personal knowledge of their God, but rather into a legalistic and judgemental form of religiosity. It 'pleased' God to introduce himself in Jesus to those of predominantly lesser scholastic achievement and social standing. These were the 'infants' ('babes' - KJV), whose consequential lack of dependency on themselves and their own standing forced them into a position of reliance upon God and his abilities. This is a place of faith through which God is pleased to act. They were under no delusions that their successes were in any way due to their own virtue or knowledge, and in consequence God would receive all the credit and glory that is rightfully his.

10:22 '"All things have been handed over to me by my Father, and no one knows who the Son is except the Father, and who the Father is except the Son, and anyone to whom the Son wills to reveal him."'

Jesus himself modelled this sense of trust and dependency, at the heart of active faith, for our benefit. All that Jesus had to do and to work with was 'handed to him' by his Father. This is *'paradidômi'*, from *'didômi'* - 'to bestow as a gift.' Jesus, like us, had been 'gifted' things to do and say in his Father's service. As Jesus said, '"Truly, truly, I say to you, the Son can do nothing of himself, unless it is something he sees the Father doing; for whatever the Father does, these things the Son also does in like manner. For the Father loves the Son, and shows him all things that he himself is doing"' (John 5:19-20). The relationship between the Father and the Son excludes all except those to whom it is the Son's intention to 'reveal' him - 'to lay open what has been veiled or covered up'.* No one can come to the Father but through Christ (John 14:6).

10:23-24 'Turning to the disciples, he said privately, "Blessed are the eyes which see the things you see, for I say to you that many prophets and kings wished to see the things which you see, and did not see them, and to hear the things which you hear, and did not hear them."'

Many of Israel's prophets and kings had looked forward to the arrival of Messiah, some, like Isaiah, had even prophesied clear information about his exact coming and ministry. But their lives had not overlapped with Messiah's, and they had had to be content with seeing his coming as if from afar. 'All these died in faith, without receiving the promises, but having seen them and having welcomed them from a distance, and having confessed that they were strangers and exiles on the earth' (Hebrews 11:13).

10:25 'And a lawyer stood up and put him to the test, saying, "Teacher, what shall I do to inherit eternal life?"'

Conversations between religious scholars were often in the form of 'tests'. A question would be posed as an introduction to a discussion of the relevant points of Law around the question. This is not at all the same thing as to 'tempt' (as in Jesus' 'testing' in the desert at the hands of the devil). 'Test' is *'ekpeirazô'*, from *'peirazô'* - 'to prove something's quality'.* This is what Jesus is doing with his disciple Philip prior to feeding the five thousand - 'He was saying to test him, for he himself knew what he was intending to do' (John 6:6). Also Paul exhorts in 2 Corinthians 13:5: 'Test yourselves to see if you are in the faith.' The lawyer is not asking the question out of a desire to trick Jesus into making an answer that would somehow compromise Jesus, rather he is using a Jewish rabbinic method of extracting from Jesus information that he wanted to know - rather important information concerning how he might enter the kingdom of heaven and gain the everlasting life (in paradise) that its residents enjoyed. As all the scholars did, he addresses Jesus by his legitimate scholastic title, *'Didaskalos'* - 'Doctor' (of Torah), recognising that Jesus had gained legal parity with the professors of rabbinic studies that he had so impressed aged twelve (Luke 2:46-47).

10:25-29 'And he said to him, "What is written in the Law? How does it read to you?" And he answered, '"You shall love the Lord your God with all your heart and with all your soul and with all your strength and with all your mind'; and your neighbour as yourself.'" And he said to him, "You have answered correctly; do this and you will live." But wishing to justify himself, he said to Jesus, "And who is my neighbour?"'

Rabbis taught through asking pertinent questions, designed to prompt the correct answer in the minds of their pupils. This is what

Jesus is doing with the Doctors of the Law in Luke 2:46-47, 'Listening to them and asking them questions. All who heard him were amazed at his understanding and his answers.' The lawyer's question ('What must I do') may well have been works oriented, as at that time this was how righteousness was thought to be derived - by keeping the Law. Jesus refers the lawyer back to what was mutually accepted ground, the law contained in Deuteronomy 6:5 (the first commandment) and Leviticus 19:18 (love of neighbour). Both these commands point to love as being the central element to pleasing God, rather than any particular legal outworking. The lawyer does not seem to have been expecting such a simple answer to what he may have thought to be an important and complex legal question. In a similar way John's Gospel (John 3:4) depicts the learned Nicodemus as being surprised by the simplicity of Jesus' teaching regarding being 'born from above'. The lawyer seeks to recover his position as an intelligent man by asking a secondary question, perhaps to deflect any impression among those listening that someone as intelligent as him should really have considered such obvious texts as Deuteronomy 6:5 and Leviticus 19:18! The question of who constituted 'a neighbour' for legal purposes was indeed a complex one. The Jews' neighbours were the Samaritans whom they despised and certainly were not put into the category of neighbour in the context of Leviticus 19:18.

10:30-35 'Jesus replied and said, "A man was going down from Jerusalem to Jericho, and fell among robbers, and they stripped him and beat him, and went away leaving him half dead. And by chance a priest was going down on that road, and when he saw him, he passed by on the other side. Likewise a Levite also, when he came to the place and saw him, passed by on the other side. But a Samaritan, who was on a journey, came upon him; and when he saw him, he felt compassion, and came to him and bandaged up his wounds, pouring oil and wine on

them; and he put him on his own beast, and brought him to an inn and took care of him. On the next day he took out two denarii and gave them to the innkeeper and said, "Take care of him; and whatever more you spend, when I return I will repay you."'

Thanks to the lawyer's question, we have handed down to us one of Jesus' most sublime and (among non-Christians) best-known teaching illustrations. It features only in Luke's Gospel, and judging by the sheer number of unique and distinctively medical terms in it, it must surely have been one of Luke's favourites to re-tell. The parable of 'The Good Samaritan' has inspired countless acts of kindness, even to the naming of charities after it. All parables are intended to make a main point, and this one is no different. The point is that following after the Law does not always lead to that life which the God who gave the Law intended. The Jews had taken some of the commands of God and embellished and added to them to the point that some of them faced the exact opposite way to that intended in the first place by the original command. An example of this was the Jewish law of 'Corban' (Mark 7:8-13), which undid the command to honour parents. It stated that adult children could give monies to God and the Temple instead of using it to care for aged and infirm parents. This legal loophole legitimately permitted them to spitefully refuse to assist estranged and needy elderly parents.

In this parable, the priest and Levite are seeking to obey the expanded command of Numbers 19:11 - 'The one who touches the corpse of any person shall be unclean for seven days.' The Oral Torah had ring-fenced and developed this by defining 'touch' as coming within a four cubit distance (approximately six feet) of prohibited proximity to that which was legally unclean [130] (in this case open wounds), in order to remain legally clean, for example, for Temple service. In circumnavigating their fellow (wounded) Jew by 'passing by on the other side', they are maintaining legal and ritual cleanliness, according to their own definition, but at the same time breaking the written commandment concerning love of neighbour.

The road from Jericho to Jerusalem passed an area of caverns and sharp turnings that were notorious for hiding highway robbers. It contained a section called in Arabic '*tal 'at ed-damm*' - 'The Ascent of Blood'. The Church historian Eusebius (263-339 AD) states that there was a castle built there, and the church father Jerome (347-420 AD) rendered the name Maledomni ('The Ascent of the Red'), so named partly because of the local rocks' colour and partly because of the blood that bandits shed there, necessitating the nearby Roman fort. Travelling alone was a sign either of folly or of pressing haste necessitating a journey prior to the departure of the next caravan of merchants, pilgrims and other travellers. However parables were told to make a central point; the dangers of extrapolating too far may be seen by the fact that the priest, Levite and Samaritan also appear to be travelling alone. The traveller is attacked and left 'half-dead' ('*hêmithanês*'), another term unique to Luke in the New Testament but used by the physician Galen. [131]

The Samaritan is the person Jesus' audience would have thought least likely to help the injured Jew. But he is unconcerned with the rigours of Oral Torah and is 'moved to compassion' - literally 'to the bowels' - '*splagchnizomai*'. The medical term 'splanchnic plexus' (the blood and nerve supply to the bowels) is derived from this. The Samaritan is brave enough to stop and risk the robbers returning, and his compassion is intensely practical, he 'binds up' (Greek: '*katadeô*') the wounds (Greek: '*trauma*'). These are medical terms unique to Luke in the New Testament but otherwise common in Greek medical texts. [132] 'Oil and wine' were common medical remedies for wounds. [133] The Samaritan was very generous; two denarii were two days full-time labourer's wages, and his credit against any excess needs is evidently good enough for the inn-keeper. 'Take care of' is '*epimeleomai*', another common medical term [134] also used in connection to pastoral care in the church (1 Timothy 3:5).

10:36-37 'Which of these three do you think proved to be a neighbour to the man who fell into the robbers' hands?" And he said, "The one who showed mercy toward him." Then Jesus said to him, "Go and do the same."'

Jesus' easy question to the lawyer is in stark contrast to the potentially complicated one the lawyer had posed. A 'neighbour' is someone who shows mercy. The challenge was then to act in like manner, crossing social and cultural boundaries to imitate God, who 'delights in mercy' (Micah 7:18, KJV).

10:38-42 'Now as they were traveling along, he entered a village; and a woman named Martha welcomed him into her home. She had a sister called Mary, who was seated at the Lord's feet, listening to his word. But Martha was distracted with all her preparations; and she came up to him and said, "Lord, do you not care that my sister has left me to do all the serving alone? Then tell her to help me." But the Lord answered and said to her, "Martha, Martha, you are worried and bothered about so many things; but only one thing is necessary, for Mary has chosen the good part, which shall not be taken away from her."'

Once again a woman's recollection appears in Luke's Gospel. This episode is only recorded in Luke, surely the influence of his female source, Jesus' mother Mary. One sister is doing all the hard work, the other is sitting at Jesus' feet - the posture of a disciple being taught by their master. Only this is a female disciple, at a time when rabbis rarely permitted women to learn Torah. In her possibly elaborate preparations for such an honoured guest, Martha was 'worried' (*'merimnaô'*, from *'merimna'* meaning 'care and anxiety')* and 'bothered' (*'turbazô'*, from *'turbê'*, meaning 'disorder and confusion'). [135] The 'one thing' that was needed was the undivided attention to him that Mary was paying. A simple meal in peace was all that was needed physically and emotionally. The good 'portion' that Mary chose is *'meris'*, from *'meros'*, which means a portion of food (Luke 24:42). This is likely to be Jesus' sense of humour coming through from the underlying Aramaic in the form a typically rabbinic play-on-words. Mary's 'portion' (Jesus' teaching) would last much longer than the 'portion' of food that Martha was busy getting ready. Food might be taken away, but Jesus' teaching had an abiding place in the hearts of those who heard it and met it with receptive faith.

11:1 'It happened that while Jesus was praying in a certain place, after he had finished, one of his disciples said to him, "Lord, teach us to pray just as John also taught his disciples."'

Human nature inevitably inclines toward making comparisons with others, however different their circumstances may be. For some of Jesus' disciples, that meant comparing themselves with John the Baptist's followers. There is no exact formula to prayer, which expresses the daily relationship between the Creator God and his children. But that did not prevent the disciples asking for one or Jesus' response in giving one. He did not intend that they treat it as a kind of incantation, but rather in the rabbinic sense where each part is a subheading in its own right. Matthew's Gospel (Matthew 6:5-14) helpfully provides the context for this teaching - a middle way between the extremes of mindless babble and repetitions of pagan prayer (Matthew 6:7) on the one hand, and on the other, the long-winded religious prayers of the Jews (Matthew 6:5). Such prayers seem to have been designed to impress a human audience rather than the God to whom they were addressed. It is a great shame when this 'Lord's prayer' is reduced to mindless repetition, and also when Christian prayer becomes something long and flowery, replete with jargon that only a few can understand. Jesus gives the many and simple elements of prayer in the following summary parts.

11:2a 'Father, hallowed be your name.'

Jesus taught this prayer as a simple prayer to a Father who already knows our needs before we have asked. The prayer is a series of natural child-to-father expressions that do not stand in isolation, but are linked together. In Luke's account the prayer simply begins 'Father'. There is no 'our' to dilute the personal, and no 'in heaven' to dilute the intimacy with distance. Jesus' will was to make the Father known. John 17:26 reads, 'I *[Jesus]* have made you *[the Father]* known to them *[the disciples]*, and will continue to make you known in order that the love you have for me may be in them and that I myself may be in them' *(words in italics are mine)*. The one word, 'Father', sums up the essence of the relationship; every line of this prayer is intended to be prayed as a child, speaking personally to their (perfect) Father out of a secure, loving relationship.

'Hallowed be your name' means, 'may your name be treated as holy'. Why? Because Father's name is the family's name, of which his children, in Christ, are part. The family's name is to be set apart as holy and represent uniquely God's essence and nature. We have a responsibility to hallow the Lord's name.

11:2b 'Your kingdom come.'

Where is this Kingdom? The Father of the family is a king, but his kingdom is not fully of this world. As Jesus said, 'My kingdom is not of this world... my kingdom is from another place' (John 18:36) - heaven. However, this kingdom has yet to be fully manifested on earth as it will be. 'The kingdom of the world has become the kingdom of our Lord and of his Christ, and he will reign forever and ever' (Revelation 11:15). The prayer is that God's children see their Father's rule and reign acknowledged and emphasized, recognised, responded to and submitted to, setting all things in right order.

'Come, your kingdom'... is rendered in the imperative mood, as is 'Be done, your will.' The use of the imperative mood in the Greek text means that these sayings are expressed as commands. The prayer insists on seeing the Father's will done, not our own, or anyone else's. Jesus once said to his disciples: 'I have food to eat you do not know about. My food is to do the will of him who sent me and to accomplish his work' (John 4:34). Doing the will of his Father was what really satisfied Jesus, the perfect Son.

Matthew's account adds, 'On earth, as it is in heaven.' In heaven, Father's will is done. It is never thwarted or frustrated. It is simply done. As his children, we ask him to act that way on earth.

11:3 'Give us each day our daily bread.'

The Greek text here contains the word '*kata*', which means 'accordingly', and so links this request to the previous phrase - 'your will be done', hence this reference to the bread or food we need in order to be doing God's will. 'Each day' is '*hemera* ', meaning a twenty-four hour day - 'today'. 'Daily bread' is '*epiousios*', a word only ever seen three times - in Luke and Matthew's versions of the Lord's Prayer and, much more recently, in an Egyptian accounting manuscript papyrus, which is what gives us an understanding of its meaning as there are no other surviving written uses. Vine's Expository Dictionary says about '*epiousios*' - 'Some would derive the word from '*epi*' - 'upon' and '*eimi*' - 'to be,' as if to signify '(bread) present,' i.e., 'sufficient bread.' But this formation is questionable. A similar dubiousness can be applied to the conjecture that it is derived from '*epi*' and '*ousia*', signifying '(bread) for sustenance.' The more probable derivation is from '*epi*' - 'upon', and '*eimi*' - 'to go' (bread) for going on, i.e. for the morrow and after, or '(bread) coming (for us) to be going on with'. History, in the form of an accounting papyrus, indicates that this last translation is correct. 'Daily' bread is that given for the needs of the day, whatever those needs may be. It is the resources advanced to us to meet the needs of the day at hand.

So, the petition reads: 'Accordingly, give us today everything we need to be going on with in doing your will for this day.' There is plenty to go around. This is in line with what Jesus was to go on to teach in Matthew 6:34 - 'Therefore do not worry about tomorrow, for tomorrow will worry about itself. Each day has enough trouble of its own.' And again in Matthew 6:32 - 'The pagans run after all these things, and your heavenly Father knows that you need them. But seek first his kingdom and his righteousness, and all these things will be given to you as well.' No child has to beg their father for their daily meals. Rather, parents often have to repeatedly ask their children to come and eat what has been prepared for them! This sad state of affairs - of people not wanting to receive from God - is also reflected in Matthew 22:23. 'The kingdom of heaven is like a king who prepared a wedding banquet for his son. He sent his servants to those who had been invited to the banquet to tell them to come, but they refused to come.' We are far more reluctant to expect and receive provision than our Father God is to give it. The prayer therefore can be rendered, 'Give us everything we need to be 'going on with' in doing the will of God.'

11:4a 'And forgive us our sins, for we ourselves also forgive everyone who is indebted to us.'

The idea of forgiveness is an important one to comprehend, not least because Jesus linked our willingness to exercise it with our being forgiven ourselves by God. Matthew's account of this teaching concludes with this salutary warning: 'For if you forgive others for their transgressions, your heavenly Father will also forgive you. But if you do not forgive others, then your Father will not forgive your transgressions' (Matthew 6:14-15).

The first 'sin' that we ask God's forgiveness for is our own *hamartia* - the areas where we have 'missed the mark' in terms of the behaviour God expects of us. The prayer then mentions forgiving others who are 'indebted' to us in terms of offenses or sins they have committed against us. This second word is *opheilô*, which is another accounting term for 'debts accrued' or to 'be indebted'. [136]

222

This 'forgiveness' of others is yet another accounting term, *'aphiemi'*, meaning to be let off the negative consequences of an omission in payment, or a debt. Those who 'sin against us' are our moral 'debtors' - still another accounting term.

The Septuagint (the Greek version of the Old Testament) uses *'aphiemi'* ('forgive/remit') in Deuteronomy 15 in relation to the Sabbath year and the release of legal debts. 'At the end of every seven years you shall grant a remission of debts. This is the manner of remission: every creditor shall release what he has loaned to his neighbour; he shall not exact it of his neighbour and his brother, because the Lord's remission has been proclaimed' (Deuteronomy 15:1-2).

This ability to forgive becomes possible through receiving God's own nature, as an adopted member of his family.

11:4b 'And lead us not into temptation.'

Thus translated, this particular prayer seems to make nonsense of what the New Testament teaches about God. Jesus was himself 'led' to a place of temptation, and he is our example in everything we do. God promises to use all things for our good: 'We know that in all things God works for the good of those who love him, who have been called according to his purpose' (Romans 8:28). Temptation and testing have a place in the plan of God to strengthen us. But Father God does not tempt anyone, as can be seen from James 3:14 - 'When tempted, no-one should say, "God is tempting me." For God cannot be tempted by evil, nor does he tempt anyone; but each one is tempted when, by his own evil desire, he is dragged away and enticed'.

The prayer is not saying that we should ask our Heavenly Father to not to do something that he cannot do, and which he promises to turn to our good when it does happen. Whereas the English reads, 'Lead us not into temptation', the preposition 'into' is duplicated in the Greek - 'do not into-bring us into temptation'. 'Into', in these cases, means a change for the person not merely of outward position, but of inward condition. 'To 'enter into' the Kingdom of God is much more than to stand within the Kingdom; it is to yield to its claims, to be dominated by it, to take its law as the law of one's being.' [137] The prayer is that we might not be brought 'into temptation', in the sense of into its power to change us so that we are mastered by it. And so the prayer asks our Father to ensure that sin's power in temptation does not cause that negative inner change.

11:5-8 'Then he said to them, "Suppose one of you has a friend, and goes to him at midnight and says to him, 'Friend, lend me three loaves; for a friend of mine has come to me from a journey, and I have nothing to set before him'; and from inside he answers and says, 'Do not bother me; the door has already been shut and my children and I are in bed; I cannot get up and give you anything.' I tell you, even though he will not get up and give him anything because he is his friend, yet because of his persistence he will get up and give him as much as he needs."'

Near-Eastern hospitality norms dictated the generous and welcoming reception of travellers, and all the more so in the case of friends and family. Times of arrival could not be anywhere near guaranteed, and usually avoided the heat of the day. The situation of a late arrival requiring a meal would have been a common one to Jesus' audience. Bread was baked in the morning for the needs of the day ahead. There would be a supply of flour from which a certain amount was taken for that day's baking requirements ('daily bread'). When the traveller arrives unexpectedly, there is no bread left to give him. And so the host turns to his neighbour.

Three loaves was sufficient bread for 6 people to eat at one meal. That is a large amount to be asking a neighbour for, especially at midnight! The point Jesus is making is that this was, in modern parlance, a 'big ask.' Why would the neighbour even have three loaves left over? 'Lend me three loaves' implies that the bread has already been made and not used (unlikely), or that the neighbour is being asked to make the bread (more likely and quite in keeping with the 'big ask' that the friend is making). And the 'ask' is made still bigger by the inconvenience of the time and circumstances. Families lived and slept in one room off the ground on a raised platform, and would often bring any animals inside with them. To get up to make bread would therefore be a major disturbance; it is not simply a case of handing over some bread from a larder and going back to bed!

Not unreasonably the friend demurs. Surely the neighbour's guest can wait until morning? But no, hospitality rules governed the society, and so the host knocks and keeps on knocking, as Jesus is about to tell his disciples to do in prayer (verse nine). By now the whole room is awake anyway, as also are the animals, and making bread will cause comparatively little further household disturbance.

Parables make a point, and the point of this one is that if a neighbour can be bothered enough to perform a 'big ask', then how much more readily will a loving Father of abundant resources help his children in their hour of need? The point is not that we need to 'twist God's arm' by means of our importunity ('perseverance') in prayer - quite the opposite! We need to come to him as his children in complete trust in his ability and willingness to provide for our needs. This does not mean that we should do so lightly or irreverently, but it does mean that our attitude should be a faith-filled confident expectation that our Father both wants and is more than able to provide abundantly for our every need, which he is in fact well aware of already. We may have to wait patiently for the answer, but we can be sure that it is coming and that it will be good.

11:9-10 'So I say to you, ask, and it will be given to you; seek, and you will find; knock, and it will be opened to you. For everyone who asks, receives; and he who seeks, finds; and to him who knocks, it will be opened.'

'So' links this saying to the parable before, indicating that the 'knocking, asking and seeking' are, like the host's bread, not one-off requests but ones that are continued, in keeping with the present tense and active voice of the Greek text. But knocking and keeping knocking does not at all imply that it is the act of persistence that causes God to open the door or grant the request. Rather, it is the confident active faith of the one who is asking, trusting in the inclination and ability of God to open and provide. We are not coming to a reluctant neighbour who must be forced into action in order to get rid of a nuisance caller. Rather, we are coming as a child to a loving and omnipotent heavenly Father.

11:11-13 '"Now suppose one of you fathers is asked by his son for a fish; he will not give him a snake instead of a fish, will he? Or if he is asked for an egg, he will not give him a scorpion, will he? If you then, being evil, know how to give good gifts to your children, how much more will your heavenly Father give the Holy Spirit to those who ask him?"'

Now Jesus arrives at the crux of the matter undergirding prayer. We are not, like the pagans, babbling vainly repetitious requests at an impotent imaginary and false deity. We are not seeking to win God around to our perspectives by impressive flowery religious language or by our ability to keep on asking the same thing over a long enough period of time. We are coming as blood-bought children, with genuine needs, to a heavenly Father who looks for an attitude of quiet, confident trust and expectant faith in his ability and willingness to meet those needs. Asking with any other attitude will only delay the answer being given, because 'without faith it is impossible to please God' (Hebrews 11:6).

Luke's account of this teaching contains a pair of items that Matthew 7:9 omits - an egg and a scorpion. Eggs were frequently prescribed to ill patients [138] and doctors such as Luke were often called upon to treat scorpion stings. [139] Thin fish look similar to small snakes, and pale desert scorpions, curled up to absorb less of the sun's heat, look similar to eggs. Human fathers, 'evil' in comparison to God because of their sinful natures, would not dream of inflicting such horrors on their needful children. 'How much more' then (i.e. immeasurably more!) does God desire to meet his children's every need, which are not always the same as their desires! God's very best gift of all is himself, dwelling in us by his Holy Spirit.

11:14 'And he was casting out a demon, and it was mute; when the demon had gone out, the mute man spoke; and the crowds were amazed.'

Expelling the unwanted intrusions of evil spirits from people's lives was nothing to the One whose word had created them long before the earth was formed. Demons evidently have the power to dictate and determine human behaviour. The demon in chapter 8 could provide supernatural strength to break chains, and the one in chapter 9 could hurl the boy into water and fire seeking to destroy him. This demon robbed the man of his ability to speak. These manifestations may accompany psychiatric illness, but are much more than the symptoms and signs associated with any such illness alone. And where such illnesses are present, they are not usually over with a single word of command, but take time to recover. Jesus is doing something very extraordinary such that the crowds are 'amazed' ('*thaumazô*' - 'to wonder at in admiration').* But not everyone in the crowd!

11:15-19 'But some of them said, "He casts out demons by Beelzebul, the ruler of the demons." Others, to test him, were demanding of him a sign from heaven. But he knew their thoughts and said to them, "Any kingdom divided against itself is laid waste; and a house divided against itself falls. If Satan also is divided against himself, how will his kingdom stand? For you say that I cast out demons by Beelzebul. And if I by Beelzebul cast out demons, by whom do your sons cast them out? So, they will be your judges."'

Such opponents of Jesus' ministry included the pharisaic religious lawyers, who in Mark 8:11 also ask Jesus for a 'sign from heaven', meaning 'from God' (whose name they would not utter). They wanted a sign performed in such a way as to make it clear that only God could be responsible and no other agency, such as 'Beelzebul'. This term for the ruler of demons is a Hebrew play-on-words around the name of a Philistine fertility god who was worshipped at Ekron. In the Hebrew, the rendering of its name '*Ba'al Zebûb*' ('lord of the flies' - hence standing for fertility) is humorously altered to mean the 'lord of the dung-heap' ('*Ba'al Zebûl*'). The humour is similar to the play-on words around the name Jezebel found in 2 Kings 9:37 in relation to the fate of Queen Jezebel's body (Je-zebel), which was eaten by dogs. 'Jezebel's body will be like dung on the ground in the plot at Jezreel.'

The Pharisees' 'thoughts' ('*dianoêma*') is another New Testament word unique to Doctor Luke (the parallel account in Matthew 12:25 has '*enthumêsis*', meaning 'deliberations'). [140] '*Dianoêma*' is a Greek medical term for the illogical and fanciful ideas of the sick. [141] Jesus countered the Pharisees' absurd thinking using two brilliant pieces of rabbinic reasoning, which they had no answer to. The 'dividing of a kingdom' is a theme found in Daniel chapter 11, and seen as having fulfilment in the (then relatively recent) breakdown of

Seleucid rule in Israel. Daniel 11:4: 'His kingdom will be broken up and parcelled out toward the four points of the compass, though not to his own descendants, nor according to his authority which he wielded, for his sovereignty will be uprooted and given to others besides them.' Any kingdom fighting against itself is finished as a recognisable entity. Clearly demons are still at work in many ways - their kingdom is therefore by no means yet finished. Therefore, the logic of the rabbinic argument concludes that Jesus cannot be using that kingdom's powers. And there was a second, more personal argument to be made. Jews did themselves attempt exorcism, as can be seen from Josephus' description of Solomon and the skills he passed down to Josephus' day. 'God also enabled him *[Solomon]* to learn that skill which expels demons, which is a science useful and sanative to men. He composed such incantations also by which distempers are alleviated. And he left behind him the manner of using exorcisms, by which they drive away demons, so that they never return; and this method of cure is of great force unto this day; for I have seen a certain man of my own country, whose name was Eleazar, releasing people that were demoniacal in the presence of Vespasian *[the Roman commander]*, and his sons, and his captains, and the whole multitude of his soldiers' (Josephus, 'Antiquities' 8, 2). Evidence of contemporary exorcism can also be seen in Acts 9:13. 'Some of the Jewish exorcists, who went from place to place, attempted to name over those who had the evil spirits the name of the Lord Jesus, saying, "I adjure you by Jesus whom Paul preaches."' So then, were those Jews serving Beelzebul too? Let them be the judge of what the Pharisees have slanderously said.

11:20-22 '"But if I cast out demons by the finger of God, then the kingdom of God has come upon you. When a strong man, fully armed, guards his own house, his possessions are undisturbed. But when someone stronger than he attacks him and overpowers him, he takes away

from him all his armour on which he had relied and distributes his plunder."'

'The finger of God' is the term used by Pharaoh's magicians for acts that only God could perform (Exodus 8:19). The truth of these two pieces of legal reasoning being undisputable, the Pharisees should acknowledge not just Jesus' ushering in of God's kingdom but also that ministry of Jesus' fore-runner, John the Baptist. But while the tax collectors and prostitutes did acknowledge this kingdom, the more learned Pharisees often did not. 'John came to you in the way of righteousness and you did not believe him; but the tax collectors and prostitutes did believe him' (Matthew 21:32).

Jesus then uses a third piece of rabbinic logic. A 'strong man' is actually '*ischuros*', simply meaning 'strong' in a 'violent' sense.* 'Man' is an interpolation, and its addition unhelpfully distorts Jesus' meaning, which is a direct continuation from his previous saying concerning Beelzebul. '*Ischuros*' occurs four times in Revelation in connection with angelic powers. While it has other New Testament applications concerning strength, it is linked here to Satan's rule and strength over that which he considers to be his, but is in fact stolen from the original owner, the Maker of all things. Such stolen goods will be recovered when someone mightier than him arrives, someone more than able to strip him of all his armour, leaving him defenseless and powerless to prevent his stolen goods being distributed as 'spoils' to those for whom they had actually been intended. Jesus was plundering the devil's kingdom.

11:23 '"He who is not with me is against me; and he who does not gather with me, scatters."'

This proverbial saying applied to those like many of the Pharisees who opposed Jesus' ministry out of a sense of religious offence. They had a choice to make. Would they recognise and embrace the signs of God's kingdom on earth or would they retreat into religious legalism and remain blind to Jesus' identity as their long-awaited Messiah?

11:24-26 '"When the unclean spirit goes out of a man, it passes through waterless places seeking rest, and not finding any, it says, 'I will return to my house from which I came.' And when it comes, it finds it swept and put in order. Then it goes and takes along seven other spirits more evil than itself, and they go in and live there; and the last state of that man becomes worse than the first."'

Jesus concludes his very practical teaching about the activity of the demonic with an illustration. Today many deny the existence of demons (surely a great benefit to their workings!), but they were well recognised by Jesus' audience. It is no use evicting an undesirable and illegal 'squatter' from someone's 'house' (*'oikos'* - 'home'), if nothing is done to prevent squatters re-occupying the building afterwards. The best deterrent to such illegal occupation is the presence of another, rightful, occupant. The human heart has been designed by God to be occupied by someone - God himself. But God will always wait to be invited, unlike an 'unclean' spirit, (*'akarthos'* - the negative form of *'kathairô'*, a word used by Jesus in John 15:2 to describe tree pruning, and denotes the 'clean' state of worshippers in Hebrews 10:2). Evil spirits do not wait for permission to invade someone's life. They will pounce on any opportunity; any sin or opening that affords them a 'foothold' in someone's life. [xvii]

Useless shoots growing from a tree do the tree no good and provide an opportunity for parasites to become attached. The same is true of

---

[xvii] 'Do not let the sun go down while you are still angry, and do not give the devil a foothold' (Ephesians 4:26-27, NIV).

human life. When an evil spirit is evicted, God must fill the void that is left. It is no use having a cleanly swept and 'tidy' house (*'kosmeô'*, meaning 'ordered', from *'kosmos'* - 'order'), if it is left empty and defenseless to re-entry by the same crowd of squatters. The entry points need to be rectified through repentance and the house filled with the light of a new occupant, the Holy Spirit, who can effectively close the gaps and defend the property.

11:27-28 'While Jesus was saying these things, one of the women in the crowd raised her voice and said to him, "Blessed is the womb that bore you and the breasts at which you nursed." But he said, "On the contrary, blessed are those who hear the word of God and observe it."'

Surely more evidence of input from Mary. This is exactly the sort of remark that a Hebrew mother in the crowd, filled with wonder and emotion at Jesus' sublime teaching, would make, and exactly the sort of remark that Jesus' own mother would remember. The other Gospels, into which Mary presumably had less input, do not include this saying. Matthew 12:43-45 and Mark 3:23-27 describes Jesus' family arriving at the packed Capernaum house of ministry, when Jesus similarly pointed the audience to the higher value of hearing and obeying the word of God - 'Come and hear' being the typical rabbinic introduction to Torah teaching. 'Jesus remarked, 'Who is my mother and who are my brothers?" And stretching out his hand toward his disciples, he said, "Behold my mother and my brothers! For whoever does the will of my Father who is in heaven, he is my brother and sister and mother."' Jesus undoubtedly gave his teachings on more than one occasion (e.g. the similar content to the Sermon on the Mount and the Sermon on the Plain), and his teaching on evil spirits, figuring here, may have prompted Mary's recollection of this saying from the other mother in the crowd. Jesus corrects the input with heaven's perspective - hearing and doing are the attributes of faith, whereby God's word is heard and so faith is generated.

('Faith comes from hearing *['akoe' - 'the thing heard']*, and hearing by the word of Christ' - Romans 10:17.) Faith is evidenced by active obedience to the word that is heard - an obedience that continues to place its trust in God rather than in self.

11:29-30 'As the crowds were increasing, he began to say, "This generation is a wicked generation; it seeks for a sign, and yet no sign will be given to it but the sign of Jonah. For just as Jonah became a sign to the Ninevites, so will the Son of Man be to this generation."'

Matthew's account (12:39-41) connects this teaching with an unwelcome request from a group of unbelieving Pharisees for a sign, despite Jesus' many signs and miraculous confirmations of his identity as Messiah. Jesus appeals to the 'sign of Jonah'. How was Jonah a sign? He appeared to the Ninevites first of all covered in whale vomit. It would have been hard to rely on your own genius with seaweed particles coating you from head to foot, and yet the men of Nineveh had, against his expectation, turned to God. Why?

Jonah had, in fact, died. Jonah 2:2: 'From the depths of Sheol I called for help, and you listened to my cry.' Sheol is the Hebrew's unseen place of the dead, which Jonah had visited, after he had sunk to the bottom of the sea. He tells us, in Jonah 2:6, 'To the roots of the mountains I sank down.'

The problem at depth is not simply the water pressure on the body itself. At around 350 feet, without any sort of protection from the water pressure or any intake of pressurised air, the relative pressures of oxygen and nitrogen in the blood reach dangerously high levels, transforming them from life-essential elements to something acutely toxic. Under a high pressure in the blood-stream, oxygen becomes poisonous and unusable to human cells, and they die.

As Jonah was dying of drowning, the Scripture tells us, 'He remembered the Lord, and his prayer came to him in his holy Temple' (Jonah 2:7). The Lord heard Jonah and commanded a whale that swallowed the (then dead) body of Jonah. Whale's stomachs, though large, will not accommodate a living moving human being. It was when Jonah was raised back to life, and so began to move, that the whale vomited him out, presumably in sight of some who reported this miracle to the inhabitants of Nineveh. Either God did a miracle in preserving Jonah's life at such pressures as the seabed (at least 1500 meters down beneath the Mediterranean Sea to the roots of the mountains - verse 6), or he did a miracle in raising him from the dead. Jesus indicates it was the second (rising from the dead), by comparing Jonah to himself, although as a very human prophet, Jonah fell far short of him. Jesus spent part of Good Friday, all of Easter Saturday and a part of Easter Sunday morning with his physical body in the tomb of Joseph of Arimathea (Matthew 27:59-60) - three parts of days, being in Hebrew thought and use three 'days'. He was then bodily resurrected after having proclaimed his victory (1 Peter 4:6) in the unseen place of the dead, where Jonah had been. The sign of Jonah is therefore the sign of the resurrection.

11:31 '"The Queen of the South will rise up with the men of this generation at the judgment and condemn them, because she came from the ends of the earth to hear the wisdom of Solomon; and behold, something greater than Solomon is here."'

The 'Queen of the South' is the Queen of Sheba (1 Kings 10:1). In Israel, they well understood the significance of this person. This Gentile woman had come to Jerusalem from Sheba, an empire comprising present-day Ethiopia and Yemen, 'south' of Judea. She had come full of herself, her own riches (with 4.5 tons of gold), and with questions and ideas, but had gone away converted to the God of Israel. It was one of the great moments in Israel's nation's history.

Jesus' Jewish audience longed to see those days again, to be rid of the Romans and be 'top nation' again, just as their prophets said would happen. 'Then the survivors from all the nations that have attacked Jerusalem will go up year after year to worship the King, the Lord Almighty, and to celebrate the Feast of Tabernacles' (Zechariah 14:16). If Gentiles, like the Queen of Sheba, could see something special, from God and respond to it, why couldn't the Jewish rulers? Was it their pride in being leaders of the nation that God had chosen? Was it their reliance on the Law, substituting human regulations for divine principles, which blinded them so much that many of them did not recognise who Jesus was? Or both?

11:32 '"The men of Nineveh will stand up with this generation at the judgment and condemn it, because they repented at the preaching of Jonah; and behold, something greater than Jonah is here."'

Jesus again uses a rabbinic argument for judgement. If Gentiles without the Torah could receive the word of such a reluctant prophet as Jonah, then how much more, by comparison, should well-informed Jews receive the word of a '*Didaskalos*' ('Doctor' - of Torah) like Jesus, and one whose miraculous signs clearly pointed to a greater status even than that?

11:33 '"No one after lighting a lamp puts it away in a cellar nor under a basket, but on the lampstand, so that those who enter may see the light."'

This is another of Jesus' very humourous teaching illustrations. Not only was light very valuable for life after sunset, but the oil lamps Jesus was referring to were dangerous sources of fire if handled incorrectly. Mark's account (Mark 4:21) includes Jesus talking about putting such a lamp under a dry matting 'bed', and the 'basket' too is a reed-bound implement used for measuring dry weights. The idea of

235

setting fire to your house by behaving in such a ridiculous way would have been quite hilarious to Jesus' local audience, who would have grasped the consequences immediately. Such light sources were placed safely in an elevated position for maximum illumination as well as for safety.

11:34-36 '"The eye is the lamp of your body. When your eye is clear, your whole body also is full of light; but when it is bad, your body also is full of darkness. Then watch out that the light in you is not darkness. If therefore your whole body is full of light, with no dark part in it, it will be wholly illumined, as when the lamp illumines you with its rays."'

There is yet more humour here, with a typically rabbinic play-on-words around light and generosity. The word for 'good' is '*haplous*', or '*haplotes*' in the noun form.* This has two meanings, firstly 'single' (in the sense of a 'singleness of purpose', for example, in performing acts of goodness) and secondly 'generous'. Jesus employs an amusing play-on-words to connect the idea that the generosity meant by a 'good eye' reflects the attitude of generosity of God the Father, and results in the spiritual blessing of inner light, if done with the right motives. A 'bad eye' was proverbial for meanness. The pun is concluded with a further humourous flourish - if the light-giver (in this instance, a generous attitude) is giving out darkness (because it is not working properly), how great is that person's (moral and spiritual) darkness! Light dispels darkness; the inner light that the Holy Spirit brings exposes that which is not of God in us. And the idea of a lamp that actually produced darkness is a further example of Jesus' creative sense of humour and his use of it in his teaching.

11:37-38 '"Now when he had spoken, a Pharisee asked him to have lunch with him; and he went in, and reclined

at the table. When the Pharisee saw it, he was surprised that he had not first ceremonially washed before the meal."'

Jesus' formal legal standing as a '***Didaskalos***' ('Doctor' of Torah, as he is addressed in verse 45) meant that he enjoyed many social privileges (such as Temple teaching) not available to uneducated men (such as most of his disciples). Peter and John were arrested for being deemed to have been teaching in the Temple in Acts 4:1-3. 'As they were speaking to the people, the priests and the captain of the temple guard and the Sadducees came up to them, being greatly disturbed because they were teaching the people and proclaiming in Jesus the resurrection from the dead. And they laid hands on them and put them in jail until the next day, for it was already evening.' To be invited to eat ('recline' as in the Roman manner) by one of the legal scholars was one such honour, one that Jesus was repeatedly afforded, despite many of them by this point having become his sworn enemies. As a senior legal scholar himself, Jesus was well acquainted with rabbinic Oral Torah, which ruled that there was a carefully prescribed pattern of hand washing to be followed prior to eating (which the water jars at the wedding in Cana *[John 2:6]* were there to provide for). Yet Jesus does not follow it, presumably partly because it was not one of God's commandments in the Jewish Scripture, and possibly partly because he was seeking a reaction from his host that would lead to a discussion about God's requirements as opposed to men's. Pharisees were highly educated too, but the rank of '***Didaskalos***' was a select one afforded only to senior, more advanced and able scholars.

11:39-41 'But the Lord said to him, "Now you Pharisees clean the outside of the cup and of the platter; but inside of you, you are full of robbery and wickedness. You foolish ones, did not he who made the outside make the inside

also? But give that which is within as charity, and then all things are clean for you."'

Again, Jesus is using a rabbinic legal style of argument. Which was more important when it comes to cleanliness - the inside of a cup (or dish) or the outside? Is it the upper surface of a plate that you need to be clean or the underneath? Clearly the inside and the upper surface. Similarly God views the inside of a person (the heart) as more important than the outside. In fact God has made both, but an ostensible 'clean' exterior is of no value to him if the inside is replete with 'robbery' ('*harpagê*' - 'extortion' of material goods) and 'wickedness' ('*ponêria*' - 'iniquity and malice').* God's intention is that we give away 'that which is within' (of what he has given us). Alms giving was held by the Jews to be one of the three main signs of 'righteousness', along with prayer and fasting. As Psalm 112:9 says of the righteous, 'He has given freely to the poor, his righteousness endures forever; his horn will be exalted in honour.' The inter-testamental Jewish book of Tobit said, 'It is better to give alms than to lay up gold; almsgiving delivers from death, and it purges away all sin.' The Talmud records 'There are four types of character in respect of almsgiving. 1) He who desires that he himself should give, but that others should not give: his eye is evil towards that which appertains to others; 2) He who desires that others should give, but that they he himself should not give: his eye is evil towards that which is their own; 3) He who desires that he himself should give, and that others should give: he is a pious man; 4) He who desires that he himself should not give and that others too should not give: he is a wicked man.' [142] If the Pharisee was to give away his ill-gotten gains to the poor, he would, like Zacchaeus (Luke 19:8), be showing proper remorse for his sins. The light of God, with his cooperation, would clean him from the inside out.

11:42 '"But woe to you Pharisees! For you pay tithe of mint and rue and every kind of garden herb, and yet

238

disregard justice and the love of God; but these are the things you should have done without neglecting the others."'

Having dealt with almsgiving, Jesus tackles the connected topic of tithing. The Law commanded that 'All the tithe of the land, of the seed of the land or of the fruit of the tree, is the Lord's; it is holy to the Lord' (Leviticus 27:30). This was paid directly to the tribe of Levi, who, in turn, paid a tithe of what they received to the priests - one-tenth of everything that could be used as food, was cultivated and grows out of the earth, as the Law taught. [143] Jesus is not dismissing tithing as legalism; rather he upholds it as 'things you should have done', being Scriptural. But there were even more important things in Scripture, such as justice and love of God, and tithing without those essentials being present simply rendered the tithe offensive to God, who had spoken through the prophet Micah. Micah 6:8: 'He has told you, O man, what is good; and what does the Lord require of you, but to do justice, to love kindness, and to walk humbly with your God?' Justice and mercy are examples of the 'things they should have done', and need first place in our lives.

11:43-44 '"Woe to you Pharisees! For you love the chief seats in the synagogues and the respectful greetings in the market places. Woe to you! For you are like concealed tombs, and the people who walk over them are unaware of it."'

The Pharisees were a powerful group of Jewish religious scholars who dedicated themselves to teaching and upholding the Law, and particularly the Oral Torah. They were a mixed group of people, and Jewish rabbinic texts [144] distinguished seven different types of Pharisee:

(a) The 'Shoulder' Pharisee, who placed signs of his piety on his shoulders in order that everyone could see them.

(b) The 'Wait-a-little' Pharisee, who always found excuse for putting off a good deed.

(c) The 'Bruised' Pharisee, who wanted to avoid looking at women in the street, and so shut their eyes and would bump into walls and buildings bruising themselves.

(d) The 'Hump-backed' Pharisee who walked bent double in ostentatious humility.

(e) The 'Ever-reckoning' Pharisee who kept count of his good deeds in a kind of heavenly balance sheet.

(f) The 'Fearful' Pharisee, who lived in dread of divine punishment.

(g) Finally, there was the 'God-loving' Pharisee; who truly loved God and delighted in God's Law.

It is the first 6 types that Jesus is taking issue with. The seventh type represented men like Nicodemus, whom Jesus discourses with in true rabbinic fashion in John chapter 3. 'Woe' (*'ouai'*) means 'alas',* - Jesus is pronouncing a Jewish lament over them, in six 'woes' concerning their underlying wrong attitudes. These were: 1) to tithing, 2) to prestige, 3) to their inner condition, 4) to giving others burdens, 5) to not renouncing their father's sins and 6) to not entering God's kingdom and hindering others who wished to. The synagogue had special seats of honour, at the front of the congregation and facing backwards. These were ideal for those wishing to adopt and show-off a particularly pious expression. Matthew 6:5 recounts Jesus saying that these men would stand on street corners and pray long prayers, in order to be seen by others; this desire for attention was also present in the market-place.

One of the scourges of Jewish religious life was unmarked graves. The Law held that to come within a prescribed distance (around 6 feet) of a grave rendered one ceremonially and religiously 'unclean' - but what if the grave was unseen and unmarked? The Pharisees lived in fear that they may have unwittingly made themselves

240

unclean and so somehow have offended God. Because of this, tombs were often marked out with whitewash (Matthew 23:27), to warn passers-by of their presence. To be described as a 'concealed tomb' was a severe judgement indeed, even worse than a 'white-washed tombs' - they at least could be clearly seen and were a warning to others to keep away from the death and uncleanness within.

11:45-46 'One of the lawyers said to him in reply, "Teacher, when you say this, you insult us too." But he said, "Woe to you lawyers as well! For you weigh men down with burdens hard to bear, while you yourselves will not even touch the burdens with one of your fingers."'

This pharisaic religious lawyer really should have stayed out of it! He was never going to win a legal argument with someone as insightful and skilled in Torah as the 'Teacher' ('*Didaskalos*') from Nazareth. Among the religious lawyers were Pharisees of type b) above, who were legalistically harsh with others, while employing pious sounding legal excuses for avoiding the demands of the Law themselves. 'Burden' is '*phortion*', the word used for loading up a ship' with the maximum amount of cargo it can carry. [145]

11:47-48 '"Woe to you! For you build the tombs of the prophets, and it was your fathers who killed them. So you are witnesses and approve the deeds of your fathers; because it was they who killed them, and you build their tombs."'

The wrong-attitude of the Pharisees spilled over to contaminate in God's eyes even the 'good deed' of honouring a prophet. All the 'righteous acts' of sinful people are as the 'filthy rag' (Isaiah 64:6) of a menstrual-cloth in the sight of a holy God. Truly they were still unchanged within, like their fathers before them who had committed the murders.

11:49-51 '"For this reason also the wisdom of God said, 'I will send to them prophets and apostles, and some of them they will kill and some they will persecute, so that the blood of all the prophets, shed since the foundation of the world, may be charged against this generation, from the blood of Abel to the blood of Zechariah, who was killed between the altar and the house of God; yes, I tell you, it shall be charged against this generation.'"'

1 Corinthians 1:24 identifies Jesus as 'the wisdom of God', and the pre-incarnate Son of God would certainly have participated in his Father's plans to send prophetic witnesses to his wayward people. The '*apostolos*' were God's messengers, some of which 'the wisdom of God' had already sent out on mission to the villages of Judea. Like the prophets before them, death would follow all of Jesus' apostles except John. Persistent rejection of God's messengers had been the theme in Israel; with the up-coming rejection of Messiah the time would be right for God's final judgement in the form of a destroying Roman army under Vespasian in 66-70 AD. The generation of rabbinic scholars that Jesus was dining with would live to see Jerusalem and the Temple laid waste in a dreadful manner. Abel had been slain by his jealous brother Cain; Zechariah by the court of Joash. 2 Chronicles 24:20-22: 'Then the Spirit of God came on Zechariah the son of Jehoiada the priest; and he stood above the people and said to them, "Thus God has said, 'Why do you transgress the commandments of the Lord and do not prosper? Because you have forsaken the Lord, he has also forsaken you.'" So they conspired against him and at the command of the king they stoned him to death in the court of the house of the Lord. Thus Joash the king did not remember the kindness that his father Jehoiada had shown him, but he murdered his son. And as he died he said, "May the Lord see and avenge!"' The Lord had seen, and now, hundreds of years later, God's patience was about to run out. The time for judgement was approaching fast.

11:52 '"Woe to you lawyers! For you have taken away the key of knowledge; you yourselves did not enter, and you hindered those who were entering."'

The final cry of lament is for the lawyers and all those who their behaviour had obstructed. Rather than make God's Law accessible and a source of spiritual life to the people they were supposed to be helping, they ring-fenced the Law with so many man-made commandments that obeying the Law had become a full-time business, which many ordinary Jews, more concerned with simply surviving, were not able to keep. So they were dismissed and despised as 'sinners' - those who 'missed the mark' in relation to the Oral Torah. The Talmud (Tractate '*Avoth*' 1, Mishnah 1) records, 'The men of the Great Synagogue used to say three things: be patient in the administration of justice, rear many disciples and make a fence round the Torah.' The men who had built the fence and then secured it with the 'key' of Torah had used it to lock themselves, and others, out of the kingdom.

11:53-54 'When he left there, the scribes and the Pharisees began to be very hostile and to question him closely on many subjects, plotting against him to catch him in something he might say.'

Jesus was gradually pressing the issues that would get him killed. As his ministry went on, he drew the authorities' fire with matters such as his co-equality with God and his right to forgive the sins of others not committed against him personally, both of which inevitably drew the capital charge of blasphemy. And now he was exposing the sin of the men whose judicial authority gave them the right to pursue him with such a charge to its inevitable legal conclusion. Legal challenges were coming that would lead to Calvary.

Chapter 12

12:1 'Under these circumstances, after so many thousands of people had gathered together that they were stepping on one another, he began saying to his disciples first of all, "Beware of the leaven of the Pharisees, which is hypocrisy."'

Vast numbers of people were drawn to Jesus' public ministry, both because of the unprecedented access to the Temple-level Torah teaching that he gave and also because of the miracles that he so readily performed. Such crowds 'stepping on each other' made the access of a group of mothers and newborn infants to Jesus (Luke 18:15) especially difficult, and so interesting to consider.

By 'leaven' Jesus is referring to the teaching of the Pharisees (Matthew 16:12), much of which was not supported by their own actions. 'Hypocrisy' is '*hupokrisis*', meaning 'play-acting' [146] from '*hupokrinomai*', meaning 'to feign or pretend'.* Many of the Pharisees evidently wore their religion like an actor's mask, hiding their unredeemed and sinful natures behind an external religious show, a kind of pretence that may have fooled the ordinary people by false piety, but which made no impression on the God who can see into the hearts of men.

12:2-3 '"But there is nothing covered up that will not be revealed, and hidden that will not be known. Accordingly, whatever you have said in the dark will be heard in the light, and what you have whispered in the inner rooms will be proclaimed upon the housetops."'

Matthew's account (Matthew 10:26-27) of this saying is: 'Do not be afraid of them. There is nothing concealed that will not be disclosed, or hidden that will not be made known. What I tell you in the dark, speak in the daylight; what is whispered in your ear, proclaim from the roofs.' Jesus' ministry as the incarnate second Person of the triune God was at that point hidden. Only on very private occasions such as on the Mount of Transfiguration (Matthew 17:2) had it been manifested. Jesus' divinity was 'covered' by his humanity, and while it was a very remarkable type of humanity (a Doctor of Torah who performed miracles), the majority of the populace of Judea were unaware that he was actually God incarnate. When his claims in that direction became clearer, that would be enough to get him killed. Previously his disciples had murmured, 'Who is this that even the winds and waves obey him?'(Mark 4:40 and had doubtless had carried on such discussions among themselves well into the night ('the dark'). But a time was coming when they would openly proclaim his identity. 'Inner rooms' were private places, a room within a room. Single room houses would sometimes have a storage-chamber within them - no better place to conduct a private conversation beyond the ears of those outside the house, and a great contrast to '*kêrussô*' - 'to herald' * the news from that very house's flat roof.

12:4 '"I say to you, my friends, do not be afraid of those who kill the body and after that have no more that they can do."'

The disciples might well have felt intimidated by the thought of announcing such controversial news as God become man in the presence of their religious society's leading actors. They would be all too familiar with the practice of summary execution by stoning for perceived blasphemy, and other violence that had already been Jesus' experience (Luke 4:9). But the human spirit is an eternal entity that will only inhabit the shell of the body for around one hundred years at most. An early entry into the kingdom of heaven should not necessarily be viewed as a bad thing, especially if it is by the Father's design with the consequential reward of a martyr's

245

crown. 'Friends' is *philos*, a tender word meaning 'beloved and dear'. [147] It is used by Jesus in John 3:29 about 'The friend of the bridegroom who stands and hears him, who rejoices greatly because of the bridegroom's voice.' The disciples were those who 'stood and heard' the voice of the bridegroom in daily life. They would hear it too in heaven having been martyred, with the exception of John who was exiled to Patmos.

12:5 '"But I will warn you whom to fear: fear the One who after he has killed, has authority to cast into hell; yes, I tell you, fear him!"'

Fear of the Pharisees could be channelled onto a healthier form - fear of God who had given them life and who could at any moment take it away. No one knows the hour of their death, which whether by natural or violent causes will bring them into the presence of the Judge against whose righteous sentences there is no right of appeal. Jesus taught more about hell than any other single topic; he did not want mankind, made in God's image, to spend eternity in the place created for the devil. 'Hell' is 'Gehenna', the deep ravine of Hinnom, just south of Jerusalem, where the rubbish and dead animals of the city were thrown and burned. A fire burned at the base, continually being re-fuelled by the steady supply of waste from the city. The term features in the Talmudic tracts, with the rabbis holding that even a problem with controlling one's temper could lead there. [148]

12:6-7 '"Are not five sparrows sold for two cents? Yet not one of them is forgotten before God. Indeed, the very hairs of your head are all numbered. Do not fear; you are more valuable than many sparrows."'

Sparrows were not hugely valuable components of the Judean economy. Matthew records that two cost one cent (an *assarion* - a small copper coin, worth one-tenth of a drachma - Matthew 10:29) - buy four and an extra was thrown in for free. Yet each was known by God. The God who takes time to feed the birds that he has made (verse 24 and Matthew 6:26) is actually far more concerned for the wellbeing of his children, even to the point of counting their hairs. Few human parents go to that length over their children!

12:8-9 '"And I say to you, everyone who confesses me before men, the Son of Man will confess him also before the angels of God; but he who denies me before men will be denied before the angels of God."'

The time was coming when such confession would indeed lead to a martyr's crown. Saul of Tarsus was so incensed by Jesus' perceived betrayal of their blasphemy laws, aggravated further by Jesus' senior academic position, that he pursued the Jewish believers (over whom he and the rest of the Sanhedrin had legal jurisdiction) to their deaths. As Paul would later say in Acts 26:10, 'This is just what I did in Jerusalem; not only did I lock up many of the saints in prisons having received authority from the chief priests, but also when they were being put to death I cast my vote against them.' 'Deny' (*'arneomai'*) means to 'refuse and reject something offered',* in this case Jesus himself and his help in time of need. The denial that this will provoke 'before' ('in the presence of') the angels (i.e. in heaven) is *'aparneomai'*, meaning 'to affirm that one has no acquaintance or connection with someone'.* Rejecting Jesus' help on earth unfortunately leaves one without any help in the courts of heaven.

12:10 '"And everyone who speaks a word against the Son of Man, it will be forgiven him; but he who blasphemes against the Holy Spirit, it will not be forgiven him."'

To 'speak against' is a very similar concept to 'slander', a common New Testament word generally denoted by the noun '*blasphêmia*', the verb form of which, '*blasphêmeô*', is used by Jesus here to refer to a particular sin against the Holy Spirit. This is equivalent to the 'sin that leads to death' of 1 John 5:16: 'If anyone sees his brother committing a sin that does not lead to death, he shall ask and God will give him life.' 1 John 2:2, however, indicates that Christ's sacrifice is for the sin (without distinction) of the whole world. [xviii] So it is the particular role of the Holy Spirit that must be looked at to understand this 'unforgivable' sin. The Spirit, Jesus tells us in John 16:8-11, 'Will convict the world concerning sin and righteousness and judgement; concerning sin, because they do not believe in me; and concerning righteousness, because I go to the Father and you no longer see me; and concerning judgement, because the ruler of this world has been judged.'

The Spirit's role is central to the preparatory work of bringing someone to salvation - convincing them of their condition of indifference or rebellion to God and their need to receive his gift of righteousness and hence avoid judgement. But that role can be resisted and refused, and to do so may involve subtle resistance ('speaking against') or even violent rejection (by 'evil speaking' or 'blasphemy'). If the person concerned persists in this, they place themselves outside the grace of repentance, and hence salvation, and so never receive forgiveness. Believers therefore can only come into this category by an active and willful rejection of their salvation, which their free will entitles them to do but is extremely rare. For them the Scripture of Hebrews 6:4-6 applies: 'For in the case of those who have once been enlightened and have tasted of the heavenly gift and have been made partakers of the Holy Spirit, and

---

[xviii] 'He himself is the propitiation for our sins; and not for ours only, but also for those of the whole world' (1 John 2:1-2).

have tasted the good word of God and the powers of the age to come, and then have fallen away, it is impossible to renew them again to repentance, since they again crucify to themselves the Son of God and put him to open shame.'

12:11-12 '"When they bring you before the synagogues and the rulers and the authorities, do not worry about how or what you are to speak in your defence, or what you are to say; for the Holy Spirit will teach you in that very hour what you ought to say."'

Jesus foresees the militant persecution that men such as his future disciple the Apostle Paul would wreak upon the fledgling Judean church, and also to the wider Gentile persecution under Nero and beyond. The disciples have no need to worry if they bring the disposition of quiet trust and total dependency that is at the heart of active faith into the situation. God will be sure not to leave you without an advocate. The same Holy Spirit that the persecutors reject will *'didasko'* you - 'hold discourse with you that you may instruct them'.* Reliance on the Father's controlling hand is key to avoidance of the anxiety and fear that so often undermines faith.

12:13-14 'Someone in the crowd said to him, "Teacher, tell my brother to divide the family inheritance with me." But he said to him, "Man, who appointed me a judge or arbitrator over you?"'

'Teacher' here is, once again, *'Didaskalos'* - 'Doctor', and the context is Torah inheritance Law. In Judean society, the firstborn received a double portion (Deuteronomy 21:17) of the estate on the death of the father. In practice this frequently led to squabbles about the material value apportioned to land and other items within the estate, especially if its value had increased following the death but before the division. In such cases, it was common to go before a court consisting of three judges who would decide the division of assets. Jesus is being appealed to here in the context of his formal role of interpreting Torah within Jewish legal society, and his ability to apply legal judgements. Without this status the man's request was largely pointless, because his brother would have been under no legal obligation to accept Jesus' ruling.

Jesus does not take issue with his legal standing in the man's sight, rather he accepts the premise on which the request is made - that he was indeed legally authorised to make a judgement. What Jesus takes issue with is a perceived covetousness in the man and also the legal need to be appointed by a court with the consent of the other brother. Jesus is not saying that he is not legally qualified; he is saying that he has not been appointed to that task. '*Meristês*' is a legal arbitrator, [149] someone appointed by a court to value assets and rule about their rightful division in the context of an inheritance dispute. Jesus had rightful legal authority as a Rabbi and '*Didaskalos*', which the man recognised, but he declined to interfere on behalf of someone without due legal process taking place, and especially when covetousness was rearing its ugly head.

12:15 'Then he said to them, "Beware and be on your guard against every form of greed; for not even when one has an abundance does his life consist of his possessions."'

Jesus seizes the opportunity to teach on covetousness (of 'every kind'). That it was serious can be seen by the double injunction - 'beware' ('*horaô*') - 'to attend to visually', [150] and so 'be on guard' ('*phulassô*') - 'to keep watch'* are very similar in meaning. Greed is a human trait that can lay dormant for years and then come back to bite us. Life is about a lot more than material things, because with them comes worries and the potential to be dominated by desire for still more, as Jesus had taught in chapter 6 verse 24 - 'Woe to the rich'. We can possess our possessions for God's use or they can 'possess' us.

12:16-21 'And he told them a parable, saying, "The land of a rich man was very productive. And he began reasoning to himself, saying, "What shall I do, since I have no place to store my crops?" Then he said, "This is what I will do: I will tear down my barns and build larger ones, and there I will store all my grain and my goods. And I will say to my soul, "Soul, you have many goods laid up for many years to come; take your ease, eat, drink and be merry." But God said to him, "You fool! This very night your soul is required of you; and now who will own what you have prepared?" So is the man who stores up treasure for himself, and is not rich toward God."'

This parable is very similar to the Jewish wisdom teaching in the apocryphal book of Sirach. 'There is one that waxes rich by his wariness and pinching, and this is the portion of his reward: Whereas he says, "I have found rest, and now will eat continually of my goods; and yet he knows not what time shall come upon him, and that he must leave those things to others, and die"' (Sirach 11:18-19). An abundance of possessions may make life easier, or the worries associated with managing them amidst the envy of others may make it worse. Undue worry shortens life rather than lengthening it. Not for nothing does the word 'miser' come from the word 'miserable'! If what we possess is to be kept from possessing us, it must be left at the disposal of the One who gave it in the first place, for his use and our enjoyment in sharing. Being 'rich toward God' involves 'storing up for oneself treasure in heaven' (Matthew 6:20) where it will bring eternal glory to God.

12:22-23 'And he said to his disciples, "For this reason I say to you, do not worry about your life, as to what you

will eat; nor for your body, as to what you will put on. For life is more than food, and the body more than clothing.'"

Worry and anxiety betray an underlying lack of trust in God's care as Father. If we genuinely believe that God is more committed to providing for his children's basic needs than even the best earthly father, then we will have no trouble being at peace in the knowledge that he is in control. All we need to do is to behave responsibly (e.g. not jumping off temples, as Satan had tempted Christ to do) and trust that he will give us all we need to live in his kingdom service. Jesus points to the spiritual values that give life in this age meaning and provide a reward in the age to come.

12:24 '"Consider the ravens, for they neither sow nor reap; they have no storeroom or barn, and yet God feeds them; how much more valuable you are than the birds!"'

Ravens seem to have no problem with stress and anxiety. Jesus reveals the fact that God the Father is a keen on feeding the birds that he has made; if that is his level of care for them, what must it be for those he says are made in his image?

12:25-26. '"And which of you by worrying can add a single hour to his life's span? If then you cannot do even a very little thing, why do you worry about other matters?"'

Worrying has been medically shown to shorten lifespan, not lengthen it. To add or subtract an hour is not a problem to the God who can make the sun reverse its course. Isaiah 38:8 - 'I will cause the shadow on the stairway, which has gone down with the sun on the stairway of Ahaz, to go back ten steps.' There really is no need to worry when we realize that God is in ultimate control of all the details of our lives.

11:27-28 '"Consider the lilies, how they grow; they neither toil nor spin; but I tell you not even Solomon in all his glory clothed himself like one of these. But if God so clothes the grass in the field, which is alive today and tomorrow is thrown into the furnace, how much more will he clothe you? You men of little faith!"'

In an age when clothing indicated wealth, not even the world's richest man, Solomon, could compete with the splendid colours of the flowers of the field. Worrying over whether or not we will lack the things that God the Father himself has pledged to provide, is a sad reflection on our lack of trust in him, to say nothing of it being a waste of time and bad for our health. Dry grass and its wild flowers were a common source of domestic fuel. God does not mind - he has plenty more where they came from. 'Oh ye of little faith' has become a common phrase in the vernacular; however the first three words (here rendered as 'You men of') are not present in the Greek text. Jesus addresses his friends with the affectionate term *'oligopistos'* - 'little faiths' - knowing that one day they would be 'big faiths'. It is not so much a rebuke, rather a humourous allusion to the size of their faith and its need to grow through being used, just as muscles grow through use.

12:29-31 '"And do not seek what you will eat and what you will drink, and do not keep worrying. For all these things the nations of the world eagerly seek; but your Father knows that you need these things. But seek his kingdom, and these things will be added to you."'

Jesus is setting out our basic human needs (food, drink, clothing, shelter) that any competent father provides through his own volition without need of reminder. In fact, to keep asking for them 'as the pagan nations do' demonstrates a lack of trust in God the Father's competence and willingness to provide, which always greatly exceeds our willingness to receive. This attitude of trusting (faith), enables us to live daily life peacefully knowing that God watches over us to provide for us. As we go about our business of following him and seeking his rule and his ways, he promises to add to us all we need to do his will. One day at a time is all that is necessary - the challenges of each day are sufficient for that day and, while some fore planning is necessary, it should be done prayerfully, without worry, allowing God to re-direct as required.

12:32 '"Do not be afraid, little flock, for your Father has chosen gladly to give you the kingdom."'

'Fear not' is a common New Testament command and especially one of Jesus'. Fear undermines faith, as happened to Peter after he had exercised sufficient faith to walk towards Jesus on Lake Galilee's stormy waters. When his gaze strayed off Jesus and onto the storm-tossed waves, fear entered and undermined his trust in the command that Jesus had given him - 'Come' (not 'drown'). In the Greek, 'little' flock is a double diminutive, emphasizing 'little'. Although great crowds followed him, they largely did so on their own terms. They left when the teaching became too challenging (e.g. John 6:68, following his teaching on being the Bread of Life). 'Good pleasure' is '*eudokeô*', the same word spoken from heaven by the Father of the Son with whom he was 'well-pleased' (Luke 3:22). The Father's decision to 'give' the kingdom (with its inherent privileges and responsibilities) is in the aorist tense, meaning that it is 'without regard to past, present and future time' * - it is an ongoing reality, in which we have the honour to represent the king.

12:33-34 '"Sell your possessions and give to charity; make yourselves money belts which do not wear out, an unfailing treasure in heaven, where no thief comes near nor moth destroys. For where your treasure is, there your heart will be also."'

Hoarding too betrays a lack of trust, and actually jeopardizes our possessions by exposing them to the risk of decay or bank collapse. 'Charity' is '*eleêmosunê*', which is more commonly translated as 'alms',* one of the three most highly regarded practices in Judaism. The Hebrew word for 'righteousness' and 'charitable giving' ('alms') is one and the same ('*tsedaqah*'), underlining the importance attached to it. The highest form of giving was held to be that where the giver gave without any direct knowledge of the recipient, and vice versa for the recipient. Jesus is not here advocating that people sell everything. He does not say 'Sell *all* you have', such that they are then completely without any resources, becoming poor themselves, like those they had wanted to help. He is teaching that their resources be put to the needs of others as well as to their own needs, and not (as is usually the case) used solely for themselves. The 'rich young ruler' (Luke 18:22) was told to sell all his possessions (presumably because Jesus could see that they 'possessed' him) but this saying of Jesus' in Luke omits the word 'all'. Possessions should be regarded as gifts from God that we are to responsibly look after on his behalf, handling them according to Scriptural principles with regard to generosity, helping the poor and responsible stewardship. This means to hold onto them lightly, so that God can take them and distribute as he wishes. The men that Jesus was teaching would later relay the crux of this to the Apostle Paul. 'They only asked us to remember the poor - the very thing I also was eager to do' (Galatians 2:10).

The 'money belt' is in fact a type of purse ('*ballantion*'), of animal skin or cloth. Repeated contact with the rough coinage of the day would indeed wear them out, if a thief did not get there first. Much better then to invest in the bank of heaven, which holds resources much more safely and for eternity. Again, this needs to be done in faith, including giving under God's particular direction. Moths were a scourge to the fancy and expensive clothing of the wealthy, including their cloth purses, inside which moth larvae might be laid.

There is a call here to simplicity in living and so maximizing one's personal resources available to heaven's agenda. Jesus understood that covetousness was the same as idolatry (Colossians 3:5), and points out the need to fill the heart with God's purposes, using a clever rabbinic play-on-words. 'Treasure' is *thêsauros*, a 'casket' for the safe-keeping of valuables.* For Jesus' Jewish audience that meant a place for their most materially and spiritually valuable possession - the Torah scroll, 'a collection of word's' (from God in this case) that has come to mean the same ('Thesaurus' - a type of dictionary) in English. This is therefore a *'midrash halakha'* of Psalm 119:11- the taking of a biblical text and clarifying what it means in respect to Jewish Law or practice (as opposed to a *'midrash aggada'* which focuses on biblical characters as they pertain to values and ideas). 'Your word I have treasured in my heart, that I may not sin against you' (Psalm 119:11). The word is stored securely in the heart, and then meditated and acted upon. The 'treasure' of the word and the kingdom should constantly fill the heart of the believer.

12:35-38 '"Be dressed in readiness, and keep your lamps lit. Be like men who are waiting for their master when he returns from the wedding feast, so that they may immediately open the door to him when he comes and knocks. Blessed are those slaves whom the master will find on the alert when he comes; truly I say to you, that he will gird himself to serve, and have them recline at the table, and will come up and wait on them. Whether he comes in the second watch, or even in the third, and finds them so, blessed are those slaves."'

Being 'dressed for readiness' ('loins girded' - KJV) meant to tuck the tunic into the belt and so provide for a greater degree of unhindered movement. A lighted oil lamp was also a sign of readiness, as shown in the parable of the wise and foolish virgins

256

(Matthew 25:1-13). Many of the men Jesus was addressing were from Galilee where the fertile soil led to a super-abundance of olive oil which was therefore cheap and plentiful. Its low value meant that it was not subject to Sabbath laws concerning things of a higher value. [151]

Wedding feasts lasted a week but a guest might have to leave a day or two early and a long journey meant that his 'slaves' (*'doulos'* - 'a bond-servant of servile position')* would not know when exactly to expect him and so had to maintain a permanent state of readiness, hence 'on the alert' or 'watching'. At this time the Jews, after the custom of the Romans, divided the night into four watches. The first watch began at six o'clock in the evening, and continued until nine; the second began at nine, and continued until twelve; the third began at twelve, and continued until three next morning; and the fourth began at three, and continued until six o'clock in the morning.

Jewish servants in Jewish households were protected by the Law and so were comparatively well treated. But they would never have heard of the absolutely extraordinary treatment handed out in this parable. Servants were there to prepare food for and wait on their masters and not the other way around! The parable points forward to the servant-like behaviour of the disciples' master, Jesus, in his service of foot washing at his final Seder meal (John 13:1-5). The servants are 'blessed' (*'makarios'* - 'happy'),* firstly in being found 'ready' to open the door immediately. Jesus would later (Luke 18:8) ask a pertinent question, 'When the Son of Man comes, will he find faith on the earth?' The active readiness to serve on the part of the servants illustrates faith on their part that the master is near. They are additionally blessed because they then find themselves in the highly unusual situation of role reversal. As Jesus also later said, 'I go to prepare a place for you' (John 14:2), which is something that the servants were doing for the master prior to his arrival.

12:39-40 '"But be sure of this, that if the head of the house had known at what hour the thief was coming, he would not have allowed his house to be broken into. You too, be ready; for the Son of Man is coming at an hour that you do not expect."'

The theme of readiness continues, only now the master of the house is at home and it is a burglar that he is thinking about waiting up for. But just as journeys often ended at an unpredictable time, so too a thief was even less likely to announce his arrival! It was not just the disciples who were unaware of the time of Jesus' (second) coming, even Jesus himself at that time was unaware of it - only the Father knew the day or hour. 'Of that day or hour no one knows, not even the angels in heaven, nor the Son, but the Father alone' (Mark 13:32). Houses at that time were often made with compacted earth, this burglar 'breaks into' '*diorussô*' ('digs through')* the house instead of coming through a door or window.

12:41-44 'Peter said, "Lord, are you addressing this parable to us or to everyone else as well?" And the Lord said, "Who then is the faithful and sensible steward, whom his master will put in charge of his servants, to give them their rations at the proper time? Blessed is that slave whom his master finds so doing when he comes. Truly I say to you that he will put him in charge of all his possessions."'

The alertness Jesus commands is a practical one - to be carrying out one's duties faithfully and fairly. That is presented as a test of true discipleship, and carries both the common-sense duties of the bond-servant with the equally sensible duties of a disciple of Christ. 'Faithfulness' is a fruit of the Holy Spirit (Galatians 5:22) and an important mark of a believer. 'Sensible' is '*phronimos*', also meaning 'prudent and wise';* the steward is doing his master's will

258

in caring for those entrusted to him - as the church should be doing. Responsibility carried out well is rewarded with more responsibility.

12:45-48 '"But if that slave says in his heart, 'My master will be a long time in coming', and begins to beat the slaves, both men and women, and to eat and drink and get drunk; the master of that slave will come on a day when he does not expect him and at an hour he does not know, and will cut him in pieces, and assign him a place with the unbelievers. And that slave who knew his master's will and did not get ready or act in accord with his will, will receive many lashes, but the one who did not know it, and committed deeds worthy of a flogging, will receive but few. From everyone who has been given much, much will be required; and to whom they entrusted much, of him they will ask all the more.'"

The punishment for the 'evil servant', as Matthew's account (24:48) refers to him, is severe. Cutting into pieces was a form of capital punishment practiced in the Near and Middle East, and is recorded also in Hebrews 11:37 - 'They (*the prophets*) were stoned, they were sawn in two.' After physical death of the evil servant comes an eternal spiritual separation from God - 'assigned a place with the unbelievers' - in a place marked by profound expressions of regret ('Weeping and gnashing of teeth' - Matthew 24:51). Such 'timed-out' remorse can be seen in Luke 16:37, where the rich man in torment asks Abraham to send a message to his still-living brothers, thus demonstrating that the experience of emotion does not end with physical life. This has been testified to by the accounts of near or after death experiences of patients who have undergone resuscitation following a cardiac arrest. They died, then were brought back to life, and testified to witnessing their leaving their dead body behind, and then re-entering it at the point of resuscitation.

The passage underscores the Italian poet Dante's idea that hell will not be a uniform place, but rather that some parts will be worse than others - some receive few lashes and others many. That the recipients are not believers is evidenced by the word for beat, '*derô*', meaning to 'thrash' or 'flay the skin'*, a severe punishment indeed. Many unbelievers know what God wants and ignore it. Far from down-playing hell or writing it out of God's agenda completely as some modern scholars try and do, Jesus warns his audience of its reality and the crucial need to avoid entering it.

There is, however, also a cautionary note for believers. As in the parable of the talents (Matthew 25:14-28), God expects a return from that which he has given us. Few have had as much 'committed' or 'entrusted' to them as believers have had, in Christ. 'Entrusted' is '*paratithêmi*', also meaning 'to set before someone (e.g. in teaching) as one sets out food'.* God expects us to live out what he has taught us, and to practice what we preach.

12:49-50 '"I have come to cast fire upon the earth; and how I wish it were already kindled! But I have a baptism to undergo, and how distressed I am until it is accomplished!"'

John the Baptist has foretold that Jesus would baptise with the Spirit and fire (Matthew 3:12). Jesus has just been speaking metaphorically of his second coming as a householder returning from a journey and as a thief in the night. Paul did the same in 1 Thessalonians 5:2 - 'You yourselves know full well that the day of the Lord will come just like a thief in the night.' The baptising with fire is symbolic of the judgement that would characterise his return as the 'one who would judge the living and the dead.' [xix] But there was a sacrifice to

---

[xix] 'Christ Jesus, who is to judge the living and the dead' (2 Timothy 4:1).

offer first, one that would test even the incarnate Son of God to the limit - that of being the sin-bearer on behalf of all humanity.

Jesus' death on the cross would be the first blow of judgement against the illegitimate rule of the devil on the earth which God had made originally devoid of sin. John 12:31-33: '"Now judgment is upon this world; now the ruler of this world will be cast out. And I, if I am lifted up from the earth, will draw all men to myself." But he was saying this to indicate the kind of death by which he was to die.' That would be a baptism of suffering, the thought of which would be enough to make Jesus sweat blood in the garden of Gethsemane. 'Being in agony he was praying very fervently; and his sweat became like drops of blood, falling down upon the ground' (Luke 22:44). Even looking ahead to it made Jesus 'distressed' - a rather weak translation of '*sunechô*' - the word Luke used to describe Peter's mother 'struck' or 'suffering' with a fever (Luke 4:38) and in Matthew 4:24 for those 'suffering with various illnesses and pains.' Vine's dictionary translates it as 'anguish'. Not until Jesus shouted, "It is finished" (John 19:30), would that anguish be over.

12:51-53 '"Do you suppose that I came to grant peace on earth? I tell you, no, but rather division; for from now on five members in one household will be divided, three against two and two against three. They will be divided father against son and son against father, mother against daughter and daughter against mother, mother-in-law against daughter-in-law and daughter-in-law against mother-in-law."'

Jesus, the Prince of Peace (Isaiah 9:6) demands a loyalty to himself that would and does divide families along that line. This would be particularly relevant in the days to come, when, as in strict Islamic and communist states today, affiliation to him would be rewarded with the death penalty.

12:54-56 'And he was also saying to the crowds, "When you see a cloud rising in the west, immediately you say, 'A shower is coming,' and so it turns out. And when you see a south wind blowing, you say, 'It will be a hot day,' and it turns out that way. You hypocrites! You know how to analyze the appearance of the earth and the sky, but why do you not analyze this present time?"'

Their skill in meteorological prediction was unfortunately not matched by skill in taking the spiritual temperature. Matthew's account has Jesus directing these comments especially to some of the Pharisees who were present, men whose religious aptitude should have been sufficient for this purpose, but which sadly was not. Since they could interpret the signs in the sky and could forecast rain, how was it that they could not see what was clearly visible and happening all around them - spiritual activity that evidenced the fulfillment of Messianic prophecy?

12:57-59 '"And why do you not even on your own initiative judge what is right? For while you are going with your opponent to appear before the magistrate, on your way there make an effort to settle with him, so that he may not drag you before the judge, and the judge turn you over to the officer, and the officer throw you into prison. I say to you, you will not get out of there until you have paid the very last cent."'

Jesus, the expert Temple '***Didaskalos***' of Torah, now brings his legal knowledge of Jewish jurisprudence into play. The signs of Messiah's coming were sufficiently obvious for children to rejoice over them (Matthew 21:15), yet the religious lawyers themselves remained blind to them. Basic common sense dictated that a defendant examine his weak legal case before coming into the presence of the judge who had the power to enact legal punishment. How much more power then does God have with which to judge those who reject his offer of new life in his Son?

The exactitude of the judgement is illustrated in Jesus' choice of word for the sum involved. There were several coins in use in Jesus' time. Being durable metal objects, some of them have survived to this day. They were, in decreasing order of value, the Hebrew 'talent' (Matthew 18:24), which was a large amount of silver weighing about 60 kilograms. Next came the 'mina' (traded by the ruler's servants in Luke 19:13) and equivalent to about 600 grams of silver or 100 drachmae (one drachma was a working man's daily wage). Then there was the shekel (in the fish's mouth - Matthew 17:27) which was worth about 11 grams of silver. For thirty shekels, the price the Law stipulated that a slave was worth, Judas betrayed Jesus. Then there was the 'didrachma', also called the half-shekel. Next came the 'drachma', the coin which the woman lost and searched for in Luke 15:8. The ten she had were likely to have been the sum paid as a marriage dowry, kept in the event of divorce. The next coin down, the 'denarius' was a day's pay for a working man (Matthew 20:2). Below that was the 'assarion' (Matthew 10:29) worth the price of two sparrows. Then there was the 'quadrans', worth two lepta and mentioned in the sum described in Matthew's account of this teaching (Matthew 5:26). Finally there was the 'lepton' (meaning 'the thin one'); the smallest coin, being the widow's offering ('mite') in Mark 12:42. This is the coin mentioned in Luke's account of this teaching. God's mill wheels of judgement may grind slowly, but, as the poem says, 'they grind exceeding small' [xx] - to the smallest coin.

[xx] 'Though the mills of God grind slowly, yet they grind exceeding small; though with patience he stands waiting, with exactness grinds he all.' ('Retribution', by Friedrich von Logau, translation by Henry Longfellow.)

Chapter 13

13:1-5 'Now on the same occasion there were some present who reported to him about the Galileans whose blood Pilate had mixed with their sacrifices. And Jesus said to them, "Do you suppose that these Galileans were greater sinners than all other Galileans because they suffered this fate? I tell you, no, but unless you repent, you will all likewise perish. Or do you suppose that those eighteen on whom the tower in Siloam fell and killed them were worse culprits than all the men who live in Jerusalem? I tell you, no, but unless you repent, you will all likewise perish."'

Josephus records that the Galileans were unruly and 'inured to war from their infancy' ('Wars' 3, 3), and that they had earlier defeated a Roman army under the command of Herod's younger brother Joseph. 'The Galileans revolted from their commanders, and took those of Herod's party, and drowned them in the lake' ('Antiquities' 14, 15). They now came under the rule of Herod's son, Herod Antipas, who was not initially on good terms with Pilate. As religious Jews, the Galileans necessarily made pilgrimage to Jerusalem for the three compulsory feasts of Passover, Pentecost and Tabernacles. The Court of Israel was connected to the Roman fort of Antonia by a broad staircase (Acts 21:35), and the garrison housed there could quickly quell unrest, often with a heavy hand. Jews slain there would indeed have their blood mixed with the sacrifices they were about to offer.

Jesus' response is to point out that all mankind are stained already by sin and that unless his (and John the Baptist's) message of repentance is heeded, a worse fate would befall them. As a *'tekton'* skilled in building large structures such as palaces, temples and towers, Jesus would have taken a keen interest in the collapse of the tower adjacent to the pool of Siloam. The pool is mentioned in John 9:1-7 in relation to Jesus' healing of the man born blind.

Water provision in Jerusalem was critical, as with any city, to its survival. Jerusalem is built on limestone, fed by underground water from the adjacent Gihon spring, which was heavily fortified and attached to the city to protect the water supply in times of war. Over time, various channels were cut to supply different parts of the city, including 'Hezekiah's tunnel' cut by King Hezekiah (c. 727-698 BC) to supply the Pool of Siloam and described in 2 Kings 20:20. 'The rest of the acts of Hezekiah and all his might, and how he made the pool and the conduit and brought water into the city, are they not written in the Book of the Chronicles, of the Kings of Judah?' Prior to 2004 the pool of Siloam was thought to be a small structure excavated under the oversight of Empress Helena of Constantinople in the early fourth century. However in the summer of 2004, a local utility crew were repairing an underground pipe in Jerusalem and in digging they hit some large rocks found to be adjacent to a huge pool, with steps leading to the Temple mount.

As Jerusalem expanded, the need for water grew. The astounding new and hugely enlarged Temple built by Herod the Great drew larger numbers of pilgrims. It is likely that the pool of Siloam was enlarged and in doing so the adjacent tower's foundations were disturbed. Or it may be that the tower had not been built with the attention to detail that Joseph, Jesus' *tekton* father, and Jesus himself, would have given. In any event a disaster occurred, the tower collapsed, and men that Jesus describes as *opheiletês* - 'debtors' (as in the Lord's Prayer - Matthew 6:12) - were killed. A 'change of thinking' of repentance with consequential behavioural change is necessary to avoid similar, only spiritual, destruction.

13:6-9 'And he began telling this parable: "A man had a fig tree which had been planted in his vineyard; and he came

looking for fruit on it and did not find any. And he said to the vineyard-keeper, 'Behold, for three years I have come looking for fruit on this fig tree without finding any. Cut it down! Why does it even use up the ground?' And he answered and said to him, 'Let it alone sir, for this year too, until I dig around it and put in fertilizer; and if it bears fruit next year, fine; but if not, cut it down.'''

In Israel fig trees produced 3 crops every year. Josephus describes them as bearing fruit over a ten-month period ('Wars' 3, 10). To plant a fig tree in a vineyard was to give it a prime position. Three years was considered plenty of time for fruiting to occur; the Jewish scholar Maimonides held that three years was the time limit for fruit bearing, [152] and a barren tree was held to needlessly deteriorate the land. Jesus ministered in public in Israel for three and a half years, having ministered in Bet Midrash within the Court of Israel prior to that, as any brilliant Jewish youth would do. [153] John the Baptist's ministry had preceded Jesus' public ministry but to little avail among the nation's leadership - there was not much spiritual fruit to show for it, largely due to the authorities' opposition. The parable warns of their 'last-chance saloon'. They were to get one more year.

13:10-13 'And he was teaching in one of the synagogues on the Sabbath. And there was a woman who for eighteen years had had a sickness caused by a spirit; and she was bent double, and could not straighten up at all. When Jesus saw her, he called her over and said to her, "Woman, you are freed from your sickness." And he laid his hands on her; and immediately she was made erect again and began glorifying God.'

As a highly respected '**Didaskalos**', Jesus was officially approved to teach Torah in the synagogues, not simply read from the scrolls. Doctor Luke notes that the woman's infirmity had a spiritual root cause; his primary source, Mary, no doubt felt great sympathy for her as a fellow older and bereaved woman. One word from her son was all it took to straighten the situation, and the woman, out - 'straighten' being '*anorthoô*', from '*orthoô*' meaning 'set straight', as in our modern 'orthopaedics' - literally 'straightening children of deformities.' 'Freed' here is '*apoluô*', also meaning 'loosed' and 'released', and is a common New Testament word but only used on one occasion in the context of healing - here. But it is a common Greek medical term for tendon and membrane division and release, and even for releasing bandaging. [154] The woman's response is '*doxazô*' - 'to praise and celebrate'.*

13:14 'But the synagogue official, indignant because Jesus had healed on the Sabbath, began saying to the crowd in response, "There are six days in which work should be done; so come during them and get healed, and not on the Sabbath day."'

Unfortunately the synagogue ruler felt unable to join her in her praise of God. He was more concerned about the petty observance of the Oral law's Sabbath regulations, rules of men that forbade all but legally prescribed essential work taking place on the Sabbath. The woman had been sick for eighteen years - surely she could have waited for one day more?

13:15-17 'But the Lord answered him and said, "You hypocrites, does not each of you on the Sabbath untie his ox or his donkey from the stall and lead him away to water him? And this woman, a daughter of Abraham as she is, whom Satan has bound for eighteen long years, should she not have been released from this bond on the Sabbath day?" As he said this, all his opponents were being humiliated; and the entire crowd was rejoicing over all the glorious things being done by him.'

As with the healing on the Sabbath of the man with the withered hand (Luke 6:6-11), Jesus uses a rabbinic legal argument to make his case. Watering animals, though work, was permitted under the Oral Torah, because of the relative value of the animal, which might die in the hot climate if unable to drink. As with the man's withered hand, a human life was infinitely more valuable; hence, doing good on the Sabbath was permitted, just as preventing harm was permitted. And a 'daughter of Abraham' was more valuable than a donkey! How the crowds must have laughed at this simple explanation from the learned Law-master who had the added quality of performing miracles, including deliverance from 'Satan's bonds'. With this, Jesus' legalistic opponents were '*kataischunô*' - 'blushed with shame' and 'disgraced'* - before the rejoicing synagogue crowd.

13:18-19 'So he was saying, "What is the kingdom of God like, and to what shall I compare it? It is like a mustard seed, which a man took and threw into his own garden; and it grew and became a tree, and the birds of the air nested in its branches."'

Jesus told several parables concerning the nature of the kingdom of God and Luke records two here. Whereas Matthew and Mark's versions have the seed being sown, Luke's account reads '*ballô*' - 'to cast' in the manner of a fishing net (Matthew 4:18), or of Barabbas being 'cast' into prison (Luke 23:19). This underlines the very different and somewhat apparently careless way the Gospels record the manner of sowing seed, as compared to the carefully targeted way it is sown in the modern Western world today. The idea is that God, the gardener of Genesis 2:8 ('The Lord God planted a garden toward the east, in Eden'), makes a super-abundance of seed that he is not miserly with, but which he is still able to watch over, knowing what will happen to each one. If some are eaten by birds (Luke 8:5) then God has plenty more.

The mustard seed was the smallest seed used in Judea at that time (Mark 4:31), and was a rabbinic metaphor for something tiny. Talmud, '*Nidah*' 5a describes 'A drop of blood of the size of a mustard seed' (in relation to menstrual blood loss and associated legal uncleanness). But like all seed, it had an in-built capacity to grow massively beyond its original size and apparent potential. The Talmud records one large enough to provide shade for a tent. [155] The kingdom of God starts small but with tremendous capacity to grow, as the early Church showed, providing spiritual and material shelter for the needy, just as the Old Testament prophet Ezekiel saw the great nations of his day as providing. [xxi]

13:20-21 '"And again he said, "To what shall I compare the kingdom of God? It is like leaven, which a woman took and hid in three pecks of flour until it was all leavened."'

More 'hidden' power. Yeast may not look like much to the naked eye, but just mix it with warm water and flour and wait a short time! The woman is making a large amount of bread. Three '*saton*' (or '*seah*' in Hebrew) was the equivalent of an '*ephah*', about 9 gallons of flour. But a small amount of yeast (often kept in warm bread dough) hence 'hidden' ('*egkruptô*' - 'concealed') within, would soon have the 'leavened' bread dough rising prior to baking.

13:22-27 'And he was passing through from one city and village to another, teaching, and proceeding on his way to Jerusalem. And someone said to him, "Lord, are there just a few who are being saved?" And he said to them, "Strive to enter through the narrow door; for many, I tell you, will seek to enter and will not be able. Once the head of the

---

[xxi] 'All the birds of the heavens nested in its *[Assyria's]* boughs, and under its branches all the beasts of the field gave birth' (Ezekiel 31:6).

house gets up and shuts the door, and you begin to stand outside and knock on the door, saying, 'Lord, open up to us!' then he will answer and say to you, 'I do not know where you are from.' Then you will begin to say, 'We ate and drank in your presence, and you taught in our streets', and he will say, 'I tell you, I do not know where you are from. Depart from me all you evildoers.'"'

Jesus was reaching every village (Matthew 9:35) with the message of his Father's kingdom. Its emphasis on personal salvation can be seen by the question put to him. The majority of the populace were ready for a popular miracle working, Torah-explaining Messiah, but not quite so ready for one who was starting to intimate a mission that would culminate in his own death. Just how many would respond? Jesus, as was often his wont, does not directly answer, but instead turns the question into an important teaching about personal responsibility. 'Strive' here is '*agônizomai*', more often translated in the New Testament as 'fight',* and was used to describe those who zealously contested in the Greek gymnastic games. Testimony to the Christian life being like a 'fight' is plentiful in the New Testament. As Jesus' disciple Paul would later write to his own disciple Timothy, 'Fight the good fight of faith; take hold of the eternal life to which you were called, and you made the good confession in the presence of many witnesses' (1 Timothy 6:12).

Entrance to God's kingdom is through a 'narrow' gate and is contrasted with the 'broad' way that leads to destruction. Jesus taught, 'Enter through the narrow gate; for the gate is wide and the way is broad that leads to destruction, and there are many who enter through it' (Matthew 7:13.) The way to life is as narrow as the space occupied by the cross of the crucified Saviour. Many indeed seek after God. But entrance to the kingdom of heaven is governed by the One who said 'No one comes to the Father but through me' (John 14:6), no matter how sincere their false worship of other gods might be. Jesus focuses on the religious people of his day who had gladly eaten with such a famous '***Didaskalos***' and Torah teacher, enjoying the new insights that he brought but without the response of personal repentance and trust in him. Their religiously motivated good deeds are to him the equivalent of an unclean menstrual cloth. 'All our righteous acts are like filthy rags' - Isaiah 64:6. Their unchanged hearts leaves them as 'evildoers' whose fate is to be expelled from the kingdom.

13:28-30 '"In that place there will be weeping and gnashing of teeth when you see Abraham and Isaac and Jacob and all the prophets in the kingdom of God, but yourselves being thrown out. And they will come from east and west and from north and south, and will recline at the table in the kingdom of God. And behold, some are last who will be first and some are first who will be last."'

Having been thus expelled ('thrown out' into the garbage dump of Gehenna - Luke 12:5), their state is eternal remorse characterised by lamentation and '***brugmos***' - 'gnashing and grinding of teeth'* in the manner of a snarling dog. Those religious Jews, tied up in man-made legalism, thought that they would have good seats in the banquet of heaven. Jesus tells them that, as the rich man in the parable of the righteous beggar could see Lazarus from afar (Luke 16:23), they will be able to see their patriarchs reclining at the kingdom's feast while they are excluded. And they will also see some unlikely characters in their company. God's kingdom was about to rapidly expand outwards from Israel to all the corners of the globe. Gentiles (the last in their minds to warrant such privilege) would occupy the seats that they had thought belonged to them - 'the first' to be called.

13:31-32 'Just at that time some Pharisees approached, saying to him, "Go away, leave here, for Herod wants to kill you." And he said to them, "Go and tell that fox,

'Behold, I cast out demons and perform cures today and tomorrow, and the third day I reach my goal.'"'

Not all the Pharisees were at enmity with Jesus. Men like Nicodemus still highly respected him and were willing to take a stand against the fast turning tide brought on by Jesus' claims to divinity. Some of the friendlier sorts want to warn Jesus about what he already knows - that he has powerful enemies. Herod here is Herod Antipas, whose jurisdiction Jesus is leaving en route to Judea and Jerusalem, over which the Sanhedrin held religious authority under the political rule of the Gentile Roman Pontius Pilate.

Jesus' reply evidences rabbinic humour as well as being a calculated put-down of Antipas, calling him a 'vixen' (the Greek word 'fox' being in the feminine tense). Herod Antipas had taken his brother Phillip's wife Salome while he was in Rome contesting his father's will. This Phillip lived as a private citizen in Rome, as distinct to the half-brother Philip to whom Rome had entrusted the rule of Iturea and Tracontis (Luke 3:1). Antipas' flagrant wife stealing and subsequent divorce from his former wife Phasaelis had caused severe political ructions in the region. Phasaelis' father was King Aretas IV, the powerful neighbouring ruler of the Nabatean Empire based in Petra in Jordan. Aretas took great exception to Antipas' treatment of his daughter, who had fled back to him, and he promptly attacked Antipas' kingdom over an ancient boundary dispute. This prompted Antipas to call upon Rome for military aid, which the incumbent Roman Emperor Tiberius granted in the form of troops under the command of Vitellius, the proconsul of Syria, though not without annoyance and ill-feeling towards Antipas for the consequences of his immoral behaviour (even by Roman standards). The real power behind Antipas' throne was his new wife Salome, who brought about the execution of Jesus' cousin, John the Baptist, hence Jesus spoke of a female fox, either as opprobrious to Antipas or as an indirect reference to Salome, or both.

Jesus was on his Father's timetable, ascertained by his daily lengthy devotion to personal prayer. He would not be hastened or deflected by anyone, but would continue in step with the Holy Spirit in performing acts of deliverance from evil spirits and miraculous healing. He was still three days away from his destination, and the final showdown with the Sanhedrin that his arrival and ministry in Jerusalem would bring. Luke's use of 'cures' ('*iasis*') is the only use in the New Testament, but was the common Greek medical term for making people well. [156]

13:33-35 '"Nevertheless I must journey on today and tomorrow and the next day; for it cannot be that a prophet would perish outside of Jerusalem. O Jerusalem, Jerusalem, the city that kills the prophets and stones those sent to her! How often I wanted to gather your children together, just as a hen gathers her brood under her wings, and you would not have it! Behold, your house is left to you desolate; and I say to you, you will not see me until the time comes when you say, 'Blessed is he who comes in the name of the Lord.'"

Days were measured in Israel as parts of days, so the third day is in two days time (being the last part of the current day, the next day and a portion of the third day). Jesus is pointing forwards to his sacrifice, in the city that had killed so many of his prophetic forerunners. He contrasts their violent and wicked hearts with his own - one of tenderness and love, like a mother hen with her chicks. This is a reference to Psalm 17:8. 'Keep me as the apple of the eye; hide me in the shadow of your wings.' Israel is the 'apple (literally 'the pupil') of God's eye ('He guarded him as the pupil of his eye' - Deuteronomy 32:10), and Jesus is still inviting them to repent. The 'house' that will be left to them desolate is the Temple, the 'holy house' believed to have been built under the oversight of Jesus' devout '*tekton*' father Joseph. [157] The sanctuary was a powerfully built place of refuge for the priests who sheltered inside against the Roman siege weapons deployed in the Roman destruction of Jerusalem (66-70 AD). Many were slain in the very act of offering sacrifices to the God whom they believed would deliver them from the pagan army. They would indeed have been crying out Psalm 118:25-26. 'O Lord, do save, we beseech you; O Lord, we beseech you, do send prosperity! Blessed is the one who comes in the name of the Lord; we have blessed you from the house of the Lord.' The very words spoken here by Jesus are quoted from a Psalm prayed at an hour when deliverance was needed. Psalm 118:10-13: 'All nations surrounded me *[the encircling Roman army under Vespasian employed many foreign mercenaries]*; in the name of the Lord I will surely cut them off. They surrounded me, yes, they surrounded me; in the name of the Lord I will surely cut them off. They surrounded me like bees; they were extinguished as a fire of thorns; in the name of the Lord I will surely cut them off. You pushed me violently so that I was falling, *[as were the walls of the city]* but the Lord helped me.' Their rejection of 'the chief corner stone' (Psalm 118:22) had brought the Roman siege and destruction upon them. 'The time' of this dire event was fast approaching. When the army broke in and slew them, they would 'see' and enter into the presence of the One who was quoting the very words they would be praying. Would they have repented?

Chapter 14

14:1-2 'It happened that when he went into the house of one of the leaders of the Pharisees on the Sabbath to eat bread, they were watching him closely. And there in front of him was a man suffering from dropsy.'

Another medical condition, another miracle, and another New Testament word unique to Doctor Luke. 'Dropsy' is '*hudrôpikos*', from '*optomai*' - 'to appear' and '*hudôr*' - 'water', and was in common use by the Greek physicians. [158] 'Dropsy' is 'congestive heart failure', sufferers of which do indeed 'appear watery', because of the oedematous fluid swelling around their lower legs, by means of the heart's insufficient pumping power to clear it away through the kidneys. Consequently the excess water seeps out into the extremities like bilge water inside a boat. This swollen man would have been audible as well as visible - fluid leaks into the lungs as well as the legs making breathing raspy and difficult. In severe cases the patient is unable to lay flat in bed because the lungs too fill up with venous fluid. Jesus' enemies among the Pharisees know of his ability to heal; they also know what the Oral Torah says about healing non-immediately life threatening conditions - you should not interrupt the Sabbath rest to remedy them. What will Jesus do?

14:3-6 'And Jesus answered and spoke to the lawyers and Pharisees, saying, "Is it lawful to heal on the Sabbath, or not?" But they kept silent. And he took hold of him and healed him, and sent him away. And he said to them, "Which one of you will have a son or an ox fall into a well, and will not immediately pull him out on a Sabbath day?" And they could make no reply to this.'

As with the man with the withered hand (Luke 6:6-11) and the woman bent double by a demon (Luke 13:10-17), Jesus takes the legal argument to the Pharisees. The Oral Law permitted certain forms of work on the Sabbath, such as pulling someone out of a well - plenty of water there! The Oral Law also contained the legal principle of relative value, and taught that it was illegal to withhold certain necessary good deeds. The man is of greater value than an ox. To withhold an opportunity to do good would have been to break the Law. So did Jesus have the power to do the good that was required? Jesus demonstrates that he does by healing the man. He is technically keeping within the Sabbath laws and at the same time showing that he has divine power to do something only God can do.

14:7-11 'And he began speaking a parable to the invited guests when he noticed how they had been picking out the places of honour at the table, saying to them, "When you are invited by someone to a wedding feast, do not take the place of honour, for someone more distinguished than you may have been invited by him, and he who invited you both will come and say to you, 'Give your place to this man,' and then in disgrace you proceed to occupy the last place. But when you are invited, go and recline at the last place, so that when the one who has invited you comes, he may say to you, 'Friend, move up higher'; then you will have honour in the sight of all who are at the table with you. For everyone who exalts himself will be humbled, and he who humbles himself will be exalted."'

Jesus is presenting a midrash (a rabbinic homiletic teaching on a passage of Scripture) on Proverbs 25:6-7. 'Do not claim honour in the presence of the king, and do not stand in the place of great men; for it is better that it be said to you, "Come up here" than for you to be placed lower in the presence of the prince, whom your eyes have seen.' It is a natural human tendency to wish to promote oneself, one that the religious scholars were prone to insofar as they loved 'taking the places of honour at banquets' (Matthew 23:6). James and John were quite willing to use their mother to gain similar places of status (Matthew 20:20). James and John's mother is recorded as Salome (Mark 15:40) and by John (19:25) as 'his mother's sister'; hence Salome was Jesus' aunt. Jesus, and the proverbial wisdom, instead recommends humility. God himself exalts the humble, as Peter would later record. 'All of you, clothe yourselves with humility toward one another, for God is opposed to the proud but gives grace to the humble' (1 Peter 5:5). Jesus' half-brother James would also echo this saying: 'Humble yourselves in the presence of the Lord, and he will exalt you' (James 4:10). What and whomever God exalts cannot be brought down, and it is God's approval that should be valued rather than man's fickle honour.

14:12-14 'And he also went on to say to the one who had invited him, "When you give a luncheon or a dinner, do not invite your friends or your brothers or your relatives or rich neighbours, otherwise they may also invite you in return and that will be your repayment. But when you give a reception, invite the poor, the crippled, the lame, the blind, and you will be blessed, since they do not have the means to repay you; for you will be repaid at the resurrection of the righteous."'

More wisdom. Jeremiah had prophesied, 'I will gather them from the remote parts of the earth, among them the blind and the lame, the woman with child and she who is in labour with child, together; a great company, they will return here... For I am a father to Israel, and Ephraim is my firstborn... He who scattered Israel will gather him... They will come and shout for joy on the height of Zion, and they will be radiant over the bounty of the Lord, over the grain and the new wine and the oil, and over the young of the flock and the herd' (Jeremiah 31:8-12). The Jews believed that God would re-pay both the righteous and the wicked for their deeds. Here Jesus uses the meal as an opportunity to teach about deeds of righteousness in the care of the needy. The notion that God would repay the righteous and the unrighteous in the age to come was a common rabbinic theme, in contrast to the Sadducean repudiation of the concept of an afterlife. The Talmud taught (Rabbi Simeon ben Lakish): [159] 'There is no Gehenna *[rubbish-dump]* in the future world, but the Holy One, blessed be he, brings the sun out of its sheath, so that it is fierce: the wicked are punished by it, the righteous are healed by it. The wicked are punished by it, as it is said: For behold, the day comes, it burns as a furnace; and all the proud, and all that work wickedness, shall be stubble; and the day that cometh shall set them ablaze, says the Lord of Hosts... The righteous are healed by it, as it is said, 'But unto you that fear my name, shall the sun of righteousness arise with healing in its wings' (Malachi 4:2).

14:15 'When one of those who were reclining at the table with him heard this, he said to him, "Blessed is everyone who will eat bread in the kingdom of God!"'

Given that there were no crippled or blind at the meal-table, Jesus' comments no doubt left his fellow diners somewhat self-conscious and embarrassed. This remark bears those hallmarks; it is hard to disagree with - all who enter the kingdom are indeed 'happy' or 'blessed' ('*makarios*') - but Jesus sees beneath the bland statement to the spiritual disconnect that belied it. The majority of religious folk present had not grasped what it meant to enter God's kingdom and if they were not careful would find themselves missing out.

14:16-24 'But he said to him, "A man was giving a big dinner, and he invited many; and at the dinner hour he sent his slave to say to those who had been invited, 'Come; for everything is ready now.' But they all alike began to make excuses. The first one said to him, 'I have bought a piece of land and I need to go out and look at it;

please consider me excused.' Another one said, 'I have bought five yoke of oxen, and I am going to try them out; please consider me excused.' Another one said, 'I have married a wife, and for that reason I cannot come.' And the slave came back and reported this to his master. Then the head of the household became angry and said to his slave, 'Go out at once into the streets and lanes of the city and bring in here the poor and crippled and blind and lame.' And the slave said, 'Master, what you commanded has been done, and still there is room.' And the master said to the slave, 'Go out into the highways and along the hedges, and compel them to come in, so that my house may be filled. For I tell you, none of those men who were invited shall taste of my dinner.'"

Since the man thought it obvious that everyone would want to enter the blessed kingdom, Jesus tells this parable to present the reality of the matter - many are too busy and have a good reason why they should be excused.. In theory they would like to be there, but in practice their activities and preferences betray their true priorities.

When those invited (who stand for the Jews to whom God's Old Covenant relationship was established) would not respond, the master turned his attention to those whom the ungrateful recipients of his invitation would have despised - the surrounding Gentile nations. They were spiritually poor and undeserving, and as Jesus had just taught, could not repay. They would not make the mistake of thinking that they had been invited on their own merits. Rather than build his kingdom on the spiritually well fed but obese and self-righteous, God would do as he had spoken through the prophet Micah. "'In that day, declares the Lord, "I will assemble the lame and gather the outcasts, even those whom I have afflicted. I will make the lame a remnant and the outcasts a strong nation, and the Lord will reign over them in Mount Zion, from now on and forever"'

(Micah 4:6-7). God's kingdom would and does have a special place for outcasts.

14:25-27 'Now large crowds were going along with him; and he turned and said to them, "If anyone comes to me, and does not hate his own father and mother and wife and children and brothers and sisters, yes, and even his own life, he cannot be my disciple. Whoever does not carry his own cross and come after me cannot be my disciple."'

The four Gospels make it clear that Jesus did not court public popularity. His teaching on 'eating the flesh of the Son of Man and drinking his blood' - 'a hard teaching' (John 6:53 and 60), seems at least in part to have been intended to whittle down the numbers of people following what might otherwise have been viewed by the Roman authorities as a populist uprising.

'Hate' can be a misunderstood term within the language of the New Testament. The term can indeed mean an intense feeling of dislike, but it is also used to express 'a relative preference for one thing over another, by way of expressing either aversion from, or disregard for, the claims of one person or thing relative to those of another'. [160] This is a form of hyperbole that rabbis often employed - a rhetorical device whereby an exaggerated statement is made to make a point, but is not intended to be taken literally. [161] Jesus uses the word in the same way in Luke 16:13 in relation to the difficulty of serving two masters ('hating one and loving the other'). Deuteronomy 5:16 commands honouring of father and mother and not hatred in the literal sense. But in the rhetorical sense the attitude toward them, when compared with what the attitude toward God should be, is as of hatred when compared to love. Jesus takes the same principle further to describe the same attitude in relation to one's own life. Love for God is supposed to far outweigh love for this temporary human existence that is, in athletic terms, a 'warm-up' for the real life of eternity.

The crowd was very familiar with the concept that disciples shared in the future of their rabbinic master. Perhaps some of them saw themselves as disciples simply because they were, at that time, following Jesus' company of disciples, surely to a glorious future in a resurgent Israel. If so, Jesus disabuses them of the notion. In the same way he would later enlighten his cousins James and John when they came with their mother (Matthew 20:20) to request the top seats in his kingdom, which they erroneously believed was soon to become a political reality. 'Carrying one's cross' was a familiar concept in an age of Roman public execution, designed to be a deterrent to other would-be insurgents. Would the crowd's love for God, in comparison with their attitude to their own love for life, lead them to that extreme an expression of discipleship, towards a rabbinic master whose own fate was to be publically executed? Would the twelve apostles' attitude extend that far? Time would tell.

14:28-30 '"For which one of you, when he wants to build a tower, does not first sit down and calculate the cost to see if he has enough to complete it? Otherwise, when he has laid a foundation and is not able to finish, all who observe it begin to ridicule him, saying, 'This man began to build and was not able to finish.'"'

Who in the large public crowd that were listening to Jesus had the means or the need to build a tower? Towers were only built by the very wealthy - by rulers or by groups of city elders for defence purposes. They were highly expensive to build because of the technical difficulties involved both in determining the necessary foundation depth in differing soil conditions, and in raising the stonework above a two storey height in days without the benefit of modern lifting equipment. If the correct work was not done, towers could and did fall down and kill people, like the one in Siloam which Jesus refers to in chapter 13 verse 4. So, given that practically no one in Jesus' audience would have been in the market for building a tower, why might Jesus have been using that particular example?

The answer lies in the Judean first-century meaning of the word *'tekton'*. Paul uses the term in 1 Corinthians 3:10 as part of a compound word *'architekon'*, which translators invariable break into two, rendering it as 'master builder' rather than the more obvious transliteration, 'architect'. Paul's context for its use is 'laying a foundation'; rather different to the wood-worker associations commonly associated with the Gospels' two references to *'tekton'* (Matthew 13:55 [xxii] and Mark 6:3), [xxiii] both of which are used without any descriptive context. Josephus' 'Antiquities' [162] uses the word in the same context as Paul's, for whom 'another' ('wise master-*tekton*') is building upon his foundation for the Corinthian church, surely the same 'master-*tekton*' who said 'I will build my church; and the gates of Hades will not overpower it' (Matthew 16:18-19). It is always the context that determines the correct translation. The first-century Judean *'tekton'* was a combination of an architect and a structural engineer, and built big buildings.

In Jesus' illustration the man gets as far, with the necessary help of a such a specialised *'tekton'*, of laying a foundation, but is not able to go further and build upon it, quite a conceivable scenario given the technical expertise and concomitant expense involved. He would certainly have been 'mocked' - *'empaizô'* - from *'paizô'* - 'playing like a child'. Disciples should not 'play' at following someone whose end was to be nailed to a Roman stake of execution.

[xxii] 'Is not this the *tekton's* son?' (Matthew 13:55).
[xxiii] 'Is not this the *tekton*, the son of Mary, and brother of James and Joses and Judas and Simon?' (Mark 6:3).

14:31-32 '"Or what king, when he sets out to meet another king in battle, will not first sit down and consider whether he is strong enough with ten thousand men to encounter the one coming against him with twenty thousand? Or else, while the other is still far away, he sends a delegation and asks for terms of peace."'

Kings not only built towers, they also led armies into battle. But not if to do so meant guaranteed wholesale slaughter! Instead, a prior agreement would be reached that saved both sides the trouble of having to incur unnecessary casualties, whereby the conquered territory would serve and pay taxes to the foreign king and agree not to wage war against him - usually the reason for the army setting out in the first place.

14:33 '"So then, none of you can be my disciple who does not give up all his own possessions."'

Willingness to give up one's life to gain an eternal reward should also encompass a willingness to give up material possessions to follow One who had done the same thing himself. The *'tekton'* family into which Jesus had been born had received large gifts from the Babylonian Magi, surely reflected in Jesus having a 'home' in Capernaum (Mark 2:1). Yet Jesus abandoned his material resources and profession to take his Father's gospel to the villages and towns of the 'lost sheep of the house of Israel' (Matthew 15:24). Thus he was able to counsel the 'rich young ruler' (Matthew 19:16-22) from his personal example of a simple lifestyle. To 'give up' one's possessions is to place them into God's hands, along with one's own life; to renounce personal ownership in the sense of allowing God to determine what is done with them. It is not the same as reflexly give everything away, except in the rare cases when God does in fact request that. Jesus himself had possessions. Some of them were very valuable, such as his one-piece tunic that the soldiers who crucified him were unwilling to tear. ('The tunic was seamless, woven in one piece. So they said to one another, "Let us not tear it, but cast lots for it, to decide whose it shall be."' - John 19:23-24.) But all that Jesus had, and was in his mission, lay at his Father's disposal, evidenced by his living a simple lifestyle when, as a widely respected Torah teacher, he could have become wealthy by means of the gifts that devout Jews bestowed on such esteemed members of their society.

The early church followed this teaching of Jesus' about possessions by pooling their resources. Other churches do not appear to have adopted this policy, as may be seen from 1 Corinthians 16:1-2. 'Concerning the collection for the saints, as I directed the churches of Galatia, so do you also. On the first day of every week each one of you is to put aside, and save, as he may prosper, so that no collections be made when I come.' The need to 'make a collection' points towards the absence of a completely common purse. But whatever the local case may be, a disciple is to '*apotassô*' his or hers possessions, meaning to 'say farewell' to them and to 'separate oneself' from them.* They now belong to their Master, who often permits us to steward them responsibly as a means of training us and resourcing others.

14:34-35 '"Therefore, salt is good; but if even salt has become tasteless, with what will it be seasoned? It is useless, either for the soil or for the manure pile; it is thrown out. He who has ears to hear, let him hear."'

Jesus quotes the Jewish proverb, 'When salt becomes unsavoury, wherewith is it salted?', also recorded in the Talmud. [163] Salt at that time was not 100% sodium chloride. Derived by evaporation from the Dead Sea, it contained other minerals as well, such as potassium compounds (mainly chlorides and carbonates found in modern 'potash'), with different solubility characteristics. If dried 'salts' became damp, the more soluble and distinctively savoury sodium chloride (modern table salt) would dissolve, be leached out and lost. This left only the less pleasant tasting residues of the various potassium salt compounds (potash) and other minerals. Jesus' followers are therefore called to retain their own distinctive 'flavour' of Christ-likeness rather than simply being 'wet'.

The passage as rendered here in the English has suffered an from English punctuation that contradicts what is known about the use of potash. Matthew records that salt, that has 'lost its saltiness', is 'no longer good for anything, except to be thrown out and trampled underfoot by men' (Matthew 5:13). 'Trampled underfoot' is '*katapateô*', literally meaning 'trodden against' (the ground). The residual potash of leached salt was trodden into the ground as a fertiliser. Luke's text can also be rendered, 'It is useless; it is thrown out either for the soil or for the manure pile', thereby making the meaning identical to Matthew's version. It was indeed 'thrown out' (as unfit for human consumption) and used instead for 'the soil' (replacing the potassium salts necessary for plant growth) or 'the manure pile' (for crop fertilisation). Its sole use was in horticulture.

In addition, 'useless' in the Luke's text is '*oute euthetos*', meaning 'not fit' (for humans to eat). Matthew 5:13 is '*ischuô*' ('good' - 'not good for anything except soil'). Doctor Luke's use of '*euthetos*' ('fit') was the common Greek medical term for a properly positioned broken bone. [164] It was also widely employed [165] by the physician, pharmacologist and botanist Pedanius Dioscorides (c. 40 - 90 AD) to describe treatments that were well suited for the need at hand. This is reflected in the modern description of something as 'fit for purpose'.

Having 'ears to hear' was something that Moses had reproached the Israelites for lacking (Deuteronomy 29:4). Rabbis invited their audiences to 'Come and hear', [166] meaning to gain understanding and then do something with it. Some of those who heard Jesus would do just that. But not as they might commonly have been expected to.

Chapter 15

15:1-2 'Now all the tax collectors and the sinners were coming near him to listen to him. Both the Pharisees and the scribes began to grumble, saying, "This man receives sinners and eats with them."'

Matthew's membership of Jesus' company of disciples would have served as a stepping stone for other Roman employed revenue collectors to hear the gospel. 'Sinners' (**'hamartôlos'**, from **'hamartanô'** - 'to miss the mark')* is, again, not referring primarily to immoral character but rather to those whose ignorance of Oral Torah led them to routinely unwittingly break it and so 'miss the mark' in relation to its requirements. The religious folk of Jesus' day would not go within 6 feet of such 'sinners', or as they were also known, 'People of the Land',[167] because of the risk of religious legal defilement. The fact that Jesus would even eat with them deeply disturbed Jesus' rabbinic peers, because it implied a disregard for their own creation, the Oral Law. And so they (in their view) quite reasonably 'grumbled' (**'diagogguzô'** - from **'gogguzô'**, 'an onomatopoeic word, representing the significance by the sound of the word, as in the word 'murmur' itself'). [168] A low rumble of discontent was being heard from the religious corner. There manmade rules were being disregarded and they were not happy about it.

15:3-7 'So he told them this parable, saying, "What man among you, if he has a hundred sheep and has lost one of them, does not leave the ninety-nine in the open pasture and go after the one which is lost until he finds it? When he has found it, he lays it on his shoulders, rejoicing. And when he comes home, he calls together his friends and his neighbours, saying to them, 'Rejoice with me, for I have found my sheep which was lost!' I tell you that in the same way, there will be more joy in heaven over one

sinner who repents than over ninety-nine righteous persons who need no repentance.'"

Sheep were often herded collectively, in which case the shepherd had a communal responsibility to the town or village as well as a personal one. Sheep, being notoriously dim-witted, would often end up in difficulties in the wild Judean rocky terrain where pasture was poor and sheep would commonly wander off in search of fresh grass. 'Open pasture' here ('wilderness' in the KJV) is *'erêmos'*, meaning 'desolate, deserted and lonely'; [169] the sparse nature of the scrub vegetation did not support flocks to remain in any one place for very long. Large flocks would have more than one shepherd - there is no suggestion in the passage that the remaining ninety-nine were being left to fend for themselves.

A lost sheep was a black-mark against a shepherd's professional competence; he would be expected to at least track the lost animal in order to bring back the skin or carcass as evidence of how the sheep had died. Shepherds (who were legally unclean), lived out with their flocks and had names for each of the sheep, for which they provided the personal level of care described in Psalm 23 (e.g. verse 5: 'He anoints my head with oil…'). The news of a lost sheep would have the village population watching eagerly for news; a safe recovery was worthy of a celebration. The joy in heaven stands in stark contrast to the Pharisees' attitude to the common folk who had not had their own educational opportunities or academic abilities in relation to Torah-learning. Like the authorities in John 7:49, they held that 'this crowd which does not know the Law is accursed.'

Once again, the term 'sinner', used here in a teaching to the Pharisees in response to their complaint about associating with those who did not know and therefore did not keep the Law (including the Oral Law), is used in the same legal sense, and not to mean the generally immoral. Similarly the term 'righteous' (*'dikaios'* - 'one who keeps the divine laws')* is used in the same legal sense - those (like the Pharisees) who were keeping the Law, and were proud of the fact. They were not truly right with God in the sense of their heart attitudes, but they were keeping the Law and hence did not need to 'repent' of that - their problems ran much deeper. The parable does not teach that such legalistic righteousness is a basis for entering the kingdom of God. Rather, the Law was given for the purpose of pointing out man's inherently corrupt nature and his fundamental inability to fix it of his own volition.

15:8-10 '"Or what woman, if she has ten silver coins and loses one coin, does not light a lamp and sweep the house and search carefully until she finds it? When she has found it, she calls together her friends and neighbours, saying, 'Rejoice with me, for I have found the coin which I had lost!' In the same way, I tell you, there is joy in the presence of the angels of God over one sinner who repents."'

The coins here are '***drachmas***', the Greek equivalent of the Roman '***denarii***', each being a day's wage for a workingman. The fact that the woman had ten indicates that they were probably part of the dowry-wedding gift from her husband's family, and therefore would have held a special sentimental as well as financial value. Part of the dowry went to the bride's family and part to the bride herself. The houses of Jesus' time were normally single-room dwellings; a lighted lamp on its stand would therefore illuminate the whole house. Search 'carefully' is '***epimelôs***', a word used solely by Doctor Luke in the New Testament, but in wide use by the physicians for the careful attention given by a physician. [170] Like the shepherd, the woman keeps up her search until she has found her lost coin, and on finding it, she considers that to be quite adequate a reason for having a celebration with her neighbours.

15:11-13 'And he said, "A man had two sons. The younger of them said to his father, 'Father, give me the share of the estate that falls to me.' So he divided his wealth between them. And not many days later, the younger son gathered everything together and went on a journey into a distant country, and there he squandered his estate with loose living."'

One of Jesus' best-known stories now unfolds to complete this 'lost' trio of parables. This time the Pharisees can engage with it personally - no 'unclean shepherding' or 'women house-cleaning', thank you - finally a story that set them out as the hero. Or did it? Two sons, one an obvious sinner, the other a good, hard-working Jewish boy - just like them! Jesus sets out the scene, painting a vivid picture of the terrible insult that asking for your inheritance before your father's actual death implied. The word 'prodigal' means 'extravagant to the point of wastefulness', and the story makes clear that it is not just the younger son who was prodigal, but the father was too. He extravagantly pours out his grace and forgiveness later in the story and extravagantly hands over monies up-front, not just to the younger but to the older son as well, who would have received double in accordance with the command of Deuteronomy 21:17. This did not render the father penniless - the money available to both sons was divided leaving the father with enough resources to continue running the family estate, and providing for his wife and servants, etc. The younger son's response to his father's extravagant generosity is to go a long way away and waste his share. 'Loose' living here is '*asôtôs*', meaning 'wasteful'. [171] It does not necessarily imply immoral living, as the older brother's seemingly dirty mind later suggests. He simply wasted his father's money.

15:14-16 'Now when he had spent everything, a severe famine occurred in that country and he began to be impoverished. So he went and hired himself out to one of the citizens of that country, and he sent him into his fields to feed swine. And he would have gladly filled his stomach with the pods that the swine were eating, and no one was giving anything to him.'

His wasteful squandering continued until the money was all gone, and he became destitute. But not yet destitute enough to repent. First he tried to fix the problem himself, by 'hiring' himself to a Gentile citizen. The Greek here is '*kollaô*', meaning 'to cleave', from '*kolla*' - 'to glue', indicating a sense of desperate need, even to the point of descending to the legally unclean state of feeding swine. The '*keration*' carob pods that the pigs ate were also known as 'locust beans', as were eaten by John the Baptist in the wilderness (see Matthew 3:4 and the earlier notes on Luke 3:2). This was a very poor class of legume, made all the worse by having been handled by Gentiles in collecting them as swine-fodder. And he was robbed again of respect; the parable stating that 'no one' (implying not even his Gentile employer) gave him anything - not even the wages due to him.

15:17-20 'But when he came to his senses, he said, 'How many of my father's hired men have more than enough bread, but I am dying here with hunger! I will get up and go to my father, and will say to him, "Father, I have sinned against heaven, and in your sight; I am no longer worthy to be called your son; make me as one of your hired men." So he got up and came to his father.'

Finally the younger son hits rock-bottom, and 'comes to himself'. Reality awakens sanity, and he compares himself and his new-found position of hired but robbed menial slave to a Gentile with those employed on his father's estate that he left behind. He recognises his state of '*appolumi*' - 'put away to destruction'* (literally, in a far-off land). He recognises that he has firstly wronged God, in dishonouring his father and living so wastefully, and secondly, sinned against his father in dishonouring the family. He resolves to return home and humble himself to a position of servitude - a '*misthios*' - a 'hireling' who works on a daily basis, rather than the somewhat more secure position of a '*doulos*' who was attached to a household on a permanent basis.

15:20-24 'But while he was still a long way off, his father saw him and felt compassion for him, and ran and embraced him and kissed him. And the son said to him, 'Father, I have sinned against heaven and in your sight; I am no longer worthy to be called your son.' But the father said to his slaves, 'Quickly bring out the best robe and put it on him, and put a ring on his hand and sandals on his feet; and bring the fattened calf, kill it, and let us eat and celebrate; for this son of mine was dead and has come to life again; he was lost and has been found.' And they began to celebrate.'

The father's extravagantly generous heart is again revealed. He is on the watch for his son, has compassion ('*splagchnizomai*' - 'moved with pity from the bowels'),* and goes to the culturally extraordinary and highly undignified length of running to him. Neither is he troubled by the smell of pigs - he 'seizes and falls upon him in an embrace' ('*epipiptô*').* 'Kissed' is in fact '*kataphileô*', meaning with 'repeated kisses'.* Before the son has had a chance to say the word 'hireling', the father is treating him in a manner worthy of both a son and an important guest. In that culture, slaves were barefoot, but the son has the ring of authority and sandals of sonship placed on him by the household servants, indicating his restored standing in the family. The 'best robe' is a '*stolê*', 'a loose outer garment for men extending to the feet, worn by kings, priests, and persons of rank'.* There was no greater honour the father could bestow. The fatted calf, possibly fattened in hope of the son's return, was the best meal a house could provide, complementing the lavish reception being bestowed upon him, in recognition of the importance of his restoration to sonship. At the command of the father, the household celebrates. But not all the household...

15:25-27 'Now his older son was in the field, and when he came and approached the house, he heard music and dancing. And he summoned one of the servants and began inquiring what these things could be. And he said to him, 'Your brother has come, and your father has killed the fattened calf because he has received him back safe and sound.''

The older son, who represents the Pharisees in Jesus' audience (who were no doubt by now thoroughly disgusted by the father's lenience toward the younger son's behaviour), is still busy working in the fields. On returning and hearing the sounds of a festivity, he learns of his brother's safe return. The older son has already received his (double) share of the inheritance, and the father doubtless acquired further wealth while the younger son was away. This is not a case of the father spending resources that belonged to the older brother. The father is too generous for that!

15:28-32 'But he became angry and was not willing to go in; and his father came out and began pleading with him. But he answered and said to his father, 'Look! For so many years I have been serving you and I have never neglected a command of yours; and yet you have never given me a young goat, so that I might celebrate with my friends; but when this son of yours came, who has devoured your wealth with prostitutes, you killed the fattened calf for him.' And he said to him, 'Son, you have always been with me, and all that is mine is yours. But we had to celebrate and rejoice, for this brother of yours was

dead and has begun to live, and was lost and has been found."

And now for the twist in the tale. Jesus has cleverly lulled his pharisaic audience into a state of self-righteous indignation. They know that they are the 'good guy' in the story; the loyal stay-at-home, work hard and keep the rules type. They loved the rules - the more the better - for the rules allowed them to lord their intellectual and moral superiority over the 'accursed' sinners who did not know the Law. They believe the older brother has a right to be upset; surely he is still the 'good guy'. But no! With a dramatic flourish, Jesus turns the tables on them. The 'good guy' they so identified with is really the 'bad guy'! In fact, he is much worse a 'bad guy' than the younger brother - a fact often lost on modern readers and commentators.

What the younger brother had done, bad as it was, had been conducted in private with the father and the consequences lived out in a distant land, far beyond the reach of public knowledge and associated family disgrace. But what the older brother does is to publicly humiliate his father in front of the household servants. He refuses to go in, and instead makes his father come out to plead with him. And he further humiliates his father by publicly accusing him of meanness, lying about his provision, knowing that the estate had been divided to him as well (verse 12), even double his brother's share, as the Law said. The Pharisees had received the Law in abundance but it had not changes their hearts for the better. The older brother's bitterness spills over into unfounded accusations against his most generous of fathers. His rancour leads him to allege unsubstantiated accusations of immoral behaviour against 'this son of yours', with not a shred of evidence. His refusal to accept the brother's restoration to a familial equality with himself as a fellow-brother is further proof of his rebellion against his father's authority. He completely humiliates and abuses his father in a way worthy of

293

death in a society which gave the father even the right of life and death over their sons for the dishonouring of the parent. Mark 7:10 - 'He who speaks evil of father or mother is to be put to death.' In a brilliant twist in the story, the supposed 'good guy' turns out to be a worse 'bad guy' than the initially supposed 'bad guy'.

Yet the father is still generous with grace and mercy. Grace because the older son gets what he does not deserve - the assurance that the bulk of the value of the estate, usually the land ('all that I have') is still his, and that he is 'always with the father' in the father's heart. And mercy because the older son does not get what he does in fact deserves - a severe punishment for blatant and extreme public dishonour of the father.

And so the story closes with the realisation that both sons are in fact 'bad guys', only one has returned and said sorry to his father. What will the older son do? Will he respond to the father's gracious invitation or not? And there the story ends, leaving a well defined question mark in the minds of Jesus' audience of Pharisees, who are still reeling from the dreadful realisation that the story has painted them to be worse, much worse, than the overtly sinful younger brother. How would they respond? It was for them to decide.

16:1-9 'Now he was also saying to the disciples, "There was a rich man who had a manager, and this manager was reported to him as squandering his possessions. And he called him and said to him, 'What is this I hear about you? Give an accounting of your management, for you can no longer be manager.' The manager said to himself, 'What shall I do, since my master is taking the management away from me? I am not strong enough to dig; I am ashamed to beg. I know what I shall do, so that when I am removed from the management people will welcome me into their homes.' And he summoned each one of his master's debtors, and he began saying to the first, 'How much do you owe my master?' And he said, 'A hundred measures of oil.' And he said to him, 'Take your bill, and sit down quickly and write fifty.' Then he said to another, 'And how much do you owe?' And he said, 'A hundred measures of wheat.' He said to him, 'Take your bill, and write eighty.'"

Jesus' teachings were rooted in real life experiences. There is more than an echo of contemporary relevance in the modern age where politicians see out their last days in office by feathering their nests for life after leaving their posts. Wheat and olives (used for oil) were the two most common items of produce in Galilee. [172] This parable is describing huge quantities. While the NASB translation above reads as 'measures', this is a poor translation for what is actually two quite different large quantities - the '**bath**' (about 40 litres) and the '**cor**' (over 400 litres). These quantities indicate that the master was extremely wealthy, and apparently not given to minutely scrutinising his servants over their shoulders. In this regard he is somewhat like God who entrusts the earth's resources to mankind with a measure of freedom for good or ill. The 'manager' ('**oikonomos**' - 'a household steward', from '*oikos*' - 'a house' and '*nemô*' - 'to manage'),* has been treating his master's goods as if they were his own. This was a common occurrence, often caused by greed or by a misplaced sense of injustice that leads to the thought that the goods should have been his and not his master's. Just as treasurers sometimes misappropriate funds, so the steward began to use them for himself. Jesus was probably well aware that Judas was behaving in the same way with the disciples' common purse. As John 12:6 relates, 'He had the money box and used to pilfer what was put into it.' If so there was a sense of home truths about the parable that made it all the more pertinent for at least one member of Jesus' audience - Judas' time for judgement had not yet come. 'Squandering' is '*diaskorpizô*', from '*skorpizô*' - 'to scatter', and was the common term for winnowing, whereby the threshed and separated wheat and chaff are together thrown into the air in order that the breeze will disperse to a distance the lighter chaff, with the heavier grain falling by the winnower. The steward is effectively throwing his master's resource around in a wasteful and dispersing manner.

But the steward is both realistic and shrewd. He knows he is finished in his present job and a reputation for dishonesty will not get him another like it. He lacks the physical stature needed for employment as a manual labourer and has no wish to be reduced to begging! But he still has time; he has not been summarily removed from his post. He has been asked to give an 'accounting' ('*logos*' - 'word'), which was an oral explanation of the master's business affairs, as used in Romans 14:12 - 'So then each one of us will give an account of himself to God.' The steward simply develops what he has been doing all along - misrepresenting his master's affairs. The exact details of their transactions are known only to himself and the debtor. By making the debtor re-write the documentation he is ensuring that the debtor is complicit in the theft. The steward only has to sign off what the debtor has declared. The steward can later, if necessary, claim he was acting in good faith and taking the debtor at face value. The debtor is now indebted to the steward not to expose any possibility of a deliberate error, for which the debtor, not the steward will be responsible. The debtors will have no choice but to 'welcome the steward into their homes.' If they don't, they might find the steward's memory of the real debt reviving, and they, not him, being accused of theft! This is because bonds of debt did not require witnesses, unless they were used as deeds for the purposes of a mortgage, whereupon three witnesses were required. These bonds are not being witnessed, and are surety against large purchases. The 'measure' of oil is '*batos*', meaning 'bath.' According to Ezekiel 45:10-11, 'You shall have just balances, a just ephah and a just bath. The ephah and the bath shall be the same quantity, so that the bath will contain a tenth of a homer and the ephah a tenth of a homer.' The 'bath' or 'ephah' equally applied to liquid and dry measures; one 'cor' equalled ten 'baths', one 'bath' equalled three 'seah', one 'seah' equalled two 'hin', one 'hin' equalled twelve 'log' and one 'log' equalled the space occupied by six eggs. [173] One hundred 'baths' of oil was therefore a lot of oil, in modern measurement equivalent of about 4,000 litres.

But not as much as the wheat the next man owed! 'Measure' there is actually 'cor', i.e. ten 'baths'. The 'cor' measured ten or eleven bushels, depending on the region, hence approximately 400 litres. The man owed 100 'cor' - around 40,000 litres of wheat - a huge amount. To reduce it by 20% was a substantial saving, one that would win the steward the friendship and future help of the debtor.

16:8-9 'And his master praised the unrighteous manager because he had acted shrewdly; for the sons of this age are more shrewd in relation to their own kind than the sons of light. "And I say to you, make friends for yourselves by means of the wealth of unrighteousness, so that when it fails, they will receive you into the eternal dwellings."'

'Shrewd' is *'phronimos'*, from *'phrên'*, meaning heart and diaphragm * - the diaphragm is supplied by the phrenic nerve. That area was held to be the seat of the understanding, and hence stood for wisdom. The steward, though dishonest, came up with a very clever way of securing his future, and it is his intelligence (not his dishonesty) that the master is 'praising' (*'epaineô'* - 'commend', from *'aineô'* - 'praise').* The master is evidently wealthy enough to take these losses 'on the chin', apparently having no legal remedy for them. He had been at the mercy of the steward, and seems to recognise that he got the due consequences of his misplaced trust. The point of the parable is that Christians are not exempt from the duty to exercise intelligence. They also have an unsurpassed access to a spiritual source of wisdom, due use of which will have eternal consequences of much greater significance than those enjoyed by the 'unjust steward', for all his worldly connivances.

Luke has already mentioned that a number of Jesus' disciples (and notably wealthy women) supported his ministry out of their own means, including one from the household of Herod Antipas (Luke 8:3). This would be a good illustration of 'the wealth of unrighteousness' reaping an eternal reward by being put to the service of the One from whom all wealth is derived. Using our resources to 'make friends' with non-Christians, so that we might convey the Gospel message to them, would be another example of wise behaviour that can have eternal consequences.

16:10-11 '"He who is faithful in a very little thing is faithful also in much; and he who is unrighteous in a very little thing is unrighteous also in much. Therefore if you have not been faithful in the use of unrighteous wealth, who will entrust the true riches to you?"'

Jesus is paraphrasing a rabbinic principle to the effect that changing the circumstances did not change the nature of the person within those circumstances. The rabbis had reasoned that the Law could not have been given to the Gentile nations of the world, since they had not observed the commandments given to Noah and his descendants, and so were consequently not worthy of the Torah brought through Moses. They told an illustrative parable in which a king had two administrators, one in charge of his gold and silver, and the other of his straw. The second administrator was believed to have behaved unfaithfully, and when suspected, said in his defence that he had not been set over the gold and silver. He was told, 'You fool, if you have rendered yourself suspected in regard to the straw, shall they commit to you the treasure of gold and silver?' The rabbis concluded that 'The Holy One, blessed be his Name, does not give great things to a man until he has been tried in a small matter.' [174]

16:12-13 '"And if you have not been faithful in the use of that which is another's, who will give you that which is your own? No servant can serve two masters; for either he will hate the one and love the other, or else he will be devoted to one and despise the other. You cannot serve God and wealth."'

Jesus asks a typically rabbinic rhetorical question, to which the answer is obvious - God will not reward unfaithfulness. If we are unfaithful with the temporal resources which we start with, and which are from him ('another's'), when everything we have has ultimately come from God, then we will not receive the eternal reward that God intends to be 'our own'. Our lives have only one throne. We can sit on it, love of money can sit on it, or God can sit on it. God will not share it with anyone or anything else. Additionally, if we try and accommodate two 'masters', we find ourselves moving outside the realm of the manufacturer's instructions and into instability. 'A double-minded man, unstable in all his ways, ought not to expect that he will receive anything from the Lord' (James 1:7-8). The reward ('that which is your own') should not be expected by the one who seeks to serve two masters.

16:14-15 'Now the Pharisees, who were lovers of money, were listening to all these things and were scoffing at him. And he said to them, "You are those who justify yourselves in the sight of men, but God knows your hearts; for that which is highly esteemed among men is detestable in the sight of God."'

The ultra-religious Pharisees, who loved money just as much as the next person and possibly a bit more, because they saw it as a sign of God's favour, deride Jesus for this teaching on freedom from love of money. 'Scoffing' is *ekmuktêrizô* from *muktêr* - 'nostril' - and literally means 'to turn up the nose at someone in the sense of sneering contemptuously' at them. [175] Certain of the Pharisees were notorious for making a public show of their supposed piety, parading it before their less religiously educated and therefore less legally correct fellow men. Matthew 6 verses 2 and 5 describes their practice of blowing a trumpet to draw attention to their alms-giving, and standing on street corners praying in order to be admired for their religious eloquence. They did this in order to 'justify' themselves (*dikaio* - 'show themselves righteous'),* wanting all to see how right they were in their legal practice of Torah. Their ritual correctness did not hide from God the state of their hearts. The praise that such ostentatious showing-off won from men made their actions no less 'detestable' (*bdelugma* - 'abominable', from *bdeô* - 'to stink') in the sight and nostrils of God, who turns away from such a stench. Men's ill-judged praise does not cut any ice with the One who sees the heart.

16:16-17 '"The Law and the Prophets were proclaimed until John; since that time the gospel of the kingdom of God has been preached, and everyone is forcing his way

into it. But it is easier for heaven and earth to pass away than for one stroke of a letter of the Law to fail."'

The announcement of good news ('*euaggelizô*' - the 'gospel preached') differed from the Law because it introduced a relationship based upon grace and faith rather than on legalistic religious practice. Such a relationship was only possible following the spiritual new birth ('from above' - John 3:3), a transformation that the 'change of mind and thinking' of repentance made possible. Such a change was possible for the religiously uneducated as well as those grounded in the practice of the religious Law. Consequently 'everyone' was able to respond to it, especially and particularly the majority of the audience who were not super-qualified in the religious society's complex legalistic practices. The Old Covenant's Scriptures (the Law and the Prophets) were preparing the ground for the repentance focussed ministry of John the Baptist. He prepared the ground for Jesus' sowing of the kingdom's seed into the now broken-up ground of his Jewish audience. As Jesus said (Matthew 11:12), 'From the days of John the Baptist until now the kingdom of heaven suffers violence, and violent men take it by force.' 'Violence' is '*biazô*', also meaning 'forceful', from '*bia*', meaning 'violent force'. God's kingdom is not somehow suffering violent abuse. On the contrary, the gracious invitation of God to a starving audience had led to a massive influx of people forcing their way into the new spiritual reality, attested to by the many signs and wonders that the author of the invitation performed in evidence of it.

So what of the Law? Now that the new and promised kingdom has come, what is its place? Is it now obsolete? Apparently not! Heaven and earth will pass away before one ever so tiny part of the Law given to and written down by Moses will pass away, 'Stroke' is '*keraia*', the term for an upward movement of a pen used to distinguish accents and letters. It is vital to remember that the written Law was given to Moses on Mount Sinai by One with whom Moses 'spoke face to face, as a man speaks with his friend' (Exodus 33:11), one whose 'finger' wrote the summary messages on tablets of stone (Exodus 31:18). This was no cloud or disembodied form of God. This was none other than the Second Person of the Triune Godhead, none other than the pre-incarnate Lord Jesus himself. In Luke chapter 2, the giver of Moses' Law can be seen teaching the teachers of Moses' Law. Jesus' words to Moses can no more pass away than can his words to the Pharisees recorded here in the Gospel of Luke. This written Law must be kept distinct from the Oral Law developed by generations of rabbinic scholars and referred to by Jesus in Mark 7:8 as 'the traditions of men' that caused them to 'neglect the commandments of God' (i.e. the written word given through Moses). The Oral Law had in some cases (e.g. 'Corban' and care of parents) been turned 180 degrees away from the written commandments that Jesus himself had given to Moses. The written Law given to Moses could not in itself save (as Paul's teachings in Romans and Galatians makes clear), but it remained the revealed word of God.

16:18 '"Everyone who divorces his wife and marries another commits adultery, and he who marries one who is divorced from a husband commits adultery."'

This verse is an example of the Law's staying power in proclaiming the mind and purposes of God. 'Divorcing a wife' was a pertinent 'hot topic' for Jews, with differences of legal interpretation at the highest level and reflected by the schools of Rabbi Hillel ('any reason at all' - Matthew 19:3) and Rabbi Shammai ('adultery only'). Mary, as Luke's source, who would have had extensive personal experience of Jewish women negatively affected by the different male rabbinic interpretations of the Mosaic Law around divorce.

For Jesus, the issue went back to the beginning, as related in the Book of Genesis, which describes the 'leaving and cleaving' that takes place within the covenant relationship of marriage. For the

Jews, covenant was sacrosanct; the concept towered over their history, going back to Abraham and beyond. God honoured covenant, and expected his people to do likewise. This is the conclusion that Jesus is presenting. Matthew's Gospel, written to a Jewish audience, gives the only grounds for divorce as *'porneia'*, meaning any kind of illicit sexual activity (and not 'adultery' - illicit sexual activity within a marriage), [176] an exception clause which is not repeated by Luke to his Gentile audience. The fidelity vows of the first century Jewish custom of betrothal were binding on the parties involved, and illicit sexual activity with another person during the betrothal stage, before the marriage ceremony occurred, was seen as a greater wrongdoing than sexual unfaithfulness after marriage (adultery). Matthew is therefore recording Jesus as stating that divorce can occur in the betrothal period (before the wedding's consummation) if one partner is sexually unfaithful to the other. Otherwise, Jesus depicts divorce and re-marriage as being equivalent to adultery.

16:19-21 '"Now there was a rich man, and he habitually dressed in purple and fine linen, joyously living in splendour every day. And a poor man named Lazarus was laid at his gate, covered with sores, and longing to be fed with the crumbs which were falling from the rich man's table; besides, even the dogs were coming and licking his sores."'

Jesus' hasn't yet finished with the Pharisees and their love of money. The parable of 'Dives and Lazarus' ('Dives' being Latin for 'rich') is told as part of his discourse with those who saw themselves as being spiritually rich and look down their noses at the spiritually impoverished 'sinners' that surrounded them. The Pharisees were rich in Torah and some used their legal knowledge to material advantage as well. Dressing in purple was a sign of serious wealth and status; in Rome a purple toga was worn only by the Emperor.

'Fine linen' is '*bussos*', from Syrian and Egyptian 'byssus' flax which was highly prized for its soft texture and pale colours. It is used to illustrate the trade in luxurious items between Syria and Tyre (Ezekiel 27:7) and of Mordecai's dress after his promotion by King Xerxes (Esther 8:15). The unnamed rich man's wealth is contrasted with the extreme poverty of the beggar Lazarus ('*ptôchos*' - 'poor', from '*ptôssô*' - 'to crouch or cower, in the manner of a beggar').* Such poverty does not lend itself to the sense of self-sufficiency that separates a man from God. Lazarus (from the Hebrew 'Eleazar' - 'God is my help') was a righteous man who had learned to put his trust in God (as his removal to paradise demonstrates) rather than those who denied him even the food that fell from their table and was eaten by their dogs.

For a Jew, being licked by a dog is not a source of comfort. It is adding an unclean insult to the injury of receiving no food or help from the rich man. Lazarus was 'covered' with sores ('*helkoô*'), a term found in a Greek medical treatise [177] and as a judgement of God in Revelation 16:2 and 11. Dogs were legally unclean; their mouths are also highly infested with bacteria. Their licking was no benefit to helping the open sores on the body of a malnourished beggar to heal.

16:22-24 '"Now the poor man died and was carried away by the angels to Abraham's bosom; and the rich man also died and was buried. In Hades he lifted up his eyes, being in torment, and saw Abraham far away, and Lazarus in his bosom. And he cried out and said, 'Father Abraham, have mercy on me, and send Lazarus so that he may dip the tip of his finger in water and cool off my tongue, for I am in agony in this flame.'"

Sheol, the Hebrew place of the dead, is presented as having two sections, one inhabited by the unrighteous (Hades, a place of torment) and one by the righteous (a place of comfort from the

Patriarch Abraham). The Jewish book of 4 Maccabees (13:17) describes the sons of the Jewish priest Eleazar bravely defying the Greek tyrant King Antiochus - 'If we die this way Abraham, Isaac and Jacob will give us a warm welcome.' To 'lie in the bosom' represented an intimacy of repose during a meal, just as the Apostle John reclined next to Jesus at the Last Supper (John 13:23). The parable evidences the fact that death is not the end of consciousness, but merely the entry into another realm where thinking and feelings still exist. The 'flame' of Hades prefigures the Lake of Fire described as the 'second death' in Revelation 20:14, and into which those in Hades find themselves thrown. The 'agony' of the flame is *'odunaô'*, meaning 'intense pain' and 'torment'.* Jesus taught more on hell than on any other single topic; he well knew the reality of it which was 'prepared for the devil and his angels' (Matthew 25:41). He was very concerned that his hearers avoided ending up there. The rich man asks only for a drop of water, possibly in return for some perceived benefit that Lazarus may have received from him. But even this small help is denied to him.

16:25-26 'But Abraham said, "Child, remember that during your life you received your good things, and likewise Lazarus bad things; but now he is being comforted here, and you are in agony. And besides all this, between us and you there is a great chasm fixed, so that those who wish to come over from here to you will not be able, and that none may cross over from there to us."'

There is no harshness in Abraham's response, no 'pay-back' for the indifference that Lazarus had perpetually been shown. Abraham can sympathise, but not help. 'Child' is *'teknon'*, also meaning 'son', thus recognising the common origin of them both. Hell was not designed for human beings, but sadly some, through their choices and omissions, will end up there. The finality is expressed by the

305

'great chasm' - '*megas chasma*', from '*chaskô*' - 'to yawn'. This term for a 'yawning abyss' [178] occurs in the Septuagint to describe the pit into which the body of David's errant son Absalom was cast. 'They took Absalom and threw him into a deep pit in the forest and erected over him a very great heap of stones' (2 Samuel 18:17).

16:27-31 'And he said, "Then I beg you, father, that you send him to my father's house, for I have five brothers, in order that he may warn them, so that they will not also come to this place of torment." But Abraham said, "They have Moses and the Prophets; let them hear them." But he said, "No, father Abraham, but if someone goes to them from the dead, they will repent!" But he said to him, "If they do not listen to Moses and the Prophets, they will not be persuaded even if someone rises from the dead."'

The parable evidences the fact that the human mind and conscience do not expire with the death of the body. Even in torment the rich man is thinking of his family and how to prevent them from sharing his fate. Surely the re-appearance of Lazarus would do the trick! Too little did he comprehend the indifferent and impervious nature of the human heart, already closed to the power of the Torah that Moses had passed on, and the power of the words spoken by those great men and women that God had anointed to speak his mind to a similarly indifferent Israel in years past. Such a resurrection would be dismissed as irrelevant by their hardness of heart, as was the case with many of Jesus' Pharisaic audience when he himself was bodily raised back to life and so widely evidenced in Judea that large numbers of the priests believed. 'The word of God kept on spreading; and the number of the disciples continued to increase greatly in Jerusalem, and a great many of the priests were becoming obedient to the faith' (Acts 6:7). The seed sown by Jesus' regular teaching in the Temple Courts had inevitably and finally germinated and born much fruit in the community of priests who worked there.

Chapter 17

17:1-2 'He said to his disciples, "It is inevitable that stumbling blocks come, but woe to him through whom they come! It would be better for him if a millstone were hung around his neck and he were thrown into the sea, than that he would cause one of these little ones to stumble."'

The concept of 'stumbling blocks' also figures prominently in Matthew's Gospel, and not just in his rendering of this portion of Jesus' teaching (Matthew 18:4-9). A *'skandalon'* ('stumbling block') is the movable trigger or baited part of a trap - the little dainty designed to trigger the violent snapping shut, and resulting imprisonment in a lifetime of sin and misery that the devil has so carefully planned for those who fall for his ruses. The word is also translated 'offence' [179] as in 'an occasion to fall' into sin. The same Greek word occurs when Paul's quotes Psalm 69:22: 'Let their table become a snare and a trap, a stumbling block and a retribution to them' (Romans 11:9).

Jesus identifies 'trap triggers' of 'stumbling' as the main means the devil uses to snare people into a spiritually compromised position. Radical steps are necessary to avoid them. Matthew's account includes the lines about 'plucking out the eye' and 'cutting off the hand or foot' if they are the means of the 'stumbling' arising, which are classic examples of rabbinic hyperbole for drastic measures of avoidance, rather than instruction to be taken literally. The rich man of the previous chapter would have done better to take stringent action than to arrive in the place of torment. 'Better for him' is *'lusiteleô'*, which is a term only appearing here in the New Testament, but which is a common medical term for a treatment of choice, advantageous to the patient over and above the other therapies. [180]

17:3-4 '"Be on your guard! If your brother sins, rebuke him; and if he repents, forgive him. And if he sins against you seven times a day, and returns to you seven times, saying, 'I repent,' forgive him."'

The devil prefers to use those closest to us to (often unwittingly) stumble us - that is far more effective than using a stranger whose words and actions are too remote to be of immediate harm. Jesus' command that we be 'on guard' (*'prosechô'* - 'beware', 'take heed to yourself') applies equally to any 'stumbling' we may do to others. Such sin (*'hamartanô'* - 'to miss the mark') should be 'rebuked'. This is a strong term - *'epitimaô'* - meaning 'to tax with fault, rate, chide, rebuke, reprove, and censure severely'.* This is supposed to produce repentance, *'metanoeô'* - meaning 'a change of mind and purpose'. [181] The fact that we as humans often err and wander off the path that God intends for us to follow is reflected in Jesus' comment on being offended against 'seven times a day' but still needing to forgive. 'Forgive' is *'aphiêmi'*, from *'hiêmi'*, to 'send away'. To forgive is literally to 'send the offence away' - to 'bid it depart.' To hold onto a sense of offence, however ostensibly justified, allows the sin to infect the one offended against. Much better then to 'send it away' and be free of the poisoned barb that would otherwise be so hard to remove, being designed by the devil to linger and allow a root of bitterness to grow, thereby defiling many. Hebrews 12:15 - 'See to it that no one comes short of the grace of God; that no root of bitterness springing up causes trouble, and by it many be defiled.'

17:5-6 'The apostles said to the Lord, "Increase our faith!" And the Lord said, "If you had faith like a mustard seed, you would say to this mulberry tree, 'Be uprooted and be planted in the sea'; and it would obey you."'

Apparently the idea of repeatedly forgiving their brother struck Jesus' chosen twelve as rather challenging! Matthew's account

(18:22) has Jesus going to 'seventy times seven' times, the point being that God does not set an arbitrary limit on the number of times he forgives, and neither should we. The disciples' request that Jesus 'increase their faith' seems to have been born out of a misunderstanding of what situational faith is and how it operates. Paul teaches in Romans 10:17 that 'faith comes from hearing (*'akoê'*, also meaning 'the thing heard')* and 'hearing *[the thing heard]* by the word of Christ'. It is not the faculty of hearing that is the key to faith, rather it is the word from God that is heard and believed that produces faith in us allowing us to make a God-empowered active response in obedience to what we have heard. A word from God can be as small as the word 'Come', which Jesus spoke to Peter from the midst of the liquid quake that was Lake Galilee in a storm. That one word, heard and believed by Peter, produced such an explosion of power in him, that it took him out of the boat and onto the water almost before he had had a chance to reflect on the physical impossibility of what he was doing.

Jesus' seed analogy makes the same point - size is not what matters, but instead the nature of the word heard (from God) and the environment of actively trusting and believing that will allow that seed to germinate. The mustard seed was the smallest seed known in Judea, yet it could grow to the size of a small tree that men could climb and birds could nest in. Its tiny size had become used in rabbinic metaphor. The Talmud records (*'Nidah'* 5a), 'A drop of blood of the size of a mustard seed' in relation to menstrual blood loss and associated legal uncleanness. God, for whom nothing is impossible (Luke 1:37), does not rely on physically impressive things. Matthew provides a version of this teaching that featured a mountain being moved; a mulberry tree is very small by comparison. If God speaks a word about a mulberry tree, that word will be accomplished - nothing can stand against it. Mulberry trees were tall and noted for their very deep root structure, but just one word from God can uproot them. This tree is a *'sukaminos'* (a 'sycamine tree',

309

also called the 'black-mulberry' owing to its berry-type fruit which were somewhat bitter), as opposed to the sycamore-fig tree that Zaccheus climbed in Luke 19:4. That was called the fig-mulberry as its leaves were similar to the mulberry tree. Luke is careful to distinguish these commonly confused trees, probably because both were used medicinally, but for different treatments. [182]

Jesus' audience would have been very familiar with one recent 'mountain moving'. King Herod the Great had decided to build a palace 12 kilometres south of Jerusalem; the site chosen because it was the site of one of Herod's military victories over the Jews. Herod 'found by experience that the Jews fell more heavily upon him than did the Parthians, and created him troubles perpetually, and this ever since he was gotten sixty furlongs from the city; these sometimes brought it to a sort of a regular battle. Now in the place where Herod beat them, and killed a great number of them, there he afterward built a citadel, in memory of the great actions he did there, and adorned it with the most costly palaces, and erected very strong fortifications, and called it, from his own name, Herodium.' [183]

The small existing hill however was not sufficient for Herod's grandiose purposes. So he did as he was wont to - he decided to turn it into a small mountain that exists to this day. Josephus further records that Herod 'did not neglect a memorial for himself, but built a fortress upon a mountain towards Arabia, and named it from himself, Herodium, and he called that hill that was of the shape of a woman's breast, and was sixty furlongs distant from Jerusalem, by the same name... He brought a mighty quantity of water from a great distance, and at vast charges, and raised an ascent to it of two hundred steps of the whitest marble, for the hill was itself moderately high, and entirely factitious. He also built other palaces about the roots of the hill, sufficient to receive the furniture that was put into them, with his friends also, insomuch that, on account of its containing all necessaries, the fortress might seem to be a city, but, by the bounds it had, a palace only.' [184]

Herod's 'factitious' mountain was constructed in a similar style to his Temple, which was based upon huge earthworks filling in the space around Mount Moriah, thereby forming a large artificial plateau on which to build. For Herodium, where he was to be buried, he went one better and made the mountain itself.

17:7-10 '"Which of you, having a slave ploughing or tending sheep, will say to him when he has come in from the field, 'Come immediately and sit down to eat'? But will he not say to him, 'Prepare something for me to eat, and properly clothe yourself and serve me while I eat and drink; and afterward, you may eat and drink'? He does not thank the slave because he did the things which were commanded, does he? So you too, when you do all the things which are commanded you, say, 'We are unworthy slaves; we have done only that which we ought to have done.'"'

This teaching illustration is commonly interpreted as showing that we are God's servants who serve in consequence of the grace we have received for salvation and that God does not owe us any debt for our service. While that is certainly true there is something much more significant in the passage. No master bids a slave to eat prior to having dined himself. But then Jesus is no ordinary master. Jesus is the type of master who stripped to his loincloth to wash his disciples feet prior to the Last Supper (John 13:4-5) in a preview of a much greater act of service that was shortly to be performed at Calvary. Jesus is the type of master who welcomes those who his defeat of death and Satan won salvation for, and invites them to his own marriage feast (Revelation 19:9), calling them his friends (John 15:14). To be sure we have the responsibility of serving him and his

311

kingdom and we are unworthy of doing so, but Jesus' shed blood propels us from a place of slavery to a place of sonship-type servanthood that bears the family name of God himself. We can take no credit for it, but we have a very different master to the conventional type that Jesus is describing. Jesus broke the mold by being a master who served his servants even unto death.

17:11-15 'While he was on the way to Jerusalem, he was passing between Samaria and Galilee. As he entered a village, ten leprous men who stood at a distance met him; and they raised their voices, saying, "Jesus, Master, have mercy on us!" When he saw them, he said to them, "Go and show yourselves to the priests." And as they were going, they were cleansed.'

Samaria separated Galilee in the north from Jerusalem, which was 120 miles to the south. The journey was difficult enough with the hostility shown by Samaritans towards those who journeyed towards Jerusalem (Luke 9:53). Now the disciples have lepers to deal with as well. This group stand at a respectful and legally required distance and call on Jesus by name, as well as with a title reflecting his authority. *'Epistatês'* ('Master') is a title only used by Luke in the New Testament and means 'Chief' or 'Commander'. [185] Luke is conveying to his Roman audience the authority that Jesus held not only legally in Jewish society as a *'Didaskalos'* ('Doctor' of Torah), but also spiritually as one who could raise the dead.

On this occasion Jesus gives no word of healing command, and there appears to have been no outward sign of the lepers receiving their healing until they had began to obey the Law's command (Leviticus 13:37), that a priest inspect them for freedom from the marks of leprosy. *Bacillus leprae* is transmitted naso-orally and attacks the body's sensory nerves leaving an area of pallor and numbness in the skin areas that those nerves supply. In an era without powerful antibacterial medication, leprosy was incurable. (In more modern times leprosy has been treatable using Dapsone, a sulphone antibiotic, since the 1940s; nowadays the anti-tuberculous agent Rifampicin is used instead.) What the priests thought of the healings is not recorded. Leprosy only very rarely spontaneously resolves and so to have nine lepers appearing at the same time would have raised a great deal of interest. Nine, because one of them decided he would prefer to go and say 'Thank you' to Jesus, than to go directly for priestly confirmation.

17:16-19 'Now one of them, when he saw that he had been healed, turned back, glorifying God with a loud voice, and he fell on his face at his feet, giving thanks to him. And he was a Samaritan. Then Jesus answered and said, "Were there not ten cleansed? But the nine - where are they? Was no one found who returned to give glory to God, except this foreigner?" And he said to him, "Stand up and go; your faith has made you well."'

Jesus clearly expected that this amazing miracle, performed upon ten diverse men, at a distance, with no touch made or word of command being spoken, warranted the return of all ten prior to them fulfilling his instruction to them to fulfil the Law's requirement that they be formally declared clean by a priest. It would be hard to imagine a clearer demonstration of divine power. Jesus' divinity is evidenced by it, or at the very least that God anointed his ministry in a unique way that pointed to his being their long awaited Messiah, whatever their understanding of that role may have been.

Jesus evidently expected that the Jewish recipients of his miraculous powers would have appreciated that perspective, but apparently they did not! We are not told why - perhaps they were keen to be re-united with their families from whom the deadly affliction would have separated them. Perhaps they were just too excited to think straight. Perhaps they came back later to thank Jesus. Perhaps one or two even joined his company of disciples. We are not told. What we do know is the one who might have been the least likely to get a correct perspective on the miracles is the one who returned, and not just to give thanks, but to 'fall on his face' at Jesus' feet, 'glorifying God', that is, giving God praise for what had happened. His bodily position, face down at the feet of Jesus, implies that he was clear that it was Jesus who was worthy of receiving this accolade on God's behalf. His giving of thanks is '*eucharisteô*', literally meaning 'to be thankful for good favour', and from which the word for the communion meal, 'Eucharist', is derived.

Jews despised Samaritans (and vice versa), but Jesus did not. The term for 'foreigner' used is not '*exô*' (an 'outsider' or 'stranger') as in Acts 26:11 - 'I kept pursuing them even to foreign cities.' Rather it is the non-emotive '*allogenês*', simply meaning 'one of another race'. [186] There is also a priestly element to Jesus' command that the Samaritan 'go' as a man 'made well' - '*sôzô*' - 'safe' from disease, 'healed and restored to health'.* Jesus himself declares the Samaritan legally clean, recognising the reluctance that any Jewish priest would have in being willing to examine a Samaritan, who they despised. The faith displayed in the active response to the word that he had heard from Jesus had made him, and the others, well.

17:20-21 'Now having been questioned by the Pharisees as to when the kingdom of God was coming, he answered them and said, "The kingdom of God is not coming with signs to be observed; nor will they say, 'Look, here it is!' or 'There it is!' For behold, the kingdom of God is in your midst."'

Not all the Pharisees were antagonistic towards Jesus, even at this later stage of his ministry. Nicodemus and the 'righteous' Joseph of Arimathea (Luke 23:50) were sufficient admirers to bury him even as one accursed to death by crucifixion. Many of the Pharisees admired Jesus highly for his Torah scholarship, and his opening the Scriptures to them in ways they had not heard before. Pharisees had already warned Jesus as to Herod Antipas' intention to kill him. These Pharisees appear to have seen in Jesus one who might well be about to usher in the kingdom of God. There was surely no one better qualified to do so! They seem to have seen that as synonymous with the expulsion of the ruling Roman power, in whose kingdom Judea very much resided. A Roman fort, Antonia, was attached to the Temple walls, and their graven image of an eagle was affixed, contrary to the Law, over the main Temple gate. [187] A Temple so defiled was certainly not what they envisaged as representing the 'kingdom of God'.

Jesus is swift to disabuse them of any such political aspirations. His was not a kingdom change in the manner of their illustrious ancestor, Judas Maccabeus, who had ejected the ruling Greek king Antiochus IV some 200 years earlier. Jesus' kingdom is not one of external political change; it is one of internal spiritual change that leads to an external change. The kingdom is 'in your midst' - '*entos*', meaning 'within' and 'among',* and is used in Matthew 23:26 to denote the 'inside' of the cup and plate that Jesus demands be made clean for use rather than simply the outside which many of the Pharisees focussed upon. There is a mistranslation of the Greek here in the NASB - the word 'signs' is not present. The text simply reads, 'The Kingdom of God comes not with observation.' Jesus' messianic ministry bore many miraculous signs - these were intended to be observed, and the correct conclusions drawn from them as to his true identity. 'Observation' is '*paratêrêsis*', from '*paratêreô*', meaning to 'watch assiduously'.* The sense is that merely watching closely, as many of Jesus' pharisaic audience were doing, would not bring about the changes needed to establish the kingdom in their lives. An internal response of repentance and faith was also required.

315

17:22-24 'And he said to the disciples, "The days will come when you will long to see one of the days of the Son of Man, and you will not see it. They will say to you, 'Look there! Look here!' Do not go away, and do not run after them. For just like the lightning, when it flashes out of one part of the sky, shines to the other part of the sky, so will the Son of Man be in his day."'

Days of persecution were coming - the lot of the crucified Master would be the lot of his disciples. When they came, the disciples would have been wishing they still had Jesus with them. There would be no need to be distracted though; by then they would have the Holy Spirit as 'another Comforter', just the same as Jesus only within them. They would not need anyone else to tell them what God was doing, it would be as clear as the sight of a lightning bolt shooting across the sky.

17:25-29 '"But first he must suffer many things and be rejected by this generation. And just as it happened in the days of Noah, so it will be also in the days of the Son of Man: they were eating, they were drinking, they were marrying, they were being given in marriage, until the day that Noah entered the ark, and the flood came and destroyed them all. It was the same as happened in the days of Lot: they were eating, they were drinking, they were buying, they were selling, they were planting, they were building; but on the day that Lot went out from Sodom it rained fire and brimstone from heaven and destroyed them all."'

Jesus' claims to divinity were about to move him out of the 'genius in Torah' category that had won him such respect with the authorities (as represented by Nicodemus in John chapter 3), and into the category of 'blasphemer', one guaranteed to bring Jesus suffering, rejection and death. For the religious leaders, that was simply 'business as usual' - doing whatever it took to maintain the status quo necessary to maintain their own standing in the Jewish community and not unduly upset the ruling Romans. But Jesus' death would seal the coming judgement upon their 'wicked and adulterous' generation; this 'evil and adulterous generation seeking after a sign would have no sign given it, except the sign of Jonah' (Matthew 16:4).

By 66 AD the Roman legions under Vespasian would besiege Jerusalem bringing unspeakable horror to its inhabitants over the four-year siege before its destruction in 70 AD. As in the days of Noah and Lot, until then the people would be taken up with normal life - simply ignoring God while they lived it. And by the time they realised that something was seriously wrong, it would be too late. Judgement would have arrived, just as the judgement upon Sodom, where Lot lived with his family, came swiftly after Abraham's intercession had failed to find even ten righteous people there.

17:30-33 '"It will be just the same on the day that the Son of Man is revealed. On that day, the one who is on the housetop and whose goods are in the house must not go down to take them out; and likewise the one who is in the field must not turn back. Remember Lot's wife. Whoever seeks to keep his life will lose it, and whoever loses his life will preserve it."'

Jesus' prophecy takes in both the coming destruction of Jerusalem under Vespasian and also his second coming, when he will return as judge. It will be precipitate, just as the Roman army encircled Jerusalem and imprisoned its inhabitants in what became a dreadful four year siege and famine from 66-70 AD. For the watching believers, who, thus warned, were able to escape the Roman military ring to safety in nearby Pella, Jesus' warning was the source of their survival. Lot's wife, caught in indecision, had been turned into a pillar of salt. 'His wife, from behind him, looked back, and she became a pillar of salt' (Genesis 19:26). 'Life' is *psuchê*, also translated as 'soul' - the spiritual life that God has given and that renders the human personality, from which we derive the term 'psyche'. It distinguishes each human being, and that which will survive after death, either with God or separated from him. Seeking to 'keep' it, in using it for one's own agendas rather than submitting it to God's, will cause it to be lost. 'Preserve' life is *zôogoneô*, another term that is only used in the Gospels by Doctor Luke. It has a medical meaning, and was used by Greek physicians to mean 'keeping a patient alive'. [188]

17:34-37 '"There will be two women grinding at the same place; one will be taken and the other will be left. Two men will be in the field; one will be taken and the other will be left." And answering they said to him, "Where, Lord?" And he said to them, "Where the body is, there also the vultures will be gathered."'

The prophetic picture now seems to fast-forward from 70 AD to Jesus' return from heaven, when his followers will 'meet him in the air'. 1 Thessalonians 4:17 - 'We who are alive and remain will be caught up together with them in the clouds to meet the Lord in the air, and so we shall always be with the Lord.' Being married to or working with a believer ought to have a significant influence on unbelievers, but evidently insufficiently in this illustration of Jesus'. Unbelievers are left behind. The disciples want to know more details, but all they get is a metaphor. When it happens it will be obvious. The sight of birds of prey on the horizon circling, then landing and taking off again, tells of the carcass on the ground that cannot be seen at that distance. Birds of prey, like the lightning of verse 24, cannot be hidden, and neither can Jesus' return. It will be obvious to all.

Chapter 18

18:1-5 'Now he was telling them a parable to show that at all times they ought to pray and not to lose heart, saying, "In a certain city there was a judge who did not fear God and did not respect man. There was a widow in that city, and she kept coming to him, saying, 'Give me legal protection from my opponent.' For a while he was unwilling; but afterward, he said to himself, 'Even though I do not fear God nor respect man, yet because this widow bothers me, I will give her legal protection, otherwise, by continually coming she will wear me out.'"'

The fact that Jesus is describing a 'judge' (singular), indicates that the judge in question was a Roman. Jewish judges judged in groups of three, to counter bias and bribery. A Jewish judge who did not himself fear God would have been a very unusual scenario, but Roman judges certainly did not and often greatly resented being in such a far-flung and obscure portion of their Empire, in what was a somewhat dangerous buffer zone against their Parthian enemies in the east. A Roman judge would make the plight of the (Jewish) widow even more dire, as she would have been unable to appeal to the protections afforded by the Jewish Law. Roman judges were called 'Dayyaney Gezeroth' - a Judge of Prohibitions. [189] Poor pay left them easy to bribe, for which reason the Jews referred to them using a rather humourous play-on-words, calling them 'Dayyaney Gezeloth' (Robber-Judges). The Talmud records that for even a dish of meat, they would pervert justice. [190]

The woman could not appeal to the Torah in her claims, and being a widow apparently has no family to speak for her. But she had one thing in her favour. She was persistent! She was apparently money-poor, but definitely time-rich. Her persistence and importunity wore the judge down. He considered his time to be more valuable and so eventually yielded to the widow's claims rather than to continually be pestered by her.

18:6-8 'And the Lord said, "Hear what the unrighteous judge said; now, will not God bring about justice for his elect who cry to him day and night, and will he delay long over them? I tell you that he will bring about justice for them quickly. However, when the Son of Man comes, will he find faith on the earth?"'

The point of this parable is that God's attitude towards his children is the diametric opposite of the judge's initial attitude to the widow. He will see justice done for them 'quickly' ('*tachos*' - 'soon'). There is a strength of intercessory prayer indicated in 'crying day and night' that may go some way to understanding why some Christians find that God's timetable of 'soon' is not always the same as theirs. There is something in a baby's cry that forces the parents to answer. The God who can see the heart knows the quality of our crying out to him - the sincerity, even desperation. It is in that attitude that Jesus promises a swift response. Jesus' reference to 'finding faith on the earth' may pertain to this quality of faith, rather than faith in general.

18:9-13 'And he also told this parable to some people who trusted in themselves that they were righteous, and viewed others with contempt. "Two men went up into the Temple to pray, one a Pharisee and the other a tax collector. The Pharisee stood and was praying this to himself: 'God, I thank you that I am not like other people: swindlers, unjust, adulterers, or even like this tax collector. I fast twice a week; I pay tithes of all that I get.' But the tax collector, standing some distance away, was even unwilling to lift up his eyes to heaven, but was beating his breast, saying, 'God, be merciful to me, the sinner!"'

Once again the Pharisees find themselves at the receiving end of a parable. Tax collectors were somewhat older, educated (that is, religiously educated) Jews - the Romans were not in the habit of entrusting their revenue collections to illiterate youngsters. Jesus' disciple Matthew is widely understood to have worked as a scribe before becoming a tax collector. The Pharisees correctly thought that religious folk should know better than to aid and abet the Gentile invaders whose golden eagle of Imperial Rome defiled the Temple gate. [191] Where they went wrong was moving into a place of judging with 'contempt'. This is *exoutheneô*, also meaning 'to despise utterly' and 'to make of no account', from *oudeis*, meaning 'nothing'.* No one made in the image of Almighty God is 'nothing' or 'to be set at nought'; they have far too much intrinsic value for that, and God does not take kindly towards those who adopt such an attitude to his estranged offspring, however out of line their lifestyle may be.

The tax collector is certainly a religious Jew - he is praying in the Temple - and has the huge advantage, in God's eyes, of humility. He knows his own failures and sins, and acknowledges them toward God. He is remorseful for them, striking himself in the chest in the Jewish manner of mourning (Luke 23:48). He does not consider himself worthy of mixing with the more overtly religious folk, but keeps at a distance from the Pharisee, who he would have seen as someone who kept the Law, and so was 'righteous' in as far as the Law could declare him so.

Paul would later speak of himself as a Pharisee, 'As to the righteousness which is in the Law, found blameless' (Philippians 3:6). The tax collector is acutely aware of his own unrighteousness, a sense aggravated by his knowing that as an educated Jew, he had no excuse for not keeping the Law. He had become *hamartôlos* - 'one who misses the mark' that the Law set out, [192] but one without the excuse of the common man who had not been fully taught the Law.

Just as the tax collector was convinced of his own unrighteousness, so the Pharisee was convinced of his own righteousness - his prayers revolve around himself. He projected his own righteousnesses onto them, forgetting the word of Isaiah 64:6 - 'All our righteous deeds are like a filthy garment.' They are offensive to God because these deeds are a product of our own sinful natures. 'Filthy' here is '*iddâ*', which means 'menstruation',* something that the Law taught rendered one ritually unclean. Lamentations 1:17 reads, 'Jerusalem has become an unclean thing among them' - 'unclean' being '*niddah*' which also means 'menstruation'.*

The Pharisee compares himself with those who were obviously unrighteous (the tax collector, whose ears his spoken prayers were intended to reach in condemnation), rather than with God by whose standards even the most devout Jew fell far short. The Apostle Paul was a student of the Doctor of Torah Gamaliel. As such he would have been privy to Jesus' Temple teaching, which no doubt covered similar grounds. He reflects this parable of Jesus in his second letter to the Corinthians. 'When they measure themselves by themselves and compare themselves with themselves, they are without understanding' (2 Corinthians 10:12). First up in the Pharisee's prayer is 'swindlers'. This is '*harpax*', also meaning 'extortioner', a form of 'robbery' where possessions are 'carried off by force'. [193] The Pharisee has 'half an eye' on the tax collector who would doubtless have been guilty of exacting such revenue collection. Next is 'unjust'. This is '*adikos*', meaning 'one who violates justice and who deals fraudulently with others.'*

Tax collectors were notorious for fraudulent dealing; either exacting more than they should or taking a bribe in return for letting people off full payment. 'And some tax collectors also came to be baptized, and they said to him, "Teacher, what shall we do?" And he said to them, "Collect no more than what you have been ordered to"' (Luke 3:12-13). With this the Pharisee has 'one whole eye' trained on the tax collector! Third in his list comes 'adulterers' ('*moichos*'). This may have been the Pharisee getting carried away in his thinking, or it is more likely being used metaphorically to denote those who were unfaithful to God - all those who were not as religious as he was. This 'spiritual adultery' is the sense of use in Ezekiel 23:43. 'Then I said concerning her who was worn out by adulteries, 'Will they now commit adultery with her when she is thus?'' If so, 'one and a half eyes' are now on the tax collector, for he had forsaken the God of Israel to serve the foreign pagan invading army and raise money for Rome. Fourthly and finally both the Pharisee's accusing eyes are now firmly trained on tax collector - 'Or even like this tax collector!' '*Yes, you over there!*'

Now comes the Pharisee's means of self-justification. The annual compulsory fast of the Day of Atonement was not enough for him; he fasted twice a week. Devout Jews often fasted on Monday and Thursday, which were market days, thus giving an opportunity to disfigure themselves in public display of their own piety. Jesus taught against this - 'Whenever you fast, do not put on a gloomy face as the hypocrites do, for they neglect their appearance so that they will be noticed by men when they are fasting' (Matthew 6:16). Devout Pharisees tithed all that they acquired, yet more devout ones would not trade with those who did not keep those standards, which went beyond those prescribed by the Law. 'You shall surely tithe all the produce from what you sow, which comes out of the field every year' (Deuteronomy 14:22). The Mishnah states of them 'He tithes all that he eats, all that he sells, and all that he buys, and he is not a guest with an unlearned person.' [194] Because if he were to be their guest he might inadvertently transgress this stricter legal interpretation by eating of something of which the whole had not been tithed from, and so break this self-imposed higher standard.

18:14 "I tell you, this man went to his house justified rather than the other; for everyone who exalts himself

will be humbled, but he who humbles himself will be exalted."'

God's word is the only true measuring rod, against which all fall short. 'All have sinned and fall short of the glory of God' (Romans 3:23-24.) No human, however devout but still touched by sin, can continually keep the tenth commandment - 'You shall not covet'. In Christ we are gifted God's own righteousness; there is therefore no possible grounds for boasting. Paul again: 'For who regards you as superior? What do you have that you did not receive? And if you did receive it, why do you boast as if you had not received it? (1 Corinthians 4:7). It was the tax collector whose prayers God heard and it was he whom God graciously forgave. He went home 'justified' (*'dikaioô'* - 'pronounced righteous').* God had seen his humility (*'tapeinoô'* - 'made low') [195] and had 'exalted' him (*'hupsoô'* - 'raised up')* from his place of lowliness, not on the grounds of his own righteousness, but of God's mercy.

18:15-17 'And they were bringing even their babies to him so that he would touch them, but when the disciples saw it, they began rebuking them. But Jesus called for them, saying, "Permit the children to come to me, and do not hinder them, for the kingdom of God belongs to such as these. Truly I say to you, whoever does not receive the kingdom of God like a child will not enter it at all."'

The theme of lowliness and humility continues, as a crèche moves through a crowd. 'Babies' is *'brephos'*, the term for a baby still in-utero (Luke 1:41 and 44) or for a newborn (Luke 2:12 and 16, Acts 7:19). Jesus in his public ministry was by now surrounded by 'many thousands' of people who were 'stepping on one another' (Luke 12:1). How did a group of mothers carrying newborn babies (of little standing in that society), even get anywhere near Jesus through such massive crowds? They must have had someone accompanying them whom the crowds would have recognised and given way to. Who could that have been? Who would have had a personal sympathy for the nursing mothers and their tiny infants? Mary was well aware of the importance of babies in the plan of God, having borne the Saviour; she was also well aware of their lowly state in a male dominated society that gave women few rights and infants even fewer. Someone with the same sympathies no doubt assisted these mothers. Someone close to Jesus, very close indeed - his own mother - now acting as Luke's primary source. To whom else would a group of mothers with babies appeal to gain access to the One now surrounded by massive crowds, and whose time was sought even by kings such as Herod Antipas? [xxiv] Mary, Jesus' own mother, was the logical person for these mothers to turn to for assistance.

By this stage in his ministry, demand for Jesus' time was so great that his disciples largely controlled access to him. John 12:20-22: 'Now there were some Greeks among those who were going up to worship at the feast; these then came to Philip, who was from Bethsaida of Galilee, and began to ask him, saying, "Sir, we wish to see Jesus." Philip came and told Andrew; Andrew and Philip came and told Jesus.' There was a hierarchy to be followed, and no doubt there were many societally important figures pressing the disciples for access to this great Temple *Didaskalos* from Nazareth. You couldn't just turn up unannounced and uninvited and expect to be escorted through the crowds into Jesus' presence. But the crowd would know who Mary was and they would have respectfully made way for her and the following group of mothers carrying their babies. Mary surely took them right to the front of the queue, before

---

[xxiv] 'Herod the tetrarch heard of all that was happening; and he was greatly perplexed, because it was said by some that John had risen from the dead, and by some that Elijah had appeared, and by others that one of the prophets of old had risen again. Herod said, "I myself had John beheaded; but who is this man about whom I hear such things?" And he kept trying to see him' (Luke 9:7-9).

the disciples had had a chance to realize what was happening and intervene. So what was the reaction of the disciples to Mary going 'under their radar', by-passing their own perceived importance as the gate-keepers to Jesus' presence and cutting their input out of the access equation? Would they have had the courage to criticize Jesus' mother directly? They would not. So instead they direct their own misplaced self-righteous sense of deflated self-importance on to the defenseless mothers. Surely babies could not be on the Master's agenda? So the disciples thought - there were many more important and worthy folk who wanted just a few minutes of Jesus' time. They couldn't squeeze all of them in! No time then for a crèche!

So the disciples unkindly rebuke the mothers, intentionally ignoring the role of the mother who had surely brought them through the crowd. 'Rebuke' is '*epitimaô*', a strong word meaning to 'censure severely'. Mary's recounting of the story to Luke sensitively omits the strength of Jesus' reaction to his less than gracious disciples. Peter however seems to have been suitably chastened and humble enough to include it in his own account of the incident in Mark's Gospel. Mark 10:14 - 'Jesus was indignant and said to them, "Permit the children to come to me; do not hinder them; for the kingdom of God belongs to such as these."' 'Indignant' is '*aganakteô*', also meaning 'much displeased', 'grieved' and 'violently irritated'. [196] It is a very strong term indeed, surely made the more so by the way his mother's godly intentions had been disregarded, in addition to the offence against these other Jewish mothers with their babies. A good opportunity indeed to teach his errant disciples the importance of humility. Babies are completely dependent upon their mothers to feed them; the infant human is the least placed to survive without its mother and remains so for a very long period of time relative to other creatures that God has made. This brings with it a lesson in the place of absolute dependence upon God that believers need to manifest if they are to be effective in their Father's service. The way to 'receive the kingdom' (dependent trust and faith) is the same as the way to live in it and to 'belong in it' (dependent trust and faith). Babies and infants epitomise this attribute of dependency. They come with nothing of themselves to bring, no sense of pride or self-importance, just a sense of total dependency and trust. There is no better way to approach the omnipotent Creator God.

18:18-21 'A ruler questioned him, saying, "Good Teacher, what shall I do to inherit eternal life?" And Jesus said to him, "Why do you call me good? No one is good except God alone. You know the commandments, 'Do not commit adultery, do not murder, do not steal, do not bear false witness, honour your father and mother.' And he said, "All these things I have kept from my youth."'

Mark says that this 'ruler' was young and 'came running' (Mark 10:17), presumably as Jesus was by then moving away from that place. He addresses Jesus as '*agathos didaskalos*' - 'Good Doctor'. 'Doctor' or 'Master' here is a title, but the young man is clearly not one of Jesus' disciples. He is addressing Jesus formally, as one asking a serious question of a Master of their Law. The term 'Master' is the same word used to describe the 'Doctors of the Law' whom the twelve-year-old Jesus had debated with and taught in the Temple courts and is the term used by Jesus to Nicodemus, a Sanhedrin scholar (John 3:10). Jesus held this same title of highest honour, which could only be awarded by the Sanhedrin and only to the most expert of the Jewish scribal lawyers.

The Gospels record on forty-six occasions that Jesus is addressed formally with this title, and eighteen of these are in formal teaching sessions, many with the antagonistic Jewish hierarchy, which he would be expected, as a Doctor of Torah, to participate in. Jesus accepts the 'Doctor' ('Master') element of the title, but takes issue with the 'good' aspect. Is the young man calling him God? Jesus knows that he is not doing so, but is challenging him to consider this possibility! Jesus then helps him review the second 'table of the Law' - those commandments that pertained to human relationships, and takes no issue with the young man's claim that those have been adhered to faithfully. The issue for Jesus is the first table of the Law - how has the young man measured up to God's commandments in terms of relating to God himself? Had he 'loved God with all his heart, soul and strength and might'? (Deuteronomy 6:5). 'Might' is '*meod*', also meaning 'exceeding abundance', including material resources. The word is translated as 'rich' in Genesis 13:2, 'Abram was very rich in livestock.' And how about that other great commandment, 'You shall love your neighbour as yourself'? (Leviticus 19:18). How had the rich young ruler dealt with his poorer neighbours? Was he, in accordance with God's word, in control of his God-given resources or were they in control of him?

18:22-23 'When Jesus heard this, he said to him, "One thing you still lack; sell all that you possess and distribute it to the poor, and you shall have treasure in heaven; and come, follow me." But when he had heard these things, he became very sad, for he was extremely rich.'

As well as seeing the ruler's evidently wealthy dress, Jesus can see that there is an idol taking up God's rightful place in his heart. Jesus lovingly wants him to be set free of its hold on him, so advises him to get rid of the obstruction to his love for God and neighbour by selling his possessions and achieving an eternal reward in their place. Jesus himself had done this in stepping out of a place of wealth and privilege in the Temple schools to travel and live in a very simple fashion proclaiming the Gospel. Unfortunately, at this point at least, the man's possessions possess him too strongly for this to be possible. We are not told what happened later, when the effect of Jesus' look of '*agapao*' love (Mark 10:21) was fully felt, but it would be surprising indeed if a response was not eventually made to those seeds that Jesus had sown into his life.

18:24-27 'And Jesus looked at him and said, "How hard it is for those who are wealthy to enter the kingdom of God! For it is easier for a camel to go through the eye of a needle than for a rich man to enter the kingdom of God." They who heard it said, "Then who can be saved?" But he said, "The things that are impossible with people are possible with God."'

Jesus contradicts the commonly held view that riches were a sign of God's blessing by making the point that they can actually hinder a spiritual response to God (in part by fostering a sense of self-reliance). He uses witty hyperbole, where an exaggerated example of impossibility is used to make a point (in this case a big animal trying to get through something very small). Fortunately, God the Father has things as important as people's eternal destiny well in hand! Some have thought that the reference is to a small gate in the wall of Jerusalem said to have been called 'The Eye of the Needle'. There has never been any good evidence for this and a similar proverb was in use elsewhere in which an elephant was substituted for a camel.

An alternative translation to 'camel' ('*kamêlos*') makes equal sense of Jesus' saying, assuming Jesus was speaking in Aramaic, in which '*gamla*' means both 'camel' and 'rope'. The application to a 'needle' (Luke's choice of '*belone*' has a surgical use in suturing wounds) [197] in attempting to thread a needle using a thick rope, carries the same sense of impossibility as a camel passing through a small opening. Whichever the original version (and both may have been used on the different occasions Jesus gave this teaching), it should, as Jesus reminds us, be remembered that 'with God all things are possible' (Mark 10:27). God is not hindered by the boundaries of human impossibility.

18:28-30 'Peter said to him, "Behold, we have left our own homes and followed you!" And he said to them,

"Truly I say to you, there is no one who has left house or wife or brothers or parents or children, for the sake of the kingdom of God, who will not receive many times as much at this time and in the age to come eternal life."'

The issue of eternal reward is one that Peter wishes to explore further, from a personal perspective. What will he and his colleagues receive? He was probably not imagining anything as lofty as the role of judge within the people of Israel, as Jesus later promised: '"Truly I say to you, that you who have followed me, in the regeneration when the Son of Man will sit on his glorious throne, you also shall sit upon twelve thrones, judging the twelve tribes of Israel"' (Matthew 19:28). But then God the Father is someone who has always been 'able to do immeasurably more than all we ask or imagine, according to his power that is at work within us!' (Ephesians 3:20, ANIV). Being a disciple means following the master, even if that means leaving one's home and family, as the apostles had done. The disciples who acted for the sake of the kingdom of God ('sake' is '*heineken*', meaning 'for the cause')* in this life would receive both a present and a future reward.

18:31-33 'Then he took the twelve aside and said to them, "Behold, we are going up to Jerusalem, and all things which are written through the prophets about the Son of Man will be accomplished. For he will be handed over to the Gentiles, and will be mocked and mistreated and spit upon, and after they have scourged him, they will kill him; and the third day he will rise again."'

Having told his disciples of their reward programme, Jesus brings them down to earth with a bump. Any illusions they may have had of messianic kingdom-glory in human terms are challenged by Jesus' stark and accurate prophetic foretelling of the suffering and indignities that he, and by extension they too, would undergo. Not for nothing does the Old Testament Scripture portray the Messiah as a suffering servant. Isaiah 53:3-6 and 10: 'He was despised and forsaken of men, a man of sorrows and acquainted with grief; and like one from whom men hide their face he was despised, and we did not esteem him. Surely our griefs he himself bore, and our sorrows he carried; yet we ourselves esteemed him stricken, smitten of God, and afflicted. But he was pierced through for our transgressions, he was crushed for our iniquities; the chastening for our wellbeing fell upon him, and by his scourging we are healed. All of us like sheep have gone astray, each of us has turned to his own way; but the Lord has caused the iniquity of us all to fall on him... But the Lord was pleased to crush him, putting him to grief; if he would render himself as a guilt offering.'

Being spat on by a Gentile was probably not at the top of the disciples' list when it came to being accounted of worth by men! Neither was being mocked, mistreated, scourged and killed. And this was God's 'plan A'? The apparent 'foolishness' in human eyes of this reversal of what the disciples must have imagined would be the glory of Messiah's kingdom would instead reveal the long-planned wisdom of God. As Paul would later write, God chooses the 'foolishness of the message preached to save those who believe. For indeed Jews ask for signs and Greeks search for wisdom; but we preach Christ crucified, to Jews a stumbling block and to Gentiles foolishness, but to those who are the called, both Jews and Greeks, Christ the power of God and the wisdom of God. Because the foolishness of God is wiser than men, and the weakness of God is stronger than men (1 Corinthians 1:21-25).

The glory of the resurrection is mentioned but the sheer scale of the shift to abuse rather than human triumph must surely have overshadowed it in the minds of the disciples, who would have been deeply shocked to hear such predictions coming from the mouth of One who only spoke truth.

18:34 'But the disciples understood none of these things, and the meaning of this statement was hidden from them, and they did not comprehend the things that were said.'

The disciples' minds could not compute the enormity of what they were hearing. Part of this would have been the shocking nature of Jesus' graphic depiction of suffering and rejection, but more than that there was the fact of God hiding it from them. God is a God who hides his truth, though he hides it for us to discover it. Proverbs 2:1-7a reads: 'My son, if you will receive my words, and treasure my commandments within you, make your ear attentive to wisdom, incline your heart to understanding. For if you cry for discernment, lift your voice for understanding. If you seek her as silver, and search for her as for hidden treasures; then you will discern the fear of the Lord, and discover the knowledge of God. For the Lord gives wisdom; from his mouth comes knowledge and understanding. He stores up sound wisdom for the upright.' God's words are likened to 'silver', and in verse 4, to 'hidden treasure' to be 'searched for'.

When we find them, we 'discover the knowledge of God': the One who 'gives wisdom', and from whom comes 'knowledge and understanding' which he has 'stored up for the upright' - for those who have set their hearts on seeking and following him. Jesus drew from this passage from the Old Testament Book of Proverbs in his teaching in Matthew 13:44 - 'The Kingdom of Heaven is like a treasure hidden in the field, which a man found and hid again; and from joy over it he goes and sells all that he has and buys that field.' The man found the treasure because he was looking for it - he did not accidently stumble over it. God chose to initially hide the meaning of Jesus' saying from the disciples, but it would not be long before they would find it and understand it.

18:35-39 'As Jesus was approaching Jericho, a blind man was sitting by the road begging. Now hearing a crowd

going by, he began to inquire what this was. They told him that Jesus of Nazareth was passing by. And he called out saying, "Jesus, Son of David, have mercy on me!" Those who led the way were sternly telling him to be quiet; but he kept crying out all the more, "Son of David, have mercy on me!"'

Mark 10:46-52 identifies this blind beggar as Bartimaeus, and Matthew's account (20:30) describes a second blind beggar with him whom Jesus also heals. Blindness was a common affliction in an era before antibiotics and drugs that can control the raised intra-ocular pressure of glaucoma. It was also one of the afflictions whose cure was specifically denoted as a messianic sign. Isaiah 42:6-7: 'I am the Lord, I have called you in righteousness, I will also hold you by the hand and watch over you, and I will appoint you as a covenant to the people, as a light to the nations, to open blind eyes, to bring out prisoners from the dungeon, and those who dwell in darkness from the prison.'

The noise of the crowd naturally aroused Bartimaeus' curiosity, and when he learns who all the fuss is about, his immediate name recognition and vigorous response demonstrates the fame that Jesus had in the region around Jericho (Matthew 20:29). 'Son of David' was a messianic title, and there was further evidence of self-important crowd-control in the response that he draws from 'those that led the way', quite possibly some of the same twelve apostles who had so recently tried to stop the mothers and babies from 'bothering' Jesus with their presence. 'Sternly telling' him is '*epitimaô*', 'to rebuke' or 'censure severely',* a humanly pompous over-reaction to the calling out of Jesus' name and title, indicating that 'those who led the way' were either uncomfortable with the title or, more likely, were more convinced of their own self-importance than they were of Bartimaeus' need of healing. Bartimaeus, like the widow in the parable of the unrighteous judge, demonstrated the importunity in asking that God looks for. He responds by re-doubling his cries ('he cried the more a great deal' - Mark 10:48-49).

18:40-43 'And Jesus stopped and commanded that he be brought to him; and when he came near, he questioned him, "What do you want me to do for you?" And he said, "Lord, I want to regain my sight!" And Jesus said to him, "Receive your sight; your faith has made you well." Immediately he regained his sight and began following him, glorifying God; and when all the people saw it, they gave praise to God.'

In contrast to the high-handed attitude of 'rebuke', Matthew's account (20:34) records that Jesus, after recognizing the importunity, was 'moved with compassion' ('*splagchnizomai*' - 'to the bowels')* in his emotions. Jesus called Bartimaeus forward, drawing from him the response that he was looking for, that crystallizes the expression of faith. Jesus performs the miracle without a prayer or contact; 'Receive' is in the imperative mood, indicating a word of command. Bartimaeus' faith had resulted in '*sôzô*' - he was 'made well', but also 'saved'. Mark 10:52 has Jesus telling him to 'Go thy way', which Bartimaeus responds to by 'following Jesus on the road' as his most recently added disciple. There are two types of praise that result. For Bartimaeus, it is '*doxazô*' ('to glorify' God or 'to esteem as glorious and praiseworthy'). [198] For the rest of the crowd it is '*ainos*', meaning 'a discourse of praise'; also used for 'a proverbial saying or story'. Jesus' 'story' was always one of glorifying his Father.

Chapter 19

19:1-4 'He entered Jericho and was passing through. And there was a man called by the name of Zaccheus; he was a chief tax collector and he was rich. Zaccheus was trying to see who Jesus was, and was unable, because of the crowd, for he was small in stature. So he ran on ahead and climbed up into a sycamore tree in order to see him, for he was about to pass through that way.'

Jericho was located on the important east-west trade route to Jerusalem, at the northern most edge of the Dead Sea, on a large area of plateau with mountains to the north and the Dead Sea to the south. In addition to its strategic location, it was well watered and fruitful, known for its roses, palm trees and especially for the trees whose sap contained the fragrant resin known as balsam. This was tapped for use in anointing oils. Josephus describes Jericho as, 'Where the palm tree grows, and that balsam which is an ointment of all the most precious, which upon any incision made in the wood with a sharp stone, distills out thence like a juice'. [199] Such prosperous cities always meant tax collectors, but only one '*architelônês*' - 'the first among revenue collectors', from '*archê*', meaning 'first' in rank, or 'the first person or thing in a series'.*

The occupying Romans' custom was to assess what they considered a particular region to be worth in revenue and then sell the right to collect that sum to those who had the wealth to pay for the privilege, and the education to manage it. Whoever bought that right could then keep whatever surpluses he was able to exact on those who frequently had no idea of what the Roman taxation system required of them. Tax collectors were therefore in league with the Roman idolaters and were viewed by the Talmud as unfit to serve as a judge or a witness. and as being no different from robbers. [200] There was a poll tax on men and women, a ground tax on grain, wine and oil, and there was income tax, all of which were fixed and fairly widely known. The real profit opportunity lay with duties that were leveled on the use of main roads, markets and vehicles such as a cart, their wheels and the animal used to pull it. There were import and export duties, and duties on particular products. These were liable to considerable distortion. There was also the added opportunity to lend the money needed to pay the duty and to charge high rates of interest on it.

As the 'chief' amongst his colleagues Zaccheus would have had the extra financial benefit that came from appointing those under his charge, and, perhaps driven by a desire to compensate for his small stature, he had prospered materially. But wealth cannot fill a spiritual void. Zaccheus knew of Jesus' reputation - his miracles meant that every Jew in the region would have heard of him. A spiritual hunger in him had been awoken by the God who calls his children from the womb (Isaiah 49:1). And so, contrary to cultural norms, he runs.

Running was not something that wealthy men did. Their importance carried a sense of dignity that expressed itself in their deportment. For the father of the prodigal to run to greet his 'lost son' was a massive expression of his love and sense of relief in recovering his youngest child. And Zaccheus runs, driven by a greater desire than love of money and one which overrides his sense of decorum.

Sycamore-fig trees (*'sukomorea'*, also known as the 'fig-mulberry' because their leaves resembled those of mulberry trees) grew low to the ground and were therefore easy for someone of short stature to climb. Their wide diameter of branches meant that they provided welcome shade and so were often planted at roadsides. Luke distinguishes this tree from the commonly mistaken *'sukaminos'* (a 'sycamine tree', also called the black-mulberry owing to its berry-type fruit which were bitter). Both were used medicinally but in different treatments. [201]

19:5-7 'When Jesus came to the place, he looked up and said to him, "Zaccheus, hurry and come down, for today I must stay at your house." And he hurried and came down and received him gladly. When they saw it, they all began to grumble, saying, "He has gone to be the guest of a man who is a sinner."'

Zaccheus had been on the lookout for Jesus but Jesus had also been on the lookout for him. Jesus' early morning prayer communions with his Father formed his daily activity; he already knew where and with whom he was having lunch. Receiving 'gladly' is a rather weak translation of '*chairô*', which means 'to rejoice' - Zaccheus danced his way home. His sense of joy at being chosen for this divine appointment is contrasted with the prevailing attitude of 'all' who witnessed it - perhaps even Jesus' disciples - such being the loathing directed at the money-grabbing quisling traitors to Imperial Rome. 'Sinner' is, again, '*hamartôlos*', the adjective form of '*hamartanô*' meaning 'to miss the mark', 'to err', and 'to wander from the Law of God.'* It is primarily a legal term for one who did not live up to the requirements of the Law ('to trespass'), and secondarily, by association, a moral issue indicating religious impurity. Jesus' status as a senior Jewish legal scholar greatly compounded the perceived impropriety of eating with such a person as Zaccheus, for whom the rigorous food purity demands of the Jewish Law would have been a distant memory.

In the public eye, Jesus would be seen as becoming stained with the legal unrighteousness of Zaccheus. In fact the spiritual reality was that Zaccheus' stains were being eradicated by the righteousness and mercy of Jesus. 'Guest' is '*kataluô*', which also means 'to destroy' or 'to throw down'* and is more commonly used to mean such in the New Testament. The reason for the dual meaning is in the origin of the word. When a traveller arrived at their overnight lodging place, they would unloose their garments and throw down their burdens, doing the same thing for their animals. In being Zaccheus' 'guest', Jesus has come to 'throw down' the things that were keeping Zaccheus from being the person God had created him to be. Jesus is 'destroying' the work of the devil in Zaccheus' life and thus unburdening him of the baggage that prevented him from knowing rest from sin.

19:8-10 'Zaccheus stopped and said to the Lord, "Behold Lord, half of my possessions I will give to the poor, and if I have defrauded anyone of anything, I will give back four times as much." And Jesus said to him, "Today salvation has come to this house, because he too, is a son of Abraham. For the Son of Man has come to seek and to save that which was lost."'

There is immediate evidence of this 'unburdening'. Zaccheus has changed his way of thinking in regard to money - he has repented of it (*'metanoia'* - 'to change one's mind').* And what repentance! According to the Law, Zaccheus, upon acknowledging his sin, was only obliged to restore the sum cheated plus one-fifth. Leviticus 6:1-5 reads, 'Then the Lord spoke to Moses, saying, "When a person sins and acts unfaithfully against the Lord, and deceives his companion in regard to a deposit or a security entrusted to him, or through robbery, or if he has extorted from his companion, or has found what was lost and lied about it and sworn falsely, so that he sins in regard to any one of the things a man may do; then it shall be, when he sins and becomes guilty, that he shall restore what he took by robbery or what he got by extortion, or the deposit which was entrusted to him or the lost thing which he found, or anything about which he swore falsely; he shall make restitution for it in full and add to it one-fifth more.' And similarly: 'He shall confess his sins which he has committed, and he shall make restitution in full for his wrong and add to it one-fifth of it, and give it to him whom he has wronged' (Number 5:7).

Theft that was not confessed to and in cases where the goods were restorable was compensated for two-fold. Exodus 22:4 records, 'If what he stole is actually found alive in his possession, whether an ox or a donkey or a sheep, he shall pay double.' Only in cases where confession had not been made and where the goods were no longer restorable was the compensation made in a four-fold quantity or greater. Exodus 22:1 states, 'If a man steals an ox or a sheep and slaughters it or sells it, he shall pay five oxen for the ox and four sheep for the sheep.'

Zaccheus is voluntarily placing himself under the stricter requirement for recompense, which was twenty times the one-fifth part he was legally obliged to restore. And in addition he was giving up half of his possessions to the poor, in a society where alms giving was so synonymous with mercy that the term was one and the same ('*eleêmosunê*').* Jesus' response to the naysayers is mixed with typical rabbinic humour. His own Hebrew name, Y'shua, means 'salvation'. Hence the text could equally well read, 'Today Jesus has come to this house.' From a legal perspective, Jesus is fulfilling a rabbinic task - to restore a descendant of Abraham to the righteousness expressed in Torah, and beyond. The One who had taught the Law concerning restoration to Moses on Mount Sinai had come to Jericho to see it worked out in a much deeper way than was possible through simply the letter of that Law.

The passage closes with Jesus' mission statement: 'to seek and to save the lost.' He had not come to judge those who had strayed from the path of Torah, either into legal transgression or into actual immorality. He had 'not come to be served, but to serve, and to give his life a ransom for many' (Matthew 20:28). It was not the healthy that needed the physician, but the sick (Luke 5:31).

19:11 'While they were listening to these things, Jesus went on to tell a parable, because he was near Jerusalem,

and they supposed that the kingdom of God was going to appear immediately.'

Jesus was well aware that his disciples had not yet grasped God's timetable or the difference between the messianic scriptures regarding a triumphant king and those describing a suffering servant. Many Jews, at the extreme of which were the Zealots, saw one of the tasks of Messiah as ridding the land of Roman impurity and the idolatry to which their Imperial Standards bore testimony. And there had been some success in this already. Josephus records: 'Now Pilate, who was sent as procurator into Judea by Tiberius, sent by night those images of Caesar that are called ensigns into Jerusalem. This excited a very great tumult among the Jews when it was day; for those that were near them were astonished at the sight of them, as indications that their laws were trodden under foot; for those laws do not permit any sort of image to be brought into the city. Nay, besides the indignation which the citizens had themselves at this procedure, a vast number of people came running out of the country. These came zealously to Pilate to Caesarea, and besought him to carry those ensigns out of Jerusalem, and to preserve them their ancient laws inviolable; but upon Pilate's denial of their request, they fell down prostrate upon the ground, and continued immovable in that posture for five days and as many nights. On the next day Pilate sat upon his tribunal, in the open market-place, and called to him the multitude, as desirous to give them an answer; and then gave a signal to the soldiers, that they should all by agreement at once encompass the Jews with their weapons; so the band of soldiers stood round about the Jews in three ranks. The Jews were under the utmost consternation at that unexpected sight. Pilate also said to them that they should be cut in pieces, unless they would admit of Caesar's images, and gave intimation to the soldiers to draw their naked swords. Hereupon the Jews, as it were at one signal, fell down in vast numbers together, and exposed their necks bare, and cried out that they were sooner ready to be slain, than that their law should be transgressed. Hereupon Pilate was greatly surprised at their prodigious superstition, and gave order that the ensigns should be presently carried out of Jerusalem.' [202]

If the witness of ordinary Jews could result in the removal of those idolatrous images, how much more would the Messiah surely accomplish? Jesus addresses the fundamental question of God's timing with a parable, relating another story to make a point.

19:12-19 'So he said, "A nobleman went to a distant country to receive a kingdom for himself, and then return. And he called ten of his slaves, and gave them ten minas and said to them, 'Do business with this until I come back.' But his citizens hated him and sent a delegation after him, saying, 'We do not want this man to reign over us.' When he returned after receiving the kingdom, he ordered that these slaves, to whom he had given the money, be called to him so that he might know what business they had done. The first appeared saying, 'Master, your mina has made ten minas more.' And he said to him, 'Well done, good slave, because you have been faithful in a very little thing, you are to be in authority over ten cities.' The second came, saying, 'Your mina, master, has made five minas.' And he said to him also, 'And you are to be over five cities.'"**

Whereas most parables 'make a point', this parable makes two points. The first is very similar to the parable of the talents (Matthew 25), which is that we are to use the gifts and resources that God has entrusted to us to the best of our ability and with his help. The second message of this parable is, as Luke says, aimed at those who mistakenly thought that Jesus' mission included political change, i.e. the expulsion of the Romans and the re-establishment of an independent kingdom that would enjoy God's particular favour as in the days of King David. In this second regard, Jesus' story has a very up to date resonance with his hearers, around a particular recent political event.

After the death of Herod the Great in 4 BC, his sons Antipas and Archelaus had disputed his will, and especially the matter of who would reign over Judea, before the Emperor Augustus in Rome. Josephus records: 'Archelaus had new sources of trouble come upon him at Rome, on the occasions following, for an embassy of the Jews was come to Rome, Varus *[the general occupying Judea]* having permitted the nation to send it, that they might petition for the liberty of living by their own laws. Now the number of the ambassadors that were sent by the authority of the nation were fifty, to which they joined above eight thousand of the Jews that were at Rome already... Now upon the liberty that was given to the Jewish ambassadors to speak, they who hoped to obtain a dissolution of kingly government betook themselves to accuse Herod *[the Great]* of his iniquities; and they declared that he was indeed in name a king, but that he had taken to himself that uncontrollable authority which tyrants exercise over their subjects, and had made use of that authority for the destruction of the Jews'... 'Herod had put such abuses upon them as a wild beast would not have put on them, if he had power given him to rule over us; and that although their nation had passed through many subversions and alterations of government, their history gave no account of any calamity they had ever been under, that could be compared with this which Herod had brought upon their nation; that it was for this reason that they thought they might justly and gladly salute Archelaus as king, upon this supposition, that whosoever should be set over their kingdom, he would appear more mild to them than Herod had been; and that they had joined with him in the mourning for his father, in order to gratify him, and were ready to oblige him in other points also, if they could meet with any degree of moderation from him; but that he seemed to be afraid lest he should not be deemed Herod's own son; and so, without any delay, he immediately let the nation understand his meaning, and this before his dominion was well established, since the power of disposing of it belonged to Caesar, who could either give it to him or not, as he pleased. That he *[Archelaus]* had given a specimen of his future virtue to his subjects, and with what kind of moderation and good administration he would govern them, by that his first action, which concerned them, his own citizens, and God himself also, when he made the slaughter of three thousand of his own countrymen at the Temple. How then could they avoid the just hatred of him, who, to the rest of his barbarity, hath added this as one of our crimes, that we have opposed and contradicted him in the exercise of his authority?'

Nicolaus, as counsellor for Archelaus, replied and said, 'That as for Herod, since he had never been thus accused all the time of his life, it was not fit for those that might have accused him of lesser crimes than those now mentioned, and might have procured him to be punished during his lifetime, to bring an accusation against him now he is dead. He also attributed the actions of Archelaus to the Jews' injuries to him, who, affecting to govern contrary to the laws, and going about to kill those that would have hindered them from acting unjustly, when they were by him punished for what they had done, made their complaints against him; so he accused them of their attempts for innovation, and of the pleasure they took in sedition, by reason of their not having learned to submit to justice and to the laws, but still desiring to be superior in all things.' [203]

When all had been said, Augustus made Archelaus ruler over Judea as 'ethnarch'; not a full king, but one who still had the power to execute as many of his Jewish subjects as he saw fit. Josephus does not relate the fate of those fifty Jews who had come from Judea to Rome to oppose his rule, but if Archelaus' track record is any guide, and in the light of Jesus' parable, it is quite likely that they were executed. The point of the parable from the political perspective is therefore that Jesus' Jewish audience should not expect any sort of political emancipation. In fact, things would get a whole lot worse, as his later teaching (Luke 21:20-24) concerning the destruction of Jerusalem would make even clearer. This was fulfilled in 66-70 AD.

The first point of the parable is the 'use of resources' aspect. A 'mina' (from the Hebrew '*maneh*') was 100 drachmae (a day's wage for a working man), not as much as a 'talent' (Matthew 25:15), which was worth 60 minas, but still a considerable sum of money. To the 'master' (who stands for God) it is actually only a 'little thing'. To the God who, in the words of Psalm 50 verse 10, 'owns the cattle on a thousand hills' (as well as the hills!), any resources entrusted to our stewardship represent only a tiny, tiny fraction of his total resources.

What matters to God is how his children handle those resources. In the parable, as with the talents of Matthew 25, two of the servants are faithful ('*pistos*', also meaning 'trustworthy') and one is not. As well as having a monetary value the 'mina' (a word only found in Luke's Gospel) was also a weight, and occurs often in physicians' dispensing manuals in apportioning amounts used in doses of medicine. [204]

19:20-24 'Another came saying, 'Master, here is your mina, which I kept put away in a handkerchief; for I was afraid of you, because you are an exacting man; you take up what you did not lay down and reap what you did not sow.' He said to him, 'By your own words I will judge you, you worthless slave. Did you know that I am an exacting man, taking up what I did not lay down and reaping what I did not sow? Then why did you not put my money in the bank, and having come, I would have collected it with interest?' Then he said to the bystanders, 'Take the mina away from him and give it to the one who has the ten minas.''

This last servant is not only unfaithful; he is also rather deficient on two other levels. He does not take the obvious step of placing the money in the first century version of a savings account, but instead does the intentionally ludicrous thing of hiding it in a place where another might easily have found it and stolen it. Furthermore he is foolish enough to condemn himself out of his own mouth and somewhat insults his master in so doing. Home truths are never going to be appreciated against a background of abject stupidity, and certainly not by a master as ruthless as is described here. 'Exacting' is '*austeros*' - 'austere' - used to describe things that were dry and rough and so which came to mean 'harsh, stern and hard'. [205] It was also used of strict diets prescribed by physicians [206] and Doctor Luke is the only writer to use it in the New Testament.

Rulers would very commonly 'reap that which they didn't sow' as a means of crop taxation, and so the master's actions are not necessarily intended to be seen as unjust but rather as an inflexible application of the law. The unfaithful (untrustworthy) servant is also described as 'worthless' ('*ponêros*', also meaning 'evil' and 'full of annoyances'* from '*ponos*', meaning 'pain'). It is used by Jesus to describe the Pharisees who asked him for a sign (Matthew 16:4), to whom no sign would be given but that of the prophet Jonah.

As in the parable of the talents, this last servant's mina is taken by the 'bystanders' of the king's court and entrusted to the servant who had performed best with his.

19:25-27 'And they said to him, 'Master, he has ten minas already.' "I tell you that to everyone who has, more shall be given, but from the one who does not have, even what he does have shall be taken away. But these enemies of mine, who did not want me to reign over them, bring them here and slay them in my presence."'

Here in summary form is presented the two points of this parable. The first is that being faithful with responsibility will lead to more responsibility and reward - It is a case of 'use it *[wisely]* or lose it'. The believer's life can produce 'gold, silver and precious stones' or 'wood, hay and stubble' - the former will last as an eternal reward that can be offered to Christ in heaven, the latter will result in salvation, but as one 'escaping through the flames.' ('Each man's work will become evident; for the day will show it because it is to be revealed with fire, and the fire itself will test the quality of each man's work. If any man's work which he has built on it remains, he will receive a reward. If any man's work is burned up, he will suffer loss; but he himself will be saved, yet so as through fire' (1 Corinthians 3:12-15).

The second point is that a judgement is coming on those Jews who would reject Jesus' message; a judgement that was much more terrible than anything Archelaus ever did. When the Roman army commanded by Vespasian approached to surround Jerusalem in 66 AD, the believers, alive to Jesus' warning of Luke 21:20-21, left the city and went to safety in Pella on the other side of the Jordan. [207] The remainder of the populace fled within the city walls and finally to the refuge of the Temple fortifications, where they perished, (many by famine) during the four year siege.

19:28-30 'After he had said these things, he was going on ahead, going up to Jerusalem. When he approached Bethphage and Bethany, near the mount that is called Olivet, he sent two of the disciples, saying, "Go into the village ahead of you; there, as you enter, you will find a colt tied on which no one yet has ever sat; untie it and bring it here."'

Jericho, on the northern side of the Dead Sea, lies 423 meters below sea level, whereas Jerusalem is about 750 meters above, a difference of 1173 meters. Ascending the seventeen miles on this road from Jericho towards Jerusalem and the Mount of Olives brings the traveller to Bethany, about 2 miles before Jerusalem, and home to Jesus' friends Mary, Martha and Lazarus. Jesus is evidently well known enough there to borrow a colt, just as he was well known enough in Jerusalem to borrow an upper room for his final Passover meal. Only this is a colt that has never been ridden, meaning it would be humanly impossible to sit upon it without being bucked off. Matthew informs us that the colt was tied with its mother (Matthew 21:2), rendering the separation even more distressing for the colt and consequently even more dangerous for the rider. But this was to be no ordinary rider.

The One whose word had calmed the storms on Lake Galilee could certainly calm a distraught colt. Jesus is very deliberately fulfilling the words of the prophet Zechariah. 'Rejoice greatly, O daughter of Zion! Shout in triumph, O daughter of Jerusalem! Behold, your king is coming to you; he is just and endowed with salvation, humble, and mounted on a donkey, even on a colt, the foal of a donkey. I will cut off the chariot from Ephraim and the horse from Jerusalem; and the bow of war will be cut off. And he will speak peace to the nations; and his dominion will be from sea to sea, and from the River to the ends of the earth' (Zechariah 9:9-10). For a king to ride on an ass rather than a horse was a sign that he came in peace. The King of Israel was coming to 'speak peace' to the nations'. But would they listen?

19:31-36 'If anyone asks you, 'Why are you untying it?' you shall say, 'The Lord has need of it.'" So those who were sent away and found it just as he had told them. As they were untying the colt, its owners said to them, "Why are you untying the colt?" They said, "The Lord has need of it." They brought it to Jesus, and they

threw their coats on the colt and put Jesus on it. As he was going, they were spreading their coats on the road.'

'Lord' here is '*kurios*', also meaning 'The Master'; such a title was enough to be known to referring to Jesus even if the disciples sent were not known to the colt's owners, which they may well have been. Throwing coats onto the back of a colt that has never been ridden is not generally considered a good idea, and one very unlikely to appease the youngster into being ridden, neither is spreading such materials in front of the animal and then expecting him to walk upon it. And definitely neither is waving palm branches in front of it! (Matthew 21:8). But by then Jesus was sitting on it and his presence and word brought peace and calm to its wild spirit, enabling him to ride an animal which could have otherwise been quite impossible to get on, let alone stay on.

19:37-38 'As soon as he was approaching near the descent of the Mount of Olives, the whole crowd of the disciples began to praise God joyfully with a loud voice for all the miracles which they had seen, shouting: 'Blessed is the king who comes in the name of the Lord! Peace in heaven and glory in the highest!''

It was the Passover custom for the residents of Jerusalem to greet pilgrims with a form of call-and-response from Psalm 118, known as the great Hallel (meaning 'praise'), being the last and longest of a series of six 'Psalms of Ascent' for such use (Psalms 113-118). Verse 26 has been changed from 'Blessed is the one who comes in the name of the Lord' to 'Blessed is the king who comes in the name of the Lord', in recognition of Jesus' messianic status. Matthew's account (21:9) adds 'Hosanna to the Son of David', this being a re-wording of Psalm 118:25 - 'O Lord, do save, we beseech you.' 'Hosanna' means 'Lord save', coupled with a further messianic allusion in the title 'Son of David.' 'Peace in heaven' indicates that they understood the pictorial reference to Zechariah 9:9-10, and that Jesus was coming in the peace that Messiah would bring from heaven to earth. They are praising God for all the 'mighty works' that Jesus has done - '***dunamis***' - meaning 'power',* from which the word 'dynamite' is derived. For these mighty works God was to be 'glorified in the highest' - praised in heaven as well as on earth.

19:39-40 'Some of the Pharisees in the crowd said to him, "Teacher, rebuke your disciples." But Jesus answered, "I tell you, if these become silent, the stones will cry out!"'

The Pharisees take issue with the messianic alterations being made to the Hallel. Surely as a senior Torah teacher, Jesus would not stand for such distortions to the Holy Scriptures? They exhort him using his academic title, '***Didaskalos***' ('Doctor' of Torah), to 'rebuke' these thoughtless, uneducated disciples of his. This is '*epitimaô*' - 'to censure severely',* such is the offence they take at the idea that Jesus' messianic claim should be openly proclaimed and that their scriptures should be modified in doing so. Jesus takes the opposite view. The rabbis [208] taught that the stones around people served as witnesses to their wrongdoing. This is based upon Habakkuk 2:10-11, which states, 'You are sinning against yourself. Surely the stone will cry out from the wall, and the rafter will answer it from the framework.' Jesus is using this saying not to imply that the stones will cry out in his praise (although no doubt they could if God willed it), but rather to express the view that for his disciples to fail to recognise his messianic status would be wrong - something for the stones to witness to against them.

19:41-42 'When he approached Jerusalem, he saw the city and wept over it, saying, "If you had known in this day, even you, the things which make for peace! But now they have been hidden from your eyes."'

Jesus is well aware of the coming judgement upon the city and its Temple, so corrupt now and guilty of shedding the blood of the prophets that God had sent to warn it. The final appeal of peace was about to be made by the Messiah himself, but Jesus knew that it too would be refused. The God who hides and reveals his truth had revealed it in the person of his Son, but the spiritual eyes of the authorities were too tightly swollen closed with religious obesity and sin to see it. Matthew 13:14-15 recalls Jesus' use of Isaiah 6:9-10 in describing their blind and deaf state: 'You will keep on hearing but will not understand; you will keep on seeing but will not perceive. For the heart of this people has become dull; with their ears they scarcely hear, and they have closed their eyes, otherwise they would see with their eyes, hear with their ears, and understand with their heart and return, and I would heal them.'

19:43-44 '"For the days will come upon you when your enemies will throw up a barricade against you, and surround you and hem you in on every side, and they will level you to the ground and your children within you, and they will not leave in you one stone upon another, because you did not recognize the time of your visitation."'

Jesus is looking forwards 39 years to the coming of the Roman army under the general and later emperor Vespasian and his son Titus. The Jewish and Roman historian Josephus Flavius records the siege of Jerusalem in gruesome detail. Towards its end he recounts the following: 'Now of those that perished by famine in the city, the number was prodigious, and the miseries they underwent were unspeakable; for if so much as the shadow of any kind of food did any where appear, a war was commenced presently, and the dearest friends fell fighting one with another about it, snatching from each other the most miserable supports of life. Nor would men believe that those who were dying had no food, but the robbers would search them when they were expiring, lest anyone should have concealed food in their bosoms, and counterfeited dying; nay, these robbers gaped for want, and ran about stumbling and staggering along like mad dogs, and reeling against the doors of the houses like drunken men; they would also, in the great distress they were in, rush into the very same houses two or three times in one and the same day. Moreover, their hunger was so intolerable, that it obliged them to chew everything, while they gathered such things as the most sordid animals would not touch, and endured to eat them; nor did they at length abstain from girdles and shoes; and the very leather which belonged to their shields they pulled off and gnawed: the very wisps of old hay became food to some; and some gathered up fibres, and sold a very small weight of them for four Attic (drachmae). But why do I describe the shameless impudence that the famine brought on men in their eating inanimate things, while I am going to relate a matter of fact, the like to which no history relates, either among the Greeks or Barbarians? It is horrible to speak of it, and incredible when heard. I had indeed willingly omitted this calamity of ours, that I might not seem to deliver what is so portentous to posterity, but that I have innumerable witnesses to it in my own age; and besides, my country would have had little reason to thank me for suppressing the miseries that she underwent at this time.'

Josephus continues: 'There was a certain woman that dwelt beyond Jordan, her name was Mary; her father was Eleazar, of the village Bethezob, which signifies the house of Hyssop. She was eminent for her family and her wealth, and had fled away to Jerusalem with the rest of the multitude, and was with them besieged therein at this time. The other effects of this woman had been already seized upon, such I mean as she had brought with her out of Perea, and removed to the city. What she had treasured up besides, as also what food she had contrived to save, had been also carried off by the rapacious guards, who came every day running into her house for that purpose. This put the poor woman into a very great passion, and by the

351

frequent reproaches and imprecations she cast at these rapacious villains, she had provoked them to anger against her; but none of them, either out of the indignation she had raised against herself, or out of commiseration of her case, would take away her life; and if she found any food, she perceived her labours were for others, and not for herself; and it was now become impossible for her any way to find any more food, while the famine pierced through her very bowels and marrow, when also her passion was fired to a degree beyond the famine itself; nor did she consult with anything but with her passion and the necessity she was in. She then attempted a most unnatural thing; and snatching up her son, who was a child sucking at her breast, she said, "O thou miserable infant! For whom shall I preserve thee in this war, this famine, and this sedition? As to the war with the Romans, if they preserve our lives, we must be slaves. This famine also will destroy us, even before that slavery comes upon us. Yet are these seditious rogues more terrible than both the other. Come on; be thou my food, and be thou a fury to these seditious varlets, and a by-word to the world, which is all that is now wanting to complete the calamities of us Jews." As soon as she had said this, she slew her son, and then roasted him, and ate the one half of him, and kept the other half by her, concealed.'

'Upon this the seditious came in presently, and smelling the horrid scent of this food, they threatened her that they would cut her throat immediately if she did not show them what food she had gotten ready. She replied that she had saved a very fine portion of it for them, and withal uncovered what was left of her son. Hereupon they were seized with a horror and amazement of mind, and stood astonished at the sight, when she said to them, "This is mine own son, and what hath been done was mine own doing! Come, eat of this food; for I have eaten of it myself! Do not you pretend to be either more tender than a woman, or more compassionate than a mother; but if you be so scrupulous, and do abominate this my sacrifice, as I have eaten the one half, let the rest be reserved for me also." After which those men went out trembling, being never so much frightened at anything as they were at this, and with some difficulty they left the rest of that meat to the mother. Upon which the whole city was full of this horrid action immediately; and while everybody laid this miserable case before their own eyes, they trembled, as if this unheard of action had been done by themselves. So those that were thus distressed by the famine were very desirous to die, and those already dead were esteemed happy, because they had not lived long enough either to hear or to see such miseries.' [209]

Jerusalem and its Temple was, as Jesus had described, 'levelled' such that its stones were torn down by the Roman siege-engines and battering rams. 'When therefore Vespasian looked upon himself as in a manner besieged by the sallies of the Jews, and when his banks were now not far from the walls, he determined to make use of his battering ram. This battering ram is a vast beam of wood like the mast of a ship, its forepart is armed with a thick piece of iron at the head of it, which is so carved as to be like the head of a ram, whence its name is taken. This ram is slung in the air by ropes passing over its middle, and is hung like the balance in a pair of scales from another beam, and braced by strong beams that pass on both sides of it, in the nature of a cross. When this ram is pulled backward by a great number of men with united force, and then thrust forward by the same men, with a mighty noise, it batters the walls with that iron part which is prominent. Nor is there any tower so strong, or walls so broad, that can resist any more than its first batteries, but all are forced to yield to it at last.' [210]

All these tragedies came about because the religious authorities of Jerusalem did not recognise the time of their 'visitation'. This is '*episkopê*', also meaning 'investigation' and 'inspection'.* It is the word from which 'episcopal' is derived, denoting a bishop, from '*skopos*', meaning 'to look' and 'to watch'. Jesus had come to 'look over' Jerusalem, and it was to be found wanting.

353

19:45-46 'Jesus entered the Temple and began to drive out those who were selling, saying to them, "It is written, 'And my house shall be a house of prayer'; but you have made it a robbers' den."'

Jesus repeats the actions that John describes him having done at the start of his public ministry (John 2:12-16), of stamping his spiritual authority, as an ordained Doctor of the Law, on the activities within the Temple. Rabbis made reference to Old Testament Scripture passages by quoting small extracts from them, and Jesus does the same thing here. Having once again separated the moneychangers from their money, he first quotes Isaiah 56:6-7. 'Also the foreigners, who join themselves to the Lord, to minister to him, and to love the name of the Lord, to be his servants, everyone who keeps from profaning the Sabbath, and holds fast my covenant; even those I will bring to my holy mountain, and make them joyful in my house of prayer. Their burnt offerings and their sacrifices will be acceptable on my altar; for my house will be called a house of prayer for all the peoples.'

The Law did not permit the sale of animals within the Temple itself (which included the Temple Courts), and this necessary activity therefore took place outside the courts along with the ritual bathing, and changing of common coins into the Temple's own currency. But such was the growth in numbers of worshippers at the three compulsory festivals that there was not sufficient space outside, and on those occasions the priests permitted (technically illegally) their own sponsored market to move inwards into the Court of the Gentiles (the outermost perimeter of what properly constituted the Temple). Jesus' concern is for 'the foreigners' about which Isaiah is prophesying in chapter 56. The outermost court of the Temple was the only part of the sacred site where it was permitted for non-Jews to enter and it was in this 'Court of the Gentiles' that the money changing and sale of sacrificial animals known as the 'Bazaars of

Annas' occurred. Annas was the father-in-law of Caiaphas, the incumbent High Priest (John 18:13). This turned the only place of prayer open to foreigners into a noisy market making profits for the family of the High Priest.

Jesus then quotes from Jeremiah 7:8-11. 'Behold, you are trusting in deceptive words to no avail. Will you steal, murder, and commit adultery and swear falsely, and offer sacrifices to Baal and walk after other gods that you have not known, then come and stand before me in this house, which is called by my name, and say, "We are delivered!" - that you may do all these abominations? Has this house, which is called by my name, become a den of robbers in your sight? Behold I, even I, have seen it, declares the Lord.'

The accusation of being 'a den of robbers' would have been a major challenge to the Jewish priesthood who ran the market and who would have had this reported to them. Jesus is making himself very clear, within a Jewish historic context. Jeremiah had preached repentance to the Jews from the very place Jesus was standing. Jeremiah 7:1-7 reads: 'The word that came to Jeremiah from the Lord, saying, 'Stand in the gate of the Lord's house and proclaim there this word and say, "Hear the word of the Lord, all you of Judah, who enter by these gates to worship the Lord!" Thus says the Lord of hosts, the God of Israel, 'Amend your ways and your deeds, and I will let you dwell in this place. Do not trust in deceptive words, saying, "This is the Temple of the Lord, the Temple of the Lord, the Temple of the Lord." For if you truly amend your ways and your deeds, if you truly practice justice between a man and his neighbour, if you do not oppress the alien, the orphan, or the widow, and do not shed innocent blood in this place, nor walk after other gods to your own ruin, then I will let you dwell in this place, in the land that I gave to your fathers forever, and ever.'' In addition to the charge made for changing ordinary money into Temple coins, the monopoly that the priests had on the sale of ritually acceptable animals for sacrifice meant that they were able to charge markedly inflated prices. Not long after Jesus' death, the Mishnah records that two doves (one of the cheapest offerings) were being sold for one gold coin, before rabbinic intervention reduced their cost to one-quarter of a silver coin. [211]

The priests and Jewish leaders of Jeremiah's day were putting their trust in their religious practices and in the imposing edifice that was the Temple of Solomon rather than in a living personal faith in the God of Abraham. This was manifest in their behaviour. They had begun to oppress the vulnerable members of their community in exactly the same way that the leaders of Jesus' day had done (e.g. 'devouring widows' houses' - Matthew 23:14). Jesus is warning them that their time is running out. If they did not change their ways then they would not be allowed to 'dwell in this place' of the Temple that they took such pride in. 'Den of robbers' served both as a description of their behaviour in grossly inflating the prices for sacrificial animals and as a warning of what was to come if they refused to listen to the prophetic word that Jesus was bringing.

Jesus was also fulfilling a third Old Testament prophecy. Zechariah (14:21) had spoken of the day when: 'Every cooking pot in Jerusalem and in Judah will be holy to the Lord of hosts; and all who sacrifice will come and take of them and boil in them. And there will no longer be a Canaanite in the house of the Lord of hosts in that day.' The Hebrew word '*kenaani*' used here has a double meaning - it can be translated as 'Canaanite' or as 'merchant'.* In the Temple cleansing described in John chapter 2, Jesus rebukes the priests for creating a 'house of merchandise'. Hence Jesus is fulfilling Old Testament prophecy by expelling the traders of the 'Bazaars of Annas', who made large profits from the ordinary Temple worshippers for the family of the High Priest, and likening those most pious of Jewish figures, the priests, to the unclean Canaanites, in their commercial pursuits.

19:47-48 'And he was teaching daily in the Temple; but the chief priests and the scribes and the leading men among the people were trying to destroy him, and they could not find anything that they might do, for all the people were hanging on to every word he said.'

When Peter and John were found speaking to the people in the Temple courts following the healing of the lame man at 'the gate called 'Beautiful' (Acts 3:2, 4:1-2), they were arrested by the Temple Guard (a body of Jewish priests trained as soldiers and authorised to police the Temple courts) on the charge of 'teaching the people'. This was because as 'unschooled' men (Acts 4:13), it was illegal for them to teach in the Temple. By contrast Jesus taught in the Temple on a daily basis while in Jerusalem, and furthermore debated matters of Torah regularly with the various authorities there. This is despite their being (later on in his public ministry) his sworn enemies who were seeking to kill him. This fact, together with the respectful titles of scholarship that they used ('Rabbi' and '*Didaskalos*'), evidences the fact that Jesus was not 'unschooled'. Had he been so, it would have meant that Mary, Joseph and all the '*Didaskalos*' he met aged 12 in the Temple school of rabbinic studies had broken their own Law, in failing to enter Jesus for higher learning as the Law demanded. [212]

By this later point in Jesus' ministry, his claims to divinity in taking the name of God to himself and forgiving other's sins in the place of God had rendered even his own brilliance in Torah of no avail in the eyes of the Jewish religious authorities. Jesus, they thought, had repeatedly committed blasphemy and so simply must be executed. They had two obstacles in bringing this to pass. The first was the fact that Jesus' brilliance in Torah simply did not permit them to win any kind of legal argument against him. The second was that Jesus was immensely popular with the Jewish people, on account of both his superb teaching and the miracles he routinely performed. 'Hanging

357

on' Jesus' words is '*ekkremannumi*', a word that only occurs in this passage in the whole New Testament but which was commonly used in Greek medical texts to describe the 'attention' a physician paid to the words, symptoms and signs of his patient. [213]

Such was the massively high regard that the general population of Judea and Jerusalem held Jesus in, as a '*Didaskalos*' who also performed remarkable miracles, that the authorities resolved to take special measures to bring about his condemnation and sentence to execution without public foreknowledge. Whatever needed to be done would have to happen in secret.

Chapter 20

20:1-2 'On one of the days while he was teaching the people in the Temple and preaching the gospel, the chief priests and the scribes with the elders confronted him, and they spoke, saying to him, "Tell us by what authority you are doing these things, or who is the one who gave you this authority?"'

Having performed many amazing miracles in the Temple, the authenticity of which could not be denied, in addition to the Temple market 'cleansing' incidents, the Jewish authorities seek to pin Jesus down on exactly who he was claiming to be. It is the same point of issue that they were pursuing in John 10:24: 'If you are the Christ, tell us plainly.' They ask, 'By what authority ('*exousia*') are you doing these things?' '*Exousia*' is translated as 'authority' 29 times in the King James Bible, but as 'power' 69 times, meaning 'the ability or strength with which one is endued'.* 'These things' that the Jews are addressing are not Jesus' teachings, which he regularly gave using the authority that been invested in him at his ordination as both a rabbi and, yet still senior, as a Doctor of Torah. As Edersheim points out, 'At whatever periods some of these practices *[rabbinic ordination]* may have been introduced, it is at least certain that, at the time of our Lord, no one would have ventured authoritatively to teach without proper rabbinic authorisation.' [214] 'The 'things' in question were the messianic signs of miraculous healing and cleansing the Temple.

20:3-8 'Jesus answered and said to them, "I will also ask you a question, and you tell me: Was the baptism of John from heaven or from men?" They reasoned among themselves, saying, "If we say, 'From heaven,' he will say, 'Why did you not believe him?' "But if we say, 'From men,' all the people will stone us to death, for they are

convinced that John was a prophet." So they answered that they did not know where it came from. And Jesus said to them, "Nor will I tell you by what authority I do these things."'

The authorities want to know whether Jesus is claiming to directly represent God in what he is doing. As always with this type of question from the religious leaders, Jesus knew that they would not believe him even if he told them directly who he really was. The evidence of the miracles themselves was not enough to change their hard hearts, and as Jesus taught in the parable of the rich man and Lazarus, neither would they be 'persuaded even if someone rose from the dead' (Luke 16:31). So Jesus tests their sincerity with a question of his own about his cousin John - where had John's spiritual power and authority come from, and in particular his ministry of baptism of repentance? Was it from God or was it merely John's own initiative? Their unwillingness to answer such a straight question revealed that they were not sincere in asking Jesus where his power and authority came from. Their comment about 'fearing the people' (Matthew 21:26) is a further sorry reflection upon their ability to govern well - they did not have sufficient fear of God. They were more concerned about maintaining their own privileged positions than in acknowledging the new thing that God was doing.

20:9-12 'And he began to tell the people this parable: "A man planted a vineyard and rented it out to vine-growers, and went on a journey for a long time. At the harvest time he sent a slave to the vine-growers, so that they would give him some of the produce of the vineyard; but the vine-growers beat him and sent him away empty-handed. And he proceeded to send another slave; and they beat him also and treated him shamefully and sent him away empty-handed. And he proceeded to send a third; and this one also they wounded and cast out."'

Parables were a useful way to get around intellectual defences. The story could filter through the hearers' conscious and subconscious thoughts allowing the truth contained within to slowly but steadily permeate the mind. Jesus gives the authorities yet another chance to consider what has been happening and what is about to happen from a spiritual and national perspective. In this case, Jesus' analogy is readily apparent to the authorities who would have been very familiar with the description of Israel. Isaiah 5:7 records, 'For the vineyard of the Lord of hosts is the house of Israel.'

Absentee landlords were a common feature in Israel, and the political turbulence of the region lent itself to scenarios such as the one Jesus depicts. What is extreme is the stubborn obduracy of the tenants. They stand for the Jewish religious authorities who had ignored and persecuted God's messengers down the ages. Rents for land and vineyards were commonly paid in the produce that the tenants gathered. But when this owner's servants arrive to claim what is rightfully their master's, they are badly abused.

20:13-16 '"The owner of the vineyard said, 'What shall I do? I will send my beloved son; perhaps they will respect him.' But when the vine-growers saw him, they reasoned with one another, saying, 'This is the heir; let us kill him so that the inheritance will be ours.' So they threw him out of the vineyard and killed him. What then will the owner of the vineyard do to them? He will come and destroy these vine-growers and will give the vineyard to others."

The parable depicts the amazing patience of the landlord, who is willing to send even his own son into what was clearly a hostile and dangerous situation. This a direct analogy with Jesus' own mission, in which he regularly claimed to represent his 'Father'. His earthly and adoptive father Joseph was by now dead. The adult son stood in their society for someone to whom the same respect was due as was owed to the father. This son is also *'agapêtos'* - 'dearly loved', [215] hence very precious to the father. His calculated murder exposes the true nature of the tenants. They are both evil, but also extremely foolish in thinking that anything other than their destruction could come of such a deliberate and heinous crime. Jesus' audience would have been in no doubt that they were the tenants being referred to. Their end was to be 'destroyed' (*'appolumi'*, also meaning 'to bring to utter ruin'). [216] Their 'tenancy' of the Temple and the city of Jerusalem was about to come to an abrupt end with the arrival in 66 AD of Roman forces under Vespasian and Titus. The kingdom of Judea would be lost to them. Jesus' comment about the 'inheritance' of the 'planted vineyard' being given to others would have reminded the rulers of the words of Moses in Exodus 15:17. 'You will bring them and plant them in the mountain of your inheritance, the place, O Lord, which you have made for your dwelling, the sanctuary, O Lord, which your hands have established.' The dwelling of God on earth - the sanctuary of their beloved Temple on the mountain of their inheritance - was going to be destroyed.

20:17-17 'When they heard it, they said, "May it never be!" But Jesus looked at them and said, "What then is this that is written: 'The stone which the builders rejected, this has become the chief cornerstone'?"'

The rulers are shocked rigid by this statement. The idea that God would destroy his own Temple and the city in which it stood was beyond their comprehension. Jesus points them to Psalm 118:22-23. 'The stone which the builders rejected has become the chief corner stone. This is the Lord's doing; it is marvellous in our eyes.' God had done something unexpected in the Temple's construction. He was about to do something even more unexpected with its destruction. The Hebrew for 'chief' here is *'ro'sh'* meaning 'head' or 'top'.* Psalm 118 had traditionally been interpreted as indicating

God's desire to make Israel the head among the nations, in keeping with the promise that Moses had given them if they obeyed God's commands. 'The Lord will make you the head and not the tail, and you only will be above, and you will not be underneath, if you listen to the commandments of the Lord your God, which I charge you today, to observe them carefully' (Deuteronomy 28:13).

This Psalm is the same one that the crowds were quoting from when they were shouting: "Blessed is he who comes in the name of the Lord!" (Psalm 118:26). When Jesus quoted Scripture, he was usually referring to the whole passage, not a single verse. The passage reads: 'Open to me the gates of righteousness; I shall enter through them, I shall give thanks to the Lord. This is the gate of the Lord; the righteous will enter through it. I shall give thanks to you, for you have answered me, and you have become my salvation. The stone which the builders rejected has become the chief corner stone. This is the Lord's doing; it is marvellous in our eyes. This is the day which the Lord has made; let us rejoice and be glad in it. O Lord, do save, we beseech you; O Lord, we beseech you, do send prosperity! Blessed is the one who comes in the name of the Lord; we have blessed you from the house of the Lord' (Psalm 118:19-26).

Jesus' use of Temple building imagery would have been doubly forceful in the minds of his hearers. They would have been well aware of his earthly father Joseph's role as a devout *tekton* in the training of the 1000 Jewish priests recruited by Herod the Great to build the Temple sanctuary - priests who needed to be given the skills of builders and '*tektons*' themselves to erect the sanctuary in the Holy Place. [217] This was where the most major and technically difficult part of the construction occurred, in an area off-limits to all except priests. Some of the priests would have had to fit the stones together, and some angled stones ('corners' - '*gônia*' - from '*gonu*', meaning 'knee') [218] would be needed to act as a corner, connecting two walls at right angles to each other.

The Jews saw the rejected 'stone' of Psalm 118 as representing the nation of Israel - a small and despised people that had been elevated to greatness by Almighty God. Jesus however is telling them that it stands for him personally, and in fact that he was going to be further rejected by the Jewish leaders ('the builders' were the priests, who had been trained to build the 165 feet tall Holy Place in the heart of the Temple). [219] Jesus had spoken openly (John 10:7) that he was the 'gate for the sheep', and 'I am the gate; whoever enters through me will be saved' (John 10:9, NIV). The prayer, 'You have answered me, and you have become my salvation' (Psalm 118:21) was fulfilled in his own person; 'salvation' being in Hebrew *'yeshuah'*,* that being his own name, Jesus. He is telling them that *he* is actually the 'top stone'; that their God has done it and the consequences are marvellous - at least in the eyes of the unbiased children present in the Temple at the time who could recognise a miracle when they saw several happen in front of them (Matthew 21:15).

20:18 '"Everyone who falls on that stone will be broken to pieces; but on whomever it falls, it will scatter him like dust."'

Jesus concludes the parable by warning them that the same fate that befell the unrighteous vineyard tenants was about to happen to them. Just as had happened in Jeremiah's day, the cycles of discipline and consequences of the disobedience described in Deuteronomy 28 would be repeated. The final and terrible judgement of verses 63-65 was about to come to pass: 'It shall come about that as the Lord delighted over you to prosper you, and multiply you, so the Lord will delight over you to make you perish and destroy you; and you will be torn from the land where, you are entering to possess it. Moreover, the Lord will scatter you among all peoples, from one end of the earth to the other end of the earth; and there you shall serve other gods, wood and stone, which you or your fathers have not known. Among those nations you shall find no rest, and there will be no resting place for the sole of your foot; but there the Lord will give you a trembling heart, failing of eyes, and despair of soul.' In AD 70 the destruction of Jerusalem and with it Herod's Temple would lead to devastation and a scattering of the people. The owner of the vineyard would then look elsewhere (to the Gentiles) for spiritual fruit. Jesus offers the Jewish leaders a choice; fall on him and his mercy and be broken in humble repentance, or be scattered like dust in judgement upon their unbelief. Isaiah 8:13-15 speaks of the Lord as being 'a rock of offence to the House of Israel': 'It is the Lord of hosts whom you should regard as holy. And he shall be your fear, and he shall be your dread. Then he shall become a sanctuary; but to both the houses of Israel, a stone to strike and a rock to stumble over, and a snare and a trap for the inhabitants of Jerusalem. Many will stumble over them, then they will fall and be broken; they will even be snared and caught.' Daniel had predicted a 'stone cut without hands' (i.e. by God, Daniel 2:45) which would break kingdoms to pieces, but the word used by Jesus here is of much smaller particles that that. 'Scattered like dust' is '*likmaô*', which also means 'to winnow',* in the sense of separating chaff from wheat using a winnowing fork, as in Matthew 3:12 - an image commonly used to describe God's judgement.

20:19 'The scribes and the chief priests tried to lay hands on him that very hour, and they feared the people; for they understood that he spoke this parable against them.'

The response of the authorities is one of an impotent fury. They know Jesus is speaking about them, and doing so in public, but his status as a Doctor of their own Torah Law permits him to teach in this way. Furthermore, just as they feared the crowd's response to anything negative that they said about John the Baptist, so now they had the same problem with opposing Jesus and needed to avoid riots. The city's huge festival crowds were hanging on Jesus' every word.

20:20 'So they watched him, and sent spies who pretended to be righteous, in order that they might catch him in some statement, so that they could deliver him to the rule and the authority of the governor.'

At this point the authorities realise afresh that they are never going to be able to entrap Jesus in a matter of their own Law. He was simply too clever for them. And so they seek to use political means, trying to trap Jesus into offending in some way against the ruling Roman power. 'Governor' here is '*hêgemôn*', used to mean a '*Legatus Caesaris*' - an officer administering a province in the name and with the authority of the Roman emperor. In Jerusalem, within the empire's small Judean province, that meant the Roman procurator, Pontius Pilate. The Jewish rulers want to 'catch' something - '*epilambanomai*' - 'to seize hold' [220] of a saying that they could use as evidence of sedition against Rome.

20:21-22 'They questioned him, saying, "Teacher, we know that you speak and teach correctly, and you are not partial to any, but teach the way of God in truth. Is it lawful for us to pay taxes to Caesar, or not?"'

Matthew's account (Matthew 22:15-22) describes this question as being brought by the Pharisees together with the Herodians, an unlikely combination on one level, given that the Herodians had a very lax view of religious purity in associating with the Gentile rulers. But 'needs must as the devil drives' goes the saying, and the Herodians had the advantage of having the ear of Pontius Pilate. Between them they devised a very loaded legal question to try and trap Jesus, based on the thorny issue of paying taxes to the heathen invaders. It was a lose-lose question: "Is it right to pay taxes to Caesar, or not?" If Jesus had answered, 'Yes', he could have been discredited as a collaborator. If he said, 'No', (the 'correct' answer from a Jewish perspective because the Romans were idolaters), he could have been arrested for inciting rebellion against the ruling power. Which way would Jesus go?

20:23-26 'But he detected their trickery and said to them, "Show me a denarius. Whose likeness and inscription does it have?" They said, "Caesar's." And he said to them, "Then render to Caesar the things that are Caesar's, and to God the things that are God's." And they were unable to catch him in a saying in the presence of the people; and being amazed at his answer, they became silent.'

Jesus handles the dilemma brilliantly. The Roman denarius was the payment for the poll tax - a tax on capitation paid simply for the privilege of being alive. The coins were stamped with the Imperial image, and it was this coin that was used to pay the tax. Jesus' answer astonishes his enemies: "Render to Caesar what is Caesar's and to God what is God's." To say 'do what is right by both secular authority and by God' was the perfect answer - one that neither the Pharisees nor the Herodians could find fault with, instead they were 'amazed', just as the Doctors of Torah had been by the 12 year old Jesus. They 'marvelled' (*'thaumazô'* - 'to wonder') at his response.

20:27-33 'Now there came to him some of the Sadducees (who say that there is no resurrection), and they questioned him, saying, "Teacher, Moses wrote for us that if a man's brother dies having a wife, and he is childless, the brother should marry the wife and raise up children to his brother. Now there were seven brothers; and the first took a wife and died childless; and the second and the third married her; and in the same way all seven died, leaving no children. Finally the woman died also. In the resurrection therefore, which one's wife will she be? For all seven had married her."'

It is now the priestly party's turn to try and bring Jesus into theological disrepute. The Sadducees held that only the Pentateuch formed God's written word, believing that any Scripture outside of these five books of Moses was not inspired. They did not believe either in angels or in the resurrection (Acts 23:8). So they attempt to discredit the concept of a resurrected body with an extreme example of Levirate marriage and a woman who out-lived her seven related husbands in their attempts to keep the eldest brother's family name alive, as the Law commanded (Deuteronomy 25:5-6). Nowadays perhaps questions would be asked over what she was putting in their food! In a society where a widow's security was contingent upon having children to provide for her in her old age, such marriages were common, and strictly regulated by the Jewish Law. [221]

The Sadducees address Jesus with his formal theological title, '**Didaskalos**' - 'Doctor' of Torah. Even as those committed to bring him to his death they remain obliged to recognise that status that his genius in Torah had necessarily won him in the years since those 5 days spent in the company of the Doctors of Torah aged 12. The theological issue of whether the resurrection was taught in the Pentateuch had long been hotly debated between the scholars among the Pharisees and the Sadducees. The Pharisees believed it was. The Talmud [222] declares 'Rabbu Simai as saying: 'Whence do we learn resurrection from the Torah? From the verse, 'And I also have established my covenant with them, *[the Patriarchs]* to give them the land of Canaan': '*[to give]* you' is not said, but 'to give them' *[personally]*; thus resurrection is proved from the Torah.' Understandably, not all of the ruling Saducean priests were convinced by this! With one clear statement Jesus would settle the matter beyond dispute.

20:34-38 'Jesus said to them, "The sons of this age marry and are given in marriage, but those who are considered worthy to attain to that age and the resurrection from the

dead neither marry nor are given in marriage; for they cannot even die anymore, because they are like angels, and are sons of God, being sons of the resurrection. But that the dead are raised, even Moses showed, in the passage about the burning bush, where he calls the Lord 'the God of Abraham, and the God of Isaac, and the God of Jacob.' Now he is not the God of the dead but of the living; for all live to him."'

God is a God of the living; hence his commonly accepted title, 'the God of Abraham, and the God of Isaac, and the God of Jacob' (Exodus 3:6), meant that the patriarchs mentioned had therefore to be alive spiritually. Jesus also enlightens the Sadducees to the fact that, yes, angels do exist, and also to the fact that there is no marriage in heaven, where an eternal state of being is entered into - death has no power to interrupt it.

20:39-40 'Some of the scribes answered and said, "Teacher, you have spoken well." For they did not have courage to question him any longer about anything.'

Scribes were highly learned in the Jewish law, but not so highly as the '*Didaskalos*', the 'Masters' of Torah law, of which Nicodemus was one: 'Jesus answered and said unto him, Art thou a master ['*Didaskalos*'] of Israel, and knowest not these things? (John 3:10, KJV). These scribes address Jesus as '*Didaskalos*', with the added complement of '*kalos*' ('beautiful')* speech. So thoroughly taken aback by Jesus' answer were they, that their desire to bring legal challenges evaporated. They lost the courage ('*tolmaô*', also meaning 'boldness')* to challenge him any further on points of Law. There was simply no out-witting Jesus' genius and grasp of Torah.

20:41-44 'Then he said to them, "How is it that they say the Christ is David's son? For David himself says in the

369

book of Psalms, 'The Lord said to my Lord: 'Sit at my right hand until I make your enemies a footstool for your feet.' Therefore David calls him 'Lord,' and how is he his son?'"

Jesus now takes the initiative. The question on the Sanhedrin's lips was, 'Are you the Christ?' (John 10:24). Jesus responds by revealing a fundamental misunderstanding in their theology. The Christ, while being a descendant of David's, and hence his 'son', was actually God, which was why David addresses him as his 'Lord'. Psalm 110:1 reads 'The Lord ('**Yahweh**') said to my Lord... ('**adon**'). '**Adon**' is used as a formal term for God in Exodus 23:17 and '**adonay**', a Hebrew name for God, is derived from it. This is a revelation that clearly identified the Messiah as divine. Once again, the authorities are faced with the fact that any attempt to discredit Jesus intellectually was unlikely to be successful; they are simply making the situation worse by provoking sayings for which they had no reply. If they wished to silence Jesus, the authorities would have to try another, more underhand, method.

20:45-47 'And while all the people were listening, he said to the disciples, "Beware of the scribes, who like to walk around in long robes, and love respectful greetings in the market places, and chief seats in the synagogues and places of honour at banquets, who devour widows' houses, and for appearance's sake offer long prayers. These will receive greater condemnation."'

Jesus' answers have the ear of ordinary worshippers as well as the authorities, and having effortlessly absorbed their legal challenges, it is now Jesus' turn to go on the offensive and take a challenge to them. Scribes, together with the majority of the legal scholars, took their own dignity very seriously. The Talmud relates: 'Rabbi Eleazar says: "One who prays behind his master, and one who gives *[the ordinary]* greeting to his master and one who returns a greeting to his master, and one who joins issue with *[the teaching of]* the Academy of his master, and one who says something which he has not heard from his master causes the Divine Presence to depart from Israel.' This sort of pride is offensive to the God who 'gives grace to the humble' (James 4:6). As a widow herself, Mary would especially remember this saying of Jesus'. Scribes, as Jewish lawyers, could act as legal executors for widows who had no known surviving family, and so could buy their houses at a low price. If such houses were located within a walled city the dwellings would then become their own property even after the Year of Jubilee; whereas otherwise the house might have been redeemed had a surviving relative been found. In this was the religious lawyers exploited the widows' estates to their own gain.

Rabbi Joshua ben Levi further said: 'A city which was first settled and then walled is reckoned as a village. What is the reason? Because it is written, 'And if a man sell a dwelling house of a walled city, one which was first walled and then settled, but not first settled and then walled' (Talmud *'Mo'ed'*, *'Megilah'* 3b). This was based upon 'If a man sells a dwelling house in a walled city, then his redemption right remains valid until a full year from its sale; his right of redemption lasts a full year. But if it is not bought back for him within the space of a full year, then the house that is in the walled city passes permanently to its purchaser throughout his generations; it does not revert in the jubilee' (Leviticus 25:29-30).

The scribes were also well-known for their long-winded prayers. Jesus had spoken out against ostentatious public prayer in Matthew 6:5-6. 'When you pray, you are not to be like the hypocrites; for they love to stand and pray in the synagogues and on the street corners so that they may be seen by men. Truly I say to you, they have their reward in full.' Religious pride in the observance of their own man-made traditions had taken over many of those in authority. Their job was to bring ordinary people into a right understanding of Torah, not keep them out of it. If such scribes did not repent, theirs would be a commensurate condemnation ('**krina**', also meaning 'a judicial sentence of damnation').* The Son of Man had come 'to seek and save the lost' (Luke 19:10). But would their pride make them deaf to his call?

Chapter 21

21:1 'And he looked up and saw the rich putting their gifts into the treasury.'

This mention of 'the treasury' places Jesus' location as 'The Court of the Women', so called because women were not allowed to enter the Temple courts any further, into 'The Court of Israel'. Edersheim records that 'according to Jewish tradition, a raised gallery ran along three sides of the court', in which women could worship without the scrutiny of the Pharisees, some of whom objected to their presence. Around the 'Court of the Women' ran a colonnade, housing thirteen chests, or 'trumpets' into which gifts were placed. 'These thirteen chests were narrow at the mouth and wide at the bottom, shaped like trumpets, whence their name. Their specific objects were carefully marked on them. Nine were for the receipt of what was legally due by worshippers; the other four for strictly voluntary gifts. Trumpets I and II were appropriated to the half-shekel Temple-tribute of the current and of the past year. Into Trumpet III those women who had to bring turtledoves for a burnt and a sin-offering dropped their equivalent in money, which was daily taken out and a corresponding number of turtledoves offered. This not only saved the labour of so many separate sacrifices, but spared the modesty of those who might not wish to have the occasion or the circumstances of their offering to be publicly known... Trumpet IV similarly received the value of the offerings of young pigeons. In Trumpet V contributions for the wood used in the Temple; in Trumpet VI for the incense and in Trumpet VII for the golden vessels for the ministry were deposited. If a man had put aside a certain sum for a sin offering, and any money was left over after its purchase, it was cast into Trumpet VIII. Similarly, Trumpets IX, X, XI, XII, and XIII were destined for what was left over from trespass-offerings, offerings of birds, the offering of the Nazarite, of the cleansed leper, and voluntary offerings.' [223]

21:2-4 'And he saw a poor widow putting in two small copper coins. And he said, "Truly I say to you, this poor widow put in more than all of them; for they all out of their surplus put into the offering; but she out of her poverty put in all that she had to live on."'

Luke's primary source, Mary, once again comes to the fore with yet another reference to a widow. Her coins are '*leptos*', meaning 'peeled' and 'thin' from '*lepis*', the 'scale of a fish', [224] and are often translated as 'mites'. Jesus' comments reflect the principle of proportional giving; this widow gave 100% of her available resources as compared with the relatively low percentage given by the wealthy, which could give abundantly without it having any significant impact on them in real terms.

The widow is also being commended for her faith in God. This episode is not necessarily the first time that this particular widow had put 'all her living' into the offering. As a Hebrew woman she would have been well acquainted with Psalm 146:9 - 'The Lord protects the strangers; he supports the fatherless and the widow.' In her giving, she was exercising trust in the God who rewards such faith with 'a good measure, pressed down, shaken together, and running over' (Luke 6:38).

21:5-6 'And while some were talking about the temple, that it was adorned with beautiful stones and votive gifts, he said, "As for these things which you are looking at, the days will come in which there will not be left one stone upon another which will not be torn down."'

Matthew's account places this saying after Jesus' denunciation of the Pharisees' hypocrisy (the 'eight woes' of Matthew chapter 23). His disciples seek to distract Jesus away from the outpouring of righteous anger by drawing his attention to the splendid religious offerings and the wonderful array of buildings in the Temple courts. Under more normal circumstances this stratagem would have been expected to be successful, given the role that '*tektons*' in general and Jesus' father Joseph (as a devout '*tekton*') in particular would have had to play in the Temple construction process, and the training of the 1000 Jewish priests needed to build the Holy Place to its height of 165 feet, [225] as well as the many other splendid buildings that adorned its courts. The Temple Courts occupied Herod's artificially in-filled plateau around Mount Moriah, consequently its building and walls required extremely deep foundations in order to be secured to the bedrock on the original valley floor some 200 feet or more below the surface. This required the skill of the '*tekton*', the first-century equivalent of an architect ('master-tekton') and structural engineer, as shown in Paul's use of the term '*architekton*' in writing to the church in Corinth, 1 Corinthians 3:10 - 'Like a wise master-builder ('*architekton*') I laid a foundation, and another is building on it.' The '*archê*' craftsman was the 'first' or 'chief' - the 'architect'.

On this occasion, Jesus was not to be drawn into a discussion of his family's specialist building skills. On the contrary, his reproaches against the religious authorities overflowed into a prophetic statement of the coming destruction about to be wrought from the Roman army under the command of Vespasian and his son Titus. Herod had re-built the Temple in a sumptuous manner, which Josephus describes. 'Now the outward face of the Temple in its front wanted nothing that was likely to surprise either men's minds or their eyes; for it was covered all over with plates of gold of great weight, and, at the first rising of the sun, reflected back a very fiery splendour, and made those who forced themselves to look upon it to turn their eyes away, just as they would have done at the sun's own rays. But this Temple appeared to strangers, when they were coming to it at a distance, like a mountain covered with snow; for as to those parts of it that were not gilt, they were exceeding white' (Josephus, 'Wars' 5, 5). The Romans would knock the Temple down and burn it, causing the gold that the stones were overlaid with to melt and run down in the midst of the rubble. In subsequent years the stones would be repeatedly turned over to recover the re-solidified lost gold, thereby literally fulfilling Jesus' prophecy.

The physical Temple, under both Solomon and Herod, was built with 'costly stones', both in the foundations (visible in Jerusalem today) and in the walls (destroyed in 70 AD). These were huge pieces of rock and marble, weighing up to hundreds of tons, skillfully cut and bevelled to aid their fitting together. 1 Kings 5:17-18 records, 'Then the king commanded, and they quarried great stones, costly stones, to lay the foundation of the house with cut stones. So Solomon's builders and Hiram's builders and the Gebalites cut them, and prepared the timbers and the stones to build the house.'

As for Herod's Temple: 'Now the temple was built of stones that were white and strong, and each of their length was twenty-five cubits, their height was eight, and their breadth about twelve; and the whole structure, as also the structure of the royal cloister, was on each side much lower, but the middle was much higher, till they were visible to those that dwelt in the country for a great many furlongs.' [226] These are the costly stones that the disciples are admiring. They were hugely expensive to produce, but are not to be confused with the jewel stones (sometimes also translated as 'costly stones') that are depicted in the foundations and walls of the heavenly city, New Jerusalem, as described in Revelation 21:18-20.

The disciples also seek to distract Jesus using the Temple's many 'votive gifts' that adorned the Temple courts. The Greek here is *'anathêma'*, meaning 'dedicated' (to God); also used to describe a dedication to evil, as in 'accursed' (Galatians 1:8) Among the best known 'votive gift' was a huge golden vine, supplied by Herod the Great himself, and described by Josephus as follows. 'The Temple had doors also at the entrance, and lintels over them, of the same height with the temple itself. They were adorned with embroidered veils, with their flowers of purple, and pillars interwoven; and over these, but under the crown-work, was spread out a golden vine, with its branches hanging down from a great height, the largeness and fine workmanship of which was a surprising sight to the spectators, to see what vast materials there were, and with what great skill the workmanship was done' (Josephus, 'Antiquities' 15, 11).

21:7-9 'They questioned him, saying, "Teacher, when therefore will these things happen? And what will be the sign when these things are about to take place?" And he said, "See to it that you are not misled; for many will come in my name, saying, 'I am he' and, 'The time is near.' Do not go after them. When you hear of wars and disturbances, do not be terrified; for these things must take place first, but the end does not follow immediately."'

Once again Jesus is addressed by his legal and theological title, '*Didaskalos*', commonly and rather simplistically translated here as 'teacher'. The question pertains to the destruction of the Temple (which was completed in AD 70). Matthew's account of this dialogue (chapter 24) makes it clear that Jesus is also speaking of the end of the present age, in relation to eternity, in other words, the end of the world. The upheavals described are likened to the labour pains of childbirth - the start of a long, slow and painful process, and one in which spiritual deception will be rife. The process can be traced to shortly after Jesus' death. Josephus records that at the time of Felix (appointed Roman procurator of Judea by Claudius in AD 53), 'There was an Egyptian false prophet that did the Jews more mischief than the former; for he was a cheat, and pretended to be a prophet also, and got together thirty thousand men that were deluded by him; these he led roundabout from the wilderness to the mount which was called the Mount of Olives.' [227]

Jesus' comment makes it clear that 'the end does not follow immediately', indeed nearly two thousand years later we are still perhaps only seeing 'the beginning of the birth-pangs' (Matthew 24:8). His statements intertwine the two strands of the imminent judgement upon Jerusalem and the Temple and what will occur much later at the second coming of Jesus, which will end the present age as we know it. With the benefit of the hindsight of history, it is possible to separate out the strands into those that occurred around the time of the destruction of Jerusalem in AD 70, and those that have yet to be fulfilled.

21:10-11 'Then he continued by saying to them, "Nation will rise against nation and kingdom against kingdom, and there will be great earthquakes, and in various places plagues and famines; and there will be terrors and great signs from heaven."'

All of these indicators of the close of the age can reasonably be said to have occurred and still be occurring in significant numbers. Wars have been many, earthquakes and their underwater equivalent, the tsunami, are increasingly common, and plagues (most recently HIV) and famines are numerous. History has been punctuated regularly by 'terrors' ('*phobêtron*' - from '*phobeô*' - 'fear'); the extermination camps of the Second World War and the gulags of the Soviet regime being recent examples. 'Signs' from heaven ('*sêmeion*' - 'miracles') are occurring more and more often where the Holy Spirit is moving powerfully in the church in different parts of the world.

21:12-15 '"But before all these things, they will lay their hands on you and will persecute you, delivering you to the synagogues and prisons, bringing you before kings and governors for my name's sake. It will lead to an opportunity for your testimony. So make up your minds not to prepare beforehand to defend yourselves; for I will

give you utterance and wisdom which none of your opponents will be able to resist or refute."'

Jesus' discourse now turns to the period before the more imminent part of the picture - the coming persecution of the (predominantly Jewish) early church prior to the judgement upon the people and the destruction of Jerusalem in AD 70. After Messiah became a condemned criminal, accursed in 'hanging upon a tree' (Galatians 3:13 and Deuteronomy 21:23), devout Jews such as Saul of Tarsus would see it as their righteous legal duty to bring his followers to judicial execution as well, for alleged blasphemy, in their confessing Jesus to be divine. As Saul (now Paul) would declare to King Agrippa while on trial in Caesarea Maritima: 'I thought to myself that I had to do many things hostile to the name of Jesus of Nazareth. And this is just what I did in Jerusalem; not only did I lock up many of the saints in prisons, having received authority from the chief priests, but also when they were being put to death I cast my vote against them. And as I punished them often in all the synagogues, I tried to force them to blaspheme; and being furiously enraged at them, I kept pursuing them even to foreign cities' (Acts 26:9-11).

Such trials were indeed 'opportunities to testify', as an angel said to Paul, 'You must stand before Caesar' (Acts 27:24). Paul would benefit from divine assistance from the greatest minds in Jewish legal history - Jesus himself. His wisdom was above other in convincing argument. Such wisdom might be rejected, but its essential nature could not be denied and would linger on in the minds of those who heard it.

21:16-19 '"But you will be betrayed even by parents and brothers and relatives and friends, and they will put some of you to death, and you will be hated by all because of my name. Yet not a hair of your head will perish. By your endurance you will gain your lives."'

Any devout Jew would see it as their clear legal duty to stop blasphemy; family bonds would not prevent that from occurring. The name of Jesus would be a rock of stumbling (Isaiah 8:14, 1 Peter 2:8) for many, and still is to this day. All of the apostles except John would be martyred for their faith. The expression, 'not a hair of your head will perish' is a recognised proverb, and was fulfilled at the destruction of Jerusalem when the entire population of Jewish believers there, forewarned by Christ's teaching, left the city, as described by the historian Eusebius. 'But the people of the church in Jerusalem had been commanded by a revelation, vouchsafed to approved men there before the war, to leave the city and to dwell in a certain town of Perea called Pella. And when those that believed in Christ had come thither from Jerusalem, then, as if the royal city of the Jews and the whole land of Judea were entirely destitute of holy men, the judgment of God at length overtook those who had committed such outrages against Christ and his apostles, and totally destroyed that generation of impious men.' [228] Their 'endurance' ('*hupomenô*' - 'to abide under, to bear up courageously under suffering' [229] resulted in their lives ('*psuchê*' - also meaning 'breath' and 'soul')* being spared.

21:20-24 '"But when you see Jerusalem surrounded by armies, then recognize that her desolation is near. Then those who are in Judea must flee to the mountains, and those who are in the midst of the city must leave, and those who are in the country must not enter the city; because these are days of vengeance, so that all things which are written will be fulfilled. Woe to those who are pregnant and to those who are nursing babies in those days; for there will be great distress upon the land and wrath to this people; and they will fall by the edge of the sword, and will be led captive into all the nations; and Jerusalem will be trampled underfoot by the Gentiles until the times of the Gentiles are fulfilled."'

'Those in Judea' did indeed 'flee to the mountains' of neighbouring Perea as Eusebius described. The concept of God using the Gentiles to judge his people Israel was one that was commonly recognised by the Jews prior to Jesus' coming. Jeremiah had prophesied that 'The destroyer of the Gentiles is on his way; he is gone forth from his place to make thy land desolate; and thy cities shall be laid waste, without an inhabitant' (Jeremiah 4:7, KJV).

The memory of the destroying Babylonian army echoed in the inter-testamental apocalyptic Jewish writings. The 'Book of Jubilee' (dated to the second century before Christ) contains the following description of the Gentiles: 'They shall name the great name, but not in truth and not in righteousness, and they shall defile the holy of holies with their uncleanness and the corruption of their pollution. And a great punishment shall befall the deeds of this generation from the Lord, and he will give them over to the sword and to judgment and to captivity, and to be plundered and devoured. And he will wake up against them the sinners of the Gentiles, who have neither mercy nor compassion, and who shall respect the person of none, neither old nor young, nor any one, for they are more wicked and strong to do evil than all the children of men. And they shall use violence against Israel and transgression against Jacob, and much blood shall be shed upon the earth, and there shall be none to gather and none to bury. In those days they shall cry aloud, and call and pray that they may be saved from the hand of the sinners, the Gentiles; but none shall be saved. And the heads of the children shall be white with grey hair, and a child of three weeks shall appear old like a man of one hundred years, and their stature shall be destroyed by tribulation and oppression. And in those days the children shall begin to study the laws, and to seek the commandments, and to return to the path of righteousness. And the days shall begin to grow many and increase amongst those children of men till their days draw nigh to one thousand years. And to a greater number of years than was the number of the days. And there shall be no old man nor one who is satisfied with his days, for all shall be *[as]* children and youths.'

The 'distress' caused by the siege of Jerusalem has already been described; Jesus' comment about 'those nursing babies' was highly pertinent in view of the cannibalism described by Josephus during the famine that the four year Roman siege produced. The city of Jerusalem was indeed trodden underfoot by the Gentiles, and to this day exists in quarters, three of which are given over to non-Jewish residents.

21:25-28 '"There will be signs in sun and moon and stars, and on the earth dismay among nations, in perplexity at the roaring of the sea and the waves, men fainting from fear and the expectation of the things which are coming upon the world; for the powers of the heavens will be shaken. Then they will see the Son of Man coming in a cloud with power and great glory. But when these things begin to take place, straighten up and lift up your heads, because your redemption is drawing near."'

Jesus' discourse now enters territory that has yet to take place in our day, but that the Jews well understood heralded the 'Day of the Lord', when God's judgements would be revealed. Isaiah (13:9-13) had prophesied: 'Behold, the day of the Lord is coming, cruel, with fury and burning anger, to make the land a desolation; and he will exterminate its sinners from it. For the stars of heaven and their constellations will not flash forth their light; the sun will be dark when it rises and the moon will not shed its light. Thus I will punish the world for its evil and the wicked for their iniquity; I will also put an end to the arrogance of the proud and abase the haughtiness of the ruthless. I will make mortal man scarcer than pure gold and mankind than the gold of Ophir. Therefore, I will make the heavens tremble, and the earth will be shaken from its place at the fury of the Lord of hosts in the day of his burning anger.' Joel too had prophesied: 'I will display wonders in the sky and on the earth, blood, fire and columns of smoke. The sun will be turned into darkness and the moon into blood before the great and awesome day of the Lord' (Joel 2:30-31). These disturbances in the created order will cause the utmost distress to those who do not see them as positive evidence of the good that will come with Jesus' return. 'Dismay' is '*sunochê*', also meaning 'anguish' and 'distress'.* 'Perplexity' is '*aporia*', from the negative of '*poros*', meaning 'a way' or 'resource', hence literally 'at a loss for a way'. [230] The nations will be 'at a loss' because there will be no rational explanation for the events in the heavens and the created order on earth, but they will not want to acknowledge God as the perpetrator of them. Their fear will cause them to '*apopsuchô*' - 'to be without breath' as it is taken from them, 'swooning' and being unable to breathe with anxiety. * This use is its only occurrence in the New Testament, but it was a very particular medical term, commonly used by Greek physicians to mean 'loss of strength due to shock'. [231]

Jesus then quotes directly from Daniel 7:13-14. 'I kept looking in the night visions, and behold, with the clouds of heaven, one like a Son of Man was coming, and he came up to the Ancient of Days and was presented before him. And to him was given dominion, glory and a kingdom, that all the peoples, nations and men of every language might serve him. His dominion is an everlasting dominion which will not pass away; and his kingdom is one which will not be destroyed.'

The reaction called out of the believer to these extraordinary events in the skies and on the sea and land is set in stark contrast to the abject terror that they cause in those who do not eagerly await Jesus' return. It is to 'straighten up' ('*anakuptô*' - 'to stoop upwards', in the sense of a reversal), hence the opposite of the fainting that will characterise the reaction of the unbelievers, and to 'lift up their heads' in eager anticipation of the second coming. This is because the final outworking of God's redemptive plan is imminent, '**apolutrôsis**', from '**apolutroô**', meaning 'a liberation procured by the payment of a ransom'.* The price of release from the power of sin and death, paid in full by Jesus' shed blood at Calvary, will have wrought its fulfilment.

21:29-33 'Then he told them a parable: "Behold the fig tree and all the trees; as soon as they put forth leaves, you see it and know for yourselves that summer is now near. So you also, when you see these things happening, recognize that the kingdom of God is near. Truly I say to you, this generation will not pass away until all things take place. Heaven and earth will pass away, but my words will not pass away."'

The nation of Israel is likened by God to a fig tree in Hosea 9:10 - 'I saw your forefathers as the earliest fruit on the fig tree in its first season.' Jesus uses the budding fig trees around the Mount of Olives as a visual aid to his 'end times' teaching. The young leaves were not yet out, but there could be no doubt that summer was on its way. The 'generation' spoken of can be seen as representing Jesus' audience with regard to the pending fall of Jerusalem; it can also be translated as 'race'. [232] In this case Jesus' words have also been fulfilled in the survival of the Jewish people despite Nazi, Communist and Islamic efforts to destroy them. Christ's words in this and all other regards have eternal longevity. As the spoken word of God, incarnate in a Jewish Torah-teacher, they have remained and will survive into eternity.

21:34-36 '"Be on guard, so that your hearts will not be weighted down with dissipation and drunkenness and the worries of life, and that day will not come on you suddenly like a trap; for it will come upon all those who

dwell on the face of all the earth. But keep on the alert at all times, praying that you may have strength to escape all these things that are about to take place, and to stand before the Son of Man.'"

'Dissipation' is '*kraipalê*', also meaning 'drunken nausea' - 'the giddiness and headache caused by drinking wine to excess'.* This occurrence is the only one in the New Testament, but it was the common medical term for such nausea. [233] 'Drunkenness' is '*methê*', which is the usual New Testament word for intoxication. Jesus recognises that the 'worries' of life can lead to self-medication with alcohol rather than a reliance on him to sort the stresses out and to guide us through them. Jesus 'end times' teaching in Matthew 24:37-40 had likened those days to those of Noah. 'As it was in the days of Noah, so it will be at the coming of the Son of Man. For in the days before the flood, people were eating and drinking, marrying and giving in marriage, up to the day Noah entered the ark; and they knew nothing about what would happen until the flood came and took them all away. That is how it will be at the coming of the Son of Man.' The 'worries' of this life are not of themselves necessarily evil, but can easily distract from the wider purposes of God if God himself is not brought into them. 'Worries' is '*merimna*', also meaning 'cares' and 'anxieties'.*

If we are so distracted we may miss some of the signs of Jesus' return and so experience that day closing in us with the suddenness of a bird 'trap' or 'snare'. The remedy is to be 'on the alert' - '*agrupneô*' - 'without sleep' (the negative form of '*hupnos*', 'to sleep'), a state of wakefulness soon to be found lacking in the disciples in their watching and praying in the Garden of Gethsemane. Prayer and strength ('*katischuô*' - 'to be strong against') are called for, a strength that God supplies in answer to our prayer, to enable us to endure until Jesus' return.

21:37-38 'Now during the day he was teaching in the Temple, but at evening he would go out and spend the night on the mount that is called Olivet. And all the people would get up early in the morning to come to him in the Temple to listen to him.'

Jesus' ability to teach freely in the closely policed Temple courts, and to debate Torah with the various Jewish authorities there, clearly evidence his legal standing in that society as a '*Didaskalos*' - a 'Doctor' of Torah. When Peter and John address a crowd in the Temple, they are arrested by the Temple Guard and charged with 'teaching the people' (Acts 4:2), something they, as 'unlearned men' (Acts 4:13) are not legally entitled to do. Jesus' popularity as the most brilliant exponent of Torah was seen in the people's willingness to rise up early from their beds to attend his teaching sessions. It need not be assumed that Jesus was sleeping out in the open air. He was staying in Bethany, some 2 miles to the east of Jerusalem, where the home of Mary, Martha and Lazarus, was located (Mark 11:1, Luke 19:29). That was a short distance from the Temple Mount, where 'all the people' could gather to hear him. His fame was now becoming a significant religious and political threat to the High Priest - Roman rulership status quo. Little by little, Jesus was forcing the authorities' hand. They were being compelled to act.

Chapter 22

22:1-2 'Now the Feast of Unleavened Bread, which is called the Passover, was approaching. The chief priests and the scribes were seeking how they might put him to death; for they were afraid of the people.'

As the numbers of pilgrim visitors to Jerusalem grew, with the impending compulsory Feast of Passover, so Jesus' admirers, particularly from Galilee in the north, grew more numerous, making the authorities' position in regards to engineering his death more difficult. Whatever steps they took would have to be without the general public's knowledge and then follow an accelerated judicial path to completion before any popular outcry could occur.

22:3-6 'And Satan entered into Judas who was called Iscariot, belonging to the number of the twelve. And he went away and discussed with the chief priests and officers how he might betray him to them. They were glad and agreed to give him money. So he consented, and began seeking a good opportunity to betray him to them apart from the crowd.'

While Judas' love of money provided Satan with a foothold in his life, it was in all likelihood also a recent development in his understanding of Jesus' mission that led him to such a drastic step. His motive may have been one of seeking to force a confrontation with the authorities, or, more likely, a sense of disappointment through learning that Jesus was not about to oust the Romans after all. He appears to have had no use for a Messiah that would suffer a criminal's death, and who foretold the destruction of Jerusalem rather than its exaltation. Judas was just the sort of person the priests needed - someone who they could manipulate with money and who could provide insider information as to Jesus' movements as well as get near enough to him for nighttime identification to be easily performed at a time when the general populace was indoors.

22:7-13 'Then came the first day of Unleavened Bread on which the Passover lamb had to be sacrificed. And Jesus sent Peter and John, saying, "Go and prepare the Passover for us, so that we may eat it." They said to him, "Where do you want us to prepare it?" And he said to them, "When you have entered the city, a man will meet you carrying a pitcher of water; follow him into the house that he enters. And you shall say to the owner of the house, 'The Teacher says to you, "Where is the guest room in which I may eat the Passover with my disciples?"' And he will show you a large furnished upper room; prepare it there." And they left and found everything just as he had told them; and they prepared the Passover.'

This passage provides good evidence for a link between Jesus as a noted '*Didaskalos*' of Torah (translated here using the usual and rather non-specific term, 'Teacher') and the most ultra-orthodox of Jewish religious groups, the Essenes. Josephus [234] comments that they 'neglected wedlock' and practiced consecrated celibacy, as did Jesus. The extremely unusual fact of a man carrying water in that society (hard for the disciples to miss!), points to an absence of women and children within the house, who would otherwise have performed that task. The Essene community regarded the traditional Jewish lunar calendar as inaccurate because it gave rise to a shorter year than the solar model, forcing the rabbis to add an extra month every 3 years. The Essenes followed a solar calendar; hence they often celebrated the Passover on a different day to the rest of Jerusalem. Accordingly their 'guest room' was available for Jesus and his disciples to use. 'Guest room' is '*kataluma*', the same word translated as 'inn' in the account of the nativity (Luke 2:7). These were first-story rooms built above the house (e.g. 1 Kings 17:23).

22:14-19 'When the hour had come, he reclined at the table, and the apostles with him. And he said to them, "I have earnestly desired to eat this Passover with you before I suffer; for I say to you, I shall never again eat it until it is fulfilled in the kingdom of God." And when he had taken a cup and given thanks, he said, "Take this and share it among yourselves; for I say to you, I will not drink of the fruit of the vine from now on until the kingdom of God comes." And when he had taken some bread and given thanks, he broke it and gave it to them, saying, "This is my body which is given for you; do this in remembrance of me."'

Passover began in the evening of the preceding day, as judged by three stars becoming visible in the twilight sky. Jesus and his disciples are eating in the Roman manner of freemen - a reclined position, and as was the custom, around the outside of a three sided table - a triclinium. The essential message of Passover, that of a lamb being sacrificed to spare the people the consequences of judgement and to open the door to freedom, was about to be played out as God had originally intended, in the sacrifice of his one and only Son.

The Seder meal's order of service contains prayers of blessing around four cups of wine, based on the four promises of God in Exodus 6:6-7. 'Say, therefore, to the sons of Israel, 'I am the Lord, and I will bring you out from under the burdens of the Egyptians *[celebrated by the cup of sanctification]*, and I will deliver you from their bondage *[celebrated by the cup of deliverance]*. I will also redeem you with an outstretched arm and with great judgments *[celebrated by the cup of blessing or redemption]* - Exodus 6:6. 'Then I will take you for my people, and I will be your God; and you shall know that I am the Lord your God, who brought you out from under the burdens of the Egyptians *[celebrated by the cup of thanksgiving or restoration]* - Exodus 6:7.

The Jewish Passover meal service contains a plate with three pieces of unleavened bread known as 'matzot' (pleural), the middle piece of which ('matzah' - singular) was broken in two. The larger part was put aside for later use as the 'afikoman' (which means 'comes after') with the smaller part of the middle matzah being returned to the Seder plate. This broken middle matzah symbolized humility, and was eaten later as the 'bread of poverty', also known as the 'bread of affliction.' The service order reads: 'This is the bread of affliction that our ancestors ate in the land of Egypt' (Deuteronomy 16:3). Jesus changed this to 'This is my body, which is broken for you, this do in remembrance of me' (1 Corinthians 11:24).

22:20-23 'And in the same way he took the cup after they had eaten, saying, "This cup which is poured out for you is the new covenant in my blood. But behold, the hand of the one betraying me is with mine on the table. For indeed, the Son of Man is going as it has been determined; but woe to that man by whom he is betrayed!" And they began to discuss among themselves which one of them it might be who was going to do this thing.'

1 Corinthians 10:16 reads, 'Is not the cup of blessing which we bless a sharing in the blood of Christ?' Paul indicates that it was the third cup of the Seder service, the cup of blessing, which Jesus took to inaugurate the new covenant in his blood. The fourth cup, the cup of thanksgiving, does not appear to have been drunk, thereby leaving it until 'the kingdom of God comes' (Mark 14:25). Drinking from the cup symbolised participating in the covenant. Matthew's account (26: 27- 28) reads, 'Drink from it, all of you. This is my blood of the covenant, which is poured out for many for the forgiveness of sins.'

The fact that Jesus was able to speak to Judas without the other disciples being aware of what was going on (Matthew 26:25, John

13:26-28), despite their general discussion as to who would betray Jesus, indicates that Judas was lying immediately on Jesus' left with John lying on Jesus' right side (John 13:25). Judas received from Jesus the portion reserved for an honoured guest (John 13:26) - the first dipping of the unleavened bread into the bitter herbs - before going out to betray him into the hands of the priests. In lying next to Jesus, his hand would have been dipping into the common dish along with Jesus' hand - 'with mine on the table'.

22:24-27 'And there arose also a dispute among them as to which one of them was regarded to be greatest. And he said to them, "The kings of the Gentiles lord it over them; and those who have authority over them are called 'Benefactors'. But it is not this way with you, but the one who is the greatest among you must become like the youngest, and the leader like the servant. For who is greater, the one who reclines at the table or the one who serves? Is it not the one who reclines at the table? But I am among you as the one who serves."'

Jesus' revelations concerning the new covenant in his own body and blood do not seem to have distracted the disciples from one of their favourite topics of conversation, namely, which of them was the greatest (Greek: '*megas*', which, fittingly, may also be translated as 'arrogant').* This disputing had raised its ugly head on previous occasions, most recently with the connivance of Jesus' aunt, the mother of James and John, who was sister to Mary the mother of Jesus (Matthew 20:20-21). Jesus' reference to 'Gentile kings', who were a by-word for heathen immorality, is a sharp rebuke for his Jewish disciples. 'Gentile kings' like the murdering and effeminate Herod Antipas [xxv] were the last people the disciples would have

---

[xxv] 'They which are gorgeously apparelled and live delicately [*'truphê'* - *'effeminately'*] are in kings' courts' (Luke 7:25, KJV).

compared themselves with, men who governed on the part of a heathen race and taxed the people into oblivion while styling themselves as doers of good.

Jesus' own example was the diametric opposite. His was a humility enshrined by stepping down from heavenly perfection into a sin-soaked world, which he had come to serve, rather than to condemn. This passage parallels the foot washing of the disciples recorded in John chapter 13, a graphic further out-working of the incarnation where the disciples, who were indeed reclining at table, were served in a way so menial that Jewish slaves were protected by Law from being forced to do.

22:28-30 '"You are those who have stood by me in my trials; and just as my Father has granted me a kingdom, I grant you that you may eat and drink at my table in my kingdom, and you will sit on thrones judging the twelve tribes of Israel."'

Many of Jesus' followers had deserted him when his teaching had been too much for them to handle, for example, in his teaching on the 'bread of life' in John chapter six. 'Jesus said to them, "Truly, truly, I say to you, unless you eat the flesh of the Son of Man and drink his blood, you have no life in yourselves. This is the bread which came down out of heaven; not as the fathers ate and died; he who eats this bread will live forever." These things he said in the synagogue as he taught in Capernaum.' 'Therefore many of his disciples, when they heard this said, "This is a difficult statement; who can listen to it?" And he was saying, "For this reason I have said to you, that no one can come to me unless it has been granted him from the Father." As a result of this many of his disciples withdrew, and were not walking with him anymore. So Jesus said to the twelve, "You do not want to go away also, do you?" Simon Peter answered him, "Lord, to whom shall we go? You have the words of eternal life'" (John 6: 53, 58-60, 65-68). Eating Jesus' flesh and drinking his blood had not been concepts that most of Jesus' Jewish audience had wanted to investigate further.

But the apostles had 'stood by him', not just when others had left but also in all the trials and tests that the incarnation caused Jesus to experience in his daily life and ministry. 'Trials' here is *peirasmos*, which is also translated as 'the test of man's fidelity, integrity, virtue, and constancy' and as 'an experiment'.* It is easy in modern times to take the concept of the incarnation for granted. But God had never become man before, had never previously lowered himself into the confines of a human body, had never subjected himself to the indignities of daily bodily physiological functions, and never had to contend with human obduracy and stupidity as a fellow human himself. The apostles had supported Jesus in what must, for the Creator of the universe, have been a somewhat trying experience.

The reward the apostles would receive was to continue to fellowship with Jesus in his true state of being, that of a king in a kingdom prepared for him by his Father. (Matthew 25:34: 'Then the King will say to those on his right, 'Come, you who are blessed of my Father, inherit the kingdom prepared for you from the foundation of the world.') And they would have a shared role with him there - that of judging the tribes of Israel. The role of a judge in a Hebrew court was not one any of Jesus' disciples, with the possible exception of Matthew, the former legal scribe, had any experience of doing, but Jesus' ministry was preparing them for it. As Paul would later write to the church at Corinth, 'Do you not know that we will judge angels?' (1 Corinthians 6:3).

22:31-34 '"Simon, Simon, behold Satan has demanded permission to sift you like wheat; but I have prayed for you, that your faith may not fail; and you, when once you have turned again, strengthen your brothers." But he said

to him, "Lord, with you I am ready to go both to prison and to death!" And he said, "I say to you, Peter, the rooster will not crow today until you have denied three times that you know me."'

'Permission' here is '*exaiteômai*', a word only used once, here, in the New Testament. It is derived from '*aiteô*', 'to ask' or 'to desire'. Satan has to ask for God's permission to 'sift' one of his children and God will only permit what is for our ultimate benefit (Job 1:11-12). Satan's motive is uniformly evil but is used by God for good. This is often as a result of the increased sense of dependency upon God that results from getting into a spiritual conflict with an angelic being that cannot be defeated in one's own human strength. The God who knows what we can bear because 'he knows our frame and is mindful that we are dust' (Psalm 103:14), protects us from the worst of Satan's attentions and brings us through them into a state of greater reliance on him, and less upon ourselves. That source of spiritual strength is then available to use to encourage our fellow travellers.

Peter, never short of self-confidence, is quick to reassure Jesus of his unfailing fidelity. Peter would eventually make it to 'prison and death', but it would not be at the first 'bite' at that particular 'cherry'. It would take a few more years of the Holy Spirit's work within him for his actions to catch up with his good intentions. Jesus prophesies with unerring accuracy the imminent denials that Peter's fears would provoke, despite his having enough bravery to follow after his fellow disciple John into the courtyard of Annas, the high priest and Jesus' arch-enemy, following Jesus' arrest.

Mark's account of Jesus' saying reads: 'Truly I say to you, that this very night, before a rooster crows twice, you yourself will deny me three times' (Mark 14:30). Male poultry crow at dawn but also in the earlier hours of the morning. The Jews traditionally recognised two crowings, as the Talmud (Tractate 'Yoma') illustrates. 'If one starts out on a journey before keriiath ha-geber [cockcrow], his blood comes upon his own head! Rabbi Josiah says: [He should wait] until he has crowed twice, some say: 'Until he has crowed thrice.' [235] 'Thrice' here signifies the repeated crowing that occurs when dawn has definitely arrived and there is sufficient light to begin a journey. Peter's first denial (Mark 14:68) was marked by the first crowing. His third denial (Mark 14:71-72) was marked by the second crowing. Peter's denials of Jesus could also be timed by the Roman watch at the neighbouring house of Pilate, the procurator, where 'cockcrow' was one of the Roman guard times of duty. The Romans divided the night into four periods or 'watches'. [236] 'Cockcrow' was the third (ending at around 3AM, a time when cocks are indeed known to crow). The fourth watch ('morning') ended at around 6AM, nearer to dawn, when cocks invariably crow.

22:35-38 'And he said to them, "When I sent you out without money belt and bag and sandals, you did not lack anything, did you?" They said, "No, nothing." And he said to them, "But now, whoever has a money belt is to take it along, likewise also a bag, and whoever has no sword is to sell his coat and buy one. For I tell you that this which is written must be fulfilled in me, 'And he was numbered with the transgressors'; for that which refers to me has its fulfilment." They said, "Lord, look, here are two swords." And he said to them, "It is enough."'

The disciples had learned an important faith lesson in terms of their reliance on God to supply their needs during their journeys in sharing the gospel, and preparing the villages in Judea to receive Jesus' coming to them. That being established as a foundation principle did not exclude the ordinary use of money and a bag to facilitate their journeys, nor a sword to deter those of their enemies cowardly enough to attack travellers without that well recognised symbol of self-defence. Two swords were evidently considered sufficient. Jesus was not promoting an unqualified pacifism that could have easily been taken advantage of by their enemies.

Having foretold to the disciples their coming reward for their faithfulness to him, Jesus quotes from the prophet Isaiah about his own reward (to be divided with them), and of the marked change of standing he was about to experience within the Jewish community. He was about to move from being a highly respected ordained Torah teacher to being seen as a reviled blasphemer, stripped of his legal title '*Didaskalos*', and condemned to death as a false teacher. 'Therefore, I will allot him a portion with the great, and he will divide the booty with the strong; because he poured out himself to death, and was numbered with the transgressors; yet he himself bore the sin of many, and interceded for the transgressors' (Isaiah 53:12).

The disciples' lot would be that of their master. John records Jesus as saying: 'Remember the word that I said to you, 'A slave is not greater than his master.' If they persecuted me, they will also persecute you; if they kept my word, they will keep yours also. But all these things they will do to you for my name's sake, because they do not know the One who sent me' (John 15:20-21). The opprobrium that was coming to Jesus would affect his disciples too.

22:39-40 'And he came out and proceeded as was his custom to the Mount of Olives; and the disciples also followed him. When he arrived at the place, he said to them, "Pray that you may not enter into temptation."'

The Mount of Olives, to the east of Jerusalem, was a regular place of prayer for Jesus. It was a place where the city's wealthier citizens kept private gardens, and one of these Jesus had access for his own use. It was named Gethsemane (Matthew 26:36), meaning 'oil-press', indicating that there were olive trees there, the fruit of which

396

could be immediately converted into the oil that had so many uses in daily life. The 'press' was a fitting image of what lay ahead for Jesus, who had his own spiritual battle to win - to choose for the cross - but his first concern was for the spiritual well-being of the eleven apostles who had continued to follow him after Judas had not returned from his treacherous errand to the priests. Jesus is concerned that none of the eleven turn aside in the coming arrest in the same way Judas had.

22:41-44 'And he withdrew from them about a stone's throw, and he knelt down and began to pray, saying, "Father, if you are willing, remove this cup from me; yet not my will, but yours be done." Now an angel from heaven appeared to him, strengthening him. And being in agony he was praying very fervently; and his sweat became like drops of blood, falling down upon the ground.'

Peter, James and John accompanied Jesus further into the garden (Matthew 26:37), and then Jesus went on further still to pray 'with his face to the ground' (Matthew 26:39). Such was the humility of the Son of God incarnate. Jesus was well aware of the torment that would accompany being the 'sin-bearer' in addition to the agonies that always attended crucifixion. Not being a masochist, he was reluctant to undergo them if another option was available. Knowing that there was not, he brought his own human wishes (to avoid such suffering, if possible) under the will of his Father. Such was his agonies that the Father sent angelic help to assist him, as had occurred following his battle with the devil in the wilderness at the start of his ministry (Matthew 4:11). 'Strengthened' here though is *'enischuô'*, a word unique to Luke in the New Testament, and is used in the same transitive sense by Hippocrates as imparting physical strength to a patient. [237]

'Agony' here is '*agônia*', another term unique to Doctor Luke in the New Testament but commonly found in Greek medical texts to denote pain severe enough to provoke sweating. [238] Ancient physicians set great store in observing the type and quantity of their patients' sweat, [239] and Luke must have found the account of Jesus 'sweating blood' fascinating - a rare medical event that he alone of the Gospel writers mentions. The agonies of Gethsemane were so great that Jesus' sweat became mixed with blood, a sign of the most acute human stress, known as haematidrosis. In this condition the constriction to the blood vessels supplying the sweat glands causes bleeding into the glands themselves, and out through the skin's pores. John's Gospel describes the Roman spear wound draining blood followed by water (serum) from Jesus' side following his death on the cross (John 19:34), a medical indication that Jesus had undergone a haemopericardium. This occurs when the heart's muscle ruptures into the pericardial sac around the heart, causing heart compression and eventual death. It is likely that this process began during the agony Jesus experienced in the garden, as he lay prostrate in prayer before his Father God reconciling himself to and preparing himself for doing his Father's will at Calvary. Luke's word for 'drops' of blood is '*thrombos*', the common term for a blood clot and from which the modern English words 'thrombus' and 'thrombosis' are derived.

22:45-46 'When he rose from prayer, he came to the disciples and found them sleeping from sorrow, and said to them, "Why are you sleeping? Get up and pray that you may not enter into temptation."'

Sorrow (combined no doubt with the effects of the cups of Passover wine) caused the disciples to succumb to sleep. Thus was not the best spiritual preparation for the trial ('temptation'), that was even then approaching from the city to the west with the arrival of Judas, together with the priests trained as soldiers who formed the Temple

Guard. Doctor Luke is the sole Gospel writer to ascribe the cause of the disciples' somnolence - *'lupê'* - 'sorrow and grief'.* The accounts of Matthew and Mark lack that diagnostic detail and simply comment that the disciples' eyes were 'heavy', without saying why.

22:47-48 'While he was still speaking, behold, a crowd came, and the one called Judas, one of the twelve, was preceding them; and he approached Jesus to kiss him. But Jesus said to him, "Judas, are you betraying the Son of Man with a kiss?"'

Passover is celebrated at the time of a full moon; John 18:3 describes the torches and lanterns that the arresting party brought, indicating that the night sky may have been cloudy. The pitch darkness of the olive grove was a difficult place to swiftly identify someone for arrest. Not realising that Jesus was planning on giving himself up, and concerned that Jesus would be alerted to their coming and try to escape under cover of darkness, the priests sent Judas ahead to signal which of the group of men was Jesus by means of a kiss. Mark 14:44: 'Now he who was betraying him had given them a signal, saying, "Whomever I kiss, he is the one; seize him and lead him away under guard."' Jesus forestalls Judas with reference to the absolute impropriety of the greeting, but was still made known by Judas' action to the soldiers that are following. Jesus had no thought of attempting an escape, or indeed any resistance to what he knew to be his Father's will.

22:49-51 'When those who were around him saw what was going to happen, they said "Lord, shall we strike with the sword?" And one of them struck the slave of the high priest and cut off his right ear. But Jesus answered and said, "Stop! No more of this." And he touched his ear and healed him.'

His disciples however, perhaps recalling Jesus' comment regarding their need of a sword, were not as in accord with the plan of God, and attempt resistance. John's account records that it was Peter, in his usual precipitate manner, who drew the blade and aiming at the servant's head, missed as he ducked, and instead succeeded in severing his ear. 'Simon Peter then, having a sword, drew it and struck the high priest's slave, and cut off his right ear; and the slave's name was Malchus. So Jesus said to Peter, "Put the sword into the sheath; the cup which the Father has given me, shall I not drink it?"' (John 18:10-11). All four Gospels record the act of severing the ear but only Doctor Luke records Jesus' restoration of it, a miracle that underlines his complete control of the situation.

While the reaction of the arresting party is not described to this miracle, John's account does describe their reaction to Jesus identifying himself to the priests that made up the soldiers from the Temple Guard. 'So Jesus, knowing all the things that were coming upon him, went forth and said to them, "Whom do you seek?" They answered him, "Jesus the Nazarene." He said to them, "I am he." And Judas also, who was betraying him, was standing with them. So when he said to them, "I am he" they drew back and fell to the ground' (John 18:4-6). Jesus, speaking in Hebrew, may well have spoken the name of God in declaring 'I am' (Exodus 3:14); in which case the priestly soldiers would have had cause to fall, either in amazement or in response to the power that accompanied such a pronouncement.

Jesus had sung the final Hallel with his disciples (Matthew 26:30), then left the upper room and closed the Passover Seder service without partaking of the fourth cup, the cup of restoration. He would drink of a different cup before the fulfilment of the feast in the Kingdom of God - the cup of God's wrath against sin. Jesus had asked James and John, upon their requests for seats at his right and left, 'You do not know what you are asking. Are you able to drink the cup that I drink, or to be baptized with the baptism with which I am baptized?' (Mark 10:38). Jesus would drain the cup of suffering to the dregs in paying the debt that mankind's sin had incurred.

22:52-53 'Then Jesus said to the chief priests and officers of the Temple and elders who had come against him, "Have you come out with swords and clubs as you would against a robber? While I was with you daily in the Temple you did not lay hands on me; but this hour and the power of darkness are yours."'

The Temple Guard were armed and accompanied by leading Temple officials, both chief priests and elders from the Sanhedrin. Jesus, as a doctor of Torah, had recently debated with some of these same figures in the Temple, but they had not had the courage to arrest him there in the presence of the people. 'Power' here is '*exousia*', more commonly translated as 'authority'.* The chief priests and elders of the Sanhedrin had legal authority, but it was being exercised as an authority of darkness - '*skotos*', a term Luke uses in Acts 13:11 to mean 'blindness'. (Acts 13:11 'Immediately a mist and a darkness fell upon him.') The rulers were blind to Jesus' true identity as Messiah, seeing him only as a senior Jewish Torah teacher who had fallen into blasphemy in taking upon himself the name of God, and forgiving the sins of others as only God could.

22:54 'Having arrested him, they led him away and brought him to the house of the high priest; but Peter was following at a distance.'

John's account indicates that Jesus was taken first to the house of Annas, the father-in-law of Caiaphus, who was high priest that year (John 18:14). Annas, being senior, was very much the power behind the throne and was immensely wealthy, profiting from the Temple market and money-changing operations known as 'The Bazaars of

Annas'. Herod the Great had taken to making High Priestly political appointments to what had originally been a hereditary position, and the practice continued to King Agrippa, who 'gave the high priesthood to Ismael, who was the son of Fabi … Such was the impudence and boldness that had seized on the high priests, that they had the hardiness to send their servants into the threshing-floors, to take away those tithes that were due to the priests, insomuch that it so fell out that the poorest sort of the priests died for want.' [240] Similarly, the Talmud records, 'Woe is me because of the house of Ishmael the son of Phabi, woe is me because of their fists! For they are High Priests and their sons are *[Temple]* treasurers and their sons-in-law are trustees and their servants beat the people with staves.' [241] Peter, apparently attempting to make good his promise of fidelity to prison and even death, followed behind.

22:55-58 'After they had kindled a fire in the middle of the courtyard and had sat down together, Peter was sitting among them. And a servant-girl, seeing him as he sat in the firelight and looking intently at him, said "This man was with him too." But he denied it, saying, "Woman, I do not know him." A little later, another saw him and said, "You are one of them too!" But Peter said, "Man, I am not!"'

John 18:15 records that John was known to the High Priest. This was Annas, who was father-in-law to Caiaphas (John 18:13), who held the formal title of High Priest but ruled in the shadow of Annas. Hence Jesus was taken first to Annas' house, before being moved to Caiaphas' house (John 18:24). John's good standing with such a powerful ruling family may have been through his mother Salome, who was sister to Mary, the mother of Jesus. Salome was therefore a fellow kinswoman to Elizabeth, wife of Zachariah, who was himself a senior priest.

John appears to have been quite at ease in the courtyard of Jesus' sworn enemy, the High Priest, who was at that very moment actively conspiring to put Jesus to death. John's favourable standing gave him influence with the girl on duty at the entrance to Annas' courtyard, who admitted Peter at John's request. Jesus was an extremely well known figure and someone in his company as prominent and out-spoken as Peter was likely to be recognised and challenged. These challenges formed the occasions for the first two of Peter's three denials, no doubt hastened by the severe stress that Peter, who was evidently not in the High Priest's favour, must have felt.

22:59-62 'After about an hour had passed, another man began to insist, saying, "Certainly, this man also was with him, for he is a Galilean too." But Peter said, "Man, I do not know what you are talking about." Immediately, while he was still speaking, a rooster crowed. The Lord turned and looked at Peter. And Peter remembered the word of the Lord, how he had told him, "Before a rooster crows today, you will deny me three times." And he went out and wept bitterly.'

Mark's account has the first of two episodes of rooster crowing after the first of Peter's denials, a kind of poultry warning to Peter of Jesus' prophecy (Mark 14:68). After the second denial, Jesus was taken from the house of Annas to the house of Caiaphus (John 18:24). Peter's third denial is recorded as containing curses called down upon himself (Mark 14:71), such was the level of Peter's desperation, and is greeted by the second round of crowing. But the God who is greater than human despair timed Peter's third denial with the emergence of Jesus from the house of Caiaphus on his way to the house of Pilate the Roman governor. One look from Jesus brought Peter to a place of remorse and eventual repentance and restoration.

22:63-65 'Now the men who were holding Jesus in custody were mocking him and beating him, and they blindfolded him and were asking him, saying, "Prophesy, who is the one who hit you?" And they were saying many other things against him, blaspheming.'

Jesus is being held by the Temple Guard under the orders of the High Priest before whom he will appear when dawn comes and the Law permitted Sanhedrin representatives to formally gather in judgement of him. The Guard consisted of priests who performed soldierly duties and kept order in the Temple Courts. These were the men who earlier in Jesus' ministry had been unable to bring him in for questioning, relating sheepishly on returning to the Sanhedrin empty-handed, 'Never has a man spoken the way this man speaks' (John 7:46). Their high regard for Jesus would have been turned on its head by a sense of religious betrayal that they felt when confronted with his claims to forgive sin and his taking upon himself the name of God. Their admiration had swung to malice, spite and ridicule. 'Blaspheming' here is '*blasphêmeô*', which can also be translated as 'to speak evil of' and 'revile',* these being much closer to the context of abuse by the priests than the more common use of 'speaking against God'.

22:66-69 'When it was day, the Council of elders of the people assembled, both chief priests and scribes, and they led him away to their council chamber, saying, "If you are the Christ, tell us." But he said to them, "If I tell you, you will not believe; and if I ask a question, you will not answer. But from now on the Son of Man will be seated at the right hand of the power of God."'

The Sanhedrin met in the '*Lishkat ha-Gazith*' - the 'Hall of Hewn Stones' - which was built into the north wall of the Holy Place, with a door into the sanctuary and another into the court beyond. The

404

Talmud speaks of proceeding 'to the great Beth-Din of the Hall of Hewn-Stones whence instruction issued to all Israel'. [242] This housed the full court of the 'Great Sanhedrin'; there were also two lesser courts of twenty-three judges, one at the entrance of the Temple Mount and one at the entrance to the Court of Israel. [243] Tractate 'Sanhedrin' 32b speaks of following the justice 'of the Sages to the Chamber of the Hewn Stones'. There would be no justice for Jesus on this occasion.

22:70-71 'And they all said, "Are you the Son of God, then?" And he said to them, "Yes, I am." Then they said, "What further need do we have of testimony? For we have heard it ourselves from his own mouth."'

Matthew 26:63 records the high priest placing Jesus under oath to answer - was he 'the Christ, the Son of God?' Jesus' affirmative answer prompts the High Priest's legal act of rending his garment. A Talmudic account records the accused and witnesses 'examined by means of a substitute for the divine Name; the accused being not executed on this evidence but after a private examination of the chief witness to 'State literally what you heard'. Thereupon he did so *[using the divine name]*. The judges then arose and rent their garments, which were not to be re-sewn.' [244] There was no need of further (false) witnesses. Jesus was, apparently, condemned out of his own mouth.

Chapter 23

23:1-2 'Then the whole body of them got up and brought him before Pilate. And they began to accuse him, saying, "We found this man misleading our nation and forbidding to pay taxes to Caesar, and saying that he himself is Christ, a king."'

After Herod the Great's cruel and unpopular son Archelaus had been exiled to Gaul by the Emperor Tiberius in 6 AD, Rome oversaw Judea by means of directly appointed governors who ruled under the more immediate oversight of the ruler (Legate) of Syria. In 1961, a block of limestone, which became known as the "Pilate Stone', was found in the Roman theatre at Caesarea Maritima, with a dedication by Pilate to the effect that he was prefect of Judea. Officials held the title of 'Prefect' where they had the authority over capital charges, as opposed to the lesser title of 'Procurator' where they were mainly responsible for tax collection and decisions of questions relative to the revenues. The Jewish authorities bring Jesus before Pilate because they are seeking a decision on a capital charge (blasphemy) that they dress up in the political terms needed to persuade the Gentile authorities to enforce it. The Judean Roman governors were based in the north-west port-city of Caesarea Maritima (where Paul was taken for trial - Acts 23:23), except during major Jewish feasts, when they occupied the governor's residence in Jerusalem.

Pontius Pilate had succeeded the rule of Valerius Gratus (who had been appointed governor under Emperor Tiberius and ruled from 15-26 AD). As earlier noted, Pilate had made an inauspicious beginning to his rule - he had brought Imperial standards into Jerusalem. These were idolatrous to the Jews because they bore the image of Caesar. Josephus further relates: 'He introduced Caesar's effigies, which were upon the ensigns, and brought them into the city; whereas the Law forbids us the very making of images; on which account the former procurators were wont to make their entry into the city with such ensigns as had not those ornaments. Pilate was the first who brought those images to Jerusalem, and set them up there; which was done without the knowledge of the people, because it was done in the night time; but as soon as they knew it, they came in multitudes to Caesarea, and interceded with Pilate many days that he would remove the images; and when he would not grant their requests, because it would tend to the injury of Caesar, while yet they persevered in their request, on the sixth day he ordered his soldiers to have their weapons privately, while he came and sat upon his judgment-seat, which seat was so prepared in the open place of the city, that it concealed the army that lay ready to oppress them; and when the Jews petitioned him again, he gave a signal to the soldiers to encompass them routed, and threatened that their punishment should be no less than immediate death, unless they would leave off disturbing him, and go their ways home. But they threw themselves upon the ground, and laid their necks bare, and said they would take their death very willingly, rather than the wisdom of their laws should be transgressed; upon which Pilate was deeply affected with their firm resolution to keep their laws inviolable, and presently commanded the images to be carried back from Jerusalem to Caesarea.' [245]

Pilate also offended Jewish sensibilities in using religiously restricted Temple revenues to build an aqueduct. Josephus records that 'Pilate undertook to bring a current of water to Jerusalem, and did it with the sacred money, and derived the origin of the stream from the distance of two hundred furlongs. However, the Jews were not pleased with what had been done about this water; and many ten thousands of the people got together, and made a clamour against him, and insisted that he should leave off that design. Some of them also used reproaches, and abused the man, as crowds of such people usually do. So he habited a great number of his soldiers in their habit, who carried daggers under their garments, and sent them to a place where they might surround them. So he bid the Jews himself go away; but they boldly cast reproaches upon him. He gave the soldiers that signal which had been beforehand agreed on; who laid upon them much greater blows than Pilate had commanded them, and equally punished those that were tumultuous, and those that were not; nor did they spare them in the least: and since the people were unarmed, and were caught by men prepared for what they were about, there were a great number of them slain by this means, and others of them ran away wounded. And thus an end was put to this sedition.' [246]

Jesus' nighttime trial was illegal on several counts of Jewish Law. Trials for life required twenty-three Sanhedrin members [247] (not all seventy-one), but could not be held at night, [248] and a whole day was required to elapse before a sentence of death could be carried out. 'Capital charges may be concluded on the same day with a favourable verdict *[acquittal]*, but only on the morrow with an unfavourable verdict.' [249] Additionally, trials were prohibited from being held on the evening of a festival. [250] The witnesses called to testify against Jesus did not agree (Mark 14:56), yet the trial was not adjourned and there is no sign that the false witnesses were punished as the Law required. [251] The same tractate also required that defence witnesses be called, yet this is not recorded as having occurred at Jesus' trial.

The Jewish authorities' opening gambit is that Jesus has been 'misleading' their nation. This is '*diastrephô*', meaning 'to pervert', 'to distort' and 'to twist',* from '*strephô*', meaning 'to turn'. They are upset that Jesus, a senior ordained Torah teacher, had deviated from their prescribed priestly and rabbinic understanding of Torah, especially in regard to his own application to himself as Messiah. Jesus had actually been untwisting their common misunderstandings that deviated away from God's original designs, brought about by generation after generation of man's wrong thinking and religious legalism. People loved to hear Jesus' expositions of Torah because he took them back to the basics in a way that wiped away the centuries of dust that obscured the true intentions of God's heart.

As 'Prefect' governing Judea on Rome's behalf, Pilate still held responsibility for revenue collections, so the Jews' accusation began with that. Jesus had not actually forbidden paying taxes to Caesar. Rather, he had said 'Give to Caesar what is Caesar's (Luke 20:25). But he had been party to both Matthew and Zaccheus leaving their posts, hence a tax related accusation was evidently felt to be a good way to secure Pilate's attention. Jesus' messianic claims are turned against him with the title '*basileus*' ('a king'), a term used by Peter (1 Peter 2:13 and 17) for the Emperor.

23:3-5 'So Pilate asked him, saying, "Are you the King of the Jews?" And he answered him and said, "It is as you say." Then Pilate said to the chief priests and the crowds, "I find no guilt in this man." But they kept on insisting, saying, "He stirs up the people, teaching all over Judea, starting from Galilee even as far as this place."'

'The King of the Jews' was the title that Mark Antony and the Roman Senate had bestowed upon Herod the Great prior to his re-taking Jerusalem from Parthian occupation in 37 BC. A non-Jew (owing to his mother being an Arab from Petra in Jordan), Herod was widely reviled by his Jewish subjects, and Pilate, who would have been well aware of Jesus' previous good standing as a legal scholar, is likely to be poking fun at Jesus' accusers in his use of this Roman-contrived title, which the Jews took great exception to being placed over Jesus' cross. 'The chief priests of the Jews were saying to Pilate, "Do not write, 'The King of the Jews'; but that he said, 'I am King of the Jews.'" Pilate answered, "What I have written I have written"' (John 19:21-22). Pilate was certainly informed by his wife of Jesus' circumstances ('While he was sitting on the judgment seat, his wife sent him a message, saying, "Have nothing to do with that righteous man; for last night I suffered greatly in a dream because of him' (Matthew 27:19). Pilate knew himself that it was out of envy that the Jewish rulers had brought Jesus to him (Matthew 27:18). He was not going to be easily persuaded by men who had almost certainly already complained to Rome about his previous behaviour with their Temple funds and the slaughter of those who had objected.

Jesus' reply to Pilate's question is an emphatic affirmative - 'It is as you say'. John's Gospel, chapter 18, describes Pilate's examination of Jesus within his house, which was sufficient to establish Jesus' innocence in Pilate's mind. The crowd of priests and elders who accompanied Jesus from the Hall of Hewn Stones to the palace of the Roman governor (John 18:28) would not enter Pilate's house for fear of ceremonial and legal defilement that might prohibit their participation in that evening's Passover service. And so Pilate comes out into his courtyard, an enclosed private area at the front, where the crowd of Jewish authority figures are waiting. The Gospel's references to 'the crowd' that called for Jesus' death refers to these men, not the general public of Jerusalem, who would not have been permitted to enter Pilate's courtyard, and in any event would still have been at home at this deliberately very early hour. 'Early in the morning the chief priests with the elders and scribes and the whole Council immediately held a consultation; and binding Jesus, they led him away and delivered him to Pilate' (Mark 15:1). The priests were determined to wrap the legal process up and have it firmly in the hands of the Roman authorities, who had powers of execution, before the ordinary populace were aware of what was happening. Jesus' huge public following would awake to a fait accompli.

The leaders' allegation that Jesus had been 'stirring up the people' is intended to imply one of sedition, something that Pilate would have known to be untrue, but their mention of Galilee gave Pilate room for manoeuvre. Galilee was under the jurisdiction of Herod Antipas, who was then in Jerusalem to celebrate the Passover. Perhaps Pilate could pass the buck to Herod.

23:6-7 'When Pilate heard it, he asked whether the man was a Galilean. And when he learned that he belonged to Herod's jurisdiction, he sent him to Herod, who himself also was in Jerusalem at that time.'

Pilate was coming under pressure from his wife, who would have had heard from the wives of the Herodian party of the Jews about Jesus' extraordinary teaching and miracles. Jesus' unusual inclusion of women in his company of disciples would have been the talk of the female population of Judea. As a Roman woman in the isolated province of Judea, Pilate's wife would have had little female company other than that provided by the wives of those Jews (known as Hellenists) who supported Roman rule. She clearly felt an urgent need to communicate with her husband about this senior rabbinic figure about whom she had heard so much. 'While he was sitting on the judgment seat, his wife sent him a message, saying, "Have nothing to do with that righteous man; for last night I suffered greatly in a dream because of him"' (Matthew 27:19). The word 'man' is an interpolation, not being present in the Greek text. Pilate's wife refers to Jesus simply as 'that *dikaios*'', the conventional description used of one considered to be 'righteous according to the Law', and hence someone highly educated in Oral Torah. This is the way that the Sanhedrin member Joseph of Arimathea is described in verse 50. It is also the way Paul described himself, as a fellow-Torah scholar from the Temple school of Gamaliel. 'As to the righteousness which is in the Law, found blameless' (Philippians 3:6). Pilate's wife is referring to Jesus' high educational standing in Jewish society in relation to the religious Law, which Jesus taught.

23:8 'Now Herod was very glad when he saw Jesus; for he had wanted to see him for a long time, because he had

411

been hearing about him and was hoping to see some sign performed by him.'

Jesus' healing in the Capernaum synagogue of the man with an unclean spirit had 'gone viral'. Mark states that 'the news about him spread to everywhere into all the surrounding district of Galilee' (Mark 1:28-29), including as far as the palaces of Herod Antipas at Machaerus and Sepphoris. It is also highly likely that the news of the healing of the son of the royal official at Capernaum had reached Herod's ears, as well as reports of the many other outstanding miracles that Jesus performed in Herod's territory. Luke has already recorded Herod Antipas as saying "I myself had John beheaded; but who is this man about whom I hear such things?" And he kept trying to see him' (Luke 9:9). Now, courtesy of Pilate, that moment had come - Herod's opportunity to perhaps see 'such things' as miracles.

23:9-10 'And he questioned him at some length, but he answered him nothing. And the chief priests and the scribes were standing there, accusing him vehemently.'

Jesus, however, remembers Herod too, as the murderer of his cousin John, and does not dignify him with a reply. Herod has to make do with the background noise of the chief priests (including former High Priests within the family of Annas), and the legal experts whose allegations would have meant little to Antipas, for whom his grandfather's forced conversion to Judaism at the time of the Maccabean kingdom was a political expediency rather than a personal spiritual conversion. Antipas was not noted for his piety, and the details of the Jewish Law that the scribes so forcibly argued would have been very likely to have gone over his head.

23:11-12 'And Herod with his soldiers, after treating him with contempt and mocking him, dressed him in a gorgeous robe and sent him back to Pilate. Now Herod

and Pilate became friends with one another that very day; for before they had been enemies with each other.'

Herod would have travelled from the fort of Machaerus with his personal bodyguard, and together they make sport of Jesus. The one who had done so many mighty deeds in Galilee is treated now as 'of no account' (*'exoutheneô'* - 'to despise and hold in contempt').* Herod is therefore one of the first to reject Jesus and so fulfil the words of Isaiah, 'He was despised and forsaken of men' (Isaiah 53:3). 'Mocked' here is *'empaizô'*, 'to trifle with', from *'paizô'*, meaning 'to play like a child'. This was quite literal in this case; a 'dressing up' game with a robe that is *'lampros'* - 'shining brilliant white', as the centurion Cornelius would later describe the clothing of the angel that appeared to him (Acts 10:30). Jesus' ministry of reconciliation worked in an unexpected way. Pilate and Herod Antipas, who were previously at odds as local rival rulers on behalf of Rome, now become best of friends.

When Archelaus was exiled to Gaul from Judea the ambitious Antipas, soon to overreach himself, would have no doubt coveted the more important territory and would have resented the arrival of a governor from Rome who exercised direct rule. Herod Antipas had controversially married his half-brother Philip's wife Herodias. Both were ambitious for greater things, so much so that Antipas had begun to stockpile weapons. But he was found out by his estranged nephew, Agrippa I, and reported to the new Emperor Caligula, who promptly banished Antipas to Lugdunum, in Gaul (modern day Lyon, in France). And so Antipas, mocker of Jesus, perished in exile, disgraced like his brother Archelaus before him.

23:13-16 'Pilate summoned the chief priests and the rulers and the people, and said to them, "You brought this man to me as one who incites the people to rebellion, and behold, having examined him before you, I have found no

413

guilt in this man regarding the charges which you make against him. No, nor has Herod, for he sent him back to us; and behold, nothing deserving death has been done by him."'

The Sanhedrin are now called to hear Pilate's judgement. They disliked Pilate and Pilate equally disliked them. Following the occasion of Pilate introducing the Emperor's standards, bearing the Emperor's image, into Jerusalem, the Jewish philosopher Philo wrote that Pilate 'was afraid that if they really sent an embassy, they would bring accusations against the rest of his administration as well, specifying in detail his venality, his violence, his thefts, his assaults, his abusive behaviour, his frequent executions of untried prisoners, and his endless savage ferocity.' There was no love lost between Pilate and his Jewish subjects. Pilate would have resented being used by the Jewish leaders to kill someone that he knew to be innocent. He equally knew that it was their jealousy of Jesus for his grasp of Torah, his miracles and his public acclaim that was behind their allegations against him (Mark 15:10). Luke, writing for the benefit of a Roman lawyer, sensitively omits the details pertinent to Roman law found in John's Gospel, "'If you release this man, you are no friend of Caesar; everyone who makes himself out to be a king opposes Caesar'" (John 19:12).

The chief priests had cleverly couched their charges to maximise their relevance to Roman rule, and so increase the likelihood of their engineering a verdict of death. 'Amicus Caesaris' ('Caesar's friend') was a coveted title in Rome, a guarantee of a job while the present Emperor Tiberius lived. In using it, the priests are piling political pressure onto Pilate. The same was true of their initial charge, 'He claims to be the Son of God', because the Emperors following Augustus referred to themselves as 'Divi Filius' - 'son of a god'. Their claim that Jesus was 'the king of the Jews' had been accepted by Jesus, but in the sense of a kingdom that was 'not of this world'

414

(John 18:36), and so was not considered by Pilate to be a threat to Rome.

23:17-19 '"Therefore I will punish him and release him." Now he was obliged to release to them at the feast one prisoner. But they cried out all together, saying, "Away with this man, and release for us Barabbas!" (He was one who had been thrown into prison for an insurrection made in the city, and for murder.)'

Matthew's Gospel recounts that Pilate offered the crowd the choice between the 'notorious prisoner' Barabbas and Jesus (Matthew 27:16-17), presumably to force their hand - how could they choose a murderer over such an esteemed Torah-teacher? But the priests were not leaving Jesus' fate to the whim of a fickle crowd. The part of the crowd within the courtyard opposite Pilate's judgement seat, at the very least, were their own followers, who had come early in the morning and remained while the leaders were locked in dialogue with Pilate. It was therefore easy for the priests, even after a larger crowd (Mark 15:8) had arrived, to orchestrate a call from before Pilate's judgement seat for the release of the murderer.

23:20-22 'Pilate, wanting to release Jesus, addressed them again, but they kept on calling out, saying, "Crucify, crucify him!" And he said to them the third time, "Why, what evil has this man done? I have found in him no guilt demanding death; therefore I will punish him and release him."'

The crowd of Sanhedrin members and supporters were driven by a sense of betrayal to the thing that they valued most highly - the Torah and all that their Jewish religion held dear. The idea that one as learned as Jesus could (in their eyes) commit blasphemy and then use his superior knowledge of Scripture to evade their accusations, infuriated them. They were experiencing the same sense of religious outrage that would later goad Saul on, in his own Sanhedrin service. As a Sanhedrin representative (Acts 22:5), Paul was dedicated to bringing about the imprisonment and death of many of Jesus' early Jewish followers. A sense of betrayal is a very powerful emotional driver of extreme behaviour, and is evidenced in Paul's own testimony to King Agrippa in Acts 26, verse 11. 'I punished them often in all the synagogues, I tried to force them to blaspheme; and being furiously enraged at them, I kept pursuing them even to foreign cities.' 'Furiously enraged' is *perissôs emmainomaï*, literally meaning a 'madness of rage beyond measure'* or 'exceedingly mad'. [252] From a human behavioural psychological perspective, an uneducated itinerant (as Jesus is often presented as by Western gentile theologians) could not possibly have provoked such an extreme response. It was Jesus' apparent betrayal of his ordained position of scholarship that was at the root of the 'madness'.

Pilate, who was not a religious Jew, was not experiencing any such extreme emotion. Rather, he perceives envy behind the technicalities of the charges of perceived blasphemy brought against Jesus, and he persists in trying to bring objectivity in the face of the strength of their emotions. He offers to 'punish' Jesus (*paideuô* - 'chastise with blows, as to a child')* which is not at all what the men of Israel's government had in mind. They want to see Jesus crucified - *stauroô* - 'the upright stake' upon which malefactors were nailed for execution. This is because the Law taught that, 'If a man has committed a sin worthy of death and he is put to death, and you hang him on a tree, his corpse shall not hang all night on the tree, but you shall surely bury him on the same day (for he who is hanged is accursed of God), so that you do not defile your land which the Lord your God gives you as an inheritance' (Deuteronomy 21:22-23). The Talmud taught: 'And if he be put to death, then thou shalt hang him on a tree. I might think that all who are put to death are to be hanged:

416

therefore Scripture states, for he is hanged *[because of]* a curse against God'. [253] The widespread Roman practice of crucifixion, borrowed from the Phoenicians, fulfilled this requirement that the wrongdoer 'hang on a tree.'

23:23-25 'But they were insistent, with loud voices asking that he be crucified. And their voices began to prevail. And Pilate pronounced sentence that their demand be granted. And he released the man they were asking for who had been thrown into prison for insurrection and murder, but he delivered Jesus to their will.'

In the end the Jewish crowd of rulers and their followers simply wore Pilate down. Like the importunate widow in Jesus' parable, they were simply not going to take 'No' for an answer. John records the priests' ironic blasphemy, 'We have no king but Caesar' (John 19:15), after which Pilate, with one eye on the possibility of a complaint to Rome, simply folded. The judicial decree was given, a murderer emerged blinking from the darkness of his cell into the bright late morning sun, and Jesus was given over to the power of the Sanhedrin to be put to death as an offender against Rome, against which he had not offended at all. Luke's Roman legal audience would not miss the significance of this, the grossest act of injustice.

23:26 'When they led him away, they seized a man, Simon of Cyrene, coming in from the country, and placed on him the cross to carry behind Jesus.'

By this time Jesus had been flogged by Pilate (Matthew 27:26). Luke's Gospel contains Jesus' prophecy that he would be 'flogged' (*'mastigoô'* - 'scourged', Luke 18:33); this chapter contains two somewhat tamer references to 'punishment' (*'paideuô'* - 'chastise') and no mention of the actual act. A Jewish flogging was restricted by the Law to three lots of thirteen blows with a plain leather thong, equally distributed between each shoulder and the back. The Talmud devotes a whole section to it. [254] The Roman flogging was quite different from the Jewish 'forty stripes save one' (2 Corinthians 11:24). There was no upper limit to the number of blows that could legally be inflicted under Roman law. Their whip itself consisted of leather thongs pierces with sharp pieces of bone and metal, which stripped away the flesh of the victim, often sufficiently severe to kill them. The church chronicler Eusebius records such punishments wounding 'even to the innermost veins and arteries, so that the hidden inward parts of the body, both their bowels and their members, were exposed to view.' [255] Luke, possibly with the sensibilities of his Roman audience in mind, draws a veil over this act of Roman savagery inflicted upon Jesus, which left Jesus too weak to carry the crossbeam of the upright wooden stake upon which he was to be crucified.

'Cyrene' was in North Africa (now Tripoli, in modern-day Libya). Simon, passing by as a Jewish pilgrim to Jerusalem for the Passover, was compelled ('pressed' under Roman law) into carrying the crossbeam on Jesus' behalf. Inhabitants of Israel, under Roman occupation, could be 'compelled' ('*angareuo*' - a term derived from Persian couriers who had the power to impress men into their service, rather like the old-English naval press-gangs) to assist the Roman army, up to distances of one mile. (Jesus had taught that his disciples should do two miles - Matthew 5:41.) Mark's account describes Simon as 'the father of Alexander and Rufus' (Mark 15:21), indicating that this experience, so unlooked for and unpleasant for Simon on the completion of his long and weary Passover pilgrimage to the holy city, led to his coming to faith in the Messiah whose cross he was forced to carry, such that his sons were well-known to the early Judean church. While 'Simon' is a common Jewish name, 'Rufus' is not; being '*Rhouphus*', meaning 'red'; in all likelihood so named because the baby boy had red hair. Paul specifically greets a 'Rufus' in his closing of his letter to the church

418

at Rome (Romans 16:13), whose mother was like a mother to Paul as well. It is possible that they were one and the same person, and if so a good illustration of God's sovereign ability to connect distant points in time and space to suit his overall purposes.

23:27 'And following him was a large crowd of the people, and of women who were mourning and lamenting him.'

The actions of the chief priests and other Sanhedrin members can be seen here to have been grossly opposed to the wishes of the general Jewish public, now rendered even further outside the equation of justice by those who were their legal representatives. Mary's influence as Luke's primary source comes across in the remembrance of the other women who followed Jesus that fateful morning, and the female emotions that surely mirrored her own at such illegal and unjust treatment of her son. 'Mourning' is '*koptô*', also meaning 'to strike' and 'to smite'* in the traditional eastern manner of 'beating the breast' in a physical outworking of the intensity of the emotion being expressed. 'Lamenting' is '*thrêneô*', also meaning 'to sing a dirge',* as commonly accompanied scenes of bereavement and other tragedies.

23:28-29 'But Jesus turning to them said, "Daughters of Jerusalem, stop weeping for me, but weep for yourselves and for your children. For behold, the days are coming when they will say, 'Blessed are the barren, and the wombs that never bore, and the breasts that never nursed.'"'

Even in his post-scourging weakened and pain-ridden state Jesus is still more concerned for other people's correct understanding of events than he is for himself. This concern would be shown again and again in the utterances made from the even more painful place of the cross itself. They too were for the benefit of others around him.

The days were coming when a woman in Jerusalem would kill and eat her own baby, such was the appalling state of the populace trapped inside the city in the famine brought about by the four year Roman siege [256] (related in chapter 19:43-44). To be responsible for a tiny dependent life as well as one's own at such a time of horror was not to be wished for. In this prophetic saying, so soon to be fulfilled, Jesus is reversing the rabbinic view that infertility was a curse and babies a blessing, based upon Jacob's blessing: 'Blessings of the breasts and of the womb' (Genesis 49:25). The Talmud recorded Hannah as appealing to the Lord, 'These breasts that thou hast put on my heart, are they not to give suck? Give me a son, so that I may suckle with them.' [257] The opposite view would prevail in the city of Jerusalem just 40 years after Jesus' death.

23:30-31 '"Then they will begin to say to the mountains, "Fall on us!" and to the hills, "Cover us!" For if they do these things when the tree is green, what will happen when it is dry?"'

The prophet Hosea had spoken of the judgement that would befall a complacent Israel, and of the people's reaction. 'Then they will say to the mountains, "Cover us!" and to the hills, "Fall on us"' (Hosea 10:8), a quick death being considered preferable to the long and drawn out death of starvation in a besieged city. Jesus' saying about the green tree is a typically rabbinic proverbial one, which meant that what would happen to a greater thing would certainly happen to a lesser thing. Ezekiel had prophesied, 'All the trees of the field will know that I am the Lord; I bring down the high tree, exalt the low tree, dry up the green tree and make the dry tree flourish' (Ezekiel 17:24). The coming of Messiah was God's last chance for the green tree, fed so long by Torah, to bear fruit. If it failed to, 'Every tree that does not bear good fruit is cut down and thrown into the fire', as Jesus had said (Matthew 7:19), and as John the Baptist had also said before him (Matthew 3:10).

23:32 'Two others also, who were criminals, were being led away to be put to death with him.'

Roman executions were performed outside the city in deference to Jewish sensibilities in regard to dead bodies and legal cleanliness laws; 'Camp outside the camp seven days; whoever has killed any person and whoever has touched any slain' (Numbers 31:19). Places of execution were by the main roads in and out of city gates, to achieve a maximum deterrent effect upon the city inhabitants.

23:33 'When they came to the place called 'The Skull', there they crucified him and the criminals, one on the right and the other on the left.'

'The Skull' is *'kranion'* (also meaning 'head'), in Latin *'Calvaria'* (hence Calvary) and in Aramaic 'Golgotha', from the Hebrew *'gulgoleth'* ('skull').* The name is likely to be derived from the fact that, as a site of Roman execution, the dead bodies of the slain were put into open common graves, from which the wild dogs of the city might feed at night and so scatter the bones around the site. The presence of dead bodies at the site of execution, a place also marked by the presence of the Imperial Roman standard (idolatrous to devout Jews), meant that it was illegal under Jewish Law for Jews to approach it, as to do so meant ritual uncleanness.

23:34 'But Jesus was saying, "Father, forgive them; for they do not know what they are doing." And they cast lots, dividing up his garments among themselves.'

Jesus' concern is, once again, not for himself. Despite the excruciating agony that he is experiencing his concern is that those who are crucifying him be forgiven by God. 'Know' what they are doing is *'oida'*, also meaning 'to perceive'.* Jesus is asking that the Roman soldiers, obeying Pilate's orders and ignorant of his identity as Messiah and attendant claims to divinity, be forgiven for their unwitting part in the priests' crime against him. He may also be asking forgiveness for the priests as well, although 'not knowing' (*'oida'*) would not be likely to include those who had diligently planned to illegally have him killed for many months. They did not know that his claims to divinity were true, but they certainly knew that what they were doing was illegal under their own Law.

The soldiers' casting of lots for Jesus' garments is a fulfilment of Psalm 22 and its prophetic description of the crucifixion many years prior to its invention ('They have pierced my hands and my feet' - verse 16), and in this instance, the handling of his clothing. Psalm 22:18: 'They divide my garments among them, and for my clothing they cast lots.' The Roman custom was for the prisoner's clothing to become the property of the execution party, which consisted of four soldiers. Jesus would have worn a head covering, sandals, a girdle and a cloak (four items, one for each soldier), and also his tunic (*'chitôn'*, the under-garment worn next to the skin). In Jesus' case this posed them a problem, because his tunic was too valuable to be torn up into sections for each soldier to have a piece. Being made from one strip of cloth ('woven without seams') it would in any case have been very difficult to tear by hand into approximately equally sized pieces. John 19:23 relates, 'The tunic was seamless, woven in one piece.' Consequently the soldiers gambled for it by 'casting' lots (*'ballô'* - 'to throw'). Jesus' expensive tunic is good evidence that the work of the *'tekton'* was a highly regarded and remunerated specialised profession, and that Joseph's family were in all probability well provided for even before the arrival of the Magi with their expensive gifts. His tunic was very valuable - too much so for the Roman soldiers to want to tear.

The High Priest too wore such a seamless garment. Exodus 28:32 reads, 'There shall be an opening at its top in the middle of it; around its opening there shall be a binding of woven work, like the opening of a coat of mail, so that it will not be torn.' The Talmud (*'Mo'ed, Yoma'* 72b) confirms this practice: 'All priestly garments must not be made by needle-work, but by weaving.' Jesus is about to perform his high-priestly sacrifice; his expensive tunic meant that he arrived at Calvary dressed in the manner of the High Priest, just as his earlier anointing with the perfume nard (John 12:3) meant that he also arrived still bearing that fragrance, anointed for the priestly role just as Aaron had been many hundreds of years earlier (Exodus 40:13).

23:35 'And the people stood by, looking on. And even the rulers were sneering at him, saying, "He saved others; let him save himself if this is the Christ of God, his Chosen One."'

Luke again illustrates the difference in response between the ordinary Judean public and the Jewish authorities. The public had 'mourned and lamented' his journey to the cross (verse 27), and would return home 'beating their breasts' in impotent fury and deep sorrow at the tremendous injustice they had witnessed, one orchestrated by their religious leaders. Those same leaders by contrast had come out to 'sneer' at Jesus. This is *'ekmuktêrizô'*, from *'muktêrizô'*, meaning 'to turn up their noses' (literally, being derived from *'muktêr'* - 'nostril' or 'snout').* Their mockery takes the form of rabbinic logic. If Jesus could genuinely do the greater work of saving others, then surely he could also do the lesser work of saving himself. They held that the fact that he appeared not to be able to save himself was evidence that his 'saving' of others in his former ministry of teaching and miracle working was counterfeit. Thus they wantonly deceived themselves. Jesus' earlier saying that 'Wisdom is justified by all her children' (Luke 7:35) was again proved true. This type of 'wisdom' was, as James would later say, 'not from above' (James 3:15), but was 'earthly, natural and demonic.'

23:36-37 'The soldiers also mocked him, coming up to him, offering him sour wine, and saying, "If you are the King of the Jews, save yourself!"'

The unlearned Roman soldiers take their cue in mocking Jesus both from the Sanhedrin rulers' mockery, whose bidding they knew that they were carrying out, and also from Pilate's mockery of the leaders themselves in his choice of inscribed title placed over the cross. Their long execution work-shift in the midday sun was a hot and thirst provoking business. It involved lifting men, together with the transverse and upright sections of the wooden cross, upright to be placed into a small excavated area of ground capable of supporting it in a vertical position and then standing in the sun until the condemned men died, or their shift ended. Jesus had already refused wine mixed with myrrh, used as a type of anaesthetic ('They tried to give him wine mixed with myrrh; but he did not take it' - Mark 15:23). The Talmud records that 'When one is led out to execution, he is given a goblet of wine containing a grain of frankincense, in order to benumb his senses, for it is written, 'Give strong drink unto him that is ready to perish, and wine unto the bitter in soul' (a rendering of Proverbs 31:6). And it has also been taught; 'The noble women in Jerusalem used to donate and bring it.' [258]

Now it is the turn of the Roman soldiers to offer him from their own wine-vinegar, which was spoiled wine that was watered down as a cheap drink for the common people. They do this as a means of making sport with him, mocking his claim to be 'The King of the Jews'. Pilate had commanded that this title be written and hung above Jesus' cross as an insult to those who had twisted his arm into the unjust verdict of crucifixion. They would offer wine vinegar to him again after Jesus' cried, 'I thirst' (John 19:28). This was in fulfilment of another prophetic Psalm of the crucifixion, Psalm 69:20-21. 'Reproach has broken my heart and I am so sick. And I looked for sympathy, but there was none, and for comforters, but I found none. They also gave me gall for my food, and for my thirst they gave me vinegar to drink.' The Roman soldiers are clearly using their own jug of wine vinegar (John 19:29) in which to soak the drinking sponge offered to Jesus, indicating that the sponge had not previously been used for any purpose other than drinking. The soldiers were not so intent on their mockery of Jesus as to contaminate their own drinks supply.

23:38 'Now there was also an inscription above him, 'This is the King of the Jews.''

John records that the inscription read ''Jesus the Nazarene, the King of the Jews.' Therefore many of the Jews read this inscription, for the place where Jesus was crucified was near the city; and it was written in Hebrew, Latin and in Greek. So the chief priests of the Jews were saying to Pilate, "Do not write, 'The King of the Jews'; but that, he said, 'I am King of the Jews.'" Pilate answered, "What I have written I have written"' (John 19:19-22). Pilate was determined to have at least this one small victory, a further insult against the priests he despised and who despised him. In mocking Jesus, the Roman soldiers are joining in the work of Pilate in mocking the Jews in general, and their leaders in particular.

23:39-41 'One of the criminals who were hanged there was hurling abuse at him, saying, "Are you not the Christ? Save yourself and us!" But the other answered, and rebuking him said, "Do you not even fear God, since you are under the same sentence of condemnation? And we indeed are suffering justly, for we are receiving what we deserve for our deed, but this man has done nothing wrong."'

Matthew's Gospel records that, initially, 'The robbers who had been crucified with him were also insulting him with the same words'

(Matthew 27:44). It is said that misery loves company, and the thieves managed to find sufficient breath, despite their being suspended from nails through their wrists, to join in the tirade of abuse being directed at Jesus. But one of them then 'changed his mind' in a '*metanoeô*' of repentance that led him into the eternal Kingdom of this 'King of the Jews' that his 'evil works' had led to his being situated adjacent to at Calvary. 'Criminal' is '*kakourgos*', from '*kakos*' - 'evil', whereas Matthew has 'robber', being '*lêstês*'. This also means 'a brigand who plunders openly by violence', [259] the same title used for Barabbas in John 18:40. It is quite possible that these two men had shared a Roman prison cell with Barabbas and perhaps had been dismayed that he had been chosen for pardon and freedom rather than one of them. Now one of them was about to be granted a pardon that bestowed an eternal freedom.

'Sentence of condemnation' is one word, '*krima*', also meaning 'a judicial judgement'.* Both had been lawfully condemned to execution, unlike Jesus, whose verdict was both unlawful and unjust. Although Jesus had been disfigured grossly by the beatings received at the hands of the Sanhedrin and the Roman soldiers, the second criminal clearly realised after a while who he really was - the well known Torah teacher in whom no offence against Torah could have been found. As Jesus had been able to say to his enemies, 'Which one of you convicts me of sin?' (John 8:46). If those religious scholars had been unable to cite any example of Jesus transgressing the Law, both written and oral, still less any moral fault, these (likely uneducated) brigands could certainly not. Jesus had done nothing deserving of death, as Pilate well knew, and had not transgressed against the Law either.

23:42-43 'And he was saying, "Jesus, remember me when you come in your kingdom!" And he said to him, "Truly I say to you, today you shall be with me in Paradise."'

The second thief has realised, or perhaps recalled something in Jesus' public teaching, to the effect that Jesus' kingdom was not of the present age, but was coming. Jesus had told Pilate that 'his kingdom was not of this world' (John 18:36), and had publically taught his disciples to pray for God's kingdom 'to come' (Luke 11:2). 'Paradise' is '*paradeisos*', a word of Persian origin ('*pairidaeza*' - a 'wall around' an area), used of the enclosed parks and garden belonging to the nobility, and is used in the Septuagint for the 'parks' that King Solomon built for himself ('I made gardens and parks for myself' - Ecclesiastes 2:5).

Jesus' body was destined for the unused tomb of Joseph of Arimathea but his Spirit was returning to his Father in heaven at the point of his death. Luke 23:46 reads: 'Into your hands I commend my Spirit', illustrating a perfect communion with the Father. Jesus' soul was, like all men's before him, going to visit Sheol, the place of the dead, where he would announce his victory over sin and death. 'He went and made proclamation to the spirits now in prison' (1 Peter 3:19), before his soul was raised together with his body which was to be re-made into an eternal body, thereby fulfilling Psalm 30:3 - 'You have brought up my soul from Sheol.' In the meantime Jesus' spirit would be in heaven to greet that of the thief when he died after the soldiers broke his legs and thereby prevented him from raising himself on his cross to breathe. 'The soldiers came, and broke the legs of the first man and of the other who was crucified with him' (John 19:32).

23:44-45 'It was now about the sixth hour, and darkness fell over the whole land until the ninth hour, because the sun was obscured; and the veil of the temple was torn in two.'

The sixth hour was 12 noon and the ninth hour was 3 pm. Solar eclipses total 8 minutes at the most, and Passover was held at the full moon, when the earth lies between the sun and the moon (i.e. when lunar, not solar, eclipses occur). The darkness that lasted 3 hours over Judea was most likely due to dark clouds, in keeping with the wrath of God towards sin that his Son was bearing on behalf of fallen humanity. The tearing of the curtain that separated the Holy Place from the Holy of Holies (entered only once a year by the High Priest) from top to bottom (Matthew 27:51) occurred down the middle, 'in two' being '*mesos*', meaning 'middle' or 'midst'.

Moses had been instructed 'You shall make a veil of blue and purple and scarlet material and fine twisted linen' (Exodus 26:31); the Jewish Gemara taught that the threads were 'twenty-four fold', [260] and that it was a man's handbreadth in thickness, 40 cubits (approximately 60 feet) long and twenty cubits (approximately 30 feet) broad. [261] 'Once the curtain had been torn open, every priest making an offering in the Holy Place could see into the Holy of Holies. Through faith in Christ all are made priests - 'He has made us to be a kingdom, priests to his God and Father' (Revelation 1:6) - and so have open access to God's presence.

23:46 'And Jesus, crying out with a loud voice, said "Father, into your hands I commit my spirit." Having said this, he breathed his last.'

Jesus is praying Psalm 31:5 - 'Into your hand I commit my spirit; you have ransomed me, O Lord, God of truth.' This was the Jewish prayer said before sleep. His addition of 'Father' shows that his relationship with his heavenly Father had not been severed by his bearing the sin of the world, but rather that 'God was in Christ reconciling the world to himself' (2 Corinthians 5:19). The Father shouldered the burden alongside the One who was 'unstained' ('undefiled') in his High Priestly role at Calvary, despite bearing the sin of the world. 'It was fitting for us to have such a high priest, holy, innocent, undefiled, separated from sinners' (Hebrews 7:26).

428

'Undefiled' is '*amiantos*', this being the negative adjective of the verb '*miainô*', which was a term used by dyers to describe a colour that had become tinged (and hence stained) with another colour.* Despite being the sin-bearer and hence becoming a curse for us (Galatians 3:13), Jesus' essential nature remained unchanged and unstained, being 'the same yesterday, today and forever' (Hebrews 13:8). His "spirit' ('*pneuma*'), is, like the soul, related to breath (which is an alternative translation of '*pneuma*'), hence Jesus' '*ekpneô*' - 'to breathe out', for the last time in his earthly body.

23:47 'Now when the centurion saw what had happened, he began praising God, saying, "Certainly this man was innocent."'

'Innocent' here is '*dikaios*', meaning 'righteous'. The Greek can also be rendered: 'Certainly this was a righteous man', in the sense of being one right with God through the minutiae of the Jewish Law. Jesus would not have been the first rabbinic scholar killed by Roman order. The manner of his death confirmed that Jesus was no ordinary man, causing the Centurion in charge of the execution party to '*doxazô*' - 'glorify' - God.

23:48-49 'And all the crowds who came together for this spectacle, when they observed what had happened, began to return, beating their breasts. And all his acquaintances and the women who accompanied him from Galilee were standing at a distance, seeing these things.'

The 'spectacle' of the crucifixion is '*theôria*'. This use of 'sight' in the noun form is peculiar to Luke in the New Testament, but was in common use in relation to medical dissection in anatomical texts. [262] The crowd of ordinary citizens and pilgrims to Jerusalem were not in accord with the priest's plans to have Jesus executed and greatly lamented his death, striking their chests in the traditional near-eastern manner of mourning. All the male apostles except John had fled, leaving the 'many women' (Matthew 27:55) to witness his death. They 'stood at a distance' because the Roman's would not have permitted entry to their site of execution. Also, for Jews, to enter would have rendered them legally unclean.

23:50-52 'And a man named Joseph, who was a member of the Council, a good and righteous man (he had not consented to their plan and action), a man from Arimathea, a city of the Jews, who was waiting for the kingdom of God; this man went to Pilate and asked for the body of Jesus.'

Not everyone was as concerned regarding legal cleanliness on that terrible day. Joseph of Arimathea (along with Nicodemus - John 19:39), went first to Pilate, then into the Roman camp itself, to recover Jesus' body from their stake of execution. Thus deliberately making themselves unclean, they were open to the criticism of their Sanhedrin colleagues. Even further, they took upon themselves the greater risk of any curse upon Jesus (as an alleged blasphemer) under Deuteronomy 21:23 ('Cursed is he who hangs upon a tree'), by taking Jesus' body for Jewish burial. Joseph is both 'good' and *'dikaios'* - 'righteous' according to the Jewish Law, and a Sanhedrin member, but one who had been out-numbered in his opposition to Jesus sentence of death and evidently not included in Jesus' trial.

23:53-54 'And he took it down and wrapped it in a linen cloth, and laid him in a tomb cut into the rock, where no one had ever lain. It was the preparation day, and the Sabbath was about to begin.'

The *'sindôn'* was a fine linen cloth used by Joseph as a shroud. The rock tomb was Joseph's own (Matthew 27:60), located in a garden 'in the place where Jesus was crucified' (John 19:41). It had never been used, in all likelihood having been cut out of the rock for his family's use at considerable expense by the wealthy Joseph, just prior to the Roman taking control of the adjacent site for use as a place of execution. As such, the garden and the tomb itself would have been rendered unclean and off-limits to his devout Jewish family. The next day was the Sabbath and a special one at that, being the Day of Passover - 'That Sabbath was a high day' (John 19:31).

23:55-56 'Now the women who had come with him out of Galilee followed, and saw the tomb and how his body was laid. Then they returned and prepared spices and perfumes. And on the Sabbath they rested according to the commandment.'

Once again the Galilean female followers of Jesus get a special mention from Luke's primary eyewitness source Mary, who was herself from Nazareth in Galilee. They do not seem to have been aware of Nicodemus' provision of 'a mixture of myrrh and aloes, about a hundred pounds weight' (John 19:39), at a cost of about £20,000 in modern terms. (Nicodemus' wealth was well-known and is mentioned in the Talmud in relation to provisions for his daughter-in-law.) [263] They return home to prepare their own embalming materials, but are necessarily forced to pause by the intervention of the Sabbath and the feast day, in accord with Leviticus 23:3. 'For six days work may be done, but on the seventh day there is a Sabbath of complete rest, a holy convocation. You shall not do any work; it is a Sabbath to the Lord in all your dwellings.'

And while they rested, Jesus, his Father and the Holy Spirit went about the work of bodily resurrection.

431

Chapter 24

24:1-3 'But on the first day of the week, at early dawn, they came to the tomb bringing the spices which they had prepared. And they found the stone rolled away from the tomb, but when they entered, they did not find the body of the Lord Jesus.'

At the first possible moment the women return to the tomb with their own embalming spices. They find the guard absent, and the stone moved away from the entrance, Pilate's seal having been broken. Despite these ominous signs of unauthorised disturbance, they are bold enough to enter the tomb. Where Jesus' body had been placed there was now simply 'the linen wrappings lying there, and the face-cloth which had been on his head, not lying with the linen wrappings, but rolled up in a place by itself' (John 20:6-7). Rock tombs were closed with a roughly circular piece of stone occupying a groove trench at the tomb's mouth; the stone had been rolled back by an angel causing the soldiers guarding it to faint and then flee.

'An angel of the Lord descended from heaven and came and rolled away the stone and sat upon it. And his appearance was like lightning, and his clothing as white as snow. The guards shook for fear of him and became like dead men' (Matthew 28:2-4). Jesus' body had gone.

24:4-5 'While they were perplexed about this, behold, two men suddenly stood near them in dazzling clothing; and as the women were terrified and bowed their faces to the ground, the men said to them, "Why do you seek the living one among the dead?"'

The absence of the priestly guard was puzzling indeed. The women would have known that Jesus' male disciples were in no condition to have overcome them physically and removed the body, and they do not immediately recognise the possibility of bodily resurrection. Where had the body gone? John's account describes Mary Magdalene looking into the tomb and seeing two angels 'sitting, one at the head and one at the feet, where the body of Jesus had been lying' (John 20:12). These angels' clothing is described as '*astraptô*', which is the word used for a lightening 'flash' in the sky in Luke 17:24, and causing predictable '*emphobos*' - 'fear'* - in the women. Unlike the guards though, the women do not faint. Rather, they '*klinô*' - 'bow'* - in godly awe and avert their gaze from the powerful brightness of the angelic forms. The rhetorical question that they hear is a good example of the humour of heaven, and the One who created humanity in his own image and hence with a sense of humour. Jesus' need for a tomb has been dispensed with; he is now very much alive.

24:6-7 '"He is not here, but he has risen. Remember how he spoke to you while he was still in Galilee, saying that the Son of Man must be delivered into the hands of sinful men, and be crucified, and the third day rise again."'

Jesus had prayed the Jewish daily bedtime prayer - 'Into your hands I commend my spirit' - prior to giving up his spirit to his Father in physical death; now he has been raised, 'risen' being '*egeirô*', also meaning 'to waken' or 'to rouse' from sleep.* All three members of the triune Godhead were involved in this momentous act. God the Father: 'If you confess with your mouth Jesus as Lord, and believe in your heart that God raised him from the dead, you will be saved' (Romans 10:9). God the Holy Spirit: 'If the Spirit of him who raised Jesus from the dead dwells in you, he who raised Christ Jesus from the dead will also give life to your mortal bodies through his Spirit who dwells in you' (Romans 8:11). And also God the Son: 'Jesus answered them, "Destroy this temple, and in three days I will raise it up." ... He was speaking of the temple of his body' (John 2:19, 21).

433

Also, "'I lay down my life so that I may take it again. No one has taken it away from me, but I lay it down on my own initiative. I have authority to lay it down, and I have authority to take it up again'" (John 10:17-18).

Jesus was raised early on the Sunday morning, having died the previous Friday afternoon. He had prophesied that 'The Son of Man will be three days and three nights in the heart of the earth' (Matthew 12:40). A 'day and a night' is a Hebrew idiom for any part of one day - one minute of one day can be expressed as a 'day and a night'. The Talmud ('*Shabbat*' 9, 3) quotes rabbi Eleazar ben Azariah (AD 100): 'A day and night are an *onah* (a portion of time) and the portion of an *onah* is as the whole of it.' 'Three days ago' can mean any time during the third day previously. Jesus spent part of Good Friday, all of Easter Saturday and a part of Easter Sunday morning with his physical body in the tomb of Joseph of Arimathea (Matthew 27:59-60) - hence three *onahs* - 'three days and nights'.

24:8-11 'And they remembered his words, and returned from the tomb and reported all these things to the eleven and to all the rest. Now they were Mary Magdalene and Joanna and Mary the mother of James; also the other women with them were telling these things to the apostles. But these words appeared to them as nonsense, and they would not believe them.'

The women become the first Jewish evangelists, led by Mary Magdalene, who John records as having been the first of all Jesus' disciples to see Jesus in his resurrected body (John 20:14-18). Joanna is mentioned in Luke 8:3 as the wife of Chuza, Herod Antipas' steward. Mary the mother of James is also mother to Joses, according to Mark 15:40, which also adds that this James was known as 'James the Less'. Perhaps predictably, the men did not believe them, dismissing their testimony as '*lêros*', meaning 'silly talk' or

434

'idle tales', [264] another medical term of Doctor Luke's to denote feverish and delirious utterances that make no sense. [265] The Apostles were disbelieving of it - '*apisteô*', literally meaning 'without faith'. *

24:12 'But Peter got up and ran to the tomb; stooping and looking in, he saw the linen wrappings only; and he went away to his home, marvelling at what had happened.'

Peter had run to the tomb with John, who had out-paced him but stopped at the tomb's entrance, while Peter upon arrival had gone inside (John 20:3-6). He saw no angels, perhaps a reflection upon his state of unbelief, but only the linen shroud and head-covering. He was changed in his perspective, going from unbelief to '*thaumazô*' - 'to wonder in admiration' at the sight. *

24:13-14 'And behold, two of them were going that very day to a village named Emmaus, which was about seven miles from Jerusalem. And they were talking with each other about all these things which had taken place.'

This particular Emmaus features in Josephus' 'Wars of the Jews' (to be distinguished from the village of Emmaus in Galilee) as a place where Vespasian founded a Roman colony in so far as he 'assigned a place for eight hundred men only, whom he had dismissed from his army, which he gave them for their habitation; it is called Emmaus, and is distant from Jerusalem threescore furlongs'. [266] The village is believed to be modern-day Quloniyeh (from 'Colonia') west of Jerusalem on the road to Jaffa; it is a more likely option than the village of Amwas, which is 16 miles from Jerusalem, too far for the disciples to have returned in time for a late meeting with the Apostles. The Greek here is three-score (sixty) '*stadion*'; each 'stadium' being one-eighth of a Roman mile, i.e. about seven and a half miles. The two disciples are still trying to make sense of the extraordinary events of the past days when someone joins them.

24:15-18 'While they were talking and discussing, Jesus himself approached and began traveling with them. But their eyes were prevented from recognizing him. And he said to them, "What are these words that you are exchanging with one another as you are walking?" And they stood still, looking sad. One of them, named Cleopas, answered and said to him, "Are you the only one visiting Jerusalem and unaware of the things which have happened here in these days?"'

Jesus catches them up walking in the same direction, but the God who opens men's eyes to the person of his Son also closes them, and they do not realise with whom they are conversing. Jesus' trial and hastily contrived execution had been the talk of Jerusalem because of his standing in their society as a '***Didaskalos***' of Torah, and the 'gloom' of '***skuthrôpos***' (literally meaning 'sullen-eyed', hence rendered 'sad')* lay heavily over them.

24:19-21 'And he said to them, "What things?" And they said to him, "The things about Jesus the Nazarene, who was a prophet mighty in deed and word in the sight of God and all the people, and how the chief priests and our rulers delivered him to the sentence of death, and crucified him. But we were hoping that it was he who was going to redeem Israel. Indeed, besides all this, it is the third day since these things happened."'

The Greek used here for the disciples' reference to Jesus is '***Iêsous Nazarênos***', equivalent to the Hebrew '*Yehoshua Na'tzeret*', 'Joshua from Nazareth'. The common Hebrew name Joshua became the name Jesus via a journey through Koine Greek (*Iēsous*) and Latin

436

(*IESVS*). 'Prophet' is '***prophêtês***', 'one who speaks forth openly' what has been heard from God, [267] but who, in Jesus' case, was mighty in deeds (miracles) as well as in word. Jesus spoke forth the word of Torah as he had given it originally to Moses on Mount Sinai. To the people it sounded 'new' (Mark 1:27), because it cut through the centuries of rabbinic variations, thus re-connecting it to the earlier revealed word of God given in the book of Genesis.

The disciples are in no doubt where the blame lay for Jesus' illegal execution. It was not with the Romans or the will of the common people, but with the majority of the Sanhedrin. They had become infuriated by Jesus' apparent betrayal of Torah in taking to himself the name of God and forgiving sins. Responsibility lay especially with the priests, who were threatened in their economic and social privileges by a messianic figure who they feared would also bring on a Roman suppression of what they would perceive as a religiously inspired uprising.

The 'redemption' of Israel that the disciples had been hoping for is '*lutroô*' - 'to release by payment of a ransom.' This is exactly what Jesus' death on the cross had achieved in a spiritual sense - release from the reign of death and sin over which the devil had for so long held sway. '***Lutroô***' is the root of '*lutrôsis*' ('redemption'), which is what both John the Baptist's father had prophetically seen in John's birth (Luke 1:68) and what the prophetess Anna had given thanks for 'all those who were looking for the redemption of Jerusalem' (Luke 2:38) on catching sight of the infant Jesus in the Temple.

24:22-24 '"But also some women among us amazed us. When they were at the tomb early in the morning and did not find his body, they came, saying that they had also seen a vision of angels who said that he was alive. Some of those who were with us went to the tomb and found it

just exactly as the women also had said; but him they did not see."'

Back to the women, whose account had so 'amazed' the men. This is '*existêmi*', also meaning 'to astound' and to 'throw into wonderment.'* The men who then went to the tomb after the women's earlier morning visit either lacked the faith that the women had or were not so favoured by God as to have their eyes opened to perceive the angels. They neither saw the body nor the angelic messengers of his resurrection.

24:25-27 'And he said to them, "O foolish men and slow of heart to believe in all that the prophets have spoken! Was it not necessary for the Christ to suffer these things and to enter into his glory?" Then beginning with Moses and with all the prophets, he explained to them the things concerning himself in all the Scriptures.'

Jesus had had plenty of experience of unbelief among his disciples, and upbraids them as suffering from '*bradus kardia*' - 'bradycardia' being the medical term for a slow heartbeat. 'Foolish' is not '*môros*', a term for a 'moral blockhead',* a pejorative term which Jesus forbade his disciples to use (Matthew 5:22), Rather, it is '*anoêtos*' - 'without understanding', from '*noeô*', 'to understand'. Jesus saw his horrendous suffering as having been a 'necessary' price to pay to release humanity from Satan's grip. The 'glory' Jesus entered is '*doxa*', which also means 'honour' and 'praise'.* Hebrews 12:2 records that it 'was for the joy set before him' that Jesus endured the cross, the joy of doing his Father's will, out of his love for fallen mankind.

Moses had been taught first-hand by the pre-incarnate Jesus for 40 days and nights on Mount Sinai and so his writings were a good place to start in enumerating the many prophetic statements that pointed to his coming in the flesh. The Old Testament is full of references to Jesus, some of which have sadly been obscured in the transition from Hebrew to English.

24:28-31 'And they approached the village where they were going, and he acted as though he were going farther. But they urged him, saying, "Stay with us, for it is getting toward evening, and the day is now nearly over." So he went in to stay with them. When he had reclined at the table with them, he took the bread and blessed it, and breaking it, he began giving it to them. Then their eyes were opened and they recognized him; and he vanished from their sight.'

Jesus does not force his presence on his disciples, but the near-east pattern of hospitality prevailed. Their eyes are opened to his true identity as he broke the bread, surely with the traditional Jewish prayer of blessing: '*Baruch atah Adonai, Eloheinu, Melech ha-olam, hamotzi lechem min ha-aretz*' - 'Blessed are you, Lord our God, King of the Universe, who brings forth bread from the earth.' Jesus' nail scarred wrists may have been revealed as he did so, in any event, that was the last they saw of him. Jesus exercised the ability of his immortal resurrection body to appear and disappear at will.

24:32-35 'They said to one another, "Were not our hearts burning within us while he was speaking to us on the road, while he was explaining the Scriptures to us?" And they got up that very hour and returned to Jerusalem, and found gathered together the eleven and those who were with them, saying, "The Lord has really risen and has appeared to Simon." They began to relate their experiences on the road and how he was recognized by them in the breaking of the bread.'

The disciples recall the manner in which the then-stranger on the road had 'explained' to them what the Scripture said - '*dianoigô*' - 'to open up completely', in such a way that all the loose ends and misunderstood concepts were cleared up. They hasten back to Jerusalem with the good news, only to find that it had reached there before them. The men are convinced, not because Jesus has appeared earlier (and indeed first) to Mary Magdalene, but because now Simon Peter has had the same experience. We are not privy to the detail, although it must have been quite well known because Paul refers to it in 1 Corinthians 15:4-5: 'He was raised on the third day according to the Scriptures, and that he appeared to Cephas, then to the twelve.'

24:36-43 'While they were telling these things, he himself stood in their midst and said to them, "Peace be to you." But they were startled and frightened and thought that they were seeing a spirit. And he said to them, "Why are you troubled, and why do doubts arise in your hearts? See my hands and my feet, that it is I myself; touch me and see, for a spirit does not have flesh and bones as you see that I have." And when he had said this, he showed them his hands and his feet. While they still could not believe it because of their joy and amazement, he said to them, "Have you anything here to eat?" They gave him a piece of a broiled fish; and he took it and ate it before them.'

Jesus' ability in his new body to appear and disappear at will is manifest again, much to the consternation of the Apostles, who, as much earlier on a stormy Lake Galilee, think that they are seeing a ghost ('*pneuma*' - 'spirit'). Spirit manifestations were associated with imminent death, when a spirit was believed to come and take the deceased to Sheol, hence the disciples' fearful reaction. Bodily resurrection was not something that exactly dominated Old Covenant theology and so Jesus offers them first-hand and tactile evidence of his material being, along with sight of the nail marks still present in his hands and feet. That not being immediately sufficient to assuage their doubts, Jesus eats a piece of fish, evidencing the reality of eating and drinking with the new body in the kingdom of heaven. Doctor Luke is careful to note that the fish was 'broiled' (*'optos'* - 'prepared by fire'); [268] broiled fish was a commonly prescribed diet by Greek physicians for patients recovering from a trauma or an illness. [269] The KJV here adds that Jesus was also given honeycomb to eat, something that was also in common use for such patients. [270]

24:44-47 'Now he said to them, "These are my words which I spoke to you while I was still with you, that all things which are written about me in the Law of Moses and the Prophets and the Psalms must be fulfilled." Then he opened their minds to understand the Scriptures, and he said to them, "Thus it is written, that the Christ would suffer and rise again from the dead the third day, and that repentance for forgiveness of sins would be proclaimed in his name to all the nations, beginning from Jerusalem."'

Jesus repeats his action of opening his disciples' minds as to the meaning of the Scripture. The Jews divide the Old Testament into three sections. First comes the Mosaic Law, consisting of the Pentateuch (Genesis, Exodus, Leviticus, Numbers and Deuteronomy). Next comes the Prophets, divided into two sections of the former prophets (Joshua, Judges, 1st and 2nd Samuel and 1st and 2nd Kings) and the latter prophets (Isaiah, Jeremiah, Ezekiel, Hosea, Joel, Amos, Obadiah, Jonah, Micah, Nahum, Habakkuk, Zephaniah, Haggai, Zechariah, and Malachi). Finally there is the Psalms, which is a collection of texts which also includes not just those prayers but also the Proverbs, Job, Song of Solomon, Ruth, Lamentations, Ecclesiastes, Esther, Daniel, Ezra, and Nehemiah, and 1st and 2nd Chronicles. This collection was also called the *Hagiographa* (holy writings). The many prophecies therein

441

concerning his first coming had now been fulfilled, leaving those that concern Jesus' second coming to be fulfilled at the proper time.

The prophet Isaiah had foretold Jesus' suffering: 'Surely he took up our infirmities and carried our sorrows, yet we considered him stricken by God, smitten by him, and afflicted. But he was pierced for our transgressions, he was crushed for our iniquities; the punishment that brought us peace was upon him, and by his wounds we are healed' (Isaiah 53:4-5). Hosea had called for a collective returning to the Lord who would 'raise us up on the third day' (Hosea 6:2). Ezekiel too had called for repentance - 'Repent and turn away from all your transgressions, so that iniquity may not become a stumbling block to you' (Ezekiel 18:30). Jeremiah had foretold a time when there would be a new relationship with the Lord who would say, 'I will forgive their iniquity, and their sin I will remember no more' (Jeremiah 31:34). Micah had prophesied that 'The word of the Lord would go forth from Jerusalem' (Micah 4:2), and Zechariah that Messiah 'will speak peace to the nations; and his dominion will be from sea to sea' (Zechariah 9:10).

24:48-53 '"You are witnesses of these things. And behold, I am sending forth the promise of my Father upon you; but you are to stay in the city until you are clothed with power from on high." And he led them out as far as Bethany, and he lifted up his hands and blessed them. While he was blessing them, he parted from them and was carried up into heaven. And they, after worshiping him, returned to Jerusalem with great joy, and were continually in the temple praising God.'

The 'things' of Messiah (his teaching and his miracles) would be 'witnessed to' ('*martus*') by the disciples, even to the point of a martyr's death. To do so in faith and reliance on God's strength rather than their own would require the coming of the Spirit, promised them three days earlier by Jesus. 'I will ask the Father, and he will give you another Helper, that he may be with you forever; that is, the Spirit of truth' (John 14:16-17). And, 'When the Spirit of truth comes, he will guide you into all the truth; for he will not speak on his own initiative, but whatever he hears, he will speak; and he will disclose to you what is to come' (John 16:13).

'Clothed' with power is *enduô* - 'endued', in the sense of 'to get into', as in 'getting dressed.' [271] God's power is quite different to human endeavour, something we must learn to cooperate with if we are to experience it fully. Jesus' ascension occurred at Bethany (on the eastern side of the Mount of Olives) as he was 'blessing' his disciples with raised hands; the 'good words' of his *eulogeô* to them continue to this day. The disciples' response is to *proskuneô*, to 'kiss towards' in worship, before returning to Jerusalem to pray together in anticipation of the promised Holy Spirit. The disciples' continuance in regular Temple worship was an important factor in demonstrating that the new faith could be seen as a subset of Judaism and hence *'religio licita'*, thus avoiding falling foul of the Roman policy against those who practice religions unaccepted by the Republic.

Thus concludes Luke's first set of chronological facts in defence of the Apostle Paul. Paul's two years under house arrest (Acts 28:30) gave Luke the time needed to write this Gospel and a second instalment (the book of Acts), bringing Theophilus completely up to date with his client's history. It was not yet God's time for Paul to die, but to take the gospel to Spain (Romans 15:24). And so 'the Lord stood with me and strengthened me, so that through me the proclamation might be fully accomplished, and that all the Gentiles might hear; and I was rescued out of the lion's mouth' (2 Timothy 4:17). Nero's court evidently accepted that the new faith born in messianic Judaism was still legally a part of Judaism - Paul had not offended Roman law. Later, a second arrest would see him martyred.

Appendix

Female word counts in the four Gospels (NASB)

	Matthew	Mark	Luke	John
She	18	31	41	23
Woman	10	7	20	23
Women	6	2	11	0
Woman's	0	0	0	0
Women's	0	0	0	0
Her	40	37	65	38
Hers	0	0	0	0
Daughter	9	8	9	1
Daughters	0	0	2	0
Wife	17	11	18	1
Wives	1	0	1	0
Wife's	1	1	1	0
Virgin	1	0	1	0
Virgins	3	0	0	0
Virgin's	0	0	1	0
Sister	1	1	2	5
Sisters	2	3	1	1
Sister's	0	0	0	0
Widow	0	2	7	0
Widows	0	0	1	0
Widows'	1	1	1	0
Widow's	0	0	0	0
Mary	11	8	17	15
Mary's	0	0	0	0
Martha	0	0	3	11
Martha's	0	0	0	0
Anna	0	0	1	0
Elizabeth	0	0	8	0

Elizabeth's	0	0	1	0
Bride	0	0	0	1
Bride's	0	0	0	0
Joanna	0	0	2	0
Mother	28	19	21	9
Mothers	0	1	0	0
Mother's	1	0	10	2
Salome	0	2	0	0
Queen	1	0	1	0
Ruth	1	0	0	0
Rahab	1	0	0	0
Tamar	1	0	0	0
Susanna	0	0	1	0
	153	116	247	130

References

* = Strong's Greek and Hebrew Dictionary

[1] Eusebius, 'History Of The Church' 3, 4
[2] Galen, 'Epidemics' 6, 'Fractures' 18
[3] Vine's Expository Dictionary of Old and New Testament Words
[4] Vine's Expository Dictionary of Old and New Testament Words
[5] Pliny, 'Natural History' 9,136
[6] Horace, 'Satires' 1.6, 28; Ovid, 'Tristia' 4.10, 35
[7] Suetonius, 'Life of Tiberius' 35; 'Life of Vespasian' 2, 4
[8] Flavius Josephus, 'Wars' 2, 14
[9] Flavius Josephus, 'Life of Flavius Josephus', 61
[10] A. T. Robertson, 'Word Pictures in the New Testament'
[11] Dr A. T. Bradford, 'According To Matthew' ISBN 9780956479839
[12] Talmud, 'Ta'anith' 15b
[13] Hippocrates, 'On Superfoetation', 265 and 'Diseases of Women', 673
[14] Edersheim, 'The Temple - Its Ministry and Services', chapter 7
[15] Edersheim, 'The Life And Times Of Jesus The Messiah'
[16] Vine's Expository Dictionary of Old and New Testament Words
[17] Talmud, 'Nazir' 4a
[18] Edersheim, 'The Life And Times Of Jesus The Messiah'
[19] Josephus, 'Antiquities' 15,11
[20] See Dr A. T. Bradford's, 'The Jesus Discovery' ISBN 9780956479808
[21] Vine's Expository Dictionary of Old and New Testament Words

[22] Galen, 'Medical Definitions' 107

[23] Hepper and Shahidullah, 'Archives of the Diseases of Childhood' 1994

[24] Hippocrates, 'Prognostics' 98; 'Diseases of Women' 642

[25] Vine's Expository Dictionary of Old and New Testament Words

[26] Vine's Expository Dictionary of Old and New Testament Words

[27] Talmud, '*Avot*' 5

[28] Dead Sea Scrolls' Library, Israel Antiquities Authority

[29] Peter Aicher, 'Rome Alive: A Source Guide to the Ancient City', vol. 1, 2004

[30] Josephus, 'Antiquities' 17, 6

[31] Josephus, 'Antiquities' 18, 1

[32] Vine's Expository Dictionary of Old and New Testament Words

[33] A. H. M. Jones, ed, 'A History of Rome through the Fifth Century' (1970)

[34] A 'targum' (paraphrase) translation note on Genesis 35:21

[35] Edersheim, 'The Life And Times Of Jesus The Messiah'

[36] Vine's Expository Dictionary of Old and New Testament Words

[37] Talmud, '*K'rithoth*' 8a

[38] Vine's Expository Dictionary of Old and New Testament Words

[39] Vine's Expository Dictionary of Old and New Testament Words

[40] Talmud, '*Avot*' 5, 21

[41] Josephus, 'Wars', 6, 9

[42] Talmud '*Avot*' 5

[43] Josephus, 'Antiquities' 17, 6

[44] Talmud, '*Avot*' 5, 21

[45] Josephus, 'Antiquities' 17, 2

[46] Josephus, 'Antiquities' 18, 2

[47] Essene Dead Sea scrolls found at Qumran date from 50 BC - 50 AD (The Earliest Gospel Manuscript?: The Qumran Papyrus 7Q5 and its Significance for New Testament Studies. Exeter: Paternoster Press)

[48] Talmud, '*Yoma*' 86b

[49] Talmud, '*Berachoth*' 17a

[50] Hippocrates, 'Morbities' 488 and 453

[51] Vine's Expository Dictionary of Old and New Testament Words

[52] See Dr A.T. Bradford's, 'The Jesus Discovery' ISBN 9780956479808

[53] Talmud, '*Megilah*' 11b, 'Satan came and danced among them and slew Vashti'

[54] Vine's Expository Dictionary of Old and New Testament Words

[55] Talmud, '*Nidah*' 24b, 'If an abortion had the likeness of Lilith *[a demon]* its mother is unclean by reason of the birth, for it is a child, but it has wings.'

[56] Talmud, '*K'rithoth*' 3b

[57] Hippocrates, 'Epidemics' 1160

[58] Aretaeus, 'Acute Morbidities' 94 (Epilepsy)

[59] Hippocrates, 'Epidemics' 948

[60] Talmud, '*Nidah*' 20a

[61] Talmud, '*Pesachim*' 8b

[62] Talmud, '*Kelim*' 23

[63] Talmud, '*Nega'im*' 13

[64] Hippocrates, 'Morbidites' 487 and 496, and 'Ancient Medicine' 11

[65] Dionysius, 'Roman Antiquities' 7

[66] Vine's Expository Dictionary of Old and New Testament Words

[67] Talmud, '*Avot*' 5

[68] Talmud, '*Nedarim*' 3, 5

[69] Talmud, '*Sukkah*' 25b

[70] Talmud, '*Nidah*' 12a

[71] Talmud, '*Kethuboth*' 3b

[72] See Dr A. T. Bradford's, 'The Jesus Discovery' ISBN 9780956479808

[73] Rabbi Shmuel Rabinowitz, Western Wall Heritage Foundation

[74] Talmud, '*Kethuboth*' 5a 'Rabbi Johanan said: 'One may do any work to save a life on Sabbath''

[75] Talmud, '*Shabbatt*' 24, 1

[76] See Dr A.T. Bradford's 'The New Testament on Woman, What Every Man Should Know.' ISBN 9780956479815

[77] Hippocrates, 'Aphorisms' 1251

[78] Vine's Expository Dictionary of Old and New Testament Words

[79] Vine's Expository Dictionary of Old and New Testament Words

[80] NASB Dictionary.

[81] Hippocrates, 'Morbidities' 504 and 'Diseases of Women' 641 and 643

[82] Vine's Expository Dictionary of Old and New Testament Words

[83] Josephus, 'Antiquities' 8, 3

[84] Josephus, 'Antiquities' 8, 3

[85] Vine's Expository Dictionary of Old and New Testament Words

[86] Galen, 'On The Powers Of Foods' 2, 13

[87] Vine's Expository Dictionary of Old and New Testament Words

[88] Aristotle, 'Politics', Book 1, section 12534b

[89] Vine's Expository Dictionary of Old and New Testament Words

[90] Hippocrates, 'Epidemics' 951, 955

[91] Vine's Expository Dictionary of Old and New Testament Words

[92] Talmud, '*Shabbath*' 153a: 'The Galileans said: 'Perform actions which shall be lamented in front of thy bier'; the Judaeans said: 'Perform actions to be lamented behind thy bier'. But they do not differ: each spoke in accordance with the usage in his locality.'

[93] Vine's Expository Dictionary of Old and New Testament Words

[94] Hippocrates, 'Acute Morbidities' 406

[95] Galen, 'Of Theriac *[an antidote for poison]* to Piso' 13

[96] Josephus, 'Antiquities' 17, 6

[97] See Dr A.T Bradford's 'The New Testament On Women, What Every Man Should Know.' ISBN 9780956479815

[98] Talmud, '*Berakhot*' 79

[99] Edersheim, 'The Life And Times Of Jesus The Messiah'

[100] Pliny's '*Natural History*' 16, 74

[101] Aretaeus, 'Signs of Diuturnal Morbities' 37

[102] Talmud, '*Sukkah*' 28a

[103] Vine's Expository Dictionary of Old and New Testament Words

[104] Henry Tristam, 'Society for the Promotion of Christian Knowledge' 1865

[105] Edersheim's 'Life And Times Of Jesus The Messiah'
[106] Professor A. Socin, Palestine Exploration Quarterly, Palestine Exploration Fund
[107] Talmud, 'Nidah' 5b
[108] Hippocrates, 'Diseases of Women' 639 and 668
[109] Talmud, 'Baba Metzia', 75b
[110] Talmud, 'Sanhedrin' 15b and 'Nedarim' 53b
[111] Talmud, 'Abhod' 44
[112] Galen, 'On the Subsistence of the Natural Faculties', 2, 4
[113] Hippocrates, 'Acute Morbidities' 399, 406 and 690
[114] Hippocrates 'Acute Morbidities' 399, 468 and 474
[115] Talmud, 'Avot' 1, 4
[116] Vine's Expository Dictionary of Old and New Testament Words
[117] Vine's Expository Dictionary of Old and New Testament Words
[118] Hippocrates, 'On The Sacred Disease'
[119] Talmud, 'Kethuboth' 77a
[120] Talmud, 'Bechoroth' 44b
[121] Talmud, 'Avodah Zarah' 12b
[122] Galen, 'On the Humours', and 'Epidemiology'
[123] Hippocrates, 'Acute Morbidities' 4 (Epilepsy)
[124] Vine's Expository Dictionary of Old and New Testament Words
[125] Vine's Expository Dictionary of Old and New Testament Words
[126] Josephus, 'Antiquities' 12, 5
[127] Hippocrates, 'Fractures' 772
[128] Dioscorides, 'Materia Medica' 2, 123 and 5, 9
[129] Vine's Expository Dictionary of Old and New Testament Words
[130] Talmud, 'Berakhot' 8,1
[131] Galen, 'Of Different Morbidities' 5, 6, 850
[132] Hippocrates, 'Morbidities' 467 and 508 respectively
[133] Hippocrates, 'Affections' 526
[134] Hippocrates, 'Morbidities' 456 and 486
[135] NASB Dictionary
[136] Vine's Expository Dictionary of Old and New Testament Words
[137] Canon A. Deane
[138] Hippocrates, 'Diseases of Women' 603
[139] Dioscorides, 'Venomous Animals' 6
[140] NASB Dictionary
[141] Hippocrates, 'Epidemics' 959
[142] Talmud, 'Avot' 5, Mishnah 13
[143] Talmud, 'Ma'aseroth' 1
[144] Talmud, 'Sotah' 22
[145] Vine's Expository Dictionary of Old and New Testament Words
[146] Vine's Expository Dictionary of Old and New Testament Words
[147] Vine's Expository Dictionary of Old and New Testament Words
[148] Talmud, 'Nedarim' 22a, 'Rabbi Samuel ben Nahmani said in the name of Rabbi Jonathan, 'He who loses his temper is exposed to all the torments of Gehenna.''

[149] NASB Dictionary

[150] NASB Dictionary

[151] Talmud '*Shabbath*' 47a

[152] '*Moreh Nebhukh*' 3:37

[153] Dr A. T. Bradford's, 'The Jesus Discovery' ISBN 9780956479808

[154] Hippocrates, 'Aphorisms' 1228; 'Articulations' 840; 'Fractures' 760

[155] Talmud, '*Peah*' 20

[156] Hippocrates, 'Sacred Diseases' 301, 'Internal Affections' 565

[157] Dr A. T. Bradford's, 'The Jesus Discovery' ISBN 9780956479808

[158] Hippocrates, 'Epidemics' 1215 and 126

[159] Talmud, '*Avodah Zarah*' 3b

[160] Vine's Expository Dictionary of Old and New Testament Words

[161] Oxford English Dictionary

[162] Josephus, 'Antiquities' 15,11

[163] Talmud, '*Bechoroth*' 8b

[164] Hippocrates, 'Fractures' 772

[165] Dioscorides, 'Materia Medica' 2, 123 and 5, 9

[166] Talmud, '*Bechoroth*' 12a (and many others)

[167] Ezekiel 46:9, Talmud '*Berachoth*' 62b

[168] Vine's Expository Dictionary of Old and New Testament Words

[169] Vine's Expository Dictionary of Old and New Testament Words

[170] Dioscorides, 'Materia Medica' 1, 24; Galen, 'Aliments' 3, 21

[171] Vine's Expository Dictionary of Old and New Testament Words

[172] Talmud, '*Sanhedrin*' 11b

[173] Theological Wordbook Of The Old Testament

[174] Edersheim, 'The Life And Times Of Jesus The Messiah'

[175] Vine's Expository Dictionary of Old and New Testament Words

[176] Vine's Expository Dictionary of Old and New Testament Words

[177] 'On Ulcers' 8, attributed to Hippocrates

[178] Vine's Expository Dictionary of Old and New Testament Words

[179] Vine's Expository Dictionary of Old and New Testament Words

[180] Hippocrates, 'Fractures' 765; 'Prognostics' 98

[181] NASB Dictionary

[182] Galen, 'Properties of Foods' 2, 11

[183] Josephus, 'Wars' 1, 13

[184] Josephus, 'Wars' 1, 21

[185] Vine's Expository Dictionary of Old and New Testament Words

[186] Vine's Expository Dictionary of Old and New Testament Words

[187] Josephus, 'Antiquities' 17, 6

[188] Galen, 'Of the Art of Medicine', 12; Aretaeus, 'Signs of Chronic Diseases' 64

[189] Talmud, '*Kethub*' 104b

[190] Talmud, '*Babha*' 114a

[191] Josephus, 'Antiquities' 17, 6

[192] Vine's Expository Dictionary of Old and New Testament Words

[193] Vine's Expository Dictionary of Old and New Testament Words

[194] Talmud, '*Demai*' 2.2

[195] Vine's Expository Dictionary of Old and New Testament Words
[196] Vine's Expository Dictionary of Old and New Testament Words
[197] Galen, 'Whether The Arteries Naturally Contain Blood' 2, 2
[198] NASB Dictionary
[199] Josephus, 'Antiquities', 14, 4
[200] Talmud, 'Sanhedrin' 25b
[201] Galen, 'Properties of Foods' 2, 11
[202] Josephus, 'Wars', 1, 9
[203] Josephus, 'Antiquities' 16, 11
[204] Hippocrates, 'Disease of Women' 626, and 'Of Internal Affections' 538
[205] Vine's Expository Dictionary of Old and New Testament Words
[206] Hippocrates, 'Food in Acute Illness' 369 and 372
[207] Eusebius, 'History Of The Church' 3, 5
[208] Talmud, 'Chagigah' 16
[209] Josephus, 'Wars', 6, 3
[210] Josephus, 'Wars' 2, 7
[211] Talmud, 'Kritut' 1, 7
[212] Talmud, 'Avot' 5
[213] Hippocrates, 'On the Instruments of Reduction' 850 and 'Morbidities' 484
[214] Edersheim, 'The Life And Times Of Jesus The Messiah'
[215] NASB Dictionary
[216] Vine's Expository Dictionary of Old and New Testament Words
[217] Dr A.T. Bradford, 'The Jesus Discovery' ISBN 9780956479808
[218] NASB Dictionary
[219] Josephus, 'Antiquities' 15, 11
[220] NASB Dictionary
[221] Talmud, 'Yebamoth'
[222] Talmud, 'Sanhedrin'
[223] Edersheim, 'The Temple - Its Ministry and Services'
[224] Vine's Expository Dictionary of Old and New Testament Words
[225] Josephus, 'Antiquities' 15, 11
[226] Josephus, 'Antiquities' 15, 11
[227] Josephus, 'Wars' 2, 13
[228] Eusebius, 'History Of The Church', 3, 5, 3
[229] Vine's Expository Dictionary of Old and New Testament Words
[230] Vine's Expository Dictionary of Old and New Testament Words
[231] Hippocrates, 'Diseases of Women', 645 and 662, Galen, 'Causes of Symptoms', 3, 7
[232] Vine's Expository Dictionary of Old and New Testament Words
[233] Hippocrates, 'Acute Morbidities' 404
[234] Josephus, 'Wars' 2, 8
[235] Talmud, 'Yoma' 21a
[236] Livy, 'History of Rome', Book IV, 9
[237] Hippocrates, 'Law', 2, and 'Affections' 526
[238] Aristotle, 'Problems' 2, 31
[239] Hippocrates 'Epidemics' 954

[240] Josephus, 'Antiquities' 20, 8
[241] Talmud, '*Pesachim*' 57a
[242] Talmud, '*Sanhedrin*' 86b
[243] Talmud, '*Sanhedrin*' 88b
[244] Talmud, '*Sanhedrin*' 56a
[245] Josephus 'Antiquities' 17, 3
[246] Josephus, 'Antiquities' 17, 3
[247] Talmud, '*Sanhedrin*' 8b
[248] Talmud, '*Sanhedrin*' 32a
[249] Talmud, '*Sanhedrin*' 32a
[250] Talmud, '*Sanhedrin*' 35a
[251] Talmud, '*Sanhedrin*' 32b
[252] Vine's Expository Dictionary of Old and New Testament Words
[253] Talmud, '*Sanhedrin*' 45b
[254] Talmud, '*Nezikin*', '*Makkoth*'
[255] Eusebius, 'The History Of The Church', 4, 15
[256] Josephus, 'Wars', 6, 3
[257] Talmud, '*Berachoth*' 31b
[258] Talmud, '*Sanhedrin*' 43a
[259] Vine's Expository Dictionary of Old and New Testament Words
[260] Talmud, '*Yoma*' 71b
[261] Talmud, '*Shakalim*', Mishnah 5
[262] Galen, 'Anatomical Procedures', 2, 1
[263] Talmud, '*Kethuboth*' 65a
[264] NASB Dictionary
[265] Hippocrates, 'Epidemics' 966, 1059, 1072
[266] Josephus, 'Wars' 7, 6
[267] Vine's Expository Dictionary of Old and New Testament Words
[268] Vine's Expository Dictionary of Old and New Testament Words
[269] Hippocrates, 'On Affections' 526 and 529
[270] Hippocrates, 'Morbidities' 496, 480 and 492
[271] Vine's Expository Dictionary of Old and New Testament Words

Also by Dr A. T. Bradford:
'The New Testament On Women - What Every Man Should Know.'
ISBN 9780956479815
'The Jesus Discovery' - Joseph the Temple '*tekton*' and Jesus the '*Didaskalos*'.
ISBN 9780956479808
'According To Matthew' - A Commentary On The Gospel Of Matthew.
ISBN 9780956479839
'Dylan, Depression And Faith' - a Scripture-based analysis of Bob Dylan's lyrics to present day. ISBN 9780956479822
'The Letter To The Hebrews' - A Commentary On The Book Of Hebrews.
ISBN 9780956479853
'Adam, Saint Or Sinner' - Adam as a 'type' of Christ (Romans 5:14).
ISBN 9780956479860

Lightning Source UK Ltd.
Milton Keynes UK
UKOW05f131270414

230645UK00001B/21/P